The Commercial Airline Industry

The Commercial Airline Industry

Managerial Practices and
Regulatory Policies

Nawal K. Taneja
Massachusetts Institute of
Technology

Lexington Books
D.C. Heath and Company
Lexington, Massachusetts
Toronto

Library of Congress Cataloging in Publication Data

Taneja, Nawal K.
 The commercial airline industry.

 Bibliography: p.
 Includes index.
 1. Air lines—United States—Management. 2. Aeronautics, Commercial—
United States. 3. Aeronautics and state—United States. I. Title.
HE9803.A4T36   387.7'0973   75-18052
ISBN 0-669-00129-5

Second printing, September 1977.

Published simultaneously in Canada.

Printed in the United States of America.

International Standard Book Number: 0-669-00129-5

Library of Congress Catalog Card Number: 75-18052

Contents

List of Figures

ix

List of Tables

Foreword

This year, and for some years to come, the future of the commercial airline industry, both domestic and international, will be clouded by the gravest uncertainties: economics, energy, the environment, and the regulatory policies of governments.

Nawal Taneja has assembled in this book the background materials important for management and the serious student to understand past practices and policies, and to chart the future.

Regardless of the outcome of the current regulatory debate in the U.S. Congress and the attempt by the Administration to establish U.S. international aviation policy, the commercial airline industry as we know it today (both here and overseas), must evolve to reflect world realities of political and economic restraints on the growth and development of the total system. This book will contribute greatly to an understanding of that evolution.

Secor D. Browne
Washington, D.C.
April 1976

Preface

Anyone who has tried to study or teach the managerial aspects of the airline industry has surely noticed the lack of an introductory book on the subject. Although a number of books exist that examine particular aspects of the airline industry, none of these books covers the overall managerial aspects with respect to economic, marketing, operational, and planning problems. Even the books dealing with specific aspects of the industry such as the regulatory framework do not go into such basic issues as the criteria and procedures for domestic and international route awards. This book is an attempt to provide the reader with an introduction to the commercial airline industry with emphasis upon managerial practices and regulatory policies.

The first chapter provides a brief review of the historical developments within the industry. In view of the current pressures to deregulate the carriers, this chapter is particularly useful for highlighting the state of the industry prior to the establishment of the Civil Aeronautics Board and the influence of this agency on the structure, performance, and market conduct of the carriers. The second chapter provides background material on the current structure of the industry with respect to the different classes of carriers, the size of the groups, and the financial and operating indices.

The next six chapters contain material that is useful in understanding how airlines operate and how typical short- and long-term decisions are made. Chapter 3 provides a brief introduction to the economic market behavior of the U.S. trunk-line carriers with some analysis of airline costs and a survey of past studies on the economies of scale in the industry. Chapter 4 introduces the intricacies of airline marketing in terms of traditional elements: product, price, promotion, and distribution. Chapter 5 deals with airline financing and provides some insight into the sources of capital and the growing area of lease financing. Chapters 6 and 7 describe the aircraft selection, fleet planning, and aircraft scheduling policies. Chapter 8 provides the reader with some insight into airline labor relations. The emphasis is on the appropriate labor legislation and its impact on labor management relations in the airline industry.

While the first eight chapters provide the reader with some understanding of how an airline operates, Chapter 9 provides an outline of the basic techniques for forecasting airline passenger traffic, a first step in the planning process. Since more and more carriers are employing the econometric method for forecasting passenger traffic, the conceptual framework of this technique is discussed at some length. This chapter also describes the major sources of data that are often used in the air transportation planning process. While the focus here is upon the data available at the Civil Aeronautics Board, other government and industry sources are also discussed briefly.

The next four chapters discuss at some length the impact of government

regulations on airline operations and management decisions. Chapter 10 highlights the procedures, policy, and discretion of the Board in determining the
need and extent of service on a route and the selection of a suitable carrier to
provide this service. The Board's policy on domestic passenger fares and freight
rates is discussed in Chapter 11. As in the case of routes, the Board's policy is
derived from an analysis of both passenger-fare and freight-rate investigations.
Chapter 12 highlights the Board's policy towards subsidy, methods of administering subsidy, and its benefits and costs to the public. Chapter 13 discusses
airline mergers. Numerous points are brought out on why two carriers decide to
merge. An attempt is also made in this chapter to examine the policies of the
Board, the Department of Transportation, and the Department of Justice toward
airline mergers.

Chapter 14 provides a broad review of the various aspects of international
aviation. The complexities of international routes, passenger fares, and cargo
rates are discussed in terms of the various international conventions and
agreements, the International Air Transport Association's traffic conference
machinery, and the interests of various governments in their flag carriers.

The final chapter attempts to identify some pressing issues in air transportation and presents an overview of the most important contemporary issue, the
debate on deregulation of the industry. This debate ties together many of the
points discussed earlier and highlights the rationale of current managerial
practices in the industry in terms of the unique characteristics of the industry
and the potential impact of economic deregulation.

This book is primarily intended for advanced undergraduate and graduate
students who are interested in exploring various aspects of the commercial
airline industry. Since the book is primarily concerned with fundamentals of the
industry, it should also be of interest to students specializing in other transportation modes as well as to students in those business schools where transportation
studies are expanding. In addition, the book should be useful to airline
management trainee programs as well as to government personnel and lawyers
entering the air transportation field. This book is hopefully unique in attempting
to pull together in one place the more important and significant issues concerned
with managerial practices and regulatory policies in the commercial airline
industry.

Acknowledgments

This book developed from a course on airline management taught by the author to graduate students in the Flight Transportation Laboratory at the Massachusetts Institute of Technology. The book also draws some material (particularly the sections on airline economics and fleet planning) from a course on air transportation economics taught by Professor Robert W. Simpson, head of the Flight Transportation Laboratory. Since the book is based upon lecture notes and class discussions, it has been contributed to by so many people (particularly students) that to thank them all individually would be impossible. However of all these individuals, Professor Simpson must receive a special note of thanks not only for his helpful comments and suggestions but also for his gracious permission to use his lecture notes throughout the book. Thanks also to: Dr. James T. Kneafsey, Economic Consultant to the Center for Transportation Studies at the Massachusetts Institute of Technology; Dr. Henry S. Marcus, Assistant Professor of Marine Systems at the Massachusetts Institute of Technology; Mr. Monte Lazarus, Senior Vice President, External Affairs, United Airlines; and Mr. Raymond A. Ausrotas, Associate Director of Flight Transportation Laboratory at the Massachusetts Institute of Technology for reading the entire manuscript and providing me with useful comments and constructive criticisms; and to Secor D. Browne, former Chairman of the Civil Aeronautics Board, for generously agreeing to write the foreword. Finally, I would like to thank Miss Rebecca Lacy, Mrs. Phyllis Scanlon, and Miss Mary Norton for typing the manuscript and for their editorial comments. Needless to say, I accept full responsibility for any and all errors.

The Commercial Airline Industry

A Review of the Historical Developments

Developments prior to 1938

With the exception of some experimental flights and routes it was not until 1918 that regularly scheduled air services were offered in the United States. Using army equipment and personnel, the air mail service was inaugurated on May 15, 1918 on the New York-Philadelphia-Washington route. Five months later the air transport aspect of the service was taken over by the Post Office Department. The fleet included war-surplus aircraft with some new aircraft specially built for the Post Office Department. By December 1918 the service was offered in the New York-Chicago market. Within two years, and in conjunction with the railroads, transcontinental air mail service was in operation between New York and San Francisco. The mail was flown during the day and transported by rail at night. While business was not too successful over short distances, great opportunities existed for long-haul transportation of the mail—aptly demonstrated by the time saved in an experimental 34-hour San Francisco-New York flight. By 1924, as a result of more reliable and durable engines, radio communication, and navigational aids, transcontinental flight time was further reduced as the operation was extended to include night service.

While there had been a number of early attempts to offer regular air passenger service, it was not until 1925 that service was offered on a year-round basis on the Los Angeles-San Diego route. The 120-mile trip took an hour and a half and cost either $17.50 one way or $26 round trip.[1] From this point on passenger traffic began to grow rapidly, and by 1930 passenger travel in the United States nearly equalled total airline passenger travel in the rest of the world. This growth in service led to a rapid development of larger and faster aircraft. Until the late 1920s Europe had maintained the lead in aircraft development, but then in a relatively short period the United States took over this leadership—beginning with the Ford Tri-Motor of 1926, followed by the Boeing 247, and in 1935 the DC-3, which received worldwide acknowledgment with its twenty-one passenger capacity and speed of almost 200 miles per hour.

The Post Office Department operated the mail flights until 1927 in spite of protests from the railroads in the early twenties regarding government supported competition in the transportation of mail. As a result of these protests the Air Mail Act of 1925 (Kelly Act) was passed to encourage commercial aviation and to transfer the air mail operation to private carriers on the basis of competitive bids. Initially the contracts were awarded for 4-year periods. Under the

1

competitive bidding system the most significant contracts were awarded to Boeing Air Transport for the San Francisco-Chicago route and to National Air Transport for the New York-Chicago route. The transcontinental route was joined by about a dozen feeder routes, with the result that almost every major city had air mail service.

The main problem during this time period was that the mail revenues were too low to justify capital expense for better equipment. Poor equipment also resulted in poor service, which in turn led to even lower revenues. Part of the unwillingness of the carriers to invest in new equipment resulted from the fear of losing mail contracts. Passenger traffic at that time had not reached a high enough level to attract investment for the development of new equipment. The carriers needed some government backing, and the public needed assurance that air transportation was safe, fast, and within their means.

There were five major factors that encouraged the development of the air transport industry at this critical time. First, the Air Commerce Act of 1926 initiated the development of civil airways, navigational aids, and provided for the regulation of safety by the federal government. This Act relieved the private carriers from heavy investments in ground facilities for air navigation. Second, Charles Lindbergh's transatlantic flight proved to be very timely in stimulating the early development of the air passenger market. Third, the Daniel Guggenheim Fund provided the funds for an experimental "model airline" designed to encourage the development of passenger traffic, which was sometimes considered a financial liability. Fourth, the Kelly Act was amended once again to include provisions to extend the original 4-year mail contracts to 10 years, resulting in increased incentive to invest in the industry. Fifth, payment for transportation of mail was made to the carriers on the basis of space available and distance flown rather than on the amount of mail carried (McNary-Watres Act).

In the summer of 1927 Juan Trippe, who was affiliated with Colonial Airways at the time, learned that the Post Office Department was considering an air mail contract between Key West, Florida and Havana, Cuba. At the time there were two carriers operating in Florida—Pan American and Florida Airways—and neither carrier had the necessary financial backing or equipment to negotiate the contract for the transportation of mail between Cuba and the United States. Although Pan American had acquired a contract from the Cuban government to fly the mail between the United States and Cuba, the carrier did not possess the landing rights. After joining Pan American, Trippe flew to Havana and negotiated an exclusive flying permit between the United States and Cuba, ensuring Pan American's exclusive rights to this route. In 1928 the Foreign Mail Act was passed authorizing the Postmaster General to award contracts for the transportation of mail by air to foreign countries and territorial possessions of the United States. Since Pan American had already acquired the necessary landing privileges in other Latin American countries, virtually all of the foreign air mail contracts were awarded to Pan American at the highest rate permissible under the Act.

Initially the federal government did not negotiate the development of the international routes with these Latin American nations. Rather Pan American, on its own initiative, had made private agreements with these nations for landing rights, and since Pan American was not in a position to offer exchange landing rights, the agreements were made without reciprocal landing rights in the United States. With mail payments authorized by the Foreign Air Mail Act of 1928 and with exclusive landing rights, Pan American displayed rapid development.

The McNary-Watres Act (amended Air Mail Act of 1925) enabled the carriers to become more stable and secure capital more easily due to their longer certificates. However, the Act also provided the Postmaster General with unlimited control over the air mail route system. In some circles the general feeling was that the Postmaster General, Walter Brown, was the chief planner of the McNary-Watres Act. He wanted to transform the industry from a random assortment of short unconnected mail routes to a more stable, integrated, self-sufficient nationwide airline system. His plan was to set up three major transcontinental routes with several coordinated and integrated feeder routes. Brown felt that the smaller carriers were under-capitalized and that nearly all of them were completely dependent upon government contracts. He was convinced that the solution was to eliminate competitive bidding and use the mail pay to support the carriers that were strong enough to contribute to the development of commercial aviation.

Postmaster Brown strengthened carriers by first awarding mail contracts to the lowest bidder who showed a daily operation for a period of at least 6 months over a route of 250 miles in length and second through extension or consolidation of routes that, in his opinion, were in the public interest. The provision for the substitution of mail contracts for 10-year route certificates had already been in existence; the extension and consolidation provision established major transcontinental routes. Finally, the airline payment was based upon space provided instead of weight carried.

Higher mail rates were available to compensate for factors such as transportation over bad terrain, inclement weather, night flying, radio equipment, and multi-engine aircraft. This rate system represented an indirect subsidy that enabled carriers to purchase and operate larger aircraft and thus develop the passenger market. Mail contracts were not always awarded to the lowest bidder, simply because there was no guarantee that the lowest bidder would be able to survive the cut-throat competition. However, it is alleged that in those cases when a contract was given to a larger carrier instead of a smaller carrier, the larger carrier was obligated to buy out the smaller carrier at a "fair" price.

In 1933 charges were made against Postmaster Brown for collusion, illegal administration, and unfair mail awards. A special investigation committee, headed by Senator Hugo Black, was formed, and hearings began in September

1933. Although during the investigation it became clear that, among other things, all of the mail contracts were awarded to three carriers, some historians claim that the investigation did not probe deeply enough into the causes of Brown's actions or the sincerity of his national plan. The result of the investigation was that the President cancelled all mail contracts held between the Post Office Department and the private carriers and asked the Army Corps to fly the mail. In the first few weeks severe weather conditions and unfamiliar routes caused some tragic accidents resulting in the gradual curtailment of air mail transportation and the complete standstill by June 1934.

The Air Mail Act of 1934 (Black-McKeller Act) set up a three-fold control of the air transport industry in the United States. The air mail contracts were to be awarded by the Post Office Department. The Interstate Commerce Commission was put in charge of setting "fair and reasonable" rates for the transportation of air mail, and the Bureau of Air Commerce (predecessor of the present Federal Aviation Administration) and the Department of Commerce were made responsible for the regulation of safety and the maintenance, operation, and development of the airway system. Under this Act, mail contracts once again were awarded on the basis of competitive bidding. However, carriers accused of collusion were not allowed to bid—a stipulation that caused many of these carriers to change their corporate names. In addition, the Act made holding companies illegal and therefore separated the historical affiliation between the major airlines and the aircraft manufacturers. Finally the Act also established a five-man Federal Aviation Commission to study and recommend future aviation policy for the federal government. The most important recommendation of this commission was the creation of a separate agency for economic regulation of the civil air transport industry.

With respect to cargo, regular scheduled air service had begun in 1927 when the American Railway Express Company had negotiated pickup and delivery contracts with a number of air carriers. Two years later the major railroads purchased this company and changed its name to Railway Express Agency (REA). The transportation of cargo by air had been fairly limited until about 1934, partially because the aircraft at the time did not have cargo bellies and cargo was carried in the cabin along with passengers. However, in 1934 American Airlines introduced an all-cargo service between Chicago and New York. The transportation of cargo by air was further encouraged when, in 1938, Lockheed introduced the L-14 (Super Electra) with the under-floor compartment for cargo (belly-hold). This was followed immediately by the introduction of the Boeing 314 and the Boeing 317 with a substantial cargo capacity in addition to passengers.

In summary, there had been no clear direction or regulation of the industry until the late thirties. Almost half of the private capital invested in the industry had been lost, and almost half of the domestic airlines carrying mail showed operating losses. The air transport industry was passing through a state of ruinous competition. Some carriers were submitting ridiculously low bids to obtain the air mail contracts and routes. Many of the smaller carriers could not bid against the giants, and public investment was beginning to shrink. Legislation that would provide control of competition and assure carrier operation was needed to stabilize the industry financially; also a single regulatory agency was deemed necessary to put an end to the confusion of responsibility.

Developments between 1938 and 1958

The Civil Aeronautics Act of 1938 placed the development, regulation, and control of air carriers under the jurisdiction of a single, independent administrative body, later known as the Civil Aeronautics Board (hereafter referred to as the CAB, or simply the Board).[a] This Act broadened the scope of safety regulation and for the first time subjected the airlines to economic regulation. Carriers offering commercial service were now required to obtain from the Board a certificate of public convenience and necessity specifying the points to be served and the services to be rendered. The carriers that received certificates to operate were also required to carry mail in accordance with Post Office Department requirements. The awarding of mail contracts was abolished. The Board exercised complete power to determine "fair and reasonable" rates for the transportation of passengers, property, and mail. The Board also had the power to regulate competition; decide on consolidations, mergers, and acquisitions; and regulate the holding of interlocking positions by officers or directors. The Board also regulated the U.S. flag carriers engaged in foreign air transportation and foreign flag carriers operating to and from the United States. These points are discussed in greater detail in subsequent chapters.

Under the "grandfather" clause, carriers who made application for a certificate of public convenience and necessity within 120 days after the date of the enactment of the Civil Aeronautics Act were entitled to receive a certificate upon demonstration of continuous and regular air service from May 14, 1938 until the effective date of the Act. Initially twenty-two carriers were granted certificates to provide air transportation service; eighteen carriers over domestic routes with respect to persons, property, and mail; two U.S. flag carriers over foreign and overseas routes; and two carriers over domestic routes with respect to persons and property only.[2] At the time grandfather certificates of public convenience and necessity were being awarded for scheduled service, several

---

[a]The Civil Aeronautics Board is an independent federal agency consisting of five members appointed for a 6-year term by the President with the consent of the Senate. No more than three members can be appointed from the same political party. One member is designated as Chairman and one as Vice Chairman. The decisions made by the Board are not normally subject to review by any executive department or agency, except in cases dealing with foreign air transportation. In such cases, it is necessary to receive the approval of the President of the United States.

carriers were providing nonscheduled air service on a demand basis. Although these carriers were not required to obtain the certificate, they were required to obtain a letter of registration and to report annually the nature and scope of their air transport operations.

With respect to air cargo, the Board in 1941 created a new classification called *indirect air carriers*, and REA became the first such carrier. In an effort to expand air cargo operations and perform long-range research studies, the Big Four carriers (American, Eastern, TWA, and United) established an organization known as Air Cargo Inc., and in subsequent years a number of other carriers joined this organization. The initial studies must have shown significant growth potential in air cargo, because in 1944 American began scheduled air freight service. This carrier applied for and received the Board's approval for the first comprehensive air freight tariff; this tariff contained commodity rates that varied according to characteristics such as weight, value, perishability, and fragility. In 1946 an all-cargo aircraft—the war surplus C-46 with a 9,300-pound capacity, a 180-miles-per-hour speed, and a 1,400-mile range—was put into service. In addition to the cargo services offered by the combination carriers, the Board in 1949 granted temporary certificates of public convenience and necessity to four all-cargo carriers: Airnews, Flying Tigers, Slick, and U.S. Airlines.

In the international area the main function of the Board was to coordinate its activities with the Department of State and other interested government agencies working on aeronautical matters. Under the Foreign Air Mail Act of 1928 all carriers that were successful in bids to offer foreign mail service were required to obtain, on their own, all landing rights in the foreign country. However, by 1940 the government's policy toward exchanging landing rights had changed. The landing privileges at foreign airports were to be negotiated by the Department of State and subject to presidential approval. It was the Board's responsibility to determine which U.S. carrier should receive the authority to operate the negotiated routes. The main reasons for this policy were: first, to provide equal opportunity for all carriers; second, to eliminate the possibility of multicarrier applications for landing rights in an individual country; and third, to eliminate the possibility of rejection by the CAB for the certificate of public convenience and necessity when a particular carrier had already obtained the necessary landing rights in a foreign country. This policy, in essence, put an end to Pan American's monopoly on negotiating and operating exclusive landing rights.

Negotiations for the North Atlantic route, begun as early as 1929, had resulted in preliminary agreements to offer service twice a week between the United States and England. However, the British insisted that Pan American could not offer the service until such time that a British carrier could also offer similar service. Since the British did not possess a commercial aircraft capable of flying the North Atlantic, service was delayed. In the meantime Juan Trippe involved himself with establishing service on the Pacific. Survey flights were made as early as 1931. While the northern Great Circle route required landing permission from Russia and Japan, the Central Pacific route contained fueling points that were U.S. territories. In 1935 Pan American received the transpacific mail contract for service from San Francisco to Manila. In 1936 the service was offered to passengers, in 1937 the route was extended to Hong Kong, and by 1940 Pan American extended its transpacific route from Hawaii to include New Zealand and Australia.

World War II disrupted civil air transportation in the United States. The armed forces took over a significant percentage of the civilian fleet, and an additional 200 aircraft were earmarked as a reserve to be held within the United States for use in possible emergency military air transportation. Service on many routes was suspended or curtailed. For example, service was suspended on markets that were primarily recreational and on short-haul routes where other alternative modes of travel were available. In addition, the air transportation priority system established a precedence of transportation of air passengers and cargo on scheduled air carriers. Finally, carriers were prohibited from operating nonscheduled services without special permission from the Military Director of Civil Aviation. On the positive side, the War was responsible for the rapid technical and operational development of transport aircraft. Many refinements were made to aircraft that had been in existence prior to the War, and new aircraft introduced during the War, such as the DC-4 and the Lockheed Constellation, possessed higher payload capacity, range, and speed. Refinements were also introduced to other areas including radio communication, navigational aids, instrument flying, and airport facilities.

Toward the end of the War, many nations were interested in formulating a universal international air transport policy that would regulate commercial air rights and establish rules governing technical and navigational aspects. In 1944, at the invitation of the United States, fifty-four nations sent their representatives to the Chicago Conference to formulate universal international air transport policy for international travel and commerce. Due to the conflicting interests of the various nations present at the conference, an agreement was not reached to provide a means for exchanging commercial rights to fly in and out of foreign nations. Basically there were two conflicting views—on the one hand, the United States' desire for relatively complete competitive freedom; and on the other, the United Kingdom's support of rather heavily regulated operations. The British wanted to set up an international agency to control capacities, frequencies, and fares. Routes were to be assigned through bilateral agreements. The United States was against the policy of regulating capacities and fares and suggested that the agency's control be limited to the technical side of air transportation.

The outcome of the Chicago Conference was the establishment of both the International Air Services Transit Agreement and the Provisional International Civil Aviation Organization (PICAO). The former agreement would allow civil aircraft of the signatories to fly across another nation's territory without landing if the nation was a participant in the agreement, and to land, when necessary, for noncommercial purposes. PICAO's functions included the coordination of the activities of the nations signing any agreement made at the Chicago Conference and the responsibility to act as an arbitrator in case of conflicts between the various member states. PICAO, however, did not possess any economic powers to be applied to the international air transport industry.

In 1945 the International Air Transport Association (IATA) was formally established at Havana, Cuba. This organization superseded the original one formed in 1919 in Europe to standardize air travel among foreign countries. Unlike the old organization, the principal function of the new IATA was to set rates on international routes. However, there were no provisions for regulating capacities or frequencies; these were to be negotiated through bilateral agreements. In addition to this new function, many of the functions of the old IATA were still to be performed by the new IATA. The machinery to set international fares is quite complex and is described in detail in Chapter 14. For the present it is sufficient to say that the two most important provisions in the functioning of IATA with regard to setting fares were: (1) a proposed tariff had to be approved unanimously by all the members, and (2) the approved tariff was still subject to the approval of the aeronautical agency of each of the member nations that would be affected by the proposed tariff.

Since the Chicago Conference did not result in an agreement to decide on a means of exchanging commercial rights, representatives from Great Britain and the United States met in Bermuda in 1946 to exchange operating rights between the two nations. The Bermuda Agreement resulted in the "five freedoms" of the air. The first two freedoms were essentially agreed upon at the Chicago Conference; namely, to fly across another nation's territory and to land for noncommercial purposes. The remaining freedoms were to disembark passengers and cargo that originated in the carrier's home country in a foreign country, to pick up passengers and cargo destined for the carrier's home country from a foreign country, and to transport passengers and cargo from one foreign country to another foreign country.

Most countries were in favor of a Bermuda-type agreement for exchanging international traffic rights for commercial civil aviation. The terms of the original Bermuda Agreement between the United Kingdom and the United States were fairly liberal. For example, the agreement did not include provisions for restricting frequency or number of carriers of either country. Since then, however, the policies of countries have changed. For instance, in 1966 a special bilateral agreement was signed between the United States and the U.S.S.R. to provide service between New York and Moscow. The agreement varies in format from the usual Bermuda type in that it contains provisions on the frequency of service between the two countries as well as a designation of the carrier that may operate these flights. Further discussion on bilateral agreements and IATA is postponed until Chapter 14.

After the War, Pan American was a strong promoter of the "chosen instrument" concept. Under this concept, all international services were to be operated by a single carrier. In international operations a country may sometimes designate one or more national carriers to offer parallel services on a given route. The United States has authorized this type of designation on the North Atlantic. London is served, for example, by National, Pan American, TWA, and Seaboard, an all-cargo carrier. The decision for multidesignation on an international route involves many factors, such as density of the route, the extent of traffic generated by each country, the market share of the carriers of each country, fifth-freedom traffic, and national interest.[3] While some of these factors are market related and based upon simple economics, others are of a political nature and, as such, are very difficult to evaluate. In the United States the CAB favored competition among the airlines. As early as 1942 American Export Airlines (formed by a shipping company) was awarded a temporary certificate to offer transatlantic service. The Board justified this on the grounds that an additional carrier would both improve the service as well as serve as a yardstick for comparison of costs. The latter reason was particularly important for calculating the level of subsidy that was set to recover the total operating costs. Soon after the War, Pan American faced further competition when another U.S. carrier, TWA, was authorized to offer scheduled service on the North Atlantic.

With expansion of routes, excess capacity, and sizeable investments in larger and faster aircraft, the domestic U.S. air transport industry was facing an economic crisis in 1948. The scheduled carriers were facing increased competition from nonscheduled carriers, who increased their level of activity at the end of the War. This increased activity was basically the result of nonscheduled operations that were initiated by former military personnel who had purchased war-surplus aircraft. In order to improve the economic situation of the industry, the Board authorized high mail rates. The additional mail revenue was supplemented by growth in passenger traffic due to the introduction of lower fares, partly a result of the economics of larger and faster aircraft and partly the result of management initiative in introducing differential pricing mechanisms, such as coach-type service and family-fare plans.

In 1951 the Board issued a report that contained a program for administrative separation of service from subsidy elements in mail rates. By this time the trunk-line carriers were no longer receiving federal subsidy. The object of this program was to identify those amounts that were compensation to the carriers for transporting mail and those amounts that represented the cost of maintaining and developing the airline industry. Service mail pay was designated solely to compensate the carrier for the service of transporting the mail. Subsidy, on the other hand, was that part of a carrier's mail pay that was designed to provide enough revenue, over and above revenue from commercial operations, to enable the carrier to meet expenses under honest, economical, and efficient management and to provide a fair return on investment. This topic is discussed in greater detail in Chapter 12.

The Board had separated the noncertificated carriers into two groups: the small, irregular carriers and the large, irregular carriers. Carriers operating aircraft over 12,500 pounds were classified as large, irregular carriers and had to comply with a greater measure of economic regulation than those operating equipment under 12,500 pounds. The large, irregular carriers, later known as the *supplemental carriers*, were required to file tariffs in addition to obtaining letters of registration. They could select the points they wished to serve and offer individually ticketed and individually waybilled transportation as long as the operations were irregular and infrequent. The small, irregular carriers were known as *air-taxi operators* and *commuter carriers* and offered service between communities not served by scheduled carriers to points receiving scheduled airline service. Under certain prescribed conditions the air-taxi operators were allowed to carry mail.

Another category of air carriers consisted of the helicopter air service operators. The Helicopter Air Service Program was started after the War with subsidies to helicopter carriers in a few major cities for the carriage of mail. Los Angeles Airways began the first certificated, regularly scheduled commercial helicopter service in the United States in October 1947. A temporary 3-year certificate authorized helicopter passenger and mail service over three circular routes, totaling about 200 miles in length and radiating out of the Los Angeles Municipal Airport to about thirty post offices in the area. Initially the carrier transported mail only. Two years later Chicago Helicopter Airways started operations between Midway and O'Hare Airports. In 1952 New York Airways began scheduled mail service and a year later became the world's first scheduled passenger helicopter service operator.

By the mid-1950s the airline industry could be considered established. In 1955 the Board issued permanent certificates to most of the local service carriers (initially established in 1945) and attempted to improve their routes. The Board proposed that those routes on the local service carriers that were also served by trunk lines should have the trunk-line service suspended to eliminate uneconomic competition. In addition the Board began to offer some relief from the point-to-point service requirements incorporated in the local service carriers' certificates. These carriers were awarded skip-stop authority that allowed skipping service to intermediate points once a minimum amount of daily service had been provided at these points. Thus the local service carriers were essentially authorized to fly nonstop in noncompetitive terminal-to-terminal markets and to offer one-stop service in the competitive terminal-to-terminal markets. The development of local service carriers is discussed in greater detail in subsequent chapters.

The Federal Aviation Act of 1958

Since the enactment of the Civil Aeronautics Act in 1938, the government's regulatory functions and responsibilities increased substantially with the result that additional regulatory tools were needed to enable the Board to deal effectively with the complex problems. Congress enacted the Federal Aviation Act of 1958 to amend and replace the Civil Aeronautics Act of 1938. However, the Board's economic regulatory authority remained essentially unchanged. The new act established the Federal Aviation Agency (FAA); its functions were to regulate airspace; acquire, operate, and develop air navigation facilities; and prescribe traffic rules for all aircraft. The FAA was also charged with carrying out research and development on matters related to the above as well as with certificating pilots, aircraft maintenance facilities, and personnel. Although regulation of safety was under the jurisdiction of the FAA, the investigation of civil aircraft accidents was still the responsibility of the CAB.

The Federal Aviation Act of 1958 has been amended a number of times. It contains fifteen Titles. The Declaration of Policy is contained in Title I. Section 102 of Title I states,

. . . in the exercise and the performance of its powers and duties under the Act, the Board shall consider the following, among other things, as being in the public interest, and in accordance with the public convenience and necessity:

a. The encouragement and development of an air transportation system proper-ly adapted to the present and future needs of the foreign and domestic commerce of the United States, of the Postal Service, and of the national defense;
b. The regulation of air transportation in such manner as to recognize and preserve the inherent advantages of, assure the highest degree of safety in, and foster sound economic conditions in, such transportation, and to improve the relations between, and coordinate transportation by air carriers;
c. The promotion of adequate, economical, and efficient service by air carriers at reasonable charges, without unjust discriminations, undue preferences or advantages, or unfair or destructive competitive practices;
d. Competition to the extent necessary to assure the sound development of an air transportation system properly adapted to the needs of foreign and domestic commerce of the United States, of the Postal Service, and of the national defense;
e. The promotion of safety in air commerce; and
f. The promotion, encouragement, and development of civil aeronautics.

The previous paragraph shows the general statement of policy, and due to its broad nature and scope, the Board has used the same policy statement to deal with many different situations as evidenced by the various Board decisions discussed in this book. As an example of the generality of the Declaration of Policy, consider part (d) dealing with competition. The Board is required to promote competition "to the extent necessary." First of all, what constitutes competition, and then exactly what is the extent necessary to assure the sound development? It should be kept in mind that one of the reasons for regulation is to protect the public interest, even in cases where public interest can only be protected by protecting the industry. While the function of the Board is to provide the public with the benefit of competition, it also has to protect the air carriers from excessive competition. Thus while the policy calls for competition, it is up to the Board to decide on the correct amount of competition.

The Board derives its economic regulatory powers from Title IV, which has seventeen separate sections. The most important sections of Title IV deal with routes, rates, subsidies, and mergers. Each one of these four areas is discussed in Chapters 10 through 13. In order to provide some background to these chapters, certain sections of Title IV are highlighted here. The reader is cautioned that only portions of Title IV are stated below as they relate to the following chapters.[b]

Section 401 gives details of the Board's functions with respect to certification of carriers on both domestic and international routes for transportation of passengers, property, and mail. The Board will issue a certificate of public convenience and necessity if it ". . . finds that the applicant is fit, willing, and able to perform such transportation properly, . . . and that such transportation is required by the public convenience and necessity. . . ." Under the "grandfather" clause of the act, certificates of public convenience and necessity were issued to domestic carriers for routes on which these carriers could show reasonable service from May 14 to August 22, 1938. In cases where an application was made for new routes or for extension of existing routes, the Board took into consideration:

1. Does a public need exist that will be served usefully by the applicant's service?
2. Can this need be fulfilled adequately by the existing carriers?
3. Will the service proposed by the applicant jeopardize the operations of the existing carriers contrary to the public interest?
4. Does the cost of the proposed service exceed the benefit?
5. Does the financial and economic need of the applicant carrier justify the award?

Section 402 empowers the Board to issue permits to foreign air carriers if it finds that the applicant is fit, willing, and able to perform the service and that

[b]For the complete text of the Act the reader is referred to other references such as Andreas F. Lowenfeld, *Aviation Law: Cases and Material*, Documents Supplement (New York: Matthew Bender, 1972).

the service is in the public interest. The Board also has the authority to modify, suspend, or revoke the authority if it is found to be in the public interest. The application from the foreign carrier is usually processed by the Department of State before any action can be taken by the Board.

The next most important area of regulation pertains to passenger fares, mail rates, and cargo rates. Section 403 requires that every air carrier file with the Board tariffs showing all rates, fares, and charges for air transportation. The Board is empowered to reject any tariff filed by the carriers if it is not consistent with the Board's requirements. Air carriers are not allowed to charge fares and rates different than the effective tariffs. The carriers are not allowed to change tariffs unless they give a 30-day notice to the Board. Section 404 states the law against discrimination by stipulating that, "no carrier . . . shall make, give, or cause any undue or unreasonable preference or advantage to any particular person, port, locality, or description of traffic in air transportation in any respect whatsoever. . . ."

Section 405 requires the carriers to file schedules with the Postmaster General, who is empowered to modify schedules for the transportation of mail. Section 406 provides the Board with authority to fix fair and reasonable rates of compensation. In fixing and determining such rates the Board considers the conditions peculiar to transportation by aircraft and to the particular air carriers or class of carriers. Among other factors, the Board is required under this section to take into consideration, "such standards respecting the character and quality of service to be produced by air carriers . . . and . . . the need rendered by air carriers . . . for compensation for the transportation of mail sufficient to ensure the performance of such service, and, together with all other revenue of the air carrier, to enable such air carrier under honest, economical, and efficient management, to maintain and continue the development of air transportation to the extent and of the character and quality required for the commerce of the United States, the Postal Service, and the national defense."

Under Section 407 the carriers are required to submit any information required by the Board in accordance with the forms prescribed by the Board. The carriers are also required to provide the Board with a list showing the names of each of their stockholders holding more than 5 percent of the entire capital stock.

The carriers are not allowed to consolidate or merge their properties unless such actions have been approved by the Board. Under Section 408 the parties interested in, ". . . merger . . . shall present an application to the Board, and thereupon the Board shall notify the persons involved in the . . . merger . . . and other persons known to have a substantial interest in the proceedings, of the time and place of a public hearing. Unless, after such hearing, the Board finds that the . . . merger . . . will not be consistent with the public interest . . . it shall by order approve such . . . merger . . . upon such terms and conditions as it shall find to be just and reasonable . . . provided, that the Board shall not approve any . . . merger . . . which would result in creating a monopoly or monopolies and thereby restrain competition or jeopardize another air carrier not party to the . . . merger . . . " This will be discussed further in Chapter 13. The remaining sections of Title IV provide the Board with various ways to exercise its regulatory control of the air carrier industry.

Finally, Title X, Section 1002(d) and (e) also provide some insight into the economic regulation of the Board as discussed in subsequent chapters. Elsewhere it has been stated that tariff charges are filed by the carriers and the Board either approves or disapproves the applications. If the Board takes no action within a specified period of time, the charges become effective. However, the Board has the power to institute an investigation if, in its opinion or through some outside complaints, it finds that the existing fares and rates are unjust or unreasonable. If after the proper hearings and investigations the Board finds this to be the case, then it has the power to ". . . determine and prescribe the lawful rate, fare, or charge (or the maximum or minimum, or the maximum and minimum thereof). . . ." In the case of international fares the Board's authority is limited to determining the maximum or minimum, or maximum and minimum rate, fare, or charge. If the Board should use its power to determine the proper fares and rates, then the following should be taken into consideration:

1. The effect of such rates upon the movement of traffic.
2. The need in the public interest of adequate and efficient transportation of persons and property by air carriers at the lowest cost consistent with the furnishing of such service.
3. Such standards respecting the character and quality of service to be rendered by air carriers as may be prescribed by or pursuant to law.
4. The inherent advantages of transportation by aircraft.
5. The need of each air carrier for revenue sufficient to enable such air carrier, under honest, economical, and efficient management, to provide adequate and efficient air carrier service.[4]

The Board performs its functions through its six bureaus. Bureau of Accounts and Statistics administers the uniform system of accounts and collects and processes both traffic and financial statistics. The Bureau of Economics deals with passenger fares, cargo rates, and subsidy and performs economic studies related to the air transportation industry. The Bureau of Enforcement ensures compliance with the regulations of the Board. The Bureau of Administrative Law Judges houses hearing examiners who are usually administrative law judges. The Bureau of International Affairs deals with foreign air transportation and coordinates its activities with the Department of State and the President. The Bureau of Operating Rights licenses air carriers, analyzes monopolies and interest conflicts, and generally maintains the proper competitive climate.[5]

Developments Following the
Act of 1958

The most significant development following the Federal Aviation Act of 1958 was the introduction of the jet aircraft. Although research and development of the jet engine were well under way during and even prior to World War II, it was not until 1952 that the public was offered commercial jet service by BOAC, which unfortunately had to be withdrawn shortly thereafter for technical reasons. In 1956 the Russians introduced the TU-104. The year 1958 is, however, referred to as the "jet revolution" year—Pan American introduced the Boeing 707 on the North Atlantic in October 1958 three weeks after BOAC introduced the second version of their jet, the DeHavilland Comet 4. For almost a full year there were no other competitors with jet aircraft on the North Atlantic, until September and November of 1959 when Qantas and TWA introduced the Boeing 707s. On the domestic scene National was the first carrier to offer jet service in December 1958 on the New York-Miami route with a Boeing 707 leased from Pan American. A month later American put in a Boeing 707 on the transcontinental route; TWA entered the market in March; and United introduced the DC-8 in September of 1959 on this route.

The mid-sixties not only set the pace for jet operations but also began to focus on the supersonic transport (SST). Pan American, BOAC, and Air France placed orders for the Concorde supersonic aircraft. Besides these three international air carriers, a U.S. domestic carrier, Continental, also placed an order for three Concorde aircraft. In the meantime, two airframe manufacturers and two engine manufacturers undertook the design studies of the SST for the United States Federal Aviation Agency. The major portion of the cost of research and development was to be borne by the federal government. The Boeing Airplane Company and General Electric were selected to design the SST. This team won the competition, but the project was abandoned in 1971 for political, environmental, and socio-economic reasons.

In the mid-1950s the Board had begun a major investigation into passenger fares. *The General Passenger Fare Investigation* had been initiated in 1956 to determine the appropriate standards on which to evaluate domestic fare changes that would provide adequate earnings by the industry to ensure its proper development consistent with the public interest. Four years later in 1960, the Board concluded its investigation and issued its decisions setting forth standards for reasonable air fares such as capital investment base, depreciation standard for rate making purposes, and reasonable level of rate of return. The Board allowed a rate of return on investment of 10.25 percent for the Big Four and 11.125 percent for the remaining trunk-line carriers (a weighted average rate of return of 10.5 percent for the domestic trunk lines as a whole). The Board also concluded that the measure for fair earnings should be a rate of return based upon investment and not on operating ratio.[6] For further details see Chapter 11.

The name "large irregular carriers" had been changed to "supplemental carriers" in 1955 and initially twenty-five of these carriers were granted temporary certificates of public convenience and necessity. The scheduled carriers challenged this decision in the courts and obtained a reversal on the Board's decision based upon technical grounds. New legislative authority was sought, and in 1962 Congress enacted Public Law 87-528 authorizing the Board to issue permanent certificates of public convenience and necessity to thirteen supplemental carriers to operate plane-load charter flights and to phase out the individual ticket part of their services.[c] Some of the thirteen carriers were also given international route authority in certain areas. In 1966 the supplemental air carriers were authorized to operate inclusive tour charters. Under the inclusive tour charters, a tour operator charters the entire capacity of the aircraft and then sells package tours to individual members of the general public.

The mid-1960s once again witnessed a further streamlining of the transportation planning process. The U.S. Department of Transportation (DOT) was created to provide total transportation planning, policy guidance, and protection of public interest with the aim of achieving an integrated national transportation system based upon economic criteria rather than on modal preferences. Prior to this organization there were numerous uncoordinated, modally oriented transportation agencies with virtually nonexistent common goals. These agencies were generally unstructured and without sufficient authority to develop an effective national transportation system. The Department of Transportation was given the responsibility of coordinating transportation leadership; cooperating and coordinating transportation projects with federal, state, and local government agencies; and identifying prodigious transportation problems.[7]

In general the U.S. policy has reflected free trade and open competition. In the case of international operations this policy was fairly clear in the various reports on U.S. international air transport policy, such as those released in 1963 and 1970. The policy was essentially nonprotectionist, promoting reasonable rates and equal opportunities for the U.S. carriers in route exchanges with foreign nations, and opposing arbitrary capacity restrictions. On the domestic routes the Board has favored competition as witnessed by the route awards in the fifties and the sixties. However, there have been two exceptions to this general trend. First, in 1959 the Board allowed the establishment of the Air Carrier Mutual Aid Pact, and then in 1971 it allowed capacity agreements between some of the carriers.

In 1959 six major airlines—American, Capital, Eastern, Pan American, TWA,

---

[c]The Congress became aware of some of the positive as well as negative aspects of the supplemental carriers. On the positive side, the group was providing low cost air transportation such as charters. On the negative side there had been a number of accidents involving this group of carriers. In addition, there was the issue of economic and financial viability. In light of this awareness the Congress decided to look into the operations of this group of carriers and enacted Public Law 87-528 which allowed the Board at first to provide temporary certificates of public convenience and necessity. These certificates were made permanent in 1966 for domestic operations.

and United—entered into an agreement called the *Air Carrier Mutual Aid Pact.* This agreement provided for financial assistance in case of a strike. The arrangement called for payment to the struck carrier of any increased windfall revenue that they received as a result of handling the struck carrier's business less the additional expense of handling such increased traffic. In 1964 the group consisted of American, Braniff, Continental, Eastern, Northwest, Pan American, TWA, and United. Since the approval of the original pact, the carriers have filed a series of amendments. Among them were amendments to broaden the strike coverage, restrict the parties to trunk-line carriers, provide for arbitration of disputes relating to payments, and revise the obligation on windfall payments by a so-called Supplemental Payments Agreement.

The second exception to the Board's favorable policy on competition took place in 1971 when, for the first time in its history, the Board approved an air carrier agreement to reduce the total aircraft capacity offered by carriers in certain heavily scheduled markets. Originally the agreement related to four markets: (1) New York-Newark-Los Angeles, (2) New York/Newark-San Francisco, (3) Chicago-San Francisco, and (4) Washington/Baltimore-Los Angeles. Later the agreement was expanded to include some two dozen markets. After having permitted capacity control agreements on domestic routes, both United States and foreign carriers were permitted for the first time to engage in capacity limitation discussions on international routes. However, in 1975 the Board decided not to renew the capacity agreements among domestic carriers. The reasons for this decision are discussed at some length in Chapter 3.

In 1970 the Airport and Airway Development and Revenue Act was passed. This presented the mechanism for providing funds for financing air navigational facilities and assistance in the development of airports. Under this Act an Airport and Airway Trust Fund was established to provide the necessary funds. The fund receives money collected in taxes according to the following schedule: the airline passenger pays 8 percent of the ticket price, and the shipper pays 5 percent on the air freight bills. Taxes are also levied on aircraft: $25 per year on any taxable civil aircraft and 3.5 cents per pound on maximum take-off weight for any turbine-engine aircraft.[8]

In recent years the airline industry has also been influenced by two other federal agencies. The Environmental Protection Agency (EPA) was established in 1970 to permit coordinated and effective governmental action on behalf of the environment. This agency endeavors to systematically abate and control pollution by the integration of a variety of research, monitoring, standard-setting, and enforcement activities. With respect to the airline industry, the agency works with the carriers and manufacturers to reduce both invisible emissions as well as the black smoke produced by jet engines. The EPA has set January 1, 1978 as the target date for retrofitting the remaining engines. The second area of concern is the noise from jet aircraft. Aircraft noise reduction efforts are aimed at reducing noise at its source as well as using flight procedures to keep aircraft higher and quieter. Noise reduction at the source has been achieved by designing engines that are quieter through the use of high by-pass ratio engines. In addition to this, changes in flight procedures, such as the use of preferential runways and routings, more power on take-offs, and two-segment approaches, are being investigated to reduce aircraft noise.

The second agency involved with the carriers in recent years is the Federal Energy Administration (which replaced the Federal Energy Office), established to ensure that the supply of energy available will continue to be sufficient to meet total energy demand. The FEA further ensures that in the case of energy shortages, priority needs are met and the burden of the shortages is borne with equity. The impact of federal regulation in this direction was felt in October 1973 when the carriers were directed to reduce their fuel usage to 1972 levels by November 1, 1973. The direct result of this was that the number of scheduled departures in November 1973 was 6 percent less than the number of departures in November 1972. Subsequent reduction in flights also forced the carriers to furlough certain categories of employees.

In 1974 the Board concluded its *Domestic Passenger Fare Investigation* initiated in 1970. While the *General Passenger Fare Investigation* established a reasonable rate of return on investment for the domestic trunk-line carriers, no standards were established for ensuring that the fare levels reflected the cost of service provided by the carriers. Thus in the *Domestic Passenger Fare Investigation* the Board made an attempt to establish such standards. The entire investigation was decided in nine separate phases, each of which is discussed in detail in Chapter 11. The Board, also in 1970, began its *Domestic Air Freight Rate Investigation.* The examiner's initial decision was released on April 15, 1975 and is also discussed in Chapter 11.[d]

This chapter represents a very brief overview of the developments that have taken place in the United States air transport industry. During this relatively short period of 60 years, progress in the commercial air transport industry has been spectacular. In 1974 the total United States scheduled airlines boarded over 200 million passengers and earned almost $15 billion in revenue. Over $1 billion of this revenue was generated through the transportation of freight. However, since the beginning of this decade the growth in passenger traffic and carrier profitability has not kept pace with rates established in the past decades, due basically to the economic recession, excess capacity, and high cost increases for labor and fuel. In spite of the decline in traffic and profit at the beginning of this decade, the United States airline industry is expected to continue to be a growth industry under normal circumstances. However, it is not clear from recent developments that the industry's regulatory framework will continue in its present form. Since the beginning of 1975 there has been strong pressure to examine, evaluate, and possibly reform the regulatory framework in the commercial airline industry.

---

[d]The examiners are now called administrative law judges.

In 1975 the President transmitted to Congress the Aviation Act of 1975, which is claimed to increase efficiency in the airline system and provide passengers and shippers improved air transportation services at a lower cost. Basically there are four principal objectives in the proposed legislation: (1) to introduce and foster price competition in the industry; (2) to provide for entry of new airline firms into the industry and provide consumers with a greater variety of domestic airline transportation services; (3) to eliminate anticompetitive air carrier agreements; and (4) to ensure that the regulatory system protects consumer interests rather than special industry interests. Chapter 15 contains a lengthy discussion on the proposed legislation and its possible ramifications.

2 Current Industry Structure

Whereas the first chapter described the major historical developments in the U.S. airline industry, this chapter provides information on the current structure with respect to the size of the industry, operating environment, and the financial data. Familiarization with this data will provide the reader with a more complete understanding of the material contained in other chapters.

Classification of Carriers

As of 1975 there are eleven different classes of air carriers operating in the United States. These classes are distinguished in general by the operating authority. First, a distinction is made between common carriers and contract carriers: a *common carrier* operates on a fixed schedule with published tariffs, whereas a *contract carrier* does not. Second, a distinction is normally made between carriers possessing a certificate of public convenience and necessity. This certificate, issued by the CAB, authorizes the performance of scheduled air transportation over specified routes. Certain nonscheduled or charter operations may also be conducted by these carriers. Third, a distinction is made between carriers regulated by the CAB and those regulated by other agencies. Fourth, distinction is made with respect to the geographic area where the service is offered. The fifth distinction is whether the company owns the aircraft it uses or simply acts as an agent between the shipper of goods and the transporting carrier. The eleven different classes of air carriers are described below.

1. Domestic Trunk-line Carriers

The domestic trunk-line carriers have a permanent certificate of convenience and necessity and operate primarily within and between the fifty states of the United States over routes serving primarily larger communities with medium and long stage lengths. In 1974 the average length of a passenger trip on domestic trunk-line carriers was 795 miles, ranging from 2,374 miles for Pan American to 587 miles for Eastern.[a] The trunk-line carriers conduct operations with large aircraft over routes that have relatively high traffic volumes. Of the twenty-two

[a]There was a marked increase in trip length in 1970 when the Board redefined domestic traffic to include all traffic between the U.S. mainland and Hawaii and Alaska.

21

airlines established under the grandfather clause, there are currently eleven carriers in operation. The rest have exited from the market through mergers. As stated at the end of the last chapter, recently there have been strong pressures to deregulate the industry. If this trend continues, some critics fear the number of domestic trunk-line carriers may possibly shrink to the three suggested originally by Postmaster Walter Brown in the late 1920s. A list of the domestic trunk-line carriers in order of revenue passenger enplanements in 1974 and average on-flight passenger trip length is shown in Table 2-1. The passenger and stage length numbers are for domestic operations only. Thus the passengers carried on Pan American refer basically to the traffic between U.S. mainland and Hawaii.

2. Local-service Carriers

Local-service carriers are permanently certificated air carriers operating routes of lesser density between the smaller traffic centers and between those centers and principal centers. They are also known as "feeder" and "regional" air carriers. Some of these carriers receive subsidy (public service revenue) for providing service to cities that do not produce sufficient revenue to cover the cost, a point discussed at some length in Chapter 12. The name *local-service carriers* is perhaps misleading since the geographic territory of many of these carriers is quite extensive. Due to short stage lengths (averaging about 300 miles) and low density routes, small equipment is used. However, permanent certificates, government guaranteed loans for the purchase of new aircraft, and the route strengthening policy of the Board have allowed these carriers to acquire capital to purchase modern aircraft and conduct profitable operations. Table 2-1 shows the current list (1974) of these carriers by size. In 1975 the Board changed the status of Air New England from a commuter carrier to a local-service carrier. The carrier took over a number of New England routes from Delta following the New England Service Investigation and was the first new local carrier certificated in three decades.

3. International and Territorial Carriers

This classification includes U.S. carriers conducting operations between the United States and foreign countries as well as carriers that offer services to U.S. territories and possessions. With the exception of United, all domestic trunk-line carriers listed in Table 2-1 also provide some international and/or territorial service. With a long average stage length of almost 1900 miles, the international and territorial carriers use large aircraft to serve these markets.

Table 2-1
Domestic Carriers by Size, 1974

Domestic Trunk-line Carrier	Revenue Passenger Enplanements (000)	On-Flight Passenger Trip Length (miles)
United Air Lines	30,588	894
Delta Air Lines	26,004	602
Eastern Airlines	23,794	587
American Airlines	19,061	954
Trans World Airlines	13,449	1,029
Northwest Airlines	8,123	835
Western Airlines	7,561	803
Braniff International	7,472	628
Continental Air Lines	6,489	859
National Airlines	4,747	812
Pan American World Airways	705	2,374
Local-service Carrier		
Allegheny Airlines	10,900	312
North Central Airlines	4,491	226
Hughes Air West	3,966	364
Piedmont Airlines	3,821	287
Frontier Airlines	3,614	384
Ozark Air Lines	3,215	269
Southern Airways	2,940	283
Texas International Airlines	2,253	337

Source: U.S. Civil Aeronautics Board, *Air Carrier Traffic Statistics*, Washington, D.C., December 1974.

4. All-cargo Carriers

These are certificated air carriers primarily engaged in the transportation of freight and express. They are also allowed to conduct nonscheduled passenger operations. At present there are three U.S. all-cargo carriers. Two of these, Airlift International and The Flying Tiger Line, are authorized to conduct both domestic and international operations. The third, Seaboard World Airlines, is exclusively an international carrier. The all-cargo carriers compete actively with the passenger carriers that carry cargo both in the passenger aircraft as well as all-freighters. Table 2-2 shows the size of the all-cargo carriers relative to the passenger carriers. The domestic all-cargo carriers account for about 2 percent of the total revenue ton miles.

Table 2-2
Market Structure, All Services, 1974

	Revenue Ton Miles (Millions)	Percent	Available Ton Miles (Millions)	Percent
Domestic Trunk-lines (11)	15,077	63.1	31,795	64.9
Local-service Carriers (8)	1,212	5.1	2,578	5.3
International Trunk-lines (10)	5,788	24.2	11,773	24.1
Domestic All-cargo (2)	533	2.2	875	1.8
International All-cargo (3)	1,113	4.7	1,602	3.3
Alaskan (4)	103	0.4	197	0.4
Hawaiian (2)	71	0.3	112	0.2
Helicopters (3)	1	–	2	–
Other	2	–	6	–
Total	23,900	100.0	48,940	100.0

Source: U.S. Civil Aeronautics Board, *Air Carrier Traffic Statistics*, Washington, D.C., December 1974.

5. Alaskan Air Carriers

This group of air carriers operates completely within the state of Alaska using small and medium size aircraft over medium stage lengths (574 miles average in 1974). At present there are four carriers with Alaska Airlines as the largest, having carried 618,000 passengers in 1974 with an average passenger length of haul of 736 miles. The other carriers are Wien Air Alaska, Kodiak-Western Alaska Airlines, and Reeve Aleutian Airways. Table 2-2 shows that of the total certificated route air carriers, the Alaskan carriers accounted for less than one-half of one percent of the total revenue ton miles.

6. Hawaiian Air Carriers

Like the scope of the Alaskan carriers, the Hawaiian carriers' operations are confined to the islands of the State of Hawaii and represent a very small fraction of the total certificated route air carriers. At present there are two carriers offering interisland service in Hawaii. Both Aloha Airlines and Hawaiian Air enplaned about 2 million passengers in 1974 with an average passenger stage length of 138 miles.

7. Helicopter Air Carriers

These are domestic certificated route air carriers employing helicopter aircraft for their primary operations to carry passengers, mail, and freight. These carriers offer intracity, intraairport, and city-airport service with extremely short stage lengths. Until 1965 these carriers received subsidy to carry mail from the airport to central post offices and outlying districts. When the subsidy was eliminated, the trunk-line carriers supported their operations in exchange for carrying passengers between airports in large metropolitan areas. At present there are three helicopter air carriers in operation: Chicago Helicopter Airways, New York Airways, and SFO Helicopter Airlines.

8. Supplemental Air Carriers

This group of carriers was established to supplement scheduled operations of the certificated route carriers on high density routes. These carriers are sometimes referred to as *charter carriers*, nonscheduled carriers, or simply "nonskeds." Although they are authorized to conduct unlimited charter services, they are also authorized to conduct on a very limited basis (more or less emergency purposes) individually ticketed passenger services and individually waybilled cargo service. The supplemental group is also exempt from the economic regulations of the Board. One noteworthy characteristic of the supplemental carriers' operation is the very high load factor. Whereas the scheduled carriers operate typically with 50 percent load factor, the supplementals operate with almost 90 percent load factor. At present there are nine supplemental carriers. Table 2-3 shows the relative size of each of the supplemental carriers in terms of revenue passenger miles, revenue passenger originations, and freight ton miles. Most of the supplemental carriers have been very active in the transportation of military troops and supplies. For 1974, while only 17 percent of the passenger traffic was under contract to the military, almost 73 percent of the freight traffic was due to the military contracts.

Table 2-3
Traffic of Individual Supplemental Carriers, 1974

Carrier	Revenue Passenger Miles (000)	Revenue Passenger Originations	Freight Ton Miles
Capitol International Airways	1,653,900	500,315	1,288,166
Johnson Flying Services	23,926	36,288	15,898
McCulloch International Airlines	99,555	35,681	–
Modern Air Transport	541,007	406,045	4,740
Overseas National Airways	1,800,055	561,208	105,233,537
Saturn Airways	698,457	201,422	244,238,748
Southern Air Transport	–	–	–
Trans International Airlines	3,545,238	753,328	14,444,075
World Airways	2,500,311	700,166	21,661,804

Source: U.S. Civil Aeronautics Board, *Air Carrier Traffic Statistics*, Washington, D.C., December 1974, pp. 93-95.

9. Intrastate Carriers

The operations of this group of carriers are restricted to an area within one state. The group is not regulated by the Board. Instead they are regulated by an agency in their own state. The largest intrastate carrier, by far, is Southwest Airlines (PSA), operating within the state of California. On the Los Angeles-San Francisco route PSA carries almost as many passengers as TWA, United, and Western put together. For example, in the year ending June 1972, PSA carried 1,128,421 passengers from Los Angeles to San Francisco; TWA carried 323,227; United carried 770,287; and Western carried 415,721. The other significant intrastate carriers are Air California, Southwest Airlines (in Texas), Air Florida, Air Illinois, and Aero Southwest (in Oklahoma). [b]

10. Commuter Carriers

Over the years, a number of local-service carriers have abandoned the very low density markets and short-haul markets. Many of these markets have been taken over by commuter air carriers that conduct services according to a published schedule on specific routes. This is different from the air-taxi operators who fly on a demand basis only. In 1969 the CAB defined a commuter air carrier as an air-taxi operator that first performs at least five round trips per week between two or more points and publishes flight schedules and second transports mail by air pursuant to a current contract with the U.S. Postal Service. The commuter carriers are not regulated by the Board as long as they operated with aircraft that have a gross take-off weight less than 12,500 pounds. In 1972 the Board changed this requirement to thirty seats or 7,500 pound payload unless the operations of larger aircraft are warranted to satisfy the needs of specific markets. The commuter carriers do not need a certificate of public convenience and necessity, and their fares and rates are not subject to the Board's regulation. They also do not receive federal subsidy. In 1974 there were about 222 commuter carriers reporting traffic data to the Board, although this number varies from quarter to quarter. About 162 of these carried passengers. Tables 2-4 and 2-5 show a summary of the service offered and traffic carried during the year ending June 30, 1974.

11. Indirect Air Carriers

Indirect air carriers are entities that do not actually transport the air freight but instead act as agents between the shipper and the air carrier. Air Freight Forwarders are indirect air carriers that conduct business under the exemption

[b]Alaskan and Hawaiian carriers are also intrastate carriers.

Table 2-4

Summary of Commuter Air Carrier Service for the Year Ended June 30, 1974

Type of Service	Carriers	Number of Airports	City-Pairs
Passenger Only	28	85	405
Cargo Only	27	45	301
Mail Only	23	77	236
Passenger and Cargo	83	268	665
Passenger and Mail	2	16	25
Cargo and Mail	10	36	55
Passenger, Cargo, and Mail	49	198	162
Total	222	725	1,849

Source: U.S. Civil Aeronautics Board, *Commuter Air Carrier Traffic Statistics*, year ended June 30, 1974, Bureau of Operating Rights, Standards Division, Washington, D.C., July 1975.

authority of the Board. An air freight forwarder collects individual shipments, consolidates them into a large load, and hands it to an airline to fly to a specific city. The air freight forwarder cannot charge rates higher than those available from the airline. Its profits come from the discounts available from the airline for large loads. At present there are 330 authorized air freight forwarders. Of these, 236 hold both domestic and international authorizations; 43 hold domestic authorizations only; and 51 hold international authorizations only. In 1973 the air freight forwarder industry consolidated just under a million tons of freight, generated $818 million, and posted an operating profit before taxes of $16.3 million.

Composite Industry Data

Although the airlines account for almost 80 percent of the passenger miles of the common carriers, their share of the U.S. passenger miles is less than 10 percent when the private automobile is included in the total traffic. In terms of passenger travel between the United States and foreign countries, airlines carry over 93 percent of the passengers. The U.S. international trunk lines carry just over half of these passengers. The rest is shared by all the foreign flag carriers operating to and from the United States.

The average domestic air passenger yield (average revenue per passenger mile) is 7.5 cents compared to 5.9 cents for Class I railroads and 4.4 cents for Class I motor buses (1974 data). The average passenger yield is higher for domestic air travel compared to international air travel (7.5 cents versus 7.3 cents). The

Table 2-5
Summary of Commuter Air Carrier Traffic for the Year Ended June 30, 1974[a]

Quarter	Number of Carriers[b]	Passengers
First	136	1,618,079
Second	136	1,359,725
Third	133	1,585,808
Fourth	134	1,731,413
Total	162	6,295,025
		Cargo (lbs.)
First	136	24,735,312
Second	135	23,564,876
Third	136	29,890,465
Fourth	137	33,406,737
Total	169	111,597,390
		Mail (lbs.)
First	63	36,270,804
Second	59	34,329,187
Third	68	39,383,831
Fourth	70	40,897,564
Total	85	150,881,386

[a]Totals exclude data for carriers reporting incorrectly.

[b]Number of carriers reporting the traffic data shown for each quarter and the year.

Source: U.S. Civil Aeronautics Board, *Commuter Air Carrier Traffic Statistics*, year ended June 30, 1974, Bureau of Operating Rights, Standards Division, Washington, D.C., July 1975.

variance in freight rates is more significant between modes. The average freight yield (average revenue per freight ton mile) for the domestic U.S. scheduled airlines is 25.9 cents compared to 1.9 cents for Class I railroads and 8.7 cents for Class I trucks.[c]

Most of the passenger and cargo traffic is carried in the 2,244 aircraft in the carrier fleet in 1974. Almost 80 percent of the fleet consists of jet aircraft. The piston and turbo-prop aircraft are mostly operated by the local service carriers.

[c]It must be remembered that the trucking industry yield figure reflects only the regulated common motor carrier portion of the total trucking industry (or about 30 percent of the total). If the other portions of the trucking industry are included, for example, the exempt carriers, the owner operators, and the private carriers (for which data are scarce), the yield figure would drop to approximately 2.5 cents per ton mile, making the trucking industry highly competitive with the railroads. See James T. Kneafsey, *Transportation Economic Analysis* (Lexington, Massachusetts: Lexington Books, D.C. Heath and Company, 1975), Chapter 22.

Most of the jet aircraft were purchased in the decade of the 1960s beginning with the Boeing 707/DC-8 type and followed by the smaller two and three engine DC-9, Boeing 737, and Boeing 727 types. The 1970s witnessed the introduction of wide-body jets beginning with the Boeing 747 and followed by the DC-10 and Lockheed 1011. The jet aircraft in the early 1960s reduced the unit operating costs. However, high inflation rates towards the end of the decade changed this earlier trend in the unit operating costs. The wide-body jets in the 1970s were supposed to reverse this trend. However, continued high inflation rates accompanied by the fuel price situation have not allowed the wide-body jets to reflect this expected change in the trend. In fact, with the exception of some very dense routes, a number of carriers are replacing the Boeing 747 with smaller jets. In light of the recent traffic growth and fuel price situation, a number of carriers claim that the most economical aircraft is the Boeing 727. By the end of 1974 U.S. carriers were flying 724 Boeing 727s out of a total of 1,988 jet aircraft. Given this trend, it is very likely that in the future any sizable order for new aircraft would have been the proposed Boeing 727-300, an enlarged version of the Boeing 727-200. However, with United backing out of the commitment to order the Boeing 727-300, it is unlikely that the aircraft will be produced.

The U.S. scheduled airline industry employs over 300,000 persons. Approximately one-third of these employees represent the aircraft traffic servicing personnel. Other major categories include: office employees (20 percent); mechanics (15 percent); cabin crew (14 percent); and pilots and copilots (9 percent). Labor costs are the largest single expense category, representing in 1973 45.7 percent for the trunk-line carriers and 48.9 percent for the local-service carriers. In 1973 the average labor cost per employee was $17,554 for trunk lines and $17,542 for local-service carriers. Among the trunk lines, American reported the highest cost per employee ($18,937); and TWA, the lowest ($16,180). Among the local-service carriers, Allegheny reported the highest cost per employee ($18,900); and Southern, the lowest ($15,070). The average revenue ton miles per employee ranged from a high of 115,530 (Northwest) to a low of 55,569 (Eastern) with 77,359 as the average for the trunk lines. For the local-service carriers, the average revenue ton miles per employee ranged from a high of 47,771 (Allegheny) to a low of 34,286 (Piedmont) with 40,327 as the average for the total group.

Route Structure

As mentioned earlier, the long-haul, high density routes are served by the trunk-line carriers and short-haul feeder routes are served by the local-service carriers. However, the Board, through its authority over the certification of new routes, has altered the competitive balance among the carriers. For instance, the

Board, in its major decisions of the 1950s and early 1960s, strengthened the small trunk lines at the expense of the Big Four. The percentage of the total passenger miles flown by the Big Four has declined from 73.8 percent in 1938 to 45.4 percent in 1972. In the late 1960s the Board expanded the route authority of the local-service carriers (either new route authority or removals of restriction on nonstop service) in an attempt to strengthen them, improve service to certain areas, and at the same time reduce the subsidy requirements. With the expansion of the route authority of the local service carriers, the share of domestic trunk lines was reduced from 81.9 percent in 1969 to 77.5 percent in 1972. Data prior to 1969 cannot be compared due to the change in the Board's definition of domestic operations. Since the beginning of this decade the Board has maintained a moratorium on major route awards.

In the United States, scheduled air service is offered on some 58,000 city-pairs. However, the top 1,000 city-pairs account for about 70 percent of the passenger traffic. Table 2-6 shows the concentration of passenger traffic in the United States domestic city-pairs ranked in terms of passenger volume. Less than 2 percent of all city-pairs account for more than 70 percent of the passengers. The densest domestic route in terms of passenger volume is Boston-New York, which accounts for more than 5,000 passengers daily. This data should be used with caution since it does not contain intrastate traffic. When intrastate traffic is included, the San Francisco-Los Angeles route is by far the densest route in the world in terms of passenger volume.

Ever since its inception, the Board has always encouraged competition. Very few routes are purely monopolistic. Table 2-7 shows the extent of competition in the top 100 domestic city-pairs. While the actual total number of competitors in a market varies from two to twelve, the effective number of competitors generally ranges from two to three. There are exceptions to this general rule, such as the Honolulu-Los Angeles market where there are six effective competitors. In Table 2-7 an *effective carrier* is defined as one that serves at least 10 percent of the total traffic carried by the largest carrier in that market.

With respect to competition, the most controversial action taken by the Board has been the approval of agreements to restrict capacity among carriers in selected markets. In September 1971 the Board allowed American, TWA, and United to agree collectively to reduce capacity in four transcontinental markets in order to improve the load factor in the industry. Proponents of capacity agreements support this action on the grounds that fuel is saved and wasteful competition is reduced. Opponents to these agreements view them as purely short-term solutions to the inefficient operation of some carriers, resulting also in the loss of desirable competition. In general the larger carriers are in favor, while the smaller carriers oppose the agreements.

Financial Structure

As shown in Table 2-2, the combination carriers account for some 93 percent of the total revenue ton miles. Although these carriers are authorized to transport

Table 2-6

Concentration of Passenger Traffic in the U.S. Domestic City-Pairs (10 Percent Sample for 12 Months Ended September 30, 1974)

Rank	City-Pair	Passengers (10% sample)	Cumulative Percent of Total
1	Boston-New York	184,311	1.39
10	Chicago-Los Angeles	69,511	9.28
20	Chicago-Washington	51,629	13.75
30	Boston-Chicago	39,446	17.04
40	Los Angeles-Washington	33,422	19.78
50	Honolulu-San Francisco	28,910	22.13
60	Los Angeles-San Diego	26,647	24.18
70	Chicago-Fort Lauderdale	24,133	26.09
80	Houston-Los Angeles	21,231	27.79
90	Indianapolis-New York	19,878	29.35
100	Miami-Orlando	17,888	30.74
200	Orlando-Philadelphia	11,207	41.38
300	San Diego-Washington	7,886	48.38
400	Chicago-Raleigh	5,993	53.62
500	Jacksonville-Washington	5,063	57.80
600	Honolulu-Kamuela	4,168	61.28
700	Cleveland-Dayton	3,595	64.19
800	Greenville-Washington	3,055	66.68
900	Phoenix-Pittsburgh	2,675	68.84
1000	Des Moines-Washington	2,312	70.71

Source: U.S. Civil Aeronautics Board, *Origin-Destination Survey of Airline Passenger Traffic, Domestic*, Volume VII-3-I, Third Quarter 1974, Washington, D.C., 1974, pp. 32-43.

both passengers and cargo, they have concentrated on passenger transportation during the last three decades. Table 2-8 shows that the U.S. domestic trunk lines derive 85.6 percent of their revenue from passenger transportation. The corresponding figures for the local-service carriers and the U.S. international trunk lines are 84.0 percent and 72.6 percent respectively. The revenue derived from freight, express, and cargo is a very small fraction of the total revenue. For the all-cargo carriers, the largest component of revenue is freight—87.5 percent for domestic operations and 64.9 for international operations. Other components of revenue for the all-cargo carriers are express, mail, and charter.

Table 2-8 also shows the breakdown of operating expenses. For all classes of carriers, the largest component of operating expense is flying operations followed by aircraft and traffic servicing. An examination of the various cost categories shows that the largest increases have been in fuel costs. The trunk-line carriers paid almost two and one-half times as much for a gallon of fuel for domestic operations in March 1975 as compared to March 1973, and almost

Table 2-7
Competition in the Top 100 U.S. Domestic City-Pairs (12 Months Ending September 30, 1974)

		Number of Competitors		
Rank	Market	Total	Effective	Airlines
1	Boston-New York	8	2	AA EA
2	New York-Washington	12	2	AA EA
3	Chicago-New York	12	3	AA TW UA
4	Miami-New York	8	3	DL EA NA
5	Los Angeles-New York	8	3	AA TW UA
6	Fort Lauderdale-New York	6	3	DL EA NA
7	Los Angeles-San Francisco	10	3	TW UA WA
8	New York-San Francisco	7	3	AA TW UA
9	Detroit-New York	9	2	AA NW
10	Chicago-Los Angeles	8	4	AA CO TW UA
11	Las Vegas-Los Angeles	6	2	RW WA
12	Chicago-Detroit	9	3	AA NW UA
13	New York-Pittsburgh	6	2	AL TW
14	Boston-Washington	8	4	AA AL DL EA
15	Cleveland-New York	8	2	AA UA
16	Atlanta-New York	9	3	DL EA UA
17	Chicago-Minneapolis	7	2	NW UA
18	Honolulu-Lihue	2	2	HA TS
19	Buffalo-New York	4	2	AA AL
20	Chicago-Washington	10	3	AA TW UA
21	Honolulu-Los Angeles	8	6	CO NW PA TW UA WA
22	Hilo-Honolulu	6	2	HA TS
23	Chicago-St. Louis	8	3	AA DL OZ
24	New York-Tampa	7	3	DL EA NA
25	New York-Rochester	3	2	AA AL
26	Boston-Philadelphia	8	2	AL DL
27	Chicago-San Francisco	7	3	AA TW UA
28	Chicago-Miami	7	3	DL EA NW
29	Honolulu-Kahului	2	2	HA TS
30	Boston-Chicago	7	3	AA TW UA
31	Chicago-Cleveland	8	2	NW UA
32	Los Angeles-Seattle	7	2	UA WA
33	Dallas-New York	5	2	AA BN
34	Chicago-Philadelphia	7	2	TW UA
35	San Francisco-Seattle	6	2	UA WA

Table 2-7 (cont.)

| Rank | Market | Number of Competitors | | Airlines |
		Total	Effective	
36	Denver-Los Angeles	5	2	CO UA
37	New York-West Palm Beach	4	2	EA NA
38	Los Angeles-Phoenix	6	4	AA CO TW WA
39	Houston-New York	5	3	BN DL EA
40	Los Angeles-Washington	7	3	AA TW UA
41	New York-Orlando	4	2	EA NA
42	Chicago-Denver	7	3	CO TW UA
43	New York-Syracuse	3	2	AA AL
44	Philadelphia-Pittsburgh	6	2	AL TW
45	Dallas-Houston	7	2	BN TT
46	New York-St. Louis	8	2	AA TW
47	Dallas-Los Angeles	6	2	AA DL
48	Chicago-Kansas City	7	3	BN CO TW
49	Chicago-Pittsburgh	6	3	AL TW UA
50	Honolulu-San Francisco	8	4	NW PA UA WA
51	Atlanta-Miami	7	2	DL EA
52	Denver-New York	6	2	TW UA
53	Miami-Philadelphia	6	3	DL EA NA
54	Atlanta-Washington	9	3	DL EA UA
55	Chicago-Dallas	6	2	AA BN
56	Boston-Los Angeles	7	2	AA TW
57	Atlanta-Chicago	8	3	DL EA NW
58	Minneapolis-New York	7	2	NW UA
59	Chicago-Las Vegas	3	2	TW UA
60	Los Angeles-San Diego	6	5	AA DL NA UA WA
61	Chicago-Tampa	6	3	DL EA NW
62	San Francisco-Washington	7	3	AA TW UA
63	Portland-Seattle	7	5	CO NW RW UA WA
64	Detroit-Los Angeles	5	2	AA UA
65	New Orleans-New York	6	2	DL EA
66	Houston-New Orleans	7	5	CO DL EA NA TT
67	Boston-Miami	6	2	DL EA
68	Miami-Washington	8	2	EA NA
69	Cincinnati-New York	7	2	AA TW
70	Chicago-Fort Lauderdale	5	3	DL EA NW
71	Seattle-Spokane	3	2	NW RW
72	Columbus-New York	8	3	AA AL TW

Table 2-7 (cont.)

Rank	Market	Number of Competitors Total	Number of Competitors Effective	Airlines
73	Chicago-Phoenix	4	2	AA TW
74	Detroit-Washington	8	2	NW UA
75	Los Angeles-Minneapolis	4	2	NW WA
76	Charlotte-New York	4	2	DL EA
77	Miami-Tampa	7	5	DL EA NA NW TW
78	Chicago-Houston	5	2	BN DL
79	Detroit-Miami	6	2	DL EA
80	Houston-Los Angeles	8	2	CO NA
81	Denver-San Francisco	5	3	TW UA WA
82	Chicago-Cincinnati	7	2	AA DL
83	New York-Raleigh	4	2	EA UA
84	Portland-San Francisco	6	2	UA WA
85	Los Angeles-Philadelphia	7	3	AA TW UA
86	Boston-San Francisco	5	3	AA TW UA
87	Los Angeles-Sacramento	3	1	WA
88	Detroit-Tampa	6	2	DL EA
89	Los Angeles-Portland	6	2	UA WA
90	Indianapolis-New York	6	2	AL TW
91	Atlanta-Tampa	6	4	DL EA NW TW
92	Baltimore-New York	8	4	AA AL EA NA
93	Detroit-Philadelphia	7	2	NW UA
94	Boston-Detroit	7	1	AA
95	Greensboro-New York	4	2	EA UA
96	New York-Norfolk	4	2	NA PI
97	Los Angeles-Salt Lake City	4	1	WA
98	Chicago-Columbus	8	2	TW UA
99	Los Angeles-Miami	8	2	NA DL
100	Miami-Orlando	4	3	EA NA SO

Source: U.S. Civil Aeronautics Board, *Origin-Destination Survey of Airline Passenger Traffic, Domestic*, Volume VII-3-2, Third Quarter 1974, Washington, D.C., 1974.

three times as much for international operations. The variance in price paid for fuel is substantial among the trunk-line carriers. In December 1974 the average price for a gallon for domestic operations varied from 18 cents for National to 36 cents for Pan American, due basically to the time at which the contracts were negotiated before the oil embargo.

Table 2-9 shows the important items in the balance sheet of domestic

Table 2-8
Operating Revenues and Expenses—Scheduled Airlines 1974

	Domestic Trunk-line		Local-service		International/Territorial	
Operating Revenues	*Amount ($000)*	*Percent*	*Amount ($000)*	*Percent*	*Amount ($000)*	*Percent*
Passenger	8,510,218	85.6	1,091,140	84.0	2,121,651	72.6
Freight	575,262	5.8	49,722	3.8	335,407	11.5
Express	26,093	0.3	4,088	0.3	297	–
Mail	158,292	1.6	16,998	1.3	91,890	3.1
Charter	133,395	1.3	14,294	1.1	233,085	8.0
Subsidy	–	–	68,508	5.3	–	–
Other	539,512	5.4	54,952	4.2	139,277	4.8
Total	9,942,772	100.0	1,299,702	100.0	2,921,607	100.0
Operating Expenses						
Flying Operations	2,874,950	31.0	364,473	30.4	1,037,441	34.6
Maintenance	1,275,136	13.8	196,332	16.4	355,187	11.9
Passenger Service	937,614	10.1	81,924	6.8	291,705	9.7
Aircraft and Traffic Servicing	1,675,714	18.1	290,889	24.3	491,359	16.4
Promotion and Sales	1,031,855	11.1	121,675	10.1	367,383	12.3
Administrative	395,796	4.3	65,271	5.4	161,650	5.4
Depreciation and Amortization	794,290	8.6	62,993	5.3	213,966	7.1
Other	277,413	3.0	15,772	1.3	76,021	2.6
Total	9,262,768	100.0	1,199,329	100.0	2,994,712	100.0
Net Operating Income	680,004		100,373		−73,105	

Source: U.S. Civil Aeronautics Board, *Air Carrier Financial Statistics*, Washington. D.C., December 1974.

Table 2-9
Balance Sheet Data, 1974

	Domestic Trunk-line Carriers		Local Service Airlines		Total All-Cargo Airlines	
	Amount ($000)	Percent	Amount ($000)	Percent	Amount ($000)	Percent
Assets						
Total Current Assets	3,279,905	24.1	305,795	29.5	105,057	25.2
Investments and Special Funds	954,250	7.0	46,624	4.5	95,340	22.8
Flight Equipment	12,424,270		773,204		252,100	
Less: Reserves for Depreciation	(4,698,263)		(279,780)		(76,620)	
Ground Property and Equipment	2,182,443		91,341		53,693	
Less: Reserves for Depreciation	(1,075,762)		(49,499)		(19,622)	
Other	317,214		29,516		3,261	
Net Property and Equipment	9,149,902	67.3	564,782	54.6	212,812	51.0
Total Deferred Charges	212,212	1.6	118,009	11.4	4,066	1.0
Total Assets	13,596,269	100.0	1,035,210	100.0	417,275	100.0
Liabilities and Equity						
Total Current Liabilities	3,013,210	22.2	283,371	27.4	73,100	17.5
Long-term Debt	4,987,386	36.7	428,462	41.4	129,235	31.0
Other Noncurrent Liabilities	239,025	1.8	9,531	0.9	30,668	7.3
Deferred Credits	1,376,204	10.1	9,198	0.9	57,132	13.7
Stockholders' Equity						
Preferred Stock	24,294		18,429		812	
Common Stock	233,116		20,613		18,384	
Other Paid-in Capital	2,071,582		230,571		61,944	
Retained Earnings	1,909,516		35,460		46,002	
Other	(258,064)		(425)		(2)	
Total	3,980,444	29.2	304,648	29.4	127,140	30.5
Total Liabilities	13,596,269	100.0	1,035,210	100.0	417,275	100.0

Source: U.S. Civil Aeronautics Board, *Air Carrier Financial Statistics*, Washington, D.C., December 1974.

trunk-line, local-service, and all-cargo carriers. The total assets of these groups are $13.6 billion for domestic trunk-line, $1 billion for local-service, and $0.4 billion for the all-cargo carriers. In each case the largest component of the assets is represented by the flight and ground equipment. The cost value of flight equipment (excluding depreciation) represents 91.3 percent of total assets for the domestic trunk-line carriers, 74.7 percent for local-service carriers, and 60.4 percent for the all-cargo carriers. Long-term debt represented 36.7 percent of the total liabilities and equity for the domestic trunk-line carriers, 41.4 percent for the local-service carriers, and 31.0 percent for the all-cargo carriers. The high proportion of long-term debt is the major drain on the net operating income of the air carriers. For instance, in 1974 the U.S. scheduled airlines earned a net operating income of $726 million, while the interest on their long-term debt amounted to $420 million.

The U.S. scheduled airlines earned their highest rate of return on investment in 1965: 11.2 percent for the domestic trunk lines, 10.4 percent for the local-service carriers, and 15.0 percent for the international and territorial airlines. Since then the rates of return on investment have declined substantially and for the domestic trunk lines have remained far below the 12 percent target set by the Board. In 1974 the domestic trunk-line carriers netted a 7.8 percent rate of return on investment on their domestic operations and 0.6 percent on their international operations. The local-service carriers have performed much better by achieving a 10.9 percent rate of return on investment during 1974, due basically to a significant improvement in load factor combined with substantial fare increases for short-haul operations. The all-cargo carriers earned the highest rate of return on investment in 1966, 17.1 percent for domestic operations and 33.0 percent for international operations. The figures for 1974 show a loss of 4.8 percent for domestic operations and a profit of 9.3 percent for international operations.

The Board compensates certain classes of carriers for maintaining service on routes that are inherently unprofitable but nevertheless eligible to receive service under the public interest concept. The Board computes the level of subsidy by forecasting the amount of funds needed for breakeven operation of the route, including a reasonable rate of return on investment and income taxes. Currently the level of subsidy is determined through a formula known as *Class Rate VII.* In 1974, through the use of this formula, the Board has established a maximum payment of $69.5 million for the local-service carriers. For further details on subsidy, see Chapter 12.

Summary

As of 1975 there are eleven different classes of air carriers operating in the United States. The domestic trunk-line carriers accounted for over 63 percent of the revenue ton miles in 1974. Although the airlines account for almost 80 percent of the passenger miles of the common carriers, their share is less than 10 percent when the private automobile is included in the total traffic. The domestic air passenger yield is 7.5 cents compared to 5.9 cents for Class I railroads and 4.4 cents for Class I motor buses (1974 data). The domestic freight yield, on the other hand, reflects 25.9 cents for airlines, 1.9 cents for Class I railroads, and 8.7 cents for Class I trucks as of 1974.

Using over 2,000 aircraft and over 300,000 employees, the airlines offer scheduled air service on some 58,000 city-pairs. The top 1,000 city-pairs account for about 70 percent, and the top 100 city-pairs account for about 30 percent of the passenger traffic. While the actual number of carriers in a market varies from two to twelve, the *effective* number of competitors generally ranges from two to three. The Honolulu-West Coast market is an exception.

Although the combination carriers are authorized to transport both passengers and cargo, they have concentrated on passenger transportation. For example, in 1974 the domestic trunk lines derived almost 86 percent of their revenue from passenger transportation. The domestic trunk lines show total assets of $13.6 billion, the cost value of flight equipment (excluding depreciation) representing about 91 percent of the total assets. In 1974 the long-term debt represented almost 37 percent of the total liabilities and equity for the domestic trunk-line carriers. These carriers netted a 7.8 percent rate of return on investment on their domestic operations in 1974—a figure substantially lower than the 12 percent allowed by the Board. One reason for the difference between the actual rate of return on investment and the maximum rate of return allowed by the Board is the way the carriers compete. The economic behavior of the carriers is discussed in the next chapter.

Airline Economics

The purpose of this chapter is to describe briefly the economic market behavior of the U.S. domestic trunk-line carriers in the context of microeconomic concepts. The economic behavior of these carriers is quite different from standard microeconomic theory, first, because the industry is regulated, and second, because it possesses some unique characteristics. In this chapter the description of the economic behavior is presented more in qualitative terms than in terms of any rigorous economic theory. This is intentional. First, in a survey type of text such as this, an exhaustive economic examination is out of place. Second, and perhaps more important, the application of traditional economic theory to the airline industry is still in its infancy. Consequently many issues regarding the economics of air transportation are far from settled among theoretician economists, government regulators, and practicing airline managers.

Economic Market Behavior

In analyzing the economic behavior of firms in a particular industry, it is a common practice to examine such factors as the number of competitors, barriers to entry and exit, cost behavior, and the characteristics of the product being produced and sold. It is occasionally said that entry into the domestic airline industry is closed. Although it is true that the Board has not allowed any new carriers in the trunk-line industry, entry on a market level where the carriers actually compete is not closed. Carriers may file for authority to offer service on a given route, and if the Board finds it in the public interest, the request will be approved. The situation can be classified as one of concentrated oligopoly, since there are two to four effective competitors on the most significant routes.

In the domestic trunk-line industry the prices are regulated by the Board. This regulation of the fares by the Board does not necessarily imply that the Board sets the fares in the industry, since the carriers themselves file fares or, more precisely, changes to existing fares; and the Board either allows to go into effect or suspends a fare. Once a particular fare is approved, all carriers are not required to charge that fare. However, because of the competitive nature of the industry, all carriers do charge the same fare. With fares the same, the carriers try to rival one another's service with respect to type of aircraft, departure time, number of flights, and such in-flight amenities as food, liquor, and movies. The Board does not regulate the industry with respect to the service characteristics, and the competition between carriers is therefore solely based upon service provided.

In the scheduled air carrier industry, market equilibrium is achieved when fares are equal to the average cost of providing the service. Normally the costs include a component for return on investment. At first it might appear that carriers would obtain excess profits with fixed fares, but in practice this is not the case. If revenues are high relative to the costs, the carriers will increase the level of service until the costs are in line with revenues and the excess profit diminishes to zero. On the other hand, if revenues are low relative to costs, the service will be reduced until once again there is a balance between revenues and costs such that excess profits cease to exist.

There is normally a significant amount of discussion among airline analysts with regard to "product differentiation" in the industry. If, for the moment, the output of an airline is defined as a seat departure (a novel idea to a lot of airline analysts), some analysts will argue that the product is undifferentiated. A seat departure on United is the same as on American or TWA. Others will argue that a seat departure in the Boston-Chicago market is not the same as one in the Chicago-Los Angeles market. Besides, a departure at ten in the morning is not the same as one at four in the afternoon. Thus the product *is* differentiated. There is some truth in both arguments. However, let us assume that the product is the same on a particular market. Suppose there are three carriers on the market and they all have similar aircraft. Suppose also that all three offer about the same level of cabin service. So on what do they compete? The answer is usually frequency of service. It is generally agreed to in the industry that frequency share is the most significant determinant of market share. This relationship is explained in the next chapter. Thus each carrier will attempt to schedule more flights than its competitor. Since the Board does not regulate capacity or frequency, each carrier will match every other carrier's frequency, and costs will increase for all the carriers on the market.

It is usually more convenient to explain the market behavior by load factors (both actual and break-even). When actual load factor is above the break-even load factors, carriers will increase frequency until the break-even load factor is approximately the same as the actual load factor. If the actual load factor is below the break-even load factor, the reverse is true. In the latter case there is usually another option. If the break-even load factor is higher than the actual, one option is to reduce frequency and thus costs, which in turn will lower the break-even load factor. The other option is for the carriers to ask the Board for higher fares that will lower the break-even load factor. Thus, since the Board does not regulate service or, more precisely, frequency, it is often faced with decisions involving tradeoffs between fares and level of service. This assumes that higher level of service is associated with higher frequency, a concept that is generally accepted in the industry.[a]

---

[a]The above discussion does not take into account the revenues generated from the transportation of cargo.

The above is the most common explanation of the market behavior of the carriers. However, this is only a partial explanation of the reality. There is nothing wrong with this line of reasoning as long as it is applied on a route-by-route basis. However, an airline does not conduct services on just one route. It offers services on a whole network of routes. Therefore it is not realistic to make an economic analysis of just one route; consideration must also be given to all other routes that are linked to the one route under consideration. One must not overlook the costs of scheduling, routing and positioning of aircraft. Network, as opposed to single route, analysis, however, is a complex task. Suppose one wanted to analyze the Chicago-Los Angeles route. This route cannot be analyzed as an entity by itself. Market behavior of each of the four carriers (American, Continental, TWA, and United) on this route must be investigated in light of each carrier's entire route system. For example, a carrier may add a flight on a given route with very little regard for the actual amount of traffic on that route. TWA flies from New York to Los Angeles and from New York to San Francisco. If TWA decides to schedule the same aircraft from New York to San Francisco and then from Los Angeles to New York, it might as well offer seats for sale between San Francisco and Los Angeles no matter how few passengers may be attracted. The alternative would be to ferry the aircraft empty.

The analysis of a whole network as opposed to a single route is also important from the standpoint of internal cross-subsidization. Whether it is economically efficient or not, the fact still remains that carriers do appear to subsidize their weak routes with the financially stronger routes. Thus any excess profit earned on the lucrative routes usually does not show up on the profit and loss statement but is used to offset the operating losses on the weak routes. Cross-subsidization is a well known fact and the Board has supported it in its past decisions with respect to route strengthening. For equity reasons some economists oppose this concept. They argue that a passenger on one route should not be made to subsidize another passenger on another route. Even if this line of reasoning were accepted, it would be extremely difficult, if not impossible, to implement it. Not enough is known about costs and cost allocation techniques within the industry to set fares appropriate to recover costs on a route-by-route basis.

The cross-subsidization argument concept merits some discussion with respect to short- and long-haul routes. Because of the nature of aircraft operating costs, the per mile operating costs decline with length of haul. Thus, per mile cost is lower for the New York to Los Angeles trip than for the Boston to New York City. To date it appears that long-haul passengers have subsidized the short-haul passengers. This is because the fare structure did not reflect the same properties as the cost structure. In a study performed by the Board's staff in 1968, it was recommended that the fare structure reflect the cost structure.[1] Since then the short-haul fares have been increasing relative to the long-haul fares. The most recent revision was adopted in Phase 9 of the *Domestic Passenger Fare Investigation* (DPFI) decided in March 1974.[2] In theory it is quite reasonable to charge high fares for short-haul operations if the costs of operations are high; nevertheless in practice it does not work out that way. For one thing there is more competition (from surface transportation) on short-haul routes. If the trunk-line carriers set short-haul fares to reflect their true costs, they could price themselves out of the market. Some of the trunk-line carriers point out that they cannot drop the short-haul routes because they need these routes to feed their long-haul routes. Dropping short-haul routes in order to lower fares on long-haul routes could, in reality, have the opposite effect: the lack of feeder traffic may in fact raise the fares.

In looking back one wonders if cross-subsidization has really worked. It may be that the carriers have used any excess profits earned on long-haul flights or on high-density routes to compete more aggressively in service. For example, on the transcontinental routes the break-even load factor is much lower than on short-haul routes. Until the recent capacity agreements (discussed later in this chapter), the actual load factor on the transcontinental routes has also been lower relative to the actual load factor on the short-haul routes. So according to the cross-subsidization theory, the carriers were supposed to take advantage of the lower break-even load factors in long-haul routes. This they did. Only the excess profit was used to increase the level of service on routes other than short-haul until the actual load factors reached fairly close to the break-even load factors. A good example of excessive service on a highly competitive route is the high density New York-Chicago market. Here again, prior to the capacity agreements, the schedule war between American, TWA, and United resulted in approximately 100 flights a day in each direction, a level of service that is substantially higher than warranted by the amount of traffic.[b]

This discussion leads to the obvious question. If the carriers do not make excess profit on their more profitable routes, then how have they supported their unprofitable routes? There is no clear answer to this question. Partly they have been bailed out over the years by the aircraft manufacturers through more and more productive aircraft. Until recently, for reasons such as inflation, the increase in aircraft productivity outpaced the increases in costs. Part of the answer may also be found in the abandonment of unprofitable routes by the trunk-line carriers. Some of these routes were taken over by the local service carriers, which in turn have also attempted to abandon a few. Finally there is always the option of applying for higher fares.

Another area where subsidization came into focus was discount fares. During the 1960s the carriers introduced numerous discount or promotional fares to fill some of the excess capacity and reduce the problem of peaking. Since the marginal costs in the airline industry are quite low, the idea of discount fares seemed quite appropriate. The discount fares were supposed to fill up the excess capacity. However, there is some evidence that a few carriers lost sight of this

[b]However, some carriers will defend such actions on the grounds that such high frequency was placed to serve other parts of the system and not just the local traffic.

objective and purchased more equipment based upon the discount traffic carried. Operations on the North Atlantic are a good example of this market behavior. Thus the full-fare passengers ended up subsidizing the passengers on discount fares.[c]

This is a qualitative description of the economic market behavior in the airline industry. In the last few years a number of investigators have attempted to explain the market behavior in terms of classical economic theory.[3] While all of these investigators have made significant contributions, there is still no definitive analytical model to explain the economic behavior of the domestic scheduled air carrier. Robert W. Simpson in *A Theory For Domestic Airline Economics*, sums up the situation as:

Thus, market conditions are far removed from the classical economical market model for perfect competition. However, it is possible to develop models for the behavior of profit seeking, oligopolistic carriers under various assumed market conditions. *While none of these may describe the conditions of a particular real market of domestic air services*, it is instructive to analyze these models because of the insight it brings to both carrier management and regulatory personnel.[4] (Emphasis added.)

Airline Costs and Profitability Analysis

Airline Costs

Historically, the total operating costs of an airline have consisted of two major components: the direct operating costs and the indirect operating costs. The *direct operating costs* are those incurred as a necessary result of, and directly related to, flying the aircraft. The *indirect operating costs* are not directly related to the operation of the aircraft but are incurred as a result of operating services on the ground and the usual overhead expenditures associated with the management of a business. These costs can be analyzed through the data submitted by carriers on operating expenses and other financial statistics in accordance with the Board's *Uniform System of Accounts and Reports.*[5] Route and supplemental carriers have different accounting and reporting procedures. See Chapter 9 for further information on the data provided by the carriers to the Board.

The cost items contained in Form 41 of the Uniform System are represented by a four-digit account number. The first two digits represent the functional classifications; the last two digits represent the objective classification which provides more information. When a fifth digit appears, it expands on the

---

[c]Incidentally, the normal fare, economy-class passenger has not only subsidized the passenger on discount fare, but until recently he has also subsidized the first-class passenger. For further discussion on discount fares, the reader is referred to the DPFI in Chapter 11.

objective classification and is used for internal purposes. The following are the major categories of the functional classifications:

Account 5100 Flying Operations
Account 5200 Direct Maintenance
Account 5300 Maintenance Burden
Account 5500 Passenger Service
Account 6100 Aircraft Servicing
Account 6200 Traffic Servicing
Account 6300 Servicing Administration
Account 6500 Reservations and Sales
Account 6600 Advertising and Publicity
Account 6800 General and Administrative
Account 7000 Depreciation and Amortization

The direct operating costs are usually some combination of Accounts 5100, 5200, 5300. The indirect operating costs for domestic trunk-line carriers are some combination of Accounts 5500, 6100, 6200, 6300, 6500, 6600, 6800, and 7000. For local service carriers Account 6400 is equivalent to the sum of Accounts 6100, 6200, and 6300 for the domestic trunk-line carriers; and Account 6700 is equivalent to the sum of Accounts 6500 and 6600. The other account numbers have the same meaning for both groups of carriers.

Although the categories of direct and indirect have been commonly used by U.S. carriers and manufacturers, the classification is, to some extent, arbitrary. Professor Robert W. Simpson of the Massachusetts Institute of Technology has developed a slightly different classification that is more useful in performing systems analysis on air transportation problems.[d] It should be emphasized that this approach, while different from the usual direct and indirect operating costs approach, is simply a rearrangement of the carrier's reported expenses.[6] Table 3-1 shows the breakdown of airline expenses under this approach.

This classification contains five categories. The flight operating costs are similar to the direct operating costs and are somewhat comparable to those costs described in the CAB's *Aircraft Operating Costs and Performance Reports.*[7] The ground operating costs incurred at the airline terminal are not included here since they represent a system administrative expense. The system operating costs represent some of the old indirect operating costs and are not directly related to the airline service. The total operating costs are now the sum of the flight operating costs, the ground operating costs, and the system operating costs. The nonoperating costs, as the name applies, are not directly associated with the operations of the airline but are related to the existence of the corporation.

---

[d]This classification has been used quite extensively in Air Transportation Economics, a class taught by Professor Simpson and the author at the Massachusetts Institute of Technology for the past 3 years.

Table 3-1
Overall Breakdown of Airline Expenses

A. Flight Operating Costs (FC)

   A.1 Direct Flying Operations
   A.2 Flight Maintenance
   A.3 Flight Equipment Ownership

B. Ground Operating Costs (GC)

   B.1 Reservations and Sales
   B.2 Traffic Servicing
   B.3 Aircraft Servicing

C. System Operating Costs (SC)

   C.1 System Promotional Costs
   C.2 System Administrative Costs
   C.3 Ground Maintenance
   C.4 Ground Equipment Ownership

D. Total Operating Costs (TOC) = Sum of A + B + C

E. System Nonoperating Costs (SNC)

   E.1 Interest and Debt Expense
   E.2 Taxes

Source: Robert W. Simpson and Y.P. Chan, *A Structure for Airline Operating Costs*, M.I.T.-FTL Technical Memorandum 71-9, December 1971.

Cost analysis is as much an art as it is a science. There is no single unique procedure for analysis. The above classification developed by Professor Simpson is not only logical but also extremely useful in analyzing the problems faced by an airline manager. Once such a classification has been developed, the next procedure is to relate the expenses in each category with those measures of airline activity that have caused the particular expense. The development of these relationships is a complex task and one that involves experience and a certain amount of familiarity with basic principles of economics and econometrics. The difficulty arises when an expense is caused by more than one activity. In this case it becomes necessary to take into consideration the joint nature of the interrelated activities through some appropriate allocation technique.

Profitability Analysis

At this point it may be useful for illustrative purposes to analyze the airline costs in terms of the structure presented in Table 3-1. The conceptual framework in the rest of this section is taken almost completely from the class notes prepared by Professor Simpson.[e] *Flight operating costs* by definition are the costs of operating an aircraft. It is common practice to measure these in terms of flight operating costs per block hour FC_{HR}, so that it is independent of the stage length for a given aircraft and a given airline. It is quite important to realize that there is a cost involved at zero distances. In other words, when a plane takes off from Boston to fly to Chicago, there is a certain expense incurred once the aircraft is airborne even though the passenger's actual trip distance covered is zero. These zero-distance costs will be discussed in some detail later. Flight operating costs per block hour are also a useful way to compare the various aircraft owned by an airline. However, since different passenger aircraft have different numbers of seats, it is sometimes more useful to talk about flight operating costs per seat hour. Table 3-2 shows typical values of these costs per hour and seat hour for 1973. The flight operating costs per seat hour vary from $4.42 to $8.70 for both jet and turbo-prop transport aircraft. The helicopter costs are much higher.

Table 3-3 is a more detailed breakdown of the hourly costs for the Boeing 727-100 series in domestic service in 1973. The total cost of $671.61 represents 53.8 percent for direct flying operations, 27.1 percent for flight maintenance, and 19.1 percent for flight equipment ownership. The total flight operating cost per block hour of $671.61 is a long-term cost. However, an airline manager, facing decisions on a short-term basis, should not consider flight maintenance burden or flight ownership costs. Thus on a short-term basis the flight operating costs are significantly lower at $465.97 per block hour. This point is important when, for example, the manager is evaluating whether or not to offer a particular flight next month. For ultra short-term decisions such as today's flight, only the fuel and oil costs are appropriate. However, this line of reasoning is not to imply that the next flight can be cancelled if there are not enough passengers, since one would then defeat the whole concept of scheduled service. What it does mean is that the flight can be operated until the next schedule change, and that it would be profitable on a marginal basis as long as it generated more than $161.05 per block hour using this particular aircraft. To complete this discussion one must also consider landing fees, which vary from airport to airport.

An investigation of the increase in total flight operating costs per block hour for the Boeing 727-100 series from 1964 to 1973 showed that the largest cost increase was experienced with respect to the flight crew. Since 1973 the largest increase has been in terms of fuel expenses. On the other hand, the ownership expense has been declining in general, due partly to the aging of this particular fleet. A small variation around the general declining trend was noticed that is probably due to the different ages of the individual aircraft in the fleet and the varying depreciation policies of different carriers operating the Boeing 727-100 series.

---

[e]Robert W. Simpson, "An Analysis of Airline Costs," lecture notes for the Massachusetts Institute of Technology, Course 16.74-Air Transportation Economics. The author thanks Professor Simpson for permission to use this material.

Table 3-2
Flight Operating Costs, 1973

Aircraft Type	Fleet Size	Cost/Hr. ($)	Seats[a]	Cost/Seat Hr. ($)	Average Stage Length (Miles)
Domestic Trunks					
Electra	19	763.60	87.8	8.70	205
B707-100B	102	837.19	120.8	6.93	933
B720	4	673.73	131.0	5.14	699
B720B	53	841.07	115.5	7.28	829
B727-100Q/C	406	671.61	98.0	6.85	556
B737-200	98	559.52	93.6	5.98	306
DC8-20	79	908.07	121.5	7.47	992
DC8-50		839.34	130.5	6.43	841
DC8-61	61	958.45	176.5	5.43	922
DC9-10	42	546.01	68.5	7.97	352
DC9-30	148	517.70	89.9	5.76	335
B747	106	1,849.89	328.4	5.63	1858
L-1011	17	1,589.81	221.8	7.17	1199
DC10-10	59	1,324.81	232.2	5.71	1003
DC10-40		1,053.88	238.4	4.42	767
Local Service					
DC9-30	79	534.38	99.7	5.36	258
CV-580	105	369.91	49.4	7.31	123
FH-227	46	315.87	44.5	7.10	104
Helicopters					
S-61	7	419.49	24.8	16.91	13
STOL					
DHC-6	13	163.55	15.0	10.90	90

[a]Seats are averaged over aircraft miles performed in 1973.

Source: U.S. Civil Aeronautics Board, *Aircraft Operating Cost and Performance Reports*, Washington, D.C., June 1974.

It is sometimes useful to relate the total operating costs per hour to the productivity of the aircraft measured in, for example, available ton miles per hour. This is shown in Figure 3-1 for different aircraft in service in 1974. Direct operating costs can be obtained by dividing the flight operating costs by aircraft productivity. A graph of direct operating costs versus aircraft productivity is shown in Figure 3-2 for various aircraft in operation in 1974. The direct operating costs have declined. The productivity has increased. Assuming that there is a linear relationship between distance and flight operating costs for a given aircraft trip (FC_{AT}) (Equation 3.1), it is possible to obtain flight operating

Table 3-3
Flight Operating Costs in Dollars per Block Hour for Boeing 727-100

	Long-term		Short-term
1. Direct Flying Operations	361.21		
Flight Crew		200.16	200.16
Fuel and Oil		161.05	161.05
2. Flight Maintenance	181.90		
Direct Airframe & Other		55.56	55.56
Direct Engine		49.20	49.20
Burden		77.14	
3. Flight Equipment Ownership	128.50		
Depreciation Airframe & Other		71.08	
Depreciation Engines		12.93	
Obsolescence & Deterioration		2.51	
Flight Equipment Rental		35.97	
Flight Insurance		6.01	
4. Long-term Average Costs		671.61	
5. Short-term Average Costs (less Burden, Ownership Costs)			465.97

Source: U.S. Civil Aeronautics Board, *Operating Cost and Performance Reports*, Washington, D.C., June 1974.

costs per seat trip (FC_{ST}) by dividing FC_{AT} by the number of seats (Equation 3.2). The flight operating costs per seat trip can be divided by distance to get the traditional direct operating cost curve that is shown in Figure 3-3 for the Boeing 727-100 series fleet in service in 1973. The coefficients C_0 to C_3 are constants and d is the trip distance. The flight operating cost per seat trip is linear, up to the design range of the aircraft. The number of seats in the aircraft are no longer constant beyond the design range. In Equation 3.2, S represents the number of seats in the aircraft.

$$FC_{AT} = C_0 + C_1 \cdot d \qquad (3.1)$$

$$FC_{ST} = \frac{C_0}{S} + \frac{C_1 \cdot d}{S} = C_2 + C_3 \cdot d \qquad (3.2)$$

Once flight operating costs have been established, ground operating costs must be determined. The *ground operating costs* are costs incurred at the terminal to prepare and terminate a trip; for all practical purposes these costs are independent of the length of trip. Normally the ground operating costs consist of the expenses incurred with respect to reservations and sales, traffic servicing,

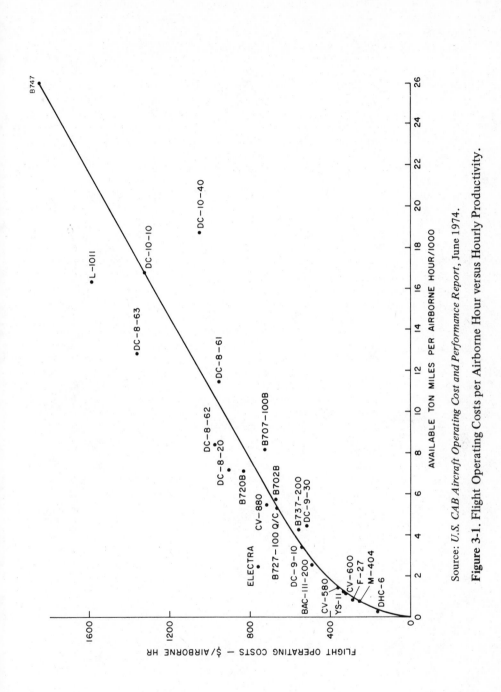

Source: *U.S. CAB Aircraft Operating Cost and Performance Report*, June 1974.

Figure 3-1. Flight Operating Costs per Airborne Hour versus Hourly Productivity.

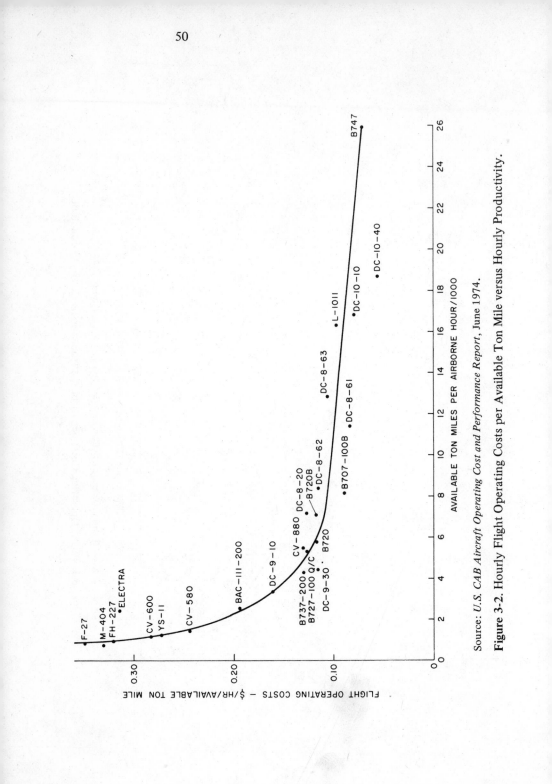

Source: *U.S. CAB Aircraft Operating Cost and Performance Report*, June 1974.

Figure 3-2. Hourly Flight Operating Costs per Available Ton Mile versus Hourly Productivity.

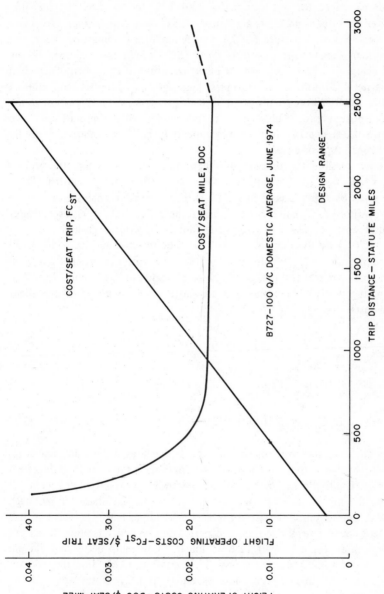

Figure 3-3. Variation of Flight Operating Costs with Trip Distance.

and aircraft servicing. In 1973 the ground operating costs for the domestic trunk-line carriers amounted to $6.46 per passenger for reservations and sales, $5.30 per passenger for traffic servicing, and $253.88 per aircraft departure. Thus the ground operating costs amounted to $11.76 per passenger (GC_p) and $253.88 per aircraft departure (GC_D), which includes landing fees. Next, one must consider the *system operating costs* *(SC)*, which are expenses of the overhead category. These costs consist of depreciation of equipment other than aircraft, general administrative expenses, passenger service costs, and indirect maintenance. In 1973 the total system operating costs were 23.39 percent of the overall transport revenue. These costs are independent of the aircraft used. The allocation of these costs against revenue appears to be logical since they are by nature overhead type of costs.

It is now possible to combine the flight operating costs and the ground operating costs to get total operating costs per aircraft trip or per seat trip. These costs are given by Equations (3.3) and (3.4). From previous analysis, not shown here, the coefficients C_2 and C_3 were found to be 2.97 and 0.01597 respectively. The ground cost per seat trip (GC_{ST}) is found by dividing ground costs per departure (GC_D) by the number of seats *(S)*. The result came out to be $2.59 per seat departure ($253.88 divided by 98). The empirical results for total operating costs per seat trip (TC_{ST}) are shown in Equation (3.5) and Figure 3-4. As shown, the ground operating costs are quite small compared to the flight operating costs.

$$TC_{AT} = FC_{AT} + GC_D \tag{3.3}$$

$$TC_{ST} = FC_{ST} + \frac{GC_D}{S} \tag{3.4}$$

$$TC_{ST} = 5.56 + 0.01597d \tag{3.5}$$

Having analyzed the costs, one must turn to the fares to be able to perform profitability analysis. Figure 3-5 shows the passenger fare structure in effect during 1974. The first-class fare was 30 percent above the standard day jet-coach fare, while the night-coach fare was 80 percent of the standard day jet-coach fare. Due to the existence of discount fares, the yield per passenger was less than the standard coach fare. While the yield per passenger depends upon the extent of discount fares, there appears to be a linear relationship between yield per passenger and trip distance as shown by Equation (3.6). For the sake of illustration, assume that the constant in Equation (3.6) is the same as the constant in the fare structure and the per mile fare is the unweighted average of all the components in the fare structure. This is shown in Equation (3.7).

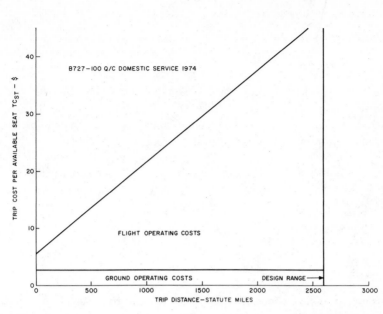

Figure 3-4. Variation of Trip Cost per Seat with Trip Distance.

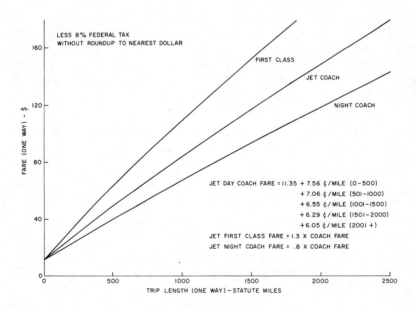

Figure 3-5. U.S. Domestic Passenger Fare Structure, 1974.

$$Y_P = C_4 + C_5 \cdot d \tag{3.6}$$

$$Y_P = 11.35 + 0.067d \tag{3.7}$$

The passenger yield, as determined in Equation (3.7), must now be reduced by the system operating costs per dollar of revenue (overhead) and the ground operating costs per passenger. This computation results in net yield per passenger (NY_P) and is shown in Equations (3.8) and (3.9). It is interesting to note that for trips less than 60 miles the net yield per passenger is negative. Figure 3-6 shows the relationship of yield, net yield, and the trip cost per seat for the Boeing 727-100. Net yield is greater than the trip cost for distances over about 250 statute miles.

$$NY_P = (1 - SC) \cdot Y_P - GC_P \tag{3.8}$$

$$NY_P = -3.06 + 0.0513d \tag{3.9}$$

It is now possible to determine income per aircraft trip, income per seat trip, and the break-even load factor. Income per aircraft trip is equal to net yield per passenger times number of passengers less the total operating costs for the aircraft. The number of passengers required to break even is found by equating the income per aircraft trip to zero. Finally, the break-even load factor is found by dividing the number of break-even passengers by the number of seats on the aircraft. Figure 3-7 shows a plot of the break-even factor with distance for the Boeing 727-100 in domestic trunk-line operation in 1974. The break-even load factor varies from over 100 percent for distances below 250 miles to 35 percent at about 2,600 miles. The reader is reminded that while this type of analysis is quite useful, the numbers are approximate and were used for illustrative purposes only. Furthermore, the analysis does not take into account the revenue derived from the transportation of air cargo.

Efficiency of Airline Operations

The efficiency of an airline will be discussed with respect to its size and the efficiency of its management. In many ways the two measures are not independent. However, the majority of investigators have focused upon the first part under the general title of economies of scale. Knowledge of economies of scale becomes particularly important in merger analysis for estimating the effect of scale of operations on the surviving carrier's cost structure. Naturally those persons favoring a particular merger proposal believe the existence of either slight economies of scale, or at least constant returns to scale. The opponents, on the other hand, claim the existence of diseconomies of scale. The differences in

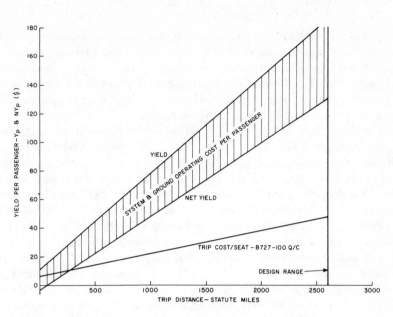

Figure 3-6. Yields and Costs versus Trip Distance.

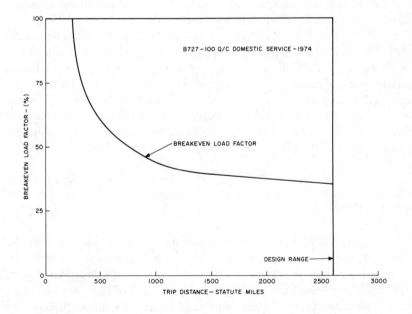

Figure 3-7. Variation of Break-even Load Factor with Trip Distance.

opinion are the result of three factors. First, the nature of the industry itself causes different analysts to reach different conclusions. Second, to date, a reasonably valid production function and associated cost function do not exist. Third, even though different investigators have concluded the existence of diseconomies, constant returns, and economies of scale, the range on either side of the constant returns is too small to draw conclusions with any confidence.

One of the earliest investigations was carried out by Harold D. Koontz. Using the cost data for 1949, Koontz concluded that there was no evidence of significant economies of scale over a range of airline sizes.[8] In 1958, using prejet cost data, Paul W. Cherington also concluded that, at best, there are constant returns to scale in the trunk-line industry.[9] According to Professor Cherington, the differences in cost among airlines were more a function of length of haul and route density than of size. The analysis performed by Professor Caves during the transition period to jets reaches the same conclusion relative to economies of scale and cost determinants.[10] Mahlon Straszheim, in a 1969 study of the international airline industry, also concluded that airline costs are influenced by size of aircraft, length of haul, and route density rather than the scale of operations.[11] Also in 1969 Eads, Nerlove, and Raduchel, in an investigation of the cost function of local-service carriers using nonlinear estimation procedure, concluded that there are slightly increasing returns to scale.[12] The Edward's report came to the conclusion in its comparison of the costs of the Big Four and the smaller domestic trunk lines that there was no evidence of either economies or diseconomies of scale of any significant magnitude.[13]

Since the beginning of the 1970s, there have been at least four significant studies that directly or indirectly investigated the question of economies of scale. Professor William Jordan, in his 1970 investigation of the California intrastate carriers, concluded that beyond four or five aircraft there was no evidence of economies of scale.[14] A year later James E. McMillen performed extensive regression analysis and concluded that the size of the carrier has very little influence on airline operating costs relative to length of haul, station, and capital and labor productivity.[15] However, McMillen warns that:

Regression analysis cannot in itself be used as proof of a theory or conviction. Rather it is a useful technique used to lend support for theories or provide forecasts of trends on historical data.[16]

McMillen applied his statistical results to evaluate the impact of both the American-Western and Northeast-Delta merger proposals on the cost structures of the surviving carriers. His analysis showed that while the American-Western merger would have saved about $20 million (economies of scale) the Northeast-Delta merger would result in a cost increase of about $24 million (diseconomies of scale). Since these results do not appear to be logical, the only explanation given was that factors other than size are more important in determining costs.

The Department of Transportation's staff, under the direction of James C. Miller III, also analyzed the issue of economies of scale as input both to the merger cases and to the *Domestic Passenger Fare Investigation*. In this study multiple regression analysis was used to determine the relationship between costs and available ton miles, average length of haul, and market density. Again, while both constant returns to scale and increasing returns to scale were observed. the range was quite small. The general conclusion was that the industry is characterized by constant returns to scale and that the critical factor determining costs is the length of haul.

In 1973, in a study of the impact of airline size on costs and profitability, Samuel R. Reid and James W. Mohrfeld examined data covering 10 years of trunk-line operations (1960-1970); they concluded that a U-shaped relationship between unit operating costs and airline size did not exist.[17] The authors also performed an analysis of size and profitability. The domestic trunk-line carriers were divided into three groups: the Big Four, the Medium Four, and the Small Three. Using regression analysis, they concluded that increasing the size of the airline beyond that of the Medium Four (Delta, Northwest, National, Western) results in decreased profits. This result suggests that mergers may not provide the solution to profitability.

As stated at the beginning of this section, it is also important to investigate managerial efficiency with respect to costs. Unfortunately this area of cost analysis has not been investigated as extensively as the issue of economies of scale. Robert J. Gordon analyzed the domestic trunk-line carriers' operations for the third quarter of 1961 with respect to managerial efficiency. Gordon maintained that after factors such as route structure and fleet composition were eliminated, the differences in costs among the various carriers must be explained by the efficiency of management. In his analysis Gordon disaggregated the reported costs into three categories: flying operations, maintenance, and aircraft and traffic servicing. The major conclusion was that inefficiency was the result of overstaffing, particularly with respect to the pilots. Using his criteria of managerial efficiency, he concluded that if all of the domestic trunk-line carriers had operated at the most efficient level, they would have posted a net profit of $67.5 million instead of a loss of $19.2 million in 1961.[18]

Interline Capacity Agreements

During the late 1960s and early 1970s the domestic trunk-line carriers were operating with substantial excess capacity resulting in low load factors and financial losses. The Board had shown its unwillingness to approve higher fares until an improvement in load factor had been achieved. For example, the Board stated in 1969:

The Board remains concerned about the declining trend of the industry's passenger load factors and the effect which this situation may be having upon the industry's continuing ability to maintain existing fare levels. . . . The Board continues to be of the view that the traveling public should not be asked to pay for the operation of a volume of capacity which is significantly out of line with market demand.[19]

With a view towards improving the excess capacity problem, some of the trunk-line carriers requested the Board's permission to discuss capacity agreements in certain markets.

In 1971 the Board approved, on a temporary basis, an agreement between American, TWA, and United to reduce the number of nonstop flights between New York and Los Angeles, New York and San Francisco, Chicago and San Francisco, and Washington and Los Angeles. In 1972 the Board renewed its approval of this agreement and also approved a similar agreement between American, Eastern, and Pan American on the New York-San Juan market. In 1973 both of these agreements were renewed. Also in 1973, due to the short supply of fuel, the Board granted antitrust immunity and encouraged carriers to decrease their schedules. In accordance with this policy, American, TWA, and United agreed among themselves to reduce capacity in twenty markets. These agreements were approved on a temporary basis. The result of the various capacity agreements was an improvement in load factor, but at the expense of reduced quality and quantity of service on the particular markets.

In November 1974 the Board examiner investigating the capacity agreements recommended that they should not be approved again. The examiner's decision was based upon a number of factors. First, the quality and quantity of air service in the agreed markets had declined, yet the level of fares in these markets had remained the same. Since the public was receiving a lower level of service, fares should also have been reduced. The examiner cited two examples of lower service. First, prior to the agreement, about 2 percent of the transcontinental passengers traveled on multistop flights, whereas after the agreements, 10 percent did. Second, the carriers reduced the number of off-peak flights instead of the peak flights.[20]

The second objection to the agreement related to the carriers' use of the "freed" capacity. In some cases the freed capacity was used to compete more aggressively on markets where the agreement did not exist. This increased the competition with carriers that were not party to the agreement. For example, the examiner cited American's 25 percent increase in capacity in the Dallas-Los Angeles market between October 1973 and April 1974. The freed capacity has also been used to increase the level of operations in charter activity, resulting in excessive competition for the supplemental carriers. Again the examiner reported a 50 percent increase in the number of aircraft devoted to charter operations by Pan American, TWA, and United. The Department of Transportation estimated the freed capacity to be 4.5 billion seat miles, enough to completely wipe out the supplemental carriers.

The third objection to capacity agreements was related to management's decision with respect to investment, marketing, and scheduling. For example, the carriers would be more willing to take risks in purchasing additional equipment on the theory that if excessive capacity should result, the Board would allow them to take anticompetitive actions. Also, the real competition under the present regulatory framework is with respect to schedule convenience. Thus, if this area of competition were eliminated, carriers would compete on cabin service only, and this action would not provide sufficient benefits of competition to the passengers. Finally, the examiner objected to the capacity agreements on the grounds that the savings in fuel as a result of these agreements were overestimated by the carriers in light of charter operations, additional flights in nonagreement markets, and greater use of multistop flights. Mindful of these criticisms, the Board disapproved the continuation of capacity agreements in July 1975.[21]

To complete the discussion on capacity agreements, it should be mentioned that the Board has approved other types of capacity agreements among carriers. In 1969 the Board approved the establishment of restrictions on maximum hourly movements at five airports to reduce air traffic congestion. The approval allowed the carriers to reach an agreement on allocations of FAA's quotas at John F. Kennedy, La Guardia, Newark, O'Hare, and Washington National Airport. In 1970 the Board allowed U.S. carriers to enter into arrangements to reduce schedules in order to relieve air traffic controllers "sickout." Also in 1970 the Board authorized carriers serving Chicago's O'Hare airport to discuss the transfer of specific flights to Midway airport in order to improve service at Midway. Finally in 1971 the Board authorized carriers using the International Arrivals Building at New York's Kennedy airport to agree to limit the flight arrivals to reduce congestion in customs clearance.

Summary

As stated at the beginning of this chapter, the application of traditional economic theory to the airline industry is still in its infancy. This is not due just to the fact that the industry is regulated but more to the unique characteristics of the industry itself. The economic regulation of the carriers and the peculiarities of the scheduling process make it difficult to analyze the operations of the carriers in terms of standard microeconomic theory. For example, one cannot perform an economic analysis on a single route since an airline does not conduct services on just one route.

Airline cost analysis is one area where a substantial amount of research has been undertaken due partly to the existence of ample data. Even here there are no unique procedures available, since cost analysis is as much an art as a science. In the chapter it was shown that costs depend not only upon the methods of allocation, but also on whether the analyst is investigating long-term, short-term, or day-to-day cases. Finally, once again due to the nature of the industry, researchers have not come to a unique conclusion with respect to economies of scale. Although some evidence exists toward constant returns, this evidence is far from being conclusive.

4

Marketing Air Transportation Services

The purpose of this chapter is to provide the reader with some perspective into the key elements of airline marketing. Years ago marketing was thought of as selling; marketing took over at the end of the production line. Once the company produced its product or service, it was the job of the marketing department to sell as much of the output as possible by changing the marketing decision variables, such as price, promotion, and distribution (marketing mix). In standard textbooks the term *marketing mix* usually refers to the types and amounts of marketing decision variables that a company is using at any given time.[1] The term *marketing strategy* is used to describe the process by which the marketing mix is changed. In recent years, however, the marketing concept has changed from one of selling the already produced goods and services to one of advising management to vary the output in light of the needs of both existing and potential customers.

Product

The marketing of air transportation services is in some ways quite unique; to begin with, the process of marketing services is quite different from marketing products. J.L. Grumbridge, for example, maintains that this difference is a result of four characteristics.[2] First, the service cannot be inventoried to match fluctuations in demand. Second, service is usually personalized. Third, there is usually no equivalent of "replacement of bad product" concept. Fourth, it is difficult to check the quality prior to the time of final sale. Grumbridge then describes those characteristics of the air transportation industry that make the marketing of air transportation services different from the marketing of other services.[3] First, the demand for air services is known as *derived demand*. Second, the industry is under considerable government control. Third, the delivery aspect cannot be guaranteed due to the unpredictability of bad weather. Fourth, the service can only be produced in batches as opposed to individual units.

For the purposes of this marketing discussion, the output of an airline is not available seat miles or ton miles but a service offered to the public by a timetable. As one industry analyst explains, a passenger does not walk up to a ticket counter and ask, "How much is an available seat mile?" The timetable published by an airline describes the characteristics of the service by listing the various fares; frequency of service; departure and arrival times; and type of aircraft, service (nonstop, multistop or connecting), and cabin service with respect to liquor, food, and in-flight entertainment. The individual service offered can be described as a reservation for a seat departure between two airports on a given day at a given time. Considered in this sense, the total system output of a carrier is the summation of all seat departures over its entire route network.

To the airline marketer the distinction between differentiated and undifferentiated service makes a big difference. Since the price charged is the same on all carriers in a given market, a marketer can increase his carriers' share of the market by showing that his service is different. Thus from a marketing point of view service can be considered differentiated. For example, on a given route the services offered at different times of the day are quite different services from a passenger's viewpoint. A seat departure between Boston and Chicago at 8:00 A.M. is a different service from an otherwise exactly similar seat departure at 5:00 P.M., and needless to say, first class service is different from coach or economy service. Even flights that depart at exactly the same time with the same equipment are different services due to the differences in cabin service, distribution channels, on-time performance, and services on the ground—that is, the passenger's image of carrier services.

The cabin service refers to food and liquor service, in-flight entertainment, and attitude and appearance of the cabin crew. Those persons who believe that the carriers scarcely dwell on such differences are reminded of Delta's slogan of professionalism, PSA's stewardesses' sex appeal, TWA's "lasagne over Los Angeles," Western's free champagne, and American's piano bars. The distribution channels refer to the different places a passenger can buy his ticket. The on-time performance refers to the reliability of service. The services on the ground refer to the quality of reservations, baggage handling, and preflight procedures. An example of the last point is American's recent implementation of a single line for ticketing and check-in, with passenger service agents directing passengers to the next available counter. Finally the overall image of the carrier is supposed to distinguish service among carriers. There is some evidence of this if you consider Delta's claim of professionalism and Pan American's claim of experience. Most of these points will be discussed in detail in the section of this chapter on promotion.

Under the new concept of marketing, it is the responsibility of the marketing department to determine the needs and wants of the carrier's existing and potential passengers. This responsibility is usually carried out through market research either in-house or through a specialized outside company. Once the desires of the passengers are known, it is necessary to determine if the services offered by the carrier are in fact fulfilling these needs and wants. Competent marketing analysts evaluate not only their own airline's service relative to the passengers' needs and wants but also the services of their competitors. If the passengers' needs are not being adequately fulfilled, it becomes the job of the marketing executive to relay their dissatisfactions to the rest of management and to advise on the appropriate adjustments to the services being offered.

It may be useful to consider some examples of changes made in the service in response to customer needs and wants: the introduction of the economy-class fare on the North Atlantic was intended to provide the public with cheaper air transportation to Europe; the K- (thrift) class service from the U.S. mainland to Hawaii was established to fulfill the needs of the traveling public; in-flight entertainment was established to eliminate boredom. The reader should be cautioned that although the carriers are seriously interested in matching their service to meet public demands, the carriers must evaluate the public needs in terms of their own objectives and constraints. For example, the seasonality problem with passenger transportation and the directionality problem with cargo transportation are very familiar. The marketing staff's job is to satisfy customer's needs while fulfilling a management objective. The following three examples describe how a marketing management has succeeded in this dual-faceted job.

The first example refers to the introduction of the one-week European GIT (Group Inclusive Tour) program. Through market research carriers found that there was a substantial U.S. market for short-duration vacations in Europe. One of the problems of the North Atlantic carriers is the low level of traffic in winter months. For example, the traffic carried in July and August on the North Atlantic has been as much as five times the amount carried in February and November. The one-week European winter GIT programs were developed to satisfy both the public's need for short-duration, inexpensive vacations and the carriers' need to reduce their seasonality problem. The attractively packaged tours (price, hotels, ground transportation, etc.) were successful immediately. In the first few months of their initiation, the carriers experienced substantial traffic growth during their low seasons. While all carriers offered similar services, they all tried to distinguish their service from all the others. Distinctions were made in terms of the departure dates and the ground services included in the package. For example, on TWA's Boston-London tour, TWA's ground services included, among other things, hotel accommodations for all seven nights. Pan American's tour, on the other hand, offered the choice of hotel accommodations for all seven nights in London or hotel accommodations including only one night in London and six nights in other English towns, and a rental car.

In a survey carried out by the European Travel Commission in June 1972, 106 travel executives within the airlines, tour operators, and travel agents were interviewed to determine their views on the one-week tours.[4] Over 90 percent of the executives reacted favorably to the tours; they attributed the success of these tours first to their low price and second to their short duration. Most of the airline executives interviewed did not consider diversion a major concern, either from the economy class in the low-season or from any class during the summer months. The same survey also interviewed 413 passengers who had returned from these trips. The tabulated results showed that 87 percent of the trips were taken for nonbusiness purposes. The major reason for selecting these tours was the low price. With the exception of the hotel accommodations, one-half of the respondents did not use the extra services offered in the package, such as sightseeing bus tours, theatre tickets, and the use of rental cars.

The second example refers to Eastern's "Leisure Class" fare based upon the conditional reservation system. Whereas the first example dealt with reducing an airline's seasonality problem, this example deals with the problems of "no-shows" and "overbooking." The *no-show* is a passenger who holds a confirmed reservation for a particular flight and who, without notice of cancellation, does not show up at the departure gate at the appropriate time. Under the present regulations the passenger is entitled to receive a full refund of the ticket price and the airline suffers the loss of revenue. Besides the loss of revenue to the carrier, the no-show passenger also inconveniences other passengers who may not be able to get a reservation if the flight is sold out. Typically, flights that are supposedly sold out can have 10 to 15 percent of their seats unfilled due to no-shows, a percentage that varies from market to market and season to season. Sometimes the failure to show up at the gate is unintentional, for example, due to enroute traffic delay; whereas at other times, it is intentional. A business traveler may make multiple reservations if it is not known what time the business will be finished. During the days when student standby fares were available, a few students, on some occasions, would make numerous reservations with the hope that some seats would be available at the time of departure.

Many of the carriers overbook their flights to compensate for the no-shows. The overbooking policy varies by carrier, market, season, and in some cases by flight. Generally carriers will overbook flights by less than 10 percent, while certain flights may be overbooked by over 100 percent. However, there is an economic penalty if all of the passengers do show up for an overbooked flight with the unfortunate result that some people must be left behind.

One carrier had a unique problem. On one of its popular flights the number of passengers holding confirmed reservations would occasionally exceed the capacity of the aircraft even after the overbooking policy was taken into account. This experience can only be explained by the fact that some other person or some agency other than the carrier issued tickets without confirming reservations with the carrier. With angry passengers at the gate time after time, the carrier adopted an "underbooking" policy for this particular flight; the flight was closed once 50 percent of the seats had been sold, with full expectation that enough passengers holding valid tickets would show up demanding seats.

The no-show and overbooking problems are two variations of the old chicken-and-egg theme. Whatever the reason, Eastern began to analyze various possible solutions and came up with the leisure-class fare, or the conditional reservation rule that can be summarized as:

When a passenger seeks a reservation on a flight he will be informed if conditional reservation space is available, and if he wishes he may purchase a conditional reservation ticket at the applicable fare and stand by for the flight. If he cannot be accommodated on that flight (in the first class if necessary), Eastern will tender the passenger compensation in the amount of the value of the remaining flight coupon(s) to the first point of stopover or inter-line connecting point, or, if there is no such point, to the passenger's destination. Eastern will also provide transportation at no charge on the next available seat.[5]

Eastern maintained that this system would reduce the no-show and overbooking problem, provide the carrier with added revenue, and enable more passengers to make reservations on flights that are supposedly full. A number of other carriers objected to Eastern's proposal on the grounds that Eastern would end up providing free transportation to some passengers (violation of Section 403(b) of the Act), discriminate against other standby passengers, and encourage some passengers to devise plans to obtain free transportation. The Board rejected these complaints and approved Eastern's proposal for a trial period.

The third example of customer-responsive marketing is the establishment of specific commodity rates that were also aimed at reducing the directionality or back-haul problem. Air freight is generally a one-way movement of goods. Commodities move from their place of production to their place of utilization. An aircraft used to transport automotive parts from Detroit to Los Angeles has to be returned to Detroit to repeat the cycle. Unless there is air freight from Los Angeles to Detroit, the carrier must charge enough on the outbound journey to compensate for the empty return flight. In a case such as this the marketing management performed marketing research to ascertain potential commodities which could be transported back to the origin of the aircraft. Once the potential commodities were determined, the marketing team had to determine rates at which these commodities could and would move. There may be plenty of strawberries in Los Angeles, but unless the price is right, they are not going to move by air. This type of process led to the establishment of *specific commodity rates*. As the name implies, these are air freight rates that apply to the transport of specific commodities on specific markets.

Returning to the role of marketing, it is evident from recent developments that, in the future, marketing management will play an even more significant role in product planning. The marketing environment is changing rapidly. For example, in 1963, 30 percent of the U.S. residents departing from New York for Europe were on vacation; in 1971 the percentage was 53.[6] It would not be surprising if during the next 10 years pleasure travel accounts for almost two-thirds of the total travel. The needs and wants of the pleasure traveler are considerably different from those of the business traveler. Thus the emphasis in airline marketing would have to reflect this trend. The convenience of a higher level of service would have to be weighted against higher prices.

High inflation rates, especially in Europe, would have a significant influence on airline marketing with respect to destinations. It is well known that demand for air transportation is a derived demand; a person pays $200 to get to a destination, not to ride around in an airplane and watch a movie. In the past many airlines have developed their marketing programs around destinations. With high inflation rates in Europe and the changing value of the dollar, cheaper alternate destinations may have to be developed. Since pleasure travelers are more concerned about the total price rather than just the price of air travel, the European markets may experience a decline in travel. The U.S. travelers may prefer to travel within the United States or visit South America or Africa on a tour. Similarly the marketing planning for air freight would also have to change. The commodities available for international air freight are changing in each country, depending upon inflation and currency exchange rates. Thus, in the future, the airline marketers will have to analyze more carefully the potential commodities for air freight.

Price

It has already been pointed out that a carrier does not have unilateral control over the prices charged. In domestic travel, fares and rates are regulated by the Board. In the international arena, fares and rates are set through the IATA machinery (although a few carriers may function outside IATA). Thus, in airline marketing, price is not a marketing decision variable that can be used for competitive purposes. Once a new price or package service is introduced, all carriers will generally offer the same price. However, price is an effective marketing tool to increase the total size of the market.

In pricing airline service one must consider both the cost of providing the service and the regulatory environment. For example, since the total cost of operating a given flight is set as soon as one passenger purchases a ticket, the marginal cost of taking on extra passengers on that particular flight is almost zero. From an economic and marketing point of view, it would seem feasible to reduce the published fare to accommodate more passengers and increase revenue to move towards the break-even point or at least attempt to contribute towards the overhead costs. However, the object of regulation is to avoid this type of situation. A scheduled carrier is obliged to offer standard, approved fares to all customers. This philosophy protects not only the passengers but also the carriers. If such a requirement did not exist, many passengers would not purchase tickets in advance but would instead wait at the gate for last-minute, drastic price reductions.

The common pricing policy is to introduce *differential fares*. The concept of differential fares on a given route is to introduce lower fares around the basic, standard, or general fare that is available to the general public without any restrictions. Both first class and normal economy or coach fall into this group The other group, called the *promotional fares*, generally carries a number of restrictions. The assumption is that certain restrictions, if applied to promotional fares, will prevent those passengers already traveling on the standard fare from diverting to the lower fares. At the same time, the market would expand to include those persons who could not afford the standard fare. The promotional fares would attract the passengers with high price elasticity of demand, while the standard fares would be retained for those with low price elasticity of demand.

The object of differential pricing policy is to promote extra traffic without diluting the revenue. The necessary conditions for an effective differential pricing policy are to identify passengers with different price elasticities of demand and to ensure, once an appropriate differential fare structure has been set up, that passengers with low price elasticity of demand do not divert to lower fares set for passengers with high price elasticity of demand. Differential fares usually take the form of excursion fares with limited validity. Restrictions usually refer to the applicability periods (minimum and maximum length of stay, time of departure, and day of the week), number of passengers in a group, family fares, and inclusive tours. These promotional fares are usually calculated by applying some fraction to the general fare.

A distinction is usually made between the terms *fare level* and *fare structure*. When this distinction is made, the term *fare level* usually refers to a carrier's average fare, or revenue per passenger mile and is called the *yield*. It is calculated by dividing the total transport revenue by the total revenue passenger miles in a given time period. The term *fare structure*, on the other hand, refers to the many different fares that exist at any given time in the category of either general fares or promotional fares. Because there are many fares in existence at any given time, it is difficult to determine overall changes in fares from one time period to the next. This difficulty is overcome by using the fare level, or yield, to calculate changes in the fares. At this point it is necessary to caution the reader that a change in yield does not necessarily imply a change in fare. The movement in yield could be due to changes in the length of haul and mix of traffic, in the fare structure, or to any combination of these different factors.

Differential pricing policy usually leads to the question of discrimination. Excursion fares are the smallest problem since any person can take advantage of the lower fare provided the necessary restrictions are met. Discrimination is usually brought to the surface when special fares are offered to certain sectors of the population, that is, students, military, and accompanying family members. Standby fares have always been a sensitive issue. Since the actual load factor of any scheduled carrier is typically less than the optimum, the object of the standby fares is to minimize this differential. The amount of discount to be allowed to a standby passenger as compensation for the uncertain status has always been the big issue. The carriers cannot make the price difference too large, otherwise they risk the possibility that full-fare passengers will opt for standby status and cancel their reservations. This issue will be discussed in greater detail in Chapter 11.

The competitive environment other than among the scheduled carriers must also be taken into account when pricing air transportation services. The scheduled airlines compete with nonscheduled carriers, other modes of travel, and with other applications of the consumer's discretionary income. The competition between the scheduled carriers and the nonscheduled carriers will change dramatically in the future for two reasons. First, the scheduled carriers are offering more and more services comparable to the nonscheduled carriers. Second, the regulatory agencies are beginning to favor the liberalization of operating restrictions for the nonscheduled carriers. Competition from other modes refers to the surface carriers, e.g., automobile for short-haul trips (as well as bus and rail to a lesser degree) and steamships for overseas travel. The steamship companies are no longer marketing their service as a mode of transportation but more as a destination per se. One area where the competition between air carriers and steamship companies may, in fact, decrease is with respect to joint marketing of fly/cruise packages. Finally the competition between air travel and other expensive items such as cars, color televisions, summer houses, and boats is likely to increase.

Promotion

Promotion and sales expenses include expenditures for advertising, publicity, reservations, and travel agent commission. As shown in Table 4-1, the domestic trunk-line carriers spend approximately 11 percent of the total operating revenue on promotion and sales. This percentage varies among the carriers; in 1974 the percentage for Northwest was 9.2, and for Pan American, 13.3. The local-service carriers spend slightly less than 9.4 percent of their total operation revenue. Again there is some variation among the carriers with Southern on the low side (7.4 percent) and Hughes Air West on the high side (11.5 percent).

The expenditures related to promotion and sales, which include advertising, are regulated by the Board. The Board's rationale for regulating this expenditure is that in rate cases it must consider the cost of producing the service. Although the Board knows that promotion and sales expenditures are a necessary part of producing the service, it has set limits on the amounts that can be spent on promotion and sales. The standards are usually set in terms of a percentage of the total revenue and vary within the industry due to factors that may be crucial in a particular case, such as the development of new routes.

Once the management appropriates a certain amount for promotion and sales, it is the function of the marketing manager to distribute this total amount into various categories, for example, advertising. Table 4-2 shows the relative amount of funds spent in advertising by the trunk-line and local-service carriers. The advertising budget is usually some percentage of the total operating revenue. It is a discretionary cost incurred to increase or maintain revenues for an airline and is subject to competitive circumstances and managerial policy. Typically the trunk-line carriers spend approximately 1.7 percent of the total operating revenue on advertising. The local-service carriers spend closer to 1 percent.

Table 4-1
Promotion and Sales Expenditures, 1974

Trunk-line Carriers	Operating Revenue (000)	Promotion and Sales Expenses (000)	Promotion as a Percentage of Revenue
American	$ 1,717,677	$ 172,435	10.0
Braniff	549,966	55,630	10.1
Continental	465,928	45,243	9.7
Delta	1,368,586	142,505	10.4
Eastern	1,530,288	175,072	11.4
National	376,910	45,030	11.9
Northwest	766,844	70,255	9.2
Pan American	1,588,033	211,868	13.3
Trans World	1,755,583	209,006	11.9
United	2,256,167	210,183	9.3
Western	488,398	62,011	12.7
Total	$12,864,380	$1,399,238	10.9
Local-service Carriers			
Allegheny	$ 372,995	$ 34,516	9.3
Frontier	156,738	14,163	9.0
Hughes Air West	164,696	18,929	11.5
North Central	151,491	13,912	9.2
Ozark	118,565	11,353	9.6
Piedmont	133,952	11,527	8,6
Southern	108,560	8,039	7.4
Texas International	92,705	9,235	10.0
Total	$1,299,702	$121,674	9.4

Source: U.S. Civil Aeronautics Board, *Air Carrier Financial Statistics*, December 1974.

There are two types of advertising—institutional and competitive. The primary objective of *institutional advertising* is to stimulate those who have not previously flown to take a trip by air and to encourage the others to take more trips. In economic terms the objective is to shift the demand curve to the right. The purpose of *competitive advertising* is two-fold. First, each carrier advertises simply to keep his share of the market. Second, each carrier, through competitive advertising, will attempt to increase its share of the market. If a carrier spends a great deal of money on competitive advertising just to maintain its market share, the obvious question that comes to mind is what would happen if all competitors on major markets reduced their advertising expenditures? It seems reasonable to assume that if, in a given market, all competitors reduced their competitive advertising expenditure by an amount proportional to their

Table 4-2
Advertising Expenditures, 1974

Trunk-line Carriers	Operating Revenue (000)	Advertising Expense (000)	Advertising as a Percentage of Revenue
American	$ 1,717,677	$ 23,673	1.4
Braniff	549,966	7,694	1.4
Continental	465,928	11,548	2.5
Delta	1,368,586	17,447	1.3
Eastern	1,530,288	21,085	1.4
National	376,910	7,417	2.0
Northwest	766,844	9,949	1.3
Pan American	1,588,033	44,327	2.8
Trans World	1,755,583	38,112	2.2
United	2,256,167	27,988	1.2
Western	488,398	9,225	1.9
Total	$12,864,380	$218,465	1.7
Local-Service Carriers			
Allegheny	$ 372,995	$ 4,686	1.3
Frontier	156,738	1,886	1.2
Hughes Air West	164,696	2,202	1.3
North Central	151,491	300	0.2
Ozark	118,565	1,395	1.2
Piedmont	133,952	1,057	0.8
Southern	108,560	1,022	0.9
Texas International	92,705	1,332	1.4
Total	$1,299,702	$13,880	1.1

Source: U.S. Civil Aeronautics Board, *Form 41 Data*, 1974.

previous investment, then the market share would not change significantly. Continuing with this line of argument, it becomes obvious that a reduction in the advertising level would decrease the overall operating expenses. The difference can be passed to the customers in the way of lower fares, or it can be used to lower the operating losses or to bring carriers closer to the allowed rate of return on investment. In theory this argument is sound; in practice it would be quite difficult to prove.

It is also the function of the marketing department to decide on the distribution of the advertising budget into institutional versus competitive advertising, by market and by medium. Of the total funds spent on advertising, the trunk-line carriers spend about one-half of it on newspapers, one-quarter on television, and the remainder on other media such as magazines, radio, and posters.[7] There has never been a clear rationale behind the distribution of the advertising expenditure. The amount spent in a given market on a particular medium is a function of the competitive circumstances and managerial policy. Coverage and community are the usual criteria used in selecting media. The term *coverage* refers to the extent of exposure, for example, circulation of a magazine. The term *community* refers to the segment of the public exposed, for example, the segment of the public attracted by a particular magazine.

The question about the effectiveness of advertising is always a hard one to answer. It is very difficult, if not impossible, to establish satisfactory quantitative devices that will measure the effects of advertising on revenue and market shares. Insufficient data are the reason for this problem. For example, a detailed breakdown of the advertising expenditures for every competitor by market and by medium is necessary, and unless this type of data were available, cross-sectional analysis could not be justified. The issue is even more complicated because the industry is continuously changing, with the result that the impact of advertising cannot be easily isolated. This problem prevents the use of time-series analysis. The analysis regarding effectiveness of advertising requires carefully planned and controlled experiments. Cross-sectional analysis can then be applied to the data obtained from these controlled experiments on advertising expenditures by competitor, market, and medium for homogenous markets. In this case it would be possible to develop and calibrate analytical models to test the effectiveness of marketing.[a]

A number of investigators have attempted to measure the impact of advertising. There is no question that advertising does influence total demand as well as market shares. The major issue is its contribution to revenue versus its cost. In an extensive study, Randall Schultz, using a simultaneous-equation model, attempted to develop demand and market share response functions.[8] In the equation used to estimate demand, total industry advertising expenditure was statistically insignificant. In equations used to estimate market share, the coefficient of share of advertising was fairly small, indicating that market share was inelastic relative to advertising. Kit Narodick, in his study on consumer motivation with respect to choice of an airline, reported that while almost all of the individuals surveyed remembered seeing an airline advertisement, only about one-half of them could recall the content of the specific advertisement.[9] Narodick also concluded that almost one-half of his respondents selected an airline based upon its schedules.

It is evident from these two studies (and from others that will be mentioned in Chapter 9) that a carrier's market share is very dependent upon its schedules,

---

[a]Readers wanting more information on the effects of advertising should refer to Julian L. Simon, *The Management of Advertising* (Englewood, New Jersey: Prentice-Hall, Inc., 1971). Professor Simon discusses advertising in clear, comprehensible language, and applies his principles to El Al, the national flag carrier for Israel.

and yet until recently very few carriers have reflected this fact in their advertisement. Delta is one carrier that has concentrated on such basic information as who, what, where, when, and how much. While in the past many of the other carriers have spent millions of dollars on such slogans as "The Friendly Skies," "The Wings of Man," and "To the Good Life," Delta has continued to stress flight frequencies and departures in its newspaper advertisements. A number of other carriers are following this trend. In 1974 the trunk-line carriers spent 23.7 percent of their advertising budget on television. Delta's budget was only 6.8 percent.[10] On the other hand, Delta's budget for newspapers and radio was far above the other trunk-line carriers. One other carrier that has consistently stressed flight frequencies and departures for a number of years is Allegheny, with a media distribution similar to Delta.

A recent editorial in *Advertising Age* explained in concise terms how ineffective some of the airline advertisements are. According to the article, some of the airline advertisements are textbook examples of how not to do it.[11] With the exception of a very few, most of the advertisements fail miserably in convincing a passenger to select a particular carrier. Even today a few carriers still send messages of little concern to the passenger. TWA's "Lasagne over Los Angeles" and "Mozart over Missouri" are alleged to be examples of this. Numerous analysts, including Kit Narodick in the study cited above,[12] have repeatedly pointed out that cabin service amenities are of minor importance in the selection of a carrier. Even if these advertisement tactics were to increase a carrier's market share, the gain would be short-lived.

Very few male television watchers would object to watching a bikini-clad girl frolicking on a sandy beach. However, how much of a long-term increase in market share can be credited to this? Likewise, advertising agencies completely exploited the appearance of cabin attendants. Who can forget PSA's seductive-looking stewardesses, Braniff's "Air Strip," and National's "Fly Me" girls? With all this glamour, one tends to forget the basic reason for the presence of cabin attendants on board the aircraft. The primary function of cabin crew personnel is not to serve meals and drinks in hot pants but to ensure the safety of passengers and provide assistance in the event of an emergency. A cabin crew is not something nice to have; rather, its presence is required by the FAA regulations. Likewise, the primary purpose of uniforms is not to create a seductive atmosphere. Uniforms are supposed to be an aid in identifying flight attendants in an emergency and should represent authority in panic situations. A good example of a carrier that has not lost this objective is Pan American with its pleasantly authoritative uniforms. However, while it is true that the primary function of cabin crew is related to safety, one must not overlook the fact that the cabin crew represents an important contact with the public. From this point of view the cabin crew can fulfill an important public relations function.

By now the reader is probably wondering what constitutes a good advertisement. There is no single answer to this question. If the purpose of advertising is to induce a passenger to select a particular carrier, then it should fulfill two requirements. First, the advertisement should highlight service features that are important to the passenger. Second, the feature should be such that it would be difficult, if not impossible, for the competitors to copy. The implementation of this concept is not as difficult as it sounds. For example, take Pan American's slogan "The World's Most Experienced Airline," this appears to be a reasonable advertisement. Many passengers still place high value on safety. Furthermore, since Pan American probably does have the most international experience, it would be almost impossible for any carrier to copy this.

Distribution

A very important element in the marketing of airline service is a distribution system that provides the mechanism for the passenger to purchase the service conveniently. The airline distribution system has two elements—the sales outlets, or channels, and its reservation system. A *sales outlet* is a place where a passenger can purchase the service offered by a carrier. The function of the *reservation system* is to provide management with the current load status of each future flight with accuracy and speed.

In the airline industry there are three basic types of sales outlets: the carrier's sales offices, the travel agents, and other carriers' sales offices. The relative importance of each one of these varies from carrier to carrier. If a ticket is purchased through a travel agent, then the carrier is obligated to give the travel agent an agreed commission that is approved by the Board. The travel agents can play an important role in three respects. First, an airline cannot possibly maintain sales offices in every town across the country, let alone the entire world. Second, the travel agent can perform an important function of producing and selling inclusive tours. Third, a travel agent can provide useful information and help in international air transportation involving traveling documents and different currencies. However, these advantages are not free. Besides the commission itself, the carrier tends to lose control over its services offered for sale. Once agreed upon, any one of the hundreds of thousands of travel agents can issue a valid ticket on the carrier, and the carrier has the obligation to honor the ticket. It is not difficult to see how communications can fail when multiple parties are able to sell space on multiple flights. Finally, on routes served by competitive carriers there is no guarantee that a given travel agent will select a particular carrier.

An airline's sales offices can be on-line or off-line. The on-line sales office is located in a city served by the carrier. Off-line sales offices are normally located only in very large cities and even then only by large carriers. An airline sales office is obviously more effective than a travel agent. However, it is a much more expensive means of outlet. Other carriers' sales offices can also be very effective outlets. These are sometimes known as interline sales. The importance of this outlet can be judged by the carriers' Clearing House interline claims that can run into billions of dollars.

The travel agents handling cargo are generally known as air freight forwarders. They provide the useful function of consolidation. For example, the airlines usually offer lower transportation rates for greater quantity shipments. The freight forwarder can therefore consolidate individual shipments going to the same destination and obtain a lower transportation rate from the carrier. The amount of profit made through grouped shipments depends upon the delay that arises from the consolidation process. Firms engaged in the consolidation process are also known as indirect carriers.

As stated earlier, the main function of an airline's reservation system is to indicate the load status of each future flight up to a given period of time such as three months or one year. Unsold seats can be accessed right up until the boarding time. Basically the reservations system keeps records of the seats sold and seats available for every scheduled flight. The unit record on confirmed seats usually contains information on the passenger's name, address, telephone number, origin, destination, connections, class of service, number of people in the party, whether tickets have been issued, and special instructions, such as the need for a wheelchair or a special meal.

The speed and accuracy of the reservations system is very important to the carrier. Speed is essential from both the passenger's and the carrier's point of view. A passenger sitting in an airline's sales office in Tokyo will demand instantaneous knowledge regarding a reservation on a future flight from London to Paris. Likewise, if a cancellation occurs in the Tokyo office, the sales office in London must be notified immediately so that the newly available seat can be offered to another passenger. Besides speed and accuracy, the reservations system also must have a very large capacity. The problem is not that a large airline with a worldwide network requires an enormous capacity, but that the airline network must be connected to other airlines for interline connections. The reservations system of American, for example, should also be able to confirm reservations on Pan American. The electronic computer lies at the heart of present-day reservations systems. It has the capacity of handling the largest of the networks of any airline as well as interline bookings. The computer also provides the necessary speed for processing an individual sale. There is virtually no time elapsed between a sale and the updating of the record.

The reservation system also provides other management services. For example, it provides information relating to demands for individual flights. This information is used in planning the capacity to be offered in a market. The system provides information on the variation in demand by season, month, week, and day. The scheduling department can utilize this information for purposes such as selecting aircraft for individual flights and preparing for extra sections. Finally, the reservation system can also be used to aid accounting (payroll and billing), maintenance (spare parts inventory), and cargo operations (determining the current status of any shipment).

Summary

The traditional definition of marketing centered on the selling of already produced services. However, newer definitions include determining the needs and wants of the carrier's existing and potential passengers and shippers and advising management to vary the output in light of these needs. A number of examples were cited to show the development of changes in service in response to customer needs and wants, such as the thrift-class service on the Pacific, the one-week European Group Inclusive Tour, and in-flight entertainment to eliminate boredom.

Although price is not a marketing decision variable in airline marketing for competitive purposes, it is an effective marketing tool to increase the total size of the market through such mechanisms as differential fares. However, while differential pricing policy can be used to promote extra traffic, it is necessary to establish sufficient conditions to keep dilution and discrimination at minimum levels.

With respect to promotion, a significant amount of effort within marketing departments appears to have focused upon maintaining and increasing the carrier's market share as opposed to the total size of the market. This is evident from the in-flight and on-the-ground services offered by the carriers. However, most studies have concluded that a majority of the passengers select carriers based upon its scheduled frequency, a factor that recently is widely being reflected in airline advertisement.

In the airline industry the distribution component of marketing consists of sales outlets and the reservation system. The sales outlets component consists of the carrier's sales offices, the travel agents, and other carriers' sales offices. The reservation system is not only an important component of the distribution system but also provides essential information used in planning the capacity to be offered in a market.

Financial Practices

As shown in Chapter 2, the largest component of industry assets is represented by flight equipment. In 1974 total assets equaled $15.2 billion; $13.5 billion of those represented cost value of flight equipment. As of 1975, according to one very large bank, the eleven U.S. trunk-line carriers are expected to spend over $2 billion per year over the next five years on flight equipment. In addition to this $10 billion for flight equipment, the trunk-line carriers will require another $14 billion for other capital requirements. Assuming that these figures are reasonable estimates of the needs of the trunk-line carriers for funds, it is of some interest to investigate the possible sources of these funds in view of the industry's earnings and rate of return on investment in recent years.

The purpose of this chapter is two-fold. First, an attempt is made to describe the different ways the industry has met its financial requirements in the past. It is hoped that this historical analysis may provide some insight as to how the industry may finance its future requirements. Second, in recent years a significant amount of the capital requirements have been met through leasing. Therefore an attempt is also made in this chapter to provide the reader with some background on leasing and on recent developments of analytical models, which can be extremely useful in the analysis of the decision to lease rather than buy the flight equipment.

Capital Requirements

The following industry analysis is performed through an examination of the financial practices concerning the acquisition of corporate capital during the last two decades. The industry considered includes the total system operations of the eleven trunk carriers, including Pan American. Although the basic data was taken from the Civil Aeronautics Board's various editions of the *Handbook of Airline Statistics* and the *Air Carrier Financial Statistics*, the reader is cautioned that the comparative balance sheet and income statement data for the industry are slightly different in this analysis due to the differences in the definition of the number of trunk line carriers in the industry. The CAB's *Handbook of Airline Statistics* reports income statement data for each carrier for its domestic and international/territorial operations separately while balance sheet data are reported on a system basis. At the same time, aggregate data on the system operations of the total trunk-line carriers are not readily available for the last two decades in any consistent form for both the balance sheets and income statements. The industry analysis presented here is based upon balance sheets and income statements constructed by adding the domestic and international/ territorial operations of each of the eleven carriers for 24 years from 1951 to 1974.

The early 1950s represented a period of strong financial stability according to the usual measure of financial risk and profitability. The data shown in Table 5-1, which measures short-term financial risk by operating ratio,[a] current ratio,[b] and interest coverage ratio,[c] are indicative of a financially stable industry. During the period 1951-1956 the operating ratio was about 90 percent, leaving 10 percent of the operating revenue for interest charges, taxes, and profit. From the bankers' point of view, a net working capital[d] of about $100 million accompanied by a current ratio of 1.3 provided an acceptable indicator of financial strength. In addition, the earning power relative to the fixed interest charges was extremely favorable, as shown by the interest coverage ratio. The long-term financial risk was fairly low, as indicated by the 0.4 ratio of long-term debt to stockholder equity, and financial leverage measured as the ratio of long-term debt to total assets, at approximately 20 percent.

During its early development, the industry had met its capital requirements primarily through equity financing. An investigation of the capitalization of major U.S. airlines shows that up until the mid-1950s less than 30 percent of the industry's capital represented long-term debt. However, during the early 1950s the industry financed a substantial part of its capital requirements through internal sources, basically depreciation and earnings. The relatively fast rate of technological change produced high depreciation charges for the airlines, and depreciation represented the single largest source of financing in the industry. Although these charges varied from carrier to carrier and from year to year, the total depreciation charges as a percent of the total operating expenses have remained in the 8 to 10 percent range. Table 5-2, which shows the uses and sources for funds, points out that for the period 1951-1956 over 40 percent of the funds came from depreciation. When interpreting the "Uses of Funds" table, the reader is cautioned that the data shown represent actual monies spent during a particular period. This clarification is necessary since a significant part of the funds used for equipment purchases is normally committed a number of years prior to equipment delivery.

The second important source of internal financing in this period was the earnings of the industry justified on the basis of its rate of return on investment during the period. Net income (income after taxes and interest on long-term debt but before special items) financed almost a quarter of the total capital

---

[a]*Operating ratio* is the ratio of operating expenses to operating revenue.

[b]*Current ratio* is the ratio of current assets to current liabilities.

[c]*Interest coverage ratio* is the ratio of operating profit to interest expenses.

[d]*Net working capital* is current assets less current liabilities.

Table 5-1
Selected Financial and Operating Ratios—Major U.S. Airlines

| | | | | Rate of Return (%) on | | | |
Year	Debt Equity	Interest Coverage	Operating Ratio (%)	Total Investment	Long-term Debt	Stockholder Equity	Current Ratio
1951	0.4	17.0	86.4	10.2	4.4	12.7	1.3
1952	0.4	14.2	90.0	7.2	3.6	8.8	1.4
1953	0.4	11.4	91.0	6.8	4.6	7.7	1.3
1954	0.4	11.7	90.3	8.0	5.0	9.2	1.4
1955	0.4	15.1	90.2	7.4	3.8	8.9	1.5
1956	0.5	12.0	91.7	5.8	3.2	7.1	1.3
1957	0.7	3.9	96.2	2.6	3.4	2.0	1.4
1958	0.9	3.8	94.8	3.2	3.7	2.8	1.6
1959	1.2	3.3	94.5	3.2	3.7	2.7	1.4
1960	1.7	1.5	96.5	2.1	3.9	−0.8	1.4
1961	2.0	0.2	99.2	1.0	4.9	−6.7	1.3
1962	2.0	1.6	94.7	4.0	5.5	1.0	1.3
1963	1.6	2.8	92.2	6.0	5.9	6.1	1.3
1964	1.4	4.9	88.4	9.3	5.2	15.1	1.2
1965	1.1	6.4	85.9	10.7	5.0	17.3	1.4
1966	1.3	6.4	86.0	9.0	4.0	15.4	1.6
1967	1.3	5.6	88.8	7.2	3.4	12.2	1.6
1968	1.5	3.0	92.4	5.1	4.0	6.9	1.3
1969	1.6	1.9	94.7	3.9	4.5	3.1	1.2
1970	1.9	0.2	99.4	1.2	4.4	−4.9	1.1
1971	1.6	1.0	96.9	3.0	5.2	−0.3	1.2
1972	1.5	1.7	95.1	4.8	4.9	4.2	1.1
1973	1.4	1.5	95.6	4.1	5.8	1.4	1.1
1974	1.3	1.7	95.3	4.6	7.0	1.2	1.1

Source: U.S. Civil Aeronautics Board, *Handbook of Airline Statistics*, Washington, D.C., Various Editions.

requirements. Table 5-1 shows the extent of profitability during this period, as measured by the average rate of return on combined investment. In this analysis ROI (return on investment) is derived by dividing the net income excluding special items plus interest expenses by the sum of net stockholders' equity and long-term debt. Special items constitute extraordinary credits and debits (including the associated special income tax credits and debits) that are of sufficient magnitude to materially distort the total operating revenues or total operating expenses if included therein. Interest expense is added back to the net income, since the overall rate of return is based upon total investment and interest expense represents a return on the debt part of the total investment.

Table 5-2
Sources and Uses of Funds for Major U.S. Airlines

	1951-1956		1956-1961		1961-1966		1966-1971		1971-1974	
	$M	%	$M	%	$M	%	$M	%	$M	%
Major Uses										
Increase In:										
Current Assets	$ 173.7	12.5	349.9	10.4	874.9	16.8	596.6	6.4	941.9	19.2
Investments and Special Funds	107.0	7.7	14.3	0.4	429.1	8.2	516.4	5.6	(188.8)	(3.8)
Flight and Ground Equipment (at Cost)	822.0	59.0	2188.1	65.1	2506.4	48.0	5709.6	61.5	1118.6	22.8
Deferred Charges	–	–	80.8	2.4	–	–	136.6	1.5	–	–
Accumulated Retained Earnings	218.8	15.7	–	–	876.9	16.8	320.0	3.4	391.7	8.0
Dividends	109.4	7.9	174.1	5.2	235.2	4.5	379.3	4.1	182.5	3.7
Other	(38.2)	(2.8)	552.6	16.5	295.5	5.7	1628.0	17.5	2467.4	50.1
Total	$1392.7	100.0	$3359.8	100.0	$5218.0	100.0	$9286.5	100.0	$4913.3	100.0
Major Sources										
Increase In:										
Current Liabilities	134.1	9.6	262.0	7.8	425.4	8.2	891.5	9.6	1038.5	21.1
Long-term Debt	191.6	13.8	1360.0	40.5	1015.7	19.5	2508.2	27.0	(3.7)	(.1)
Deferred Credits	31.5	2.3	132.6	3.9	344.5	6.6	543.5	5.9	312.0	6.4
Deferred Charges	14.3	1.0	–	–	21.9	0.4	–	–	4.7	.1
Stockholder's Equity (not including Retained Earnings)	100.9	7.2	191.2	5.7	424.0	8.1	877.9	9.5	232.1	4.7
Retained Earnings (Accumulated)	–	–	24.5	0.7	–	–	–	–	–	–
Depreciation Expenses (total FH & Ground)	595.8	42.8	1222.4	36.4	1933.4	37.1	3704.4	39.8	2729.0	55.4
Net Income (after Int. & Tax & Spec. Items)	324.5	23.3	167.1	5.0	1053.1	20.1	761.0	8.2	600.7	12.2
Total	$1392.7	100.0	$3359.8	100.0	$5218.0	100.0	$9286.5	100.0	$4913.3	100.0

Source: U.S. Civil Aeronautics Board, *Handbook of Airline Statistics*, Washington, D.C., Various Editions.

Table 5-1 also shows the separate rate of return on investment for the debt holders and the stockholders. The rate of return on long-term debt is determined by dividing the interest by the long-term debt. The rate of return on stockholders equity is calculated by dividing net income by stockholders equity. This provides information on the cost of debt and equity financing. Since debt has a lower cost relative to equity capital, the debt-to-equity ratio has a considerable influence on the overall rate of return. The data shown illustrate the effect of this financial leverage on the overall rate of return on investment.

Although major portions of the funds were generated internally, relatively small amounts of external funds were raised. For instance, long-term debt and new stock issues accounted for about one-fifth of the total sources. The amount and source of external financing naturally varied within the industry. For example, American did not use long-term debt, while Eastern relied heavily upon this source. TWA financed only about 10 percent of its funds from external sources, most of which were derived from the sale of common stock. In this case the choice of the financial instrument was due basically to the limited availability of debt capital. The carrier was experiencing a high operating ratio, which is indicative of a higher than average business risk. At the same time, the current ratio was extremely low—a sign of high degree of financial risk. The amount of debt that TWA could raise was therefore limited. Another carrier going against the industry trend was Delta. During this period the carrier financed over 60 percent of its requirements from external sources. Most of Delta's debt was financed through bank loans.

During the mid-1950s, the industry turned its attention to planning for the jet aircraft. The carriers committed themselves to almost $2 billion for flight equipment and the associated ground equipment. This was a considerable amount of capital to be raised through pure equity—without causing excessive dilution of earnings. Besides, the rate of return on investment had dwindled to about 3 percent, with return on stockholder equity even lower. This situation implied that a good portion of the funds had to be raised as external debt. While the banks were relatively uninterested in financing this huge long-term debt, the industry was not in desperate straits, since the carriers had not yet exploited the insurance companies who were very interested in negotiating the long-term debt on the basis of extremely high interest coverage ratio in the previous 5-year period. The period 1956-1961 was a time of debt financing. A little over 40 percent, or $1.4 billion, was raised through new debt. This was more than seven times the amount raised in the previous five years.

The period 1961-1966 was financed heavily through internal sources, due basically to the high profits earned during this period. Over one-third of the funds came from depreciation, about 20 percent from net earnings, and 6.6 percent from deferred credits, which were mostly deferred income taxes. Profitability was important in this period not only as an internal source of funds but also because of its critical influence on the availability of debt financing. In addition, the existence of profits enabled the industry to raise almost $350 million through deferred credits, a figure almost three times larger than the previous 5-year period. Most of this resulted from the reported difference in depreciation charges to stockholders and the Internal Revenue Service. External sources during this period provided less than one-third of the total requirements with 19.5 percent derived from long-term debt and 8.1 percent from new stock issue. See Table 5-2.

Between 1966 and 1971 the industry placed orders amounting to $10 billion for the larger wide-body equipment. This tremendous commitment was made soon after the industry had realized substantial profits. However, toward the end of the 1960s the financial position of the industry began to deteriorate. The high operating ratios, fluctuating and uncertain earnings, inflation, and declining airline stock prices resulted in a tight supply of money for industry. Capital in the form of debt or equity was not as readily available as in the previous decade, and the industry began to investigate different and more expensive instruments of financing its capital requirements, including subordinated convertible debenture financing, bank financing, and lease financing.

Subordinated convertible debenture financing was used when the insurance companies did not want to buy straight senior debt. The convertible debenture is a hybrid type of security with characteristics both of straight debt and common equity. This source of financing can be superior to both straight debt and common equity. However, if improperly used, it can produce the worst features of both alternatives. The carriers used this instrument as a sweetener in attracting money from the insurance companies. A sizeable amount of funds were still obtained from the insurance companies, although part of the securities were now convertible debentures. There are many advantages in using convertibles as a source of financing. For example, even if conversion is exercised, convertible debentures can result in a lesser number of additional common shares compared to a straight sale of common stock in the same amount. Furthermore, the convertibles can be issued at a lower effective interest cost and sinking fund rates compared to straight long-term debt because of the convertible feature. In 1971 convertible debt amounted to more than $1 billion and represented 21.2 percent of the total debt. Of the trunk-line carriers, Braniff, Delta, National, Northwest, and United did not negotiate any convertible debt.

During the 1966-1971 period, about 27.0 percent of the capital required was financed through long-term debt. The share of the capital provided by the banks increased from 8.9 percent in 1967 to 16.0 percent in 1971. This source of financing was expensive, since not only are short-term interest rates usually high, but also the loan has to be negotiated two or three times during the life of the flight equipment. The other major source of equipment financing was the use of leasing. The value of leased aircraft increased from 7.7 percent in 1966 to 18.7 percent in 1971. The importance of this source of financing is discussed in detail in the next section.

The financial position of the industry looked fairly gloomy at the end of 1970. Because of the slowdown in the economy, excess capacity, and substantial increase in operating costs, earnings in the past few years had been declining steadily. The interest coverage ratio had dropped down to an unacceptable level of 0.2, and the operating ratio stood at an all-time high of 99.4 percent. The highly leveraged position of the industry (debt to equity ratio of 1.9) accompanied by a lower average rate of return on investment relative to the interest rate on debt produced substantial losses for the stockholders. During the period 1971-1974, most of the capital requirements of the industry were met through depreciation and increase in current liabilities.

The industry made a turn in 1971 when the U.S. scheduled airlines posted a net income of $28 million compared to a loss of more than $200 million in 1970. Subsequently the industry earned $215 million in 1972, $227 million in 1973, and $322 million in 1974, although still substantially less than the highest earnings recorded in 1966 at $428 million.[1] The improvement between 1970 and 1974 was due basically to the drastic cost-cutting measures initiated by the carriers and to the improvement in operating revenue. The reduction in operating costs was the result of tight capacity control and a cutback in the number of employees. However, the operating costs have been going up again since 1973 because of the increased price of fuel. The improvement in operating revenue was the result of increases in traffic growth accompanied by substantial fare increases. A substantial part of the fare increases was justified to cover the added costs of fuel. However, despite this obvious financial improvement between 1970 and 1974, the industry began to show a reverse trend again in 1975.

Estimates made in 1975 for the capital requirements of the industry stand at over $25 billion for the second half of the 1970s.[2] The question is: What sources will the industry use to meet these mammoth capital requirements? In considering the possible alternative instruments of financing, one can only rely on the experience of 20 years. The historical analysis is especially useful for a cyclical industry, and based upon the past analysis, it appears that the airlines portray the cyclical trend, with the cycle running from 5 to 10 years. However, while the equipment cycle has a significant influence on the carriers' earning cycle, the existence of an economic cycle on top of the equipment cycle makes interpretation of the results very difficult. The key factor determining the ability and needs of the carriers to raise the necessary funds will be the future profitability, which will not only be a significant source of internal financing as during the 1951-1956 and 1961-1966 periods but also will exert substantial influence in attracting external funds. As seen from the historical analysis, the airlines represent a high-risk industry. Earnings fluctuate considerably, operating ratios are high, and the industry is highly susceptible to the business cycle. Furthermore the industry is highly competitive and subject to rapid technological change. It is, therefore, difficult to forecast correctly the extent and timing of future profitability.

The difficulty in forecasting lies in the inability to forecast accurately the operating costs, traffic growth, trends in yield, and the operating load factors. Within operating costs, the single largest uncertainty is the price of fuel. In other areas where the labor costs are expected to increase, the carriers will have to maximize their cost control efforts in areas that are subject to management discretion. Current forecasts of passenger traffic growth are 6 to 7 percent through 1980. The upward trend in yield is expected to continue through fare increases, which are necessary to offset increasing labor and fuel prices. Thus despite the anticipated losses during 1975, reasonable earnings for the next 5 years are expected, even though they probably will not reach the 12 percent rate of return allowed by the Board.

Most of the $25 billion required for the rest of this decade will have to be generated from internal sources. One current estimate of the amount to be generated through internal sources stands at $19 billion. By far the single largest source of internal funds will still be depreciation. Historically this source has provided between 30 and 40 percent of the total funds needed. In the future the percentage of the funds raised through this source may decline slightly due to the greater use of lease financing. Although the extent of funds raised through this source will depend upon CAB regulations and will vary by carrier as a reflection of individual management policies, this will remain the major source of internal funds. With respect to external financing, a slowdown is expected in the acquisition of long-term debt. There are two reasons for this expectation. First, the current level of fixed interest expense is becoming fairly large relative to such expenses in light of the high operating ratio. In 1974 this expense amounted to $270 million, more than three times the amount for 1961. Second, because of the volatility of the earnings relative to capital investment, the industry would be forced to improve its debt to equity ratio if it is to attract the insurance companies and the banks.

In the past there has been a substantial concentration of the debt held by these institutions. For example, at the end of 1973 the top three insurance companies held 60 percent of the total debt held by these institutions, and 36 percent of the total bank debt was held by the top three banks. With so much at stake, these institutions maintain financial specialists in the airline industry to determine the relative risk of the industry. It is therefore unlikely that the industry as a whole will be able to tap the insurance companies and banks for any substantial amount of long-term debt in the future. However, certain carriers such as Delta represent very favorable risk/return characteristics from the point of view of these institutions, due to their low debt to equity ratios and high interest coverage ratios. Conservative carriers with low financial leverages, such as Delta, Northwest, Continental, and possibly National and Western, should be able to attract debt capital more easily than the high financially leveraged carriers, such as TWA and Eastern. In addition, the debt could be of the convertible type if the straight long-term debt were too expensive or the industry could not easily attract common equity.

Since airline stocks are generally considered short-term trading vehicles, equity financing should increase with improved earnings. It is difficult, however, to forecast the extent of this source, since it would depend upon the financial position of the industry. Again, carriers that have shown a relatively low level of business and financial risk should have no problems in attracting equity capital. Delta and Northwest are certainly examples of investment grade; these two carriers are practically the only ones that have continually paid dividends, even through the recent recession periods.

Leasing as a source of equipment financing should continue to be popular as long as the investment tax credit is in existence and the tax laws do not change enough to alter its attractiveness to lessors. Furthermore, since leases can extend over many years, they could prove to be a significant source accounting for as much as 30 to 40 percent of the new aircraft.

Lease-or-Purchase Decisions

Aircraft leasing as a source of financing became significant in the mid-1960s due basically to the existence of Investment Tax Credit (ITC). In 1961 leased aircraft represented about 3 percent of the value of total aircraft, whereas in 1971 the figure was closer to 20 percent. Although some of the smaller trunk-line carriers had been using leasing as a source of financing since the early 1960s, the extent of this source was small until the mid-1960s when the Big Four began to use this instrument. A few carriers have entirely avoided leasing. For example, the number of leased aircraft operated by Continental, Delta, National, and Northwest has been minimal compared to Eastern and TWA. In comparing the rate of return and the extent of leasing, carriers earning higher rate of return than the industry average have generally been the ones that avoid leasing aircraft. Their higher-than-average earnings have provided them with more desirable sources of financing. Furthermore, carriers with poor or no earnings were not able to take advantage of the ITC laws. For example, a carrier has to make a profit in order to have tax obligations and before it can benefit from the ITC shields. For these carriers, leases provided a partial benefit since the tax advantages obtained by the lessor (for example, the bank) were generally shared with the lessee (the air carrier) through lower effective interest rates. Toward the end of the 1960s, leasing for some carriers was not only a way of obtaining aircraft at lower effective interest rates, but perhaps the only way of acquiring an aircraft.

There are many reasons for leasing flight equipment. First, by leasing, the airline eliminates the need to borrow. Second, if the carrier's level of profit is low or non-existent, leasing may provide a partial ITC benefit. The introduction in 1962 of the ITC allowance provided an incentive for the U.S. corporations to increase investment in exchange for a substantial tax benefit. Third, leasing avoids the progress payments to the manufacturer. This can be as much as 20 percent of the cost of the aircraft. Fourth, leasing offers a hedge against inflation, since the payments remain fixed throughout the contract even if interest rates rise. Fifth, leasing simplifies bookkeeping for tax purposes. Sixth, leasing can reduce the risk of technical obsolescence. The disadvantages of leasing, besides the "pride of ownership" or the "security of ownership," are the loss to the lessee of the salvage value of the aircraft or the additional services from the remaining life of the aircraft and the partial loss of the ITC benefit. The latter depends upon the profitability of the carrier. In addition, some banks consider the value of leased aircraft as part of the airline's long-term debt, thus making the capital structure of the carrier appear weaker. The reader should be cautioned that leasing should not be considered a disadvantage from the point of view of depreciation deductions, since lease payments are tax deductible.

The investment tax credit is perhaps the most important cause of widespread leasing. The tax benefit is very attractive to investors in the high-income tax bracket. In 1963 the commercial banks were allowed to lease equipment to the carriers and take the benefit of the tax credit. In 1970 the amendments to the Bank Holding Company Act allowed banking organizations to form leasing subsidiaries separate from the bank. Through this law the holding company subsidiaries could issue commercial paper and use other capital markets in ways that banks could not. For example, if the subsidiary can provide 20 percent of the cost of the asset and borrow the remaining 80 percent from other lenders by placing the equipment under a chattel mortgage as security on the loans, the subsidiary becomes the owner of the asset and qualifies for full tax benefits. This type of lease is sometimes called a *leverage lease*.

The airlines were attracted to leasing for the following reasons. First, because of the competitive nature of the business, they felt forced to buy the expensive equipment, especially the wide-body jets. Second, due to the poor financial position of many of the carriers, they could not attract the necessary capital to buy the equipment. Third, the fluctuating and low level of profit did not allow the carriers to take advantage of the investment tax credit. Fourth, during the recession the supply of money was tight and interest rates were extremely high. During the years when the ITC was not available, the lessors charged the carriers an amount 1 to 3 percent above the interest paid by the lessors for funds obtained to purchase the aircraft. However, during those times when the ITC was in operation, the effective interest rate paid by the carriers was often below the prime interest rate, reflecting the shared tax benefits.

While specific terms in the leasing contracts vary within the industry, there are some general terms that are contained in almost all contracts. Before discussing these terms, it is necessary to distinguish between a financial lease and an operating lease. An *operating lease* is usually a relatively short-term agreement. Airlines usually enter into this type of agreement to meet capacity demands during peak periods. The *financial lease*, on the other hand, is an instrument by which the carrier acquires the services of the flight equipment for the major portion of its useful life without actually purchasing it. The difference between the two types of leases is not just one of time span but also of cost. Because of the lower risk faced by the lessor, the cost of a financial lease is less than the cost of an operating lease. The following discussion is limited to the financial lease.

The term of the financial lease can vary from 4 to 18 years. While the average term is between 10 and 12 years, the minimum duration is always over 3 years. The reasons for minimum time period come from the fact that in order for the lessors to claim an ITC on the purchase price of an aircraft being leased to some airline, it is essential that the agreement be for at least 3 years. The rental payments can be monthly, quarterly, semiannually, or annually. A typical basic rent payment may be stated as:

... lessee hereby agrees to pay lessor in 48 equal consecutive quarterly installments, each in an amount equal to 3.148% of the lessor's cost of the aircraft. ...

Other provisions contained in the financial lease are (1) residual value of the aircraft; (2) the option for the lessee to purchase the aircraft; (3) costs with respect to maintenance, spare parts, and insurance; (4) default clauses; and (5) cancellation clauses. Regarding the residual value of the aircraft, the Internal Revenue Service requires that the residual value of the asset 2 years after the expiration date of the lease be at least 15 percent of the original purchase cost of the asset. Furthermore, the IRS requires that no "bargain" option may exist within the lease contract enabling the lessee to purchase the asset or renew the lease at the end of, or during, the term of the lease. With respect to maintenance and insurance, it can either be the responsibility of the lessee or of the lessor. In the case of leases negotiated through the subsidiaries of aircraft manufacturers, the lessor will sometimes provide for maintenance and overhauls. These provisions are typical points included in many lease agreements.

The question as to whether an airline should lease or buy flight equipment is complex; to answer it a sound knowledge of the institutional and operating structure of the industry is required as well as a thorough understanding of the principles of financial theory. For example, regarding the former point, one must consider the high cost of flight equipment, the lead time between design and delivery, and the high risk of obsolescence, partially due to the institutional nature of the industry. With respect to the latter point, one must be able to differentiate between the usefulness and appropriateness of various financial models involving such controversial issues as the appropriate discount rate for obtaining the present values of the relevant cash flow.

Since the use of lease financing has been increasing in recent years, it may be helpful to investigate the feasibility of using some of the existing financial models to determine a rational way of making the lease-or-purchase decision in the airline industry. While a number of fairly acceptable lease-or-buy decision models have appeared in recent financial literature, their application to the airline industry relative to the widespread use of some other analytical techniques, such as demand analysis, has been virtually nonexistent. With a heavy debt of appreciation to the theoretical work published in recent financial literature, an attempt is made here to describe for the reader some basic analytical tools that may be useful in making a rational choice between leasing and buying flight equipment.[3] In addition, the analytical models provide the decision maker with the ability to perform sensitivity analysis, which can be extremely useful in investigating the influence of individual parameters in the model on the decision between leasing and buying.

The first problem in investigating the lease-versus-buy decision is to determine what criteria should be used in analyzing leasing decisions. At first one is tempted to determine the desirability of leasing by comparing the effective rate of interest with the rate of interest that a carrier would pay to borrow if the decision were made to purchase the aircraft, assuming that the carrier is able to borrow the funds. This analysis would compare leasing with borrowing. However, borrowing is a method of financing the asset, whereas leasing is a method of acquiring the asset. Thus the question of financing lease payments is a separate issue. With this the case, the comparison of effective rate of interest with borrowing rate of interest is an inappropriate method of analysis.

One reasonable method of evaluating alternative capital budgeting proposals is commonly known as *present value method*. In this method the object is to determine the future cash flows and discount these at an appropriate rate of return to obtain the net present value. The idea behind the present value method is to take into account the time value of money. Today's dollar is worth more than next year's dollar. Substantial amounts of the analytical work using this approach in leasing decisions has been performed by Johnson and Lewellen; the analytical framework discussed here is an overly simplified version of their theoretical model.[4]

In evaluating the lease-versus-buy decision, the reader is cautioned in the use of any analytical model for a number of reasons. First, a significant amount of controversy exists over the appropriate terms to be included in a model and the treatment of each term with respect to discounting. Second, there is the problem of empirical data to run the various models. Third, the translation of the terms of a leasing contract into a model can be quite complex. Therefore, given the present state of the art, it may be appropriate not to use a specific model in making a go or no-go decision; rather one should merely make use of the model to perform sensitivity analysis.

The first step in developing a financially rational method of analyzing leasing is to define an objective function for the lease-or-buy decision. The usual criterion here is the maximization of the market value of the carrier. Even if this criterion were not the desired variable, the model based upon it would at least indicate to management the cost of adopting a less financially rational decision criterion. The second step is to identify the important variables that affect the decision. Only those factors that are quantifiable and have economic value are considered; pride of ownership, for example, is not included in the analysis. The third step is to determine the total cost, using the present value approach under both alternatives (lease and buy), and then take action on the least cost alternative. Assuming that an airline decides to maximize its market value, the following variables can be defined in the net present value equation for the decision to buy an aircraft:

A = purchase price of aircraft
W = additional working capital needed (spare parts, inventory)
t_c = tax rate applicable to the carrier
I = Investment Tax Credit (if airline shows profits)
n = length of period considered
SV = salvage value of aircraft at end of period n
BV = book value of aircraft at end of period n
t_g = tax rate applicable to the capital gains realized by the carrier
R_i = revenue realized from the use of aircraft in period i
C_i = costs (operating, insurance, administrative, etc.) allocated to the aircraft in period i
D_i = amount of aircraft depreciated in period i
k = appropriate discount rate
NPV_P = net present value expected from purchase of the aircraft

$$NPV_P = \sum_{i=1}^{n} \frac{(R_i - C_i) - t_c(R_i - C_i - D_i)}{(1 + k)^i} + \frac{SV - t_g(SV - BV)}{(1 + k)^n} - A - W + I$$

(5.1)

In order to keep the model as simple as possible, the discount rate k should be the rate used by management to evaluate all major capital expenditures. It is the after-tax cost of capital, a weighted average of cost of debt and cost of equity. Although this is not an easy number to determine, the cost of debt can be approximated by the yield on the oustanding debt, while the dividend rate and the market price of the outstanding stock can be used to approximate the cost of equity.[e] For purposes of simplicity and illustration all terms are discounted by the single cost of capital figure k. However, this condition can be relaxed. Suppose that the financial manager feels that since not all of the items are equally predictable (that is, they do not have the same degree of risk associated with them), they should be discounted at a different rate. For example, since revenue and costs are not predictable to the same degree as

---

[e]Readers unfamiliar with this should refer to a standard text in finance, such as Wilbur G. Lewellen, *Cost of Capital* (Belmont, California: Wadsworth Publishing Company, 1969).

depreciation, they should be discounted at a different rate. Such modifications can easily be made, provided one is convinced of the validity of these assumptions.

There are many other assumptions incorporated into the net present value shown in Equation (5.1). For example, the sales costs associated with buying the aircraft are not included. The advance payments required by the aircraft manufacturer are also not included in this equation. Assuming that these and other assumptions built into the model are satisfactory, Equation (5.1) can be used to determine the net present value of the proposed purchase. If this is greater than zero, then the decision to purchase the aircraft is valid. This action would in theory increase the value of the carrier by the amount of the net present value if the aircraft is purchased.

The decision to lease the aircraft can now be investigated in a similar manner. In addition to the above terms, it is necessary to define the following terms:

L_i = lease payment in period i

n = term of the lease contract

LD_i = leasing discounts in cost in period i (for example, maintenance, insurance, or property tax discounts paid by the lessor as specified in the lease contract)

r = after-tax interest rate on the carrier's borrowings

NPV_L = net present value expected if the aircraft is leased

$$NPV_L = \sum_{i=1}^{n} \frac{[R_i - (C_i - LD_i)](1 - t_c)}{(1 + k)^i} - \sum_{i=1}^{n} \frac{L_i(1 - t_c)}{(1 + r)^i} - W \qquad (5.2)$$

In Equation (5.2) the lease term payment L_i is separated since a number of financial experts believe that this term should be discounted at a rate different than k, the overall cost of capital. This belief is usually justified on the grounds that the lease payments and tax savings should be capitalized at the discount rate r (after-tax interest rate on the carrier's borrowings) to reflect their relatively higher predictability. The reader should be cautioned that this issue is extremely controversial and that the debate is far from settled. However, if this reasoning is accepted, the depreciation factor in Equation (5.1) should also be discounted at the rate r, due to its degree of predictability. In Equation (5.2) the lease payments L_i, are not separated into interest and principal components on the grounds that the entire payment is a cash outflow and is tax deductible. Finally, just as the first equation, Equation (5.2) is also an oversimplified version of reality. One example of its limitations is that the costs of negotiating a lease are not included.

The two equations developed above can now be used to evaluate the benefit of leasing over purchasing the aircraft. This can be achieved by taking the difference between the two net present values shown by Equation (5.3). By taking the difference between the first two equations, terms common to both equations will drop out. A positive value in Equation (5.3) will indicate the decision to purchase; a negative value will indicate the decision to lease. This equation should be used with caution. Suppose the difference in net present value turns out to be negative, an indication that leasing would be superior to purchasing the aircraft. This is not to imply, though, that the aircraft should be acquired; its only significance is that if the aircraft is acquired, it should be leased rather than purchased. If one is interested in the decision whether or not to acquire the aircraft, it is necessary to use Equation (5.1).

$$\Delta NPV = NPV_P - NPV_L = \sum_{i=1}^{n} \frac{D_i t_c - LD_i(1 - t_c)}{(1 + k)^i} + \frac{SV - t_g(SV - BV)}{(1 + k)^n}$$

$$+ \sum_{i=1}^{n} \frac{L_i(1 - t_c)}{(1 + r)^i} - A + I \tag{5.3}$$

Summary

This chapter reviewed briefly the past methods of long-term financing the industry's capital requirements to provide the reader with some understanding of how the industry arrived at its present financial position and the possible alternatives available to finance the future requirements. Over the years, the major carriers have changed emphasis in financing sources from equity to long-term debt, followed by internal sources such as earnings and depreciation, to more recent sources, such as convertible debenture and lease financing.

For the carrier, leasing can provide a number of benefits, such as: the elimination of the need to borrow money; a partial ITC benefit; the avoidance of progress payments to the manufacturer; a hedge against inflation; simplified bookkeeping; and reduced risk of technical obsolescence. The disadvantages of leasing, besides the loss of the pride of ownership, include the loss of the salvage value of the aircraft or the additional services from the remaining life of the aircraft and the partial loss of ITC benefit. In recent years a number of analytical models have become available to determine a rational way of making the lease-or-purchase decision in the airline industry. Even though the present state of the art restricts financial analysts from using these models to make a go or no-go type of decision, they can still be used profitably to perform sensitivity analysis.

6

Aircraft Selection and Fleet Planning

The two major assets of an airline are its routes and its aircraft. Consequently, it is not surprising to learn that a great deal of thinking, analysis, and planning must take place before an airline makes an investment in either of these items. Furthermore because profitability is a function both of routes and of aircraft, it is necessary to consider the two assets jointly. While many factors must be considered in reaching a decision to acquire a particular aircraft, the dominant factor is always the routes on which the aircraft must fly. Finally, since the proposed aircraft must fit properly into the airline's overall corporate plan, it becomes necessary to evaluate the new aircraft in light of the entire route structure and fleet composition. The process by which this analysis is performed is generally known as *fleet planning*. The purpose of this chapter is first to outline the various factors influencing a carrier's selection of a particular aircraft, and second to describe very briefly the general framework of typical airline fleet planning models.

Aircraft Selection Criteria

The decision to procure new aircraft is generally based upon an expected growth in traffic, a new route authority, the desire to increase capacity, frequency, or market share, or the desire or need to replace some of the existing aircraft either for reasons of efficiency or of age. Whatever the reason, once a decision has been made to acquire new aircraft, the problem facing the airline fleet planner is to choose among the various available alternatives. It is important to realize that the emphasis is on alternative "available" aircraft. Due to enormous development costs, it is not possible to have an airplane or even a number of airplanes tailor-made, even for a large carrier. Since the break-even production run for the manufacturer can be anywhere from 200 to 500, depending upon the requirements relative to existing technology, a number of carriers must be interested in a particular design before a manufacturer will make the necessary investments. This large break-even number does not imply that a carrier the size of United or Pan American has no influence on the operating characteristics of new aircraft they feel are needed. On the contrary, both United and Pan American have played key roles in the production plans of the Boeing 727-300 and the Boeing 747SP, respectively.

Assuming that a carrier is evaluating a number of existing aircraft, what factors are considered in making the final choice? Among the various factors usually considered, technical performance, financial costs, contribution of overall profitability, and external influences play a major role in the final analysis. The influence of each factor varies from carrier to carrier. Furthermore, it is often necessary to make trade-offs between the various factors. It is very rare that an aircraft will score high on each of these considerations simultaneously.

In the past, technical performance has always been very important. The technical parameters usually considered are *cruise performance, runway requirements,* and *noise performance.* Under cruise performance the analysis is usually performed on payload-range diagrams. These diagrams show the relationship of payload (number of passengers and cargo) to the distance the aircraft can fly. Figure 6-1 shows typical payload-range diagrams for some of the existing jet transport aircraft. In each case, there is a maximum payload that can be carried up to a specific range. Beyond this the payload must be reduced to accommodate more fuel. Finally there is the maximum distance that the aircraft can fly.

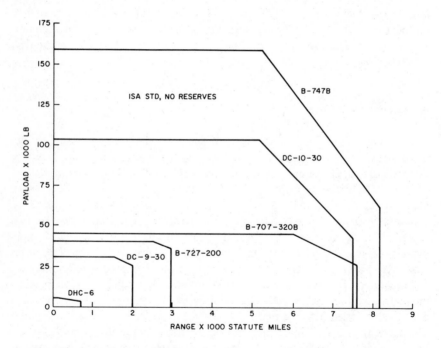

Source: Simpson, Robert W., *Technology for Design of Transport Aircraft,* Lecture Notes, M.I.T., July 1972, p. 25.

Figure 6-1. Payload-Range Diagrams for Selected Jet Transport Aircraft.

The object here is not to select an aircraft that meets the specific requirements of just one or two routes. A carrier such as TWA serves a variety of domestic markets, such as Columbus-Dayton and Boston-San Francisco. Besides the difference in range, there is also a difference in the density of traffic. While it is not essential that every aircraft be able to serve all markets, a certain amount of flexibility is always desirable. In addition, one must consider the trade-off between high capacity-low frequency and low capacity-high frequency. The other two areas of technical performance relate to the runway requirements and noise, which are self-explanatory. Noise performance has begun to get higher ratings in recent years.

Having narrowed the choice on the basis of technical factors, consideration is then given to the financial costs of both acquisition and operation. The financial cost includes the costs of the aircraft itself, spare parts, ground equipment, maintenance, training, and last but not least, the cost of money itself. Thus it is quite possible that while the actual price of one aircraft may be less than another, the total price, including all other factors, may in fact be more. The following two examples illustrate this fact. If a carrier's existing fleet consisted entirely of Boeing aircraft (various versions), maintenance costs of additional Boeing aircraft are likely to be less than for a Douglas or Lockheed aircraft. If an airline already has a dozen Boeing 747s, the additional spare parts required for another Boeing 747 would be small compared to those for an additional DC-10 or Lockheed 1011. Similar arguments apply to ground equipment and pilot training. The cost of money refers to various financial arrangements offered by different manufacturers. If there are any trade-ins, then the purchase price offered for those must also be taken into consideration.

In addition to the acquisition price, it is also necessary to consider the direct operating costs of the various candidates. The reader is cautioned against the use of *only* the direct operating costs per seat mile to evaluate alternative aircraft. There is nothing wrong with this parameter per se, except that its use in this context can be misleading. First, there is no single direct operating cost per available seat mile. For a given aircraft, it varies with range. Thus, if this parameter were used, the comparison should be made at a particular range. Second, choosing an aircraft on the basis of its very low value of direct operating costs per seat mile is not very useful if the seats cannot be filled with paying passengers. High capacity aircraft show lower direct operating costs per seat mile. However, they require greater passenger loads to break even. These aircraft, therefore, limit their potential use to high-density markets.[1]

One component of direct operating costs that has been receiving substantial attention in recent years is the cost of fuel. In light of recent fuel shortages and significant increases in the price of fuel, a number of airline managers are focusing upon specific fuel consumption, in particular, and fuel efficiency, in general. Again, one must be cautious in using these parameters. While it is important to select a more efficient aircraft, the decision must be based upon a cost-effective basis. The possibility of excessive maintenance, excessive spares or replacement support, and excessive down time should also be taken into consideration.

At some point during the evaluation procedure it is necessary to perform a profitability analysis. The usual procedure is to investigate an aircraft with respect to the total airline system, that is, over a wide range of length of hauls taking into account the carrier's indirect operating costs as well as the effective fare structure. One method used in the Flight Transportation Laboratory at MIT is to combine the break-even load diagrams (as discussed in Chapter 3) with the payload-range diagrams for various aircraft. The resulting plots are known as the *profitability-load diagrams.* Figure 6-2 shows the general shape and characteristics of such diagrams.[2] For any given route *AB*, the profitability-load diagrams show the profit that can be made using different aircraft available. If the shaded areas do not overlap, the decision is fairly simple. On the other hand, if the areas do overlap, as shown, then all other things being equal, the aircraft selected should be the one where the point of intersection of traffic on route and trip distance lies close to the upper boundary of the payload-range limits. For the route *AB* shown in Figure 6-2, the medium, long-range aircraft should be selected over the

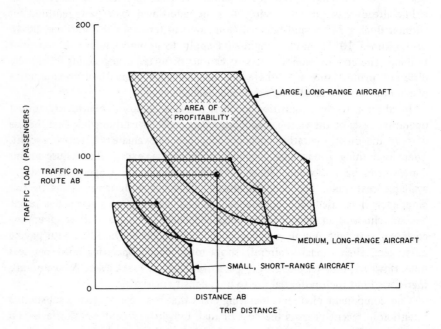

Source: Simpson, Robert W., *Technology for Design of Transport Aircraft*, Lecture Notes, M.I.T., July 1972, p. 44.

Figure 6-2. Profitability-Load Diagrams.

large, long-range aircraft. However, one should not overlook the potential growth in market that can increase the traffic load.

These are some of the major criteria used by air carriers in selecting flight equipment. There are two other factors that can influence the decision to acquire one aircraft over another. First, some analysts claim that passenger comfort or passenger appeal can also have an impact on the choice of a particular aircraft, but a number of market surveys that have been taken give no conclusive evidence of this. Second, government pressure can sometimes play an important role for some carriers in the decision to acquire a particular aircraft.[3] If a carrier is substantially controlled by the government, its choice of aircraft can be significantly influenced by government pressure. An example of this is British Airways with respect to its choice of VC-10 and Lockheed 1011.

Fleet Planning

Given the resources of an airline, a forecast of the market environment and the carrier's corporate plan, the process of fleet planning can provide the management with a timetable of fleet acquisitions and phase-outs for a given planning horizon. Historically, the fleet planning process has been carried out by hand. Each time management changed its corporate strategy, the fleet planning process was undertaken to produce a fleet plan to implement the new strategy. In recent years the fleet planning process has become very sophisticated. Analytical computer models have been developed that are continuously updated as changes in the internal and external environment take place.[4] The purpose of this section is to describe, in layman's terms, the analytical framework of fleet planning models with their associated inputs and outputs. Due to the broad scope of this book and the varied backgrounds of the readers, the focus in this section is on a conceptual framework rather than on elegant mathematical and operations-research formulation. Fleet planning through the use of analytical models is becoming more and more accepted by the air carriers, and an increasing number of large airlines maintain a full complement of professional operations research analysts. In addition, all major aircraft manufacturers possess fleet planning models that are used to produce fleet plans for their customers.

A *fleet planning model* is usually some sort of a mathematical computer simulation model of an airline system. In layman's terms the object is to find the optimal balance between projected market demand and fleet size and composition. Or, in other words, given a set of inputs such as route structure, existing fleet, costs, and fare structure, the object is to determine future fleet acquisition requirements, fleet assignment requirements, financial requirements, and operating conditions over a planning horizon. Although fleet planning models provide management with many useful outputs, the basic output is related to aircraft—the number and type to be acquired, the times of acquisition, and timing of trade-in or phase-out of existing aircraft by number and type. The analytical formulation of the model provides management with an opportunity to assess the impact of alternative policy actions.

Fleet planning models can also provide an optimal assignment of aircraft to routes; therefore, they are sometimes called *fleet assignment models.* The assignment of aircraft to routes is generally made on the basis of profitability. However, if a need exists to assign a specific fleet to a particular set of routes, this can also be incorporated into the model. For instance, management may decide that the DC-9 should not serve the New York-Chicago market, or it may exclude the use of the DC-9 west of Kansas City because of the lack of appropriate maintenance facilities. Finally, if these models are integrated with scheduling models, the end result is a complete timetable of schedules over the entire network of an airline.

There are basically four types of input to the fleet planning model. These are shown in Figure 6-3. The resources of an airline are its aircraft and route authority. The following type of information is required with respect to aircraft: initial fleet size and composition, aircraft on order with availability dates, acquisition costs (purchase or lease), start-up costs, direct operating costs, landing-fee structure, block time versus range diagrams, capacity, and initial utilization. Conditions on route authority are required with respect to operating restrictions, whether nonstop, multistop, or special routings.

The second set of inputs refers to the forecast of market demand with respect to passengers and cargo. Characteristics of this market demand such as seasonality, directionality (in the case of cargo), business versus pleasure classification (for passenger travel), and price elasticity of demand are also required. A critical input with respect to market demand is the relationship with the level of service offered. At the very least, it is necessary to incorporate the relationship between the number of flights and total passenger demand for each market. It is also necessary to supply some sort of a relationship between frequency share and market share for each market. Sometimes it is more convenient to classify markets by length of haul (short, medium, and long) and then make assumptions with respect to frequency-share-market-share relationships. Finally, it is necessary to include fare and rate structure and level for both passenger and cargo service.

The third set of inputs includes the financial policies—whether they are management controlled or regulated by the Board or other government agencies, such as the Internal Revenue Service. These include a carrier's initial debt and repayment plans, depreciation policies (service life and residual value), method of payment for the aircraft (predelivery, on delivery, leasing), market value of used aircraft, maximum allowable debt-equity ratio, and tax structure (including the Investment Tax Credit). Additional information is required for local service carriers with respect to subsidy, government assistance in purchasing aircraft, and any capital gains tax status. Finally, information on indirect operating costs

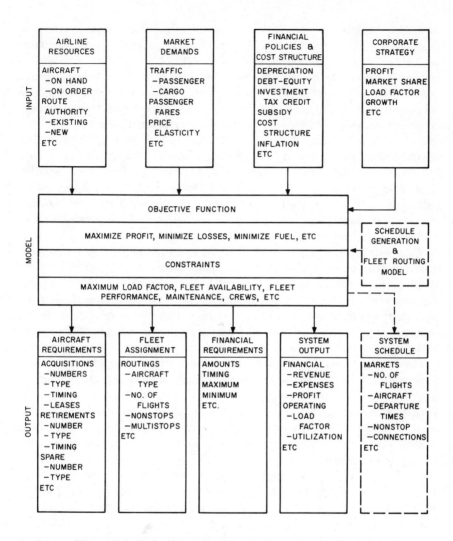

Figure 6-3. General Framework of Fleet Planning Models.

is required both for present and future operations. The last set of inputs to the model is on the corporate strategy. Under this, management must provide its objectives, such as to maximize profits, market share, load factor, revenue, growth, or to minimize fuel, cost, and financial losses.

The model itself is usually one of the linear programming type. Based upon the inputs discussed above, the analyst establishes an objective function.[a] This is

---

[a]For an economic discussion of alternative objective functions available to an airline, see James T. Kneafsey, *The Economics of the Transportation Firm* (Lexington, Massachusetts: Lexington Books, D.C. Heath and Company, 1974) Chapter 6.

a mathematical statement of the objective of carrier management, such as to maximize profits or maximize the contribution to overhead. The program then, as the case may be, maximizes or minimizes the objective function subject to numerous constraints. Some of the constraints are external to the program and based upon management policy; such as, the average load factor must not exceed 75 percent, cash on hand must not fall below a set value, the debt to equity ratio must not exceed a given value, or a particular type of aircraft must not be flown on certain routes. These constraints are usually dictated by financial considerations, marketing strategies, maintenance requirements, crew requirements, environmental considerations, technical considerations, and fleet standardization considerations. Other constraints are internal to the program, e.g., total capacity offered must be greater than total demand and final number of aircraft must equal initial number plus number purchased and leased less number sold or traded in.

Even with large computers, the fleet planning problem is quite sizable for a carrier the size of United. A number of techniques can be used to reduce the size of the problem. One common technique is known as a *decomposition technique.* Readers who are not familiar with this should refer to a standard text on operations research. Briefly, the idea is to divide the constraints, for example, into two groups. Other possibilities of reducing the size of the problem are to group the aircraft and routes into categories. For example, aircraft can be grouped according to characteristics such as range, capacity, and direct operating costs. Similarly, routes can be grouped according to market density or length of haul.

The output from the model consists essentially of future aircraft requirements, including numbers, type, and timing of acquisition and the number, type, and timing of the retirement of the existing fleet. Other outputs typically available from the model are shown in Figure 6-3. The model will provide the optimal solution given the inputs and the constraints. Whether the solution can be implemented exactly as stated is another story. This does not imply that all fleet planning models should be discredited. On the contrary, they can be extremely useful, even if the solution cannot be implemented in its exact form. Suppose the solution calls for the acquisition of ten Boeing 747 jets. Because the management cannot raise the funds to make this purchase, it decides to lease these aircraft. The model can then be used to produce the profit and loss statement under the new set of conditions and compare the results with those had it been in a position to buy the aircraft outright.

Airline fleet planners have come a long way from performing the fleet planning process by hand to the current use of large-scale computer-based models. However, while the level of sophistication has increased dramatically, some of the assumptions incorporated into the models are still fairly crude. Two examples of this are assumptions of the market response to changes in the level of service and the competitive behavior of other carriers when one carrier changes its flight schedules. This criticism is not to imply that until all assumptions are perfected the models are completely useless. To the contrary, models can be extremely useful in analyzing the impact of various policies. In short, while the models may be unable to provide absolute solutions that are acceptable, they can nevertheless be used quite profitably for performing sensitivity analysis. One reason for the restrictive use of these models is the way they have been presented to upper-level management. If professional airline operations research analysts would only set aside for a moment their elegant mathematical details and explain the fundamental concepts in terms comprehensible to upper-level management, perhaps these models would achieve greater acceptance and wider use. One other comment that may be worth making is that most of the development work in this area has been performed by manufacturers and by the more analytically oriented carriers. Due to the corporate confidentiality of these models, their availability has been restricted. Thus it is fairly difficult to write on the exact state of development of fleet planning models.

The extent to which fleet planning and fleet assignment models can be used is amply demonstrated by the work of Professor Simpson at the Flight Transportation Laboratory at MIT. Professor Simpson has used his "FA" series of models (of which there are currently seven) to analyze a variety of issues in the air transportation industry. In the late 1960s these models were used to analyze new routings for Northeast in its service to Florida. In recent years the models have been used to study the policy options available to the local service carriers. With the full cooperation of management, case studies have been performed on the operations of Frontier, Hughes Air West, Ozark, and Southern.[5] To move to the other end of the scale, United's operations were analyzed to determine the impact of fuel limitations. Presently there are two areas where the FA series of models are being used. First, investigations are underway to determine the impact of various policies regarding airport operations at selected terminals. Second, the models are being modified to allow for variances in passenger fares. It is hoped that this will provide some insight into the present deregulation issue discussed in Chapter 15.

Summary

Among the many factors considered in selecting aircraft, technical performance, financial costs, and contribution to overall profitability in light of the given route structure play a major role in the final decision. However, occasionally external influences such as government pressure, particularly in the case of government carriers, can also influence the aircraft selection process. In recent years analytical computer fleet planning models have become an integral part of the corporate planning process at major carriers. Given the resources of an airline, a forecast of the market environment, and a carrier's corporate plan, a fleet planning model can provide management with a timetable of fleet acquisitions and phase-outs for a given planning horizon. A typical fleet planning model is one of the linear programming type, with an objective function and a set of constraints. While the output of the model is essentially aircraft requirements, it can also include fleet assignment, financial requirements, and a system schedule.

7 Problems in Airline Scheduling

Airline scheduling is perhaps one of the most complex and critical tasks faced by management. It is complex because it involves a balancing of conflicting objectives such as public requirements, economic efficiency, and operational feasibility. It is critical because of its financial leverage on profitability. The purpose of this chapter is to highlight the problems faced by a typical airline scheduler in order to provide the reader with some appreciation of why schedules appear the way they do. Although there are some computer models available to help the airline scheduler, they are very complex mathematically, and no attempt is made here to discuss them.[a]

The scheduling department of an airline receives input from numerous sources both within and outside of the company before any changes can be made to the existing schedule. It should be pointed out that airlines do not generally develop the entire schedule from scratch. For each scheduling cycle, it is a common practice to take the existing schedule and make the appropriate changes. In revising the schedule, the scheduler first receives input from within the company. This information is related to factors such as availability of aircraft, performance characteristics, maintenance requirements, operating costs, size and type of the markets to be served, route restrictions, availability of crew, ground equipment limitations, and time zones over the route system. Information from external sources consists of input from passengers, shippers, travel agents, hotels, the Post Office Department, airport authorities, the community, and advanced published schedules of other carriers.

Public Requirements

One of the most important inputs to the development of a schedule is the information of traffic volumes and their related characteristics. The importance of this information should be obvious, since the first objective of any scheduler is to attempt to match the amount of service offered to the amount of service required. However, while the objective here is clear, the implementation of this objective is quite difficult. For example, what is the volume of passenger traffic in any city-pair? To consider only the local origin-destination traffic is not sufficient. One must also consider the amount of connecting traffic at each

[a]See Warren Hyman and Larry Gordon, "Commercial Airline Scheduling Technique," *International Journal of Transportation Research*, Vol. 2 (1969), pp. 23-29.

point. Depending upon the city and the arrival and departure time of a particular flight, there may be literally dozens of connecting flights. At major connecting gateways, such as Atlanta, Chicago, and Dallas, the connecting traffic can average as high as 70 percent of the total traffic. This percentage can be even higher on individual flights. Therefore schedules are constructed on the concepts of servicing "areas" rather than individual city-pairs. Connecting patterns will influence the total daily flights, their departure and arrival times, and the number of stops enroute. The following example illustrates the impact of connecting flights. Suppose that by rearranging the flight departure time in New York, United could carry ten extra passengers every day from New York to Los Angeles, providing the airline with an additional revenue of well over $0.5 million per year. Since the cost of transporting ten additional passengers is nominal, the increase in potential operating profit in this case would be almost the entire $0.5 million.

The advantages produced by the concept of traffic flow or back-up traffic depends upon the geographic location of the individual cities, the carrier's route structure, and the alternatives available to the passengers. For example, prior to the availability of nonstop transcontinental service, flights from Chicago to the West Coast received back-up traffic not only from points in the midwest, but also from major points in the east. Then in the 1960s the expansion of nonstop transcontinental service tended to diminish the importance of the traffic flow concept. However, in recent years, with the initiation of capacity control agreements due to the fuel crisis, the importance of the total traffic flow concept is once again evident.

The scheduling of flights to serve international markets, such as over the North Atlantic, is essentially a function of traffic density and time zones. With the exception of two or three markets, such as New York-London, New York-Paris, and New York-Frankfurt, the traffic density on the various transatlantic markets is very thin relative to many of the U.S. domestic markets. The result of this thin traffic density is that each of the competitors usually ends up by scheduling one daily round trip. Due to the size of the long-range aircraft, sometimes even one round trip is not economically justifiable. In such cases, service is changed from a daily to a weekly basis with the number of weekly flights ranging from two to five. If six flights a week could be justified, the carrier would probably offer daily service for marketing reasons. Table 7-1 shows TWA's daily transatlantic nonstop flights during June 1975. As shown, even during the summer months, with the exception of three cities, the service is only one flight a day each way. The departure times are determined substantially by the time zones. Eastbound flights to Europe leave U.S. eastern cities late in the evening. Westbound flights from Europe leave European capitals during the morning.

The total traffic volume provides the scheduler with some idea of the total number of flights to be scheduled. The next concern is the time at which flights

Table 7-1
TWA Transatlantic Service, August 1975

Market	Nonstop Daily[a] Frequency
New York-London	3
Boston-London	1
Philadelphia-London	1
Chicago-London	1
Los Angeles-London	1
New York-Paris	2
Boston-Paris	1
Chicago-Paris	1
Washington-Paris	1
New York-Geneva	1
New York-Zurich	1
New York-Milan	1
New York-Rome	2
New York-Lisbon	1
New York-Madrid	1
New York-Shannon	2
New York-Athens	1
New York-Malaga	1

[a]Frequency less than daily is not counted.
Source: Trans World Airlines, *System Timetable*, August 1, 1975.

should be scheduled. Here again, it is necessary to investigate the passengers' and shippers' desired departure and arrival times. The carriers and, in some cases, the airport authorities are frequently criticized for bunching flights at certain peak periods. There are good reasons for the existence of this pattern. First, the passengers themselves want to leave at particular hours. For example, in the short-haul markets the business traveler wants to leave in the morning, do a day's work, and then return home the same day. Consequently, flights are scheduled at peak hours because that is when the passengers want to depart. Now, if passengers did not care about their departure times, no rational airline scheduler would permit a $10 million aircraft to sit empty on the ground waiting for the peak hour. Needless to say, marginal cost of operating a flight at 2 A.M. would be small. However, the demand for such flights would be negligible and, as stated before, the output cannot be stockpiled.

Coupled with the departure time is the arrival time. The need for this coordination becomes critical in markets where flights cross time zones, for example, the scheduled arrival and departure times of the transcontinental flights. Since eastbound nonstops from the West Coast take "eight" hours—5 hours of flight time and 3 hours lost because of time changes—a departure at midnight from Los Angeles would arrive in Boston at 8 A.M. the next morning. Eastbound departures after midnight are undesirable. Subsequent flights can be scheduled to depart from the West Coast between 8 A.M. and 1 P.M. This means that during a 24-hour cycle, there are almost 18 hours that cannot be used for the scheduling of eastbound flights. The only two spots open to the scheduler are between 11 P.M. and midnight and between 8 A.M. and 1 P.M. The same constraints apply to transatlantic flights where time zones are even more restricting.

Freight shippers and the Post Office Department have their own unique requirements. Shippers generally prefer flights in the late afternoon and early evening after the close of the business day. For those shippers who require the use of all-freighters, this is a difficult requirement to satisfy. Consider a transcontinental all-cargo flight. If the flight leaves Los Angeles at 10 P.M., it will arrive in Boston at around 6 A.M. Now, if the shipments are not ready to leave Boston until 8 P.M., a very expensive piece of equipment is likely to sit idle for 14 hours. Shippers also prefer nonstop flights, not so much for the reduced travel time, but for the reduced likelihood of loss and damage in making connections. The Post Office Department is interested in flight departures ranging from 6 P.M. to 1 A.M. (times when the mail is available for departure) and in arrivals from 4 A.M. to 6 A.M. (to ensure first delivery of the mail in the morning).

Having considered the prime customers, the scheduler must now direct his attention to input from other parties. First, there are airport authorities who will attempt to discourage the establishment of peaking. In addition, some of the airports have hourly quotas on the number of total operations. Second, because of noise problems, the local community is not very anxious to have flights depart after 11 P.M. and before 7 A.M. Then there are the large hotel operators who would like the airline to schedule flights to integrate with their check-out times. C.H. Glenn of Air Canada cites a few more parties who usually have something to say about airline scheduling.[1] Thus the airline scheduler is faced with the impossible task of having to satisfy numerous parties simultaneously.

Economic Considerations

The public requirements provide an essential input to the scheduling process. However, these inputs have to be balanced against the economic considerations, on the one hand, and operational feasibility, on the other. Under the economic considerations it becomes necessary to analyze both the costs as well as the potential revenue to be generated from each flight. The airline scheduler looks at the profitability of a flight in terms of aircraft utilization and the load factor, which are not independent of one another. For example, a very high utilization rate, that is, 18 hours per day, is completely useless if the aircraft are flying virtually empty. At the other extreme, very high average load factors, for example, 80 percent, are also not desirable if the utilization is very poor. Needless to say, this situation would not exist for very long if the market had more than one carrier certificated to offer the service. Consequently, the scheduler must strike a good balance between utilization and load factor.

The other facet of utilization and load factor is related to the length of haul. It is difficult to achieve high utilization on short-haul operations because a higher percentage of the total block to block time is spent on the ground and in the climb and descent. The reverse is true for long-haul operations. Suppose a transcontinental flight is operated with intermediate stops. On the one hand, utilization would be low, but on the other hand, load factors are likely to be high due to connecting traffic at intermediate stops. However, while the revenue will be higher (due to additional traffic), the expenses will also be higher due to numerous stops. Thus, assuming that the passengers inconvenienced as a result of the added intermediate stops remain on the flight, the schedule still has to weigh the additional revenue against the additional costs.

Finally, the average load factor is also a function of the size of the aircraft. On a given route the scheduler has a choice of various sizes of aircraft. For example, the Boston-Chicago-Denver-San Francisco markets can be served in numerous ways with aircraft ranging in size from the Boeing 727 to the Boeing 747. Load factor is therefore a function of the on-board passenger load, which in turn is a function of the aircraft routing and the size of the aircraft. Suppose that the total operating costs per seat mile of two different sizes of aircraft were the same, the scheduler would then face a choice between high frequency with a smaller-sized aircraft and low frequency with a larger-sized aircraft. Since demand varies by time of day and from day to day, higher frequency would probably be preferable to lower frequency, especially if the environment is highly competitive. In the final analysis, economic efficiency would necessitate some trade-off between utilization, load factor, and frequency; the weight attached to each of these factors would vary by market.

One of the major objectives of any carrier's management is to achieve high load factors relative to break-even load factors. High load factors imply lower operating costs per passenger. However, high load factors also raise the probability of turning away passengers. Therefore the optimal load factor is not 100 percent for scheduled service. The optimal load factor depends upon a number of factors such as management's policy on the service to be provided and overbooking and market characteristics such as traffic density, traffic mix (business versus pleasure), seasonality, directionality (applicable more in the case of cargo), length of haul, number of competitors, and route authority. Because of the variation of optimal load factors in light of these considerations, it is difficult to state an exact figure. Typically the optimal load factor for a scheduled carrier may lie in the 60 to 75 percent range. There exist some fairly sophisticated statistical models that can be used to aid the scheduling department in determining the value of optimal load factors by market and by season.

Operating Constraints

So far the discussion has been limited to achieving the balance between the various components of public requirements, between the various components of economic efficiency, and between public requirements and economic efficiency. Now consideration must be given to a third element, the operating constraints. Like the others, the operating constraints also have a number of components, of which, to the scheduler, the most important input comes from the maintenance department. Because the carriers can neither purchase an excessive number of aircraft as spares, nor operate extensive maintenance facilities at every airport they serve, the scheduling of maintenance work can substantially influence the availability of a particular aircraft at a particular airport at a particular time. Typically, a jet aircraft requires 300 hours of maintenance work for every 3,000 hours of flight time. However, the maintenance work cannot all be done at the end of these 3,000 flight hours. A certain number of maintenance hours must be spent after a certain number of flying hours. The complexities of routing aircraft even for planned maintenance should not be taken lightly. Different types of maintenance must be performed at different times on different aircraft at different terminals. Not all locations can handle all types of maintenance on all types of aircraft. Besides the necessary equipment, one must also have all the necessary spare parts and the appropriate FAA-approved personnel.

Assuming that a "perfect" maintenance schedule could be achieved, one must also face the possibility of unexpected mechanical breakdowns. Therefore the schedule must be flexible enough to allow for unforeseen situations. How much time should be allowed for this? Delays due to mechanical breakdowns can vary from a few minutes to an indefinite period of time. While on the subject of unplanned interruptions, it is necessary to point out that the scheduler must also provide some flexibility to allow for bad weather, particularly at airports where the weather is frequently bad during certain periods of the year. An unexpected change in the schedule at these stations can have repercussions in the entire network. Unexpected fog in London can easily inconvenience passengers waiting to depart at Honolulu.

The next critical component of the operating constraints is the integration of crew scheduling. A flight deck crew is usually qualified to fly only one type of aircraft. Thus, not unless all crew members have gone through the appropriate flight training programs can a standard Boeing 727 crew fly a Boeing 747. Second, there are very strict flight crew timing limits. For example, there are strict rules concerning how often a pilot can fly within any 7-day period.

Second, there are union-management employment agreements that must be obeyed. Third, the "bidding" system creates complex problems. Under this system the flight crews bid for domiciles, flights, and aircraft. The decisions are usually made on seniority. Fourth, there are only a certain number of domiciles at which crews can be based. It is very important that flights, crews, and domiciles be matched. "Dead heading" crews back and forth can be very expensive, since the crew is on the payroll from the time it leaves the base to the time it finally returns; a crew that must be flown from Boston to New York in order to take out a flight from New York to Denver and back to New York receives pay for the time spent in getting to and from New York. Finally, a certain number of aircraft must be kept back for pilot training either for upgrading purposes or for proficiency checks.

The next component of operating constraints concerns ground facilities and personnel. Here the scheduler must consider the availability of ground equipment, gate positions, and terminal facilities such as ticket counters. For each of these categories consideration must also be given to personnel to operate these facilities. For obvious economic reasons the ground equipment and facilities at each station cannot be established to handle all types of service at peak periods. Ground support for a Boeing 747 can cost a few hundred thousand dollars, and providing for sufficient ground equipment, facilities, and personnel to meet peak-period demands can substantially lower their utilization.

Finally, there are three other operating constraints that influence the scheduler. First, a route authority influences not only the number of intermediate stops but also the ground time for various types of stops, that is, turn-around, connecting, or through flights. The amount of ground time depends upon many factors, such as aircraft type, length of trip completed as well as upcoming trip, refueling policy, maintenance checks, crew changes, possibilities of late arrivals, availability of gates, and connecting flights. The minimum ground time for through flights is about 20 minutes for domestic flights and about 1 hour for international operations. For connecting flights and turn-around flights, the ground time is much longer. For transatlantic turn-around flights using narrow-body equipment, the minimum ground time would be about 90 minutes. The second constraint refers to the positioning of aircraft. Some passengers will observe that certain flights are scheduled at very peculiar hours and consistently carry very few revenue passengers. These peculiar departure times are forced upon the scheduler due to the fact that the aircraft may be required at another station for an early morning flight or that it cannot be overnighted at a particular station for maintenance reasons. The third constraint refers to the number of slots available at any given airport.

The above items are some of the usual problems faced by an airline scheduler. There is no such thing as a schedule that satisfies everybody; a perfect schedule is impossible. The next best thing is to compromise and attempt to produce an optimal balance between the various considerations discussed above. Once a schedule has been developed and implemented, is it possible to make a change? That depends upon the change. A small change can usually be accommodated albeit with numerous obstacles. The following is a hypothetical example of the incredible complications that can arise if only a minor change is desired.

Suppose the routing of Flight 101 is as shown in Table 7-2. It may be a useful exercise to investigate the implications of a minor change in the departure time at Chicago. A departure at 6 P.M. instead of 5 P.M. would eventually land the aircraft at Honolulu after midnight. Not only is this in itself undesirable, but the flight would break connections from three other flights, and a change in each of these would have its own repercussions. In addition to other problems caused by this extremely late arrival, the aircraft could also not leave Honolulu at 8 A.M. the next morning because the flight crew layover limits would be violated. On the other hand, the flight could not be scheduled to depart Chicago at 4 P.M. because this would mean a 9 A.M. departure from London. This is unrealistic because the flight is a turn-around and requires 2 hours on the ground after arriving from New York the previous night. In addition, two flights, one from Frankfurt and the other from Paris, arrive in London at 9:30 A.M. and make a connection with Flight 101.

The flight cannot arrive at Chicago between 4 P.M. and 5 P.M. because of the quota on the number of flights arriving in Chicago during this hour. In any case, Flight 101, because of the unavailability of a gate position, cannot arrive in Los Angeles before 7 P.M. In order to free a gate for Flight 101, flights have to be changed at San Diego, Phoenix, and Dallas. Even if a gate were available, the flight could not depart Los Angeles until 8 P.M. because no flight crew is available until then. Due to federal flight time limits, 8 P.M. is the earliest departure time the available crew can take out the flight; it would not be economical to have an additional crew based in Los Angeles.

Table 7-2
Routing of Flight 101

Station		Local Time		Connecting Flights
London	LV	10:00	A.M.	Frankfurt, Paris
New York	AR	12:00	Noon	Boston, Providence, Hartford
	LV	2:00	P.M.	
Detroit	AR	3:30	P.M.	Toronto, Cleveland, Toledo,
	LV	4:00	P.M.	Syracuse
Chicago	AR	4:00	P.M.	Indianapolis, Columbus
	LV	5:00	P.M.	Washington, Oklahoma City, St. Louis
Los Angeles	AR	7:00	P.M.	New York, Denver
	LV	8:00	P.M.	
Honolulu	AR	11:30	P.M.	

Flight 101 cannot leave Detroit earlier than 4 P.M. because it connects with flights from Toronto, Cleveland, Toledo, and Syracuse. Moving back a little to New York, although the minimum ground time is only 75 minutes for an international arrival, the flight is scheduled to depart at 2 P.M. because there are three flights that arrive in New York at 1:15 P.M. and would connect with Flight 101. In order to accommodate an earlier departure, changes would have to be made to flights from Boston, Providence, and Hartford. Although there is another potential connecting flight at 1:45 P.M., Flight 101 cannot be delayed any longer because this would leave the through-passengers to Detroit and Chicago dissatisfied enough to switch to the competitor's flight from London to Detroit and Chicago via Boston. Because of a highly competitive environment, the amount of flexibility available to the schedule planner is very limited. Even though it may be very costly from every aspect, flights are scheduled to meet competition.

These considerations are only a few of the problems that would occur if Flight 101 were changed in (on the surface) a seemingly insignificant way. This hypothetical example illustrates the interrelationship and chain reactions that can take place to accommodate a change in arrival or departure time of as little as 30 minutes. In analyzing the costs involved in making a change to the schedule, one must remember to also consider the administrative costs of publications, promotion, and notification. If a number of small changes have been made, it may become necessary to publish a new system timetable. The publication and distribution costs of the revised timetable can be quite substantial. Advertisement and promotion affected by these revisions may also be changed. Finally, the new changes must also be filed with the appropriate government agencies, such as the Board and the Post Office Department.

Demand Scheduling

In recent years TWA has been experimenting with a new concept in scheduling known as *demand scheduling*. The object is to reduce the uncertainty of flight loads by having passengers make firm plans for their day of departure. The reduced uncertainty regarding available passengers raises the load factors, which in turn allows the cost per passenger to be lowered. The savings are passed on to the passengers. Once the scheduler knows with certainty the number of passengers in each market for any given day, he or she is able to schedule flights much more efficiently.

The system works in the following manner. A passenger makes a confirmed reservation to fly from A to B on a certain day at least 3 months in advance and places a $20 nonrefundable deposit. At the time the reservation is made, only the day of departure is guaranteed. The passenger at this point does not know the flight number, time of departure, or routing of the aircraft. Two months prior to the flight departure the passenger is given the exact flight plan. At this time he or she is also required to pay the balance of the fare. In case of cancellation on the part of the passenger, the $20 deposit is forfeited. This system provides TWA's schedulers with sufficient time to analyze demand on each market and produce a schedule that results in an optimal load factor.

Initially the service was offered in six transcontinental markets between Boston, New York, Washington/Baltimore, Los Angeles, and San Francisco. The one-way fares were set between $90 and $120, depending upon the day of departure and season. The prices were based upon a load factor of 75 percent with high-density configured aircraft. In-flight amenities would be less than those available to the rest of the passengers on the carrier's system. The prices were based upon fully allocated costs, that is, including capacity costs. According to the carrier, the only cost category expected to increase on a unit cost basis was the cost of reservations due to several transactions for each passenger. This additional cost was estimated to be $5 per passenger.

At first it appeared that the concept of demand scheduling would be received by the nonbusiness travelers with great enthusiasm. The fare differential between the standard reservation system and demand scheduling was large enough to attract new passengers, yet small enough to discourage the business traveler from taking advantage of the new service. This anticipation was also based upon the fact that the Board, in its decision in Phase 5 of the *Domestic Passenger Fare Investigation*, reduced significantly the availability of discount fares. One would assume that the inconvenience of a small difference between the desired time of departure and the allocated time of departure would be minor, as long as the day of departure was confirmed. Furthermore, since the service was restricted to four east coast cities and two west coast cities, it was not expected that the carrier would make numerous intermediate stops in the middle of the country. Despite its expected appeal, demand scheduling has not been very successful. This illustrates in some ways the value passengers place on the current scheduled service that with its low load factors, allows passengers to make last-minute reservations.

Summary

Airline scheduling is a complex and critical process involving a balancing of conflicting objectives, such as public requirements, economic efficiency, and operational feasibility. The input from public requirements consists of such items as the traffic characteristics, desired arrival and departure times (taking into account time zones), the needs of freight shippers and the Post Office Department, the problems of airport authorities, and the desires of hotel operators. The economic considerations revolve around the analysis of both the costs and the potential revenue to be generated from each flight. The focus here is to achieve a good balance between utilization and load factor. Finally, the operating constraints encompass factors such as maintenance requirements, crew availability and restrictions, ground facilities, route structure, and aircraft positioning. There is no such thing as a schedule that satisfies everybody. Instead a compromise is made to produce an optimal balance between the various considerations discussed above.

8 Airline Labor Relations

Labor-management relations in the air transport industry are influenced by a number of factors, such as regulation, the Airline Mutual Air Pact, and other unique characteristics of the industry. The purpose of this chapter is to provide the reader with a broad overview of air transport labor legislation and the impact of economic regulation on collective bargaining in the industry.

Labor Legislation and the Airlines

The Railway Labor Act (RLA) was enacted in 1926 to regulate the labor-management relations in the railroad industry subject to the Interstate Commerce Act. Ten years later, in 1936, Title II of the RLA was passed, which applied most of the provisions of the Act to the air carriers. Except for minor changes made in the provisions, the RLA remains the same today as it was in 1936 and has provided the basic framework for the airline labor relations. In general, the railroad and air carriers are excluded from the provisions of the National Labor Relations Act (NLRA). The NLRA, passed in 1935 and also known as the Wagner Act, was designed to protect the unions by prohibiting employers from carrying out certain anti-union practices designated as "unfair labor practices." Since under the NLRA the employers had no protection against unfair use of economic power by unions, the Taft-Hartley Act was passed in 1947 to protect employers, individual workers, and the general public. In contrast to the Wagner Act, the Taft-Hartley Act imposed a variety of restrictions on union operations.

The air carriers in their labor relations are also subject to the Norris-La-Guardia Act of 1932, which limits the use of injunctions in labor disputes. Under this Act the employers were required to prove that they were unable to protect their property through regular means before the courts could issue injunctions. The Norris-LaGuardia Act in effect removed certain governmental restraints on trade union action giving the unions more latitude to exert their power against the employer. In addition to the above legislation, the airline labor relations are to some extent controlled by the Civil Aeronautics Board, which requires that carriers with a certificate of public convenience and necessity (PC&N) comply with the provisions of the Railway Labor Act. The CAB also exercises control of carriers' labor relations in cases involving mergers and subsidies. Finally, the Federal Aviation Administration exercises a certain amount of control over the carriers' labor relations.

In addition to the above legislation, an important ruling issued in the airline labor relations deals with the regulation of wages and flying hours for pilots and copilots. On May 10, 1934, Decision Number 83 of the National Labor Board fixed 85 hours of flying as the monthly maximum for pilots and copilots and also fixed their base and hourly rates of pay. Decision 83 was subsequently incorporated into the Civil Aeronautics Act of 1938 and the Federal Aviation Act of 1958, Section 401(k). Thus every air carrier engaged in interstate air transportation is required to maintain rates of compensation, maximum hours, and other working conditions and relations of all of its pilots and copilots to conform with Decision 83. The significance of this requirement can easily be seen since it contains both mileage pay and an hourly pay rate which increase with the speed of the aircraft. Therefore Decision 83 provides the pilots and copilots with a share of the productivity gains associated with faster aircraft. After World War II an additional pay factor was incorporated into pilot pay formula to provide certificated gross weight as a pay factor. Thus, pilots pay is governed by all factors related to the productivity of aircraft—speed, miles and weight.

At the time that Title II of the Railway Labor Act was passed, there were virtually no collective bargaining agreements in the airline industry. The Air Line Pilots Association (ALPA) was the only union of any strength in the industry, and it was the leading proponent of Title II of the RLA. The Act is based solely upon "craft or class." Each craft or class has the right to select a union to represent them without any interference from the carriers. The Act, however, fails to define the term *craft* or *class* except to state that in cases of dispute over representation of a craft, the National Mediation Board (NMB) will determine the collective bargaining representative. Over the years there have been many criticisms of the RLA. Had only the NMB defined the term craft or class more specifically, many of these criticisms would have been avoided in the industry. The cause of many of these criticisms is due to the interpretation of the craft or class concept rather than to the concept itself.

The Railway Labor Act has established certain guidelines to be followed in negotiating the settlement of labor disputes. However, these guidelines are quite vague in their interpretation and application and thus have often created many problems. For example, while the RLA does not require that an agreement be reached by the parties, it does require the management of an airline to meet and confer with the appropriate employee representative and make and maintain agreements. Both parties are compelled to bargain in "good faith." However, what constitutes "good faith" is not clear. Sometimes it is defined as the absence of "bad faith." Refusal to bargain and failure to comply with Section 6 procedures are considered bargaining in bad faith. In such cases, the failure to bargain in good faith is failure to comply with the RLA and the actions are enjoinable. The aggrieved party is entitled to an injunction, while the party refusing to bargain is restricted from obtaining judicial relief in stopping the aggrieved party from striking.

There are many cases involving parties claiming bad faith bargaining. However, it is difficult to make a definitive analysis, since the cases do not generally contain enough information concerning the circumstances involved. In any case, the RLA does not contain any standards to evaluate allegations regarding bad faith bargaining. The only way to comprehend what constitutes bargaining in bad faith is to go through a number of cases. Pan American was charged guilty of bad faith bargaining because the carrier called for the NMB mediation too early.[1] The carrier could not prove that there was sufficient reason to believe that negotiations would not result in an agreement. In another case American was charged with bargaining in lack of good faith because the carrier, voluntarily and under the auspices of the NMB, formed a committee to negotiate issues affecting pilots and flight engineers.[2] Later the flight engineers became dissatisfied with the committee and demanded separate negotiations, while the carrier and the pilots demanded continuation of the joint negotiations to settle joint issues.

Having discussed the requirements of good faith bargaining, the subject of bargaining is now considered. The RLA is of no help in establishing whether a particular subject is bargainable. The courts' interpretation is that while the RLA does not undertake governmental regulation of rates of pay, rules, or working conditions, the Act does provide a means by which an agreement can be reached. But one is never really certain of what falls within the phrase, "rates of pay, rules, or working conditions." In the past, topics that have been held to be bargainable under the RLA have included management's right to make changes affecting working conditions, seniority rights after a merger, grounds for discharge, qualifications for a particular position, pension plans and retirement conditions, and the right to discipline strikers. Those areas involving safety that are under the direct control of the FAA are not considered to be bargainable.

Another area of confusion in the Railway Labor Act is whether the provisions of the Act cover international air transportation. Since international operations make it necessary that some of an airline's employees work in foreign cities, the problem arises as to whether or not the Act is applicable in such cases and, if so, how shall it be applied. There are two views on this, and the answer is not clear. As will be explained in Chapter 14, according to the Chicago Convention, the operation of aircraft of foreign nationality is subject to local laws and regulations. In addition, before any foreign carrier can offer service to and from the United States, it must obtain an operating permit from the CAB. In providing these permits, the CAB does not normally impose any conditions relating to labor relations. Therefore, since neither the Federal Aviation Act nor the bilateral agreements specifically state that the Act does not apply, it can be taken that the Act does apply to foreign commerce. However, the language of the Act, as applied to the railroads, leads to the conclusion that the Act does not extend beyond the continental United States and its territories. Therefore, if the standards of the Interstate Commerce Act are applied to the Railway Labor Act, employees of U.S. carriers based outside of the United States are excluded from coverage under the RLA. Thus, while it is not clear whether the employees of U.S. carriers based permanently outside the United States are covered under the Act, there are some cases that have resulted in the decision that certain employees (such as mechanics) of foreign carriers based permanently in the U.S. are covered by the Act. For nonunion type of employees of foreign carriers (such as corporate staff) based in the United States, the bilateral agreements normally exempt employees from U.S. laws relating to labor.

The National Mediation Board

The National Mediation Board is an independent agency under the executive branch. It consists of three members (and a staff of about twenty mediators) appointed by the President for 3-year terms. While the NMB serves a number of functions under the RLA, such as mediation in major disputes, designation of arbitrators, organization of meetings between the parties when and if necessary, and repository of contracts and legal notices, its major function is to settle representation disputes. In the past, the NMB has been severely criticized for its establishment and administration of procedures for the selection of a union to represent employees for collective bargaining with carriers.

The National Mediation Board is sometimes criticized for being pro-union. Although under the RLA employees have the right not to be represented by a union, the NMB has encouraged union representatives in the past. For example, on representation ballots, the NMB has not provided for a place to mark "no union." While it is possible to vote for "no union" by not voting at all, it is hardly practical since voting is not secret and it is fairly easy to determine who did not vote. Even if the majority of the employees did not vote, the NMB still has two other methods of encouraging unions. It can allow the union currently representing the class in question to continue its representation. Also, the NMB may hold another election. The NMB does not require that a union receive a majority vote in order to be certified. Only a "no union" status needs a majority to win. Therefore, as long as "no union" vote is less than 50 percent, a union with a much lower percentage of the vote can win, since a vote for a particular union can be considered as a vote for any union compared to the "no union" vote. Finally, the NMB has not allowed the carriers to initiate an election or to challenge the results of an election.

Union representation in the airline industry under the RLA is based upon a craft or class basis. However, as mentioned earlier, the RLA does not define the classes and has left this to the judgment of the NMB, which has applied railroad precedent to the airline industry. The confusion begins with the RLA's definition of "employees," which includes the subordinate officials who generally are both first-line supervisors and middle-management personnel. However, under this definition every one except the president of an airline is an employee.

Second, the carriers, undoubtedly the most familiar with the functions of the various groups of employees and other factors essential to determining classes, are not allowed active participation in the craft or class proceedings. In spite of these difficulties the NMB has exercised substantial power (which is not subject to court review) in specifying classes.

Over the years the NMB has developed nine major categories of class or craft. While the crew in the aircraft and certain types of ground employees, such as dispatchers and radio operators, have been classifed separately, the majority of the other ground employees are lumped together into a unit called *clerical, office, stores, fleet,* and *passenger service.* The first significant case on craft or class litigation, known as the NMB Case No. R-1706 (1947), established the major classification of ground employees for the airlines. In its decision, the NMB divided the janitors, represented by a small union at Pennsylvania Central Airlines (later known as Capital Airlines), and turned them over to the Railway Clerks and the International Association of Machinists (IAM). The Railway Clerks, on the other hand, having captured a small group of clerks from a small union, lost its own representative status when Capital merged with United, since most of the clerks at United were unrepresented. While the NMB has to some extent deviated from the ruling made in the Case No. R-1706, the disputes on classification for representation purposes are far from settled.

One dispute worthy of consideration is the dispute between the pilots and flight engineers over the qualification of a third man in the cockpit. In the mid-1950s, ALPA adopted a policy that all active cockpit crew members must be pilot-qualified. The Flight Engineers International Association (FEIA) recognized this as a threat to its existence and persuaded its nonpilot flight engineers to demand that all flight engineers be licensed as airframe and powerplant mechanics. The FEIA felt that this move would secure its existence since the pilots were not expected to fulfill this job qualification. United, after a strike, satisfied both groups by first licensing the flight engineers as pilots, and second recognizing the FEIA as the representative of the flight engineers. The pilots could hardly object to this agreement. However, Eastern, on the recommendation of the Emergency Board (explained later), agreed to train their flight engineers as pilots to satisfy ALPA's demands that all flight engineers on the new jet aircraft be pilot-qualified. Contrary to the initial reasoning behind their demands, the pilots accepted this proposal. However, the FEIA rejected the proposal on the grounds that this would lead to the eventual loss of the flight engineers' jobs and their bargaining power.

Eastern hesitated in the implementation of its free pilot training program resulting in a threat to strike by ALPA. The carrier obtained a temporary restraining order against ALPA on the grounds that ALPA was illegally seeking to bargain with Eastern over job qualifications of another class. The carrier finally settled the dispute (as did some other carriers) by agreeing to add a fourth man (an ALPA pilot) to the cockpit to satisfy the pilots' association and to not force flight engineers to accept free pilot training. However, ALPA then demanded that the fourth man in the crew (presumably an ALPA pilot) also be trained as a flight engineer and refused to take training on the new jets until this demand was met. Eastern obtained a court order against ALPA on the grounds that interpretation of the agreement was a System Board (explained later) issue that was finally settled through arbitration.

The original fears of the FEIA that ALPA's insistence on pilot training for flight engineers would eventually result in the loss of union status began to materialize in the early 1960s. Continental eliminated the FEIA by having all three ALPA pilots on the jets. The flight engineers underwent an unsuccessful strike for 103 days in 1960. Similarly in 1961 a committee appointed by the NMB decided that since the cockpit crew members at United were integrated, the pilots and the flight engineers at United were a single class, resulting in an end of FEIA representation. This action resulted in a massive strike by the flight engineers at seven carriers. The President appointed a commission that called for even more pilot training for the flight engineers, but with provisions for flight engineers: job representational security. The massive protest by the flight engineers was really a strike against the NMB and its committee. Not only can the NMB decide on the extent to which an airline may bargain with one union, it can also exercise substantial power in deciding between the bargaining jurisdiction of the two unions. The courts have avoided intervention in the jurisdictional or representation disputes by leaving the decisions up to the NMB.

The second major function of the NMB is mediation. The RLA divides labor-management disputes into two types commonly referred to as *minor* and *major disputes*. Major disputes are generally described as disagreements in the negotiation of new contracts. The RLA is unique in the manner in which each type of dispute is handled. In both types of disputes the parties are initially required to attempt to reach a settlement between themselves without assistance. However, should the parties fail to reach a settlement at the first stage, the subsequent procedures are different for the two types of disputes. It should be pointed out that it is not a simple matter to determine whether a dispute is minor or major. In any case, the real difficulty arises when a disagreement contains elements of both a major and a minor dispute.

In disagreements involving major disputes, the party desiring to change the terms issues a *Section 6 Notice*. This is a formal notice to the other party for negotiations to change the pay, rules, or working conditions. Once a Section 6 Notice is issued, the parties must, within 10 days, either meet or at least agree on a place and time to meet. Neither party is allowed to make changes at this point or to resort to self-help, that is, strike. If the parties cannot agree on the time and place of the meeting, the decision is made by the NMB. In the event that an agreement is not reached after good faith negotiations have taken place, the NMB will mediate either on its own or at the request of either or both parties. If mediation by the NMB does not resolve the problems, it can recommend voluntary arbitration. Once arbitration is accepted, its decision is binding on both parties. However, if arbitration is not accepted, the NMB withdraws from the negotiations and the parties can resort to self-help and make changes 30 days after the withdrawal by the NMB.[a]

Emergency Board and System Board

In certain cases, if the NMB feels that the dispute may lead to a strike resulting in the interruption of interstate commerce to the extent that part of the nation would be deprived of essential transportation service, the NMB can notify and recommend that the President appoint an Emergency Board to investigate, possibly mediate, and report on the dispute. While the parties are not required to accept the decision of the Emergency Board, they are required to maintain status quo during the Emergency Board's investigation and for 30 days thereafter. In the past, the Presidential Emergency Boards have generally not been effective in bringing about an acceptable settlement. While carriers have acceded to the recommendations of the Emergency Board, the unions have taken the Board's decisions as base offers from which to begin further bargaining.

The procedures for handling minor disputes are somewhat different from those described above. To begin with, minor disputes regarding the interpretation or application of an existing contract and including disciplinary action resulting in discharges are generally not allowed to develop into strike situations. These minor disputes are generally handled through the grievance procedure. Grievance procedures are generally distinguished between disciplinary grievances, such as discharge cases and contract interpretation grievances. The procedures for handling grievances can differ between the two types and also vary by carrier and union. Normally an attempt is first made to settle the grievance through the company machinery. If this does not work out, it goes to the System Board of Adjustment, which produces a binding and final settlement of minor disputes. Normally there is one separate System Board of Adjustment for every agreement. Thus, if the employees of a carrier are represented by half a dozen unions, there will be half a dozen System Boards. A System Board functions according to the rules provided for in the work agreement that established the Board and contains an equal number of airline and union representatives. In the event of a deadlock with even membership in the System Board, a referee (aribtrator) can be appointed by the NMB or the American Arbitration Association (AAA).

The machinery for seeking grievances differs from carrier to carrier, and the description contained here represents the typical cases. For disciplinary grievances, for example, there are generally four steps, but the number can vary from carrier to carrier. If the grievance reaches the System Board (the final step), the Board generally has exclusive and primary jurisdiction to settle it. In rare cases

---

[a]In this context, a strike is referred to as self-help by the union. An example of a carrier's self-help would be a unilateral change in rates of pay, rules, or working conditions.

the federal or state courts have invaded this jurisdiction. While the RLA does not require the decisions of the System Board to be final and binding, the airline agreements have generally considered this to be the case. Prior to 1966 a carrier could obtain judicial review of the System Board's decision and the union could not. Therefore, if a grievant lost a case before the System Board, judicial review could not be obtained. However, if the grievant won the case, the carrier could refuse to comply with the decision, in which case the grievant had to turn to the courts to enforce the decision of the System Board. In 1966 this discrimination was ended by allowing both parties the same right of judicial review.

The Effects of the Railway Labor Act and Regulation

Having reviewed the labor legislation, it is now necessary to consider the impact of the RLA and regulation on labor-management relations in the air transport industry. The basic question is: What is the impact of the RLA and regulation on the bargaining power of the unions and carriers? Before this question can be answered, it becomes necessary to define the determinants of bargaining power that, in turn, depend upon the nature of the industry under investigation. Furthermore it is difficult to talk about the bargaining power of the unions in the airlines in general. There are approximately eighteen unions representing the employees of the U.S. airlines. Because of their members' input into the production process, some unions, such as ALPA, are more influential than others, such as reservation workers. In general, it appears that the applications of the procedures in the RLA as well as the regulation by the CAB and to some extent by the FAA have increased the bargaining power of the unions. One exception to this generalization is the existence of the Airline Mutual Aid Pact, which has increased the carriers' bargaining power.

The RLA, as discussed in the last section, has allowed employees of the same class to be collectively represented, with the result that employees have been fragmented into eighteen unions within the industry. Since the RLA does not provide for compulsory arbitration and since the decisions of the Presidential Emergency Board are final and binding, the impact of the RLA has been to increase the bargaining power of the unions. This conclusion appears reasonable for several reasons. First, some craft unions, particularly those representing the flight deck crew, can shut down the whole operation. Second, since there are so many unions in the industry and the carriers are always bargaining with someone, the unions are able to whipsaw between the carriers. Third, not only are decisions of the Presidential Emergency Board not binding, but the unions have used these recommendations as a basis for further bargaining.

With regard to the nature of the industry, there are a number of factors that have a significant influence over the bargaining power of the unions, but the most important one is the inability of an airline to stockpile its output or build up inventory in anticipation of a strike. Airline service once produced must be used at the time of production. It is possible that some travel could be postponed if all carriers were not offering service simultaneously. However, with the exception of the IAM strike in the mid-1960s, the unions rarely strike against more than one carrier at a time. Because most routes have more than one carrier, passengers generally do not have to postpone their trips. Therefore, during a strike a carrier faces a complete loss of traffic. Furthermore, additional losses result from cancelled reservations due to a strike threat prior to the strike; there is also the loss of initial reservations after the strike is over. The inability to stockpile the output gives tremendous bargaining power to the unions. Part of this power is offset by the existence of the Airline Mutual Aid Pact, which will be discussed later in this chapter.

The second characteristic of the industry influencing the bargaining power relates to price elasticity of demand for air transportation. If the market demand is inelastic, management can generally pass on the higher costs of settlements to the passengers. However, if the market demand is elastic, higher wage settlements cannot be completely passed on to the passengers without serious impact on profits. Although no definitive answers exist on the value of price elasticities in air transportation, it is generally agreed that business travel is inelastic relative to pleasure and personal travel, and long-haul travel is inelastic relative to short-haul travel. If one couples this generalization with the facts that one-half of the travel within the United States is for business purposes and one-half of the travel within the United States is less than 500 miles in trip length, one can begin to appreciate the impact of price elasticity of demand on the bargaining power of the unions. For international operations, the proportion of business travelers is much lower—only about 25 percent.

The third characteristic of the industry influencing the bargaining power relates to the seasonality of travel. Certain carriers face a high seasonality problem, and a strike or even a strike threat during the peak period could be very costly. The existence of high seasonality, such as on the North Atlantic, can become very critical in the timing of bargaining. Seasonality and the price elasticity of demand are, of course, not independent. For example, during the summer months large numbers of students travel to Europe. This student traffic (highly price elastic) and the fact that the number of passengers carried on the North Atlantic in July and August can be almost five times the amount carried in February and November provide the unions with significant bargaining power.

In addition to the above factors, there are numerous other factors that are important in the investigation of the bargaining power of the unions and management. Examples of these are availability of alternative income for union workers, ratio of union labor costs to total costs, and ratio of the carrier's liquid assets to fixed costs.[3] The latter refers to the ability of an airline to endure a strike by using its liquid assets to meet short-term obligations. In the airline industry the ratio of liquid assets to fixed costs is quite low; this has been especially true in recent years. This phenomena is basically the result of high fixed costs because of the high value of leased equipment on which payments must be made—even if the carrier is on strike.

Next it is also important to consider the impact of federal regulation on labor-management relations in the industry. The Federal Aviation Act of 1958 requires compliance with the provisions of the RLA as a condition for holding a certificate of public convenience and necessity. However, there are no specific guidelines to help the CAB determine if an airline has violated the RLA, and it is also not clear how much of a violation constitutes the revocation of the certificate of PC&N. Furthermore, it is also not clear whether the CAB is the appropriate agency to establish whether or not an airline has violated the RLA. On the second point, the CAB decided in *Air Line Pilot's Association v. Southern Airways* that in appropriate cases it is indeed the proper agency to hear and determine complaints alleging violation of the RLA.[4] In this case the CAB did establish that a carrier's refusal to bargain in good faith calls for revocation of the carrier's certificate. However, in this case the CAB demanded that Southern either begin good faith bargaining within 30 days or face the consequences of losing its certificate.

The second area of the CAB's control over airline labor relations arises in cases involving mergers. In such cases, as will be shown in Chapter 13, the CAB generally imposes labor protection conditions under the public interest clause. A common enough reality in the railroad industry under the Interstate Commerce Act, this practice only began in the airline industry in 1950 with the settlement of the United-Western acquisition case.[5] Western Airlines applied for CAB's approval for the transfer of a certain route and property to United. The Air Line Pilots Association demanded that Western pilots receive full employment and seniority rights as a condition of CAB's approval. The CAB concluded that the issues should be settled between the parties. However, the parties were unable to settle among themselves and the CAB imposed labor protection conditions. These conditions were again brought up in the *North Atlantic Route Transfer* case involving the acquisition of all assets and the certificate of PC&N of American Overseas Airlines by Pan American.[6] Once again, voluntary efforts having failed, the CAB integrated the seniority of certain classes of employees on the basis of length of service. These provisions were standardized in 1961 in the *United Capital* case.[7]

The third area of the CAB's impact on airline labor relations is related to the Board's approval of fare increases due to cost increases. In regulating the industry the Board has had a dual role of both protecting as well as promoting the air transportation industry. The protection of the industry is related to the restrictions on entry and regulation of rates to guarantee survival. Therefore, if the industry faces cost increases due to higher wage settlements with the unions, these can usually be passed on to the consumers, eventually through fare increases. The existence of this financial security has tended to increase the bargaining power of the unions subject only to the price elasticity considerations discussed earlier.

The fourth area of the CAB's impact on airline labor relations is related to the existence of the Airline Mutual Aid Pact (MAP), which was designed to increase the bargaining power of airline management by increasing the ability of a carrier to withstand a strike. Prior to the existence of MAP, consensus among airline management was that labor had far greater bargaining power than management. This opinion was based partially on the nature of the industry and partially on the RLA. With regard to the nature of the industry, it was concluded that the imbalance in bargaining power existed because of such factors as the inability of the industry to stockpile its output and the necessity of union labor in the production process. With respect to the RLA, the imbalance existed because of the fragmentation of unions in the industry and the lack of provisions for compulsory arbitration.

In order to shift the balance in favor of management, the airlines, as early as 1947, began to look for ways to cooperate among themselves. A number of carriers formed the Airline Negotiating Conference to present a united front to the unions. Although approved by the CAB, this conference proved ineffective because the unions refused to bargain with management on a collective basis. This conference was replaced in 1950 by the Airline Personnel Relations Conference, which in 1956 became a committee of the Air Transportation Association—the Personnel Relations Conference (PRC). One of the tasks of this special committee was to investigate the possibility of joint airline negotiations, in general, and *strike insurance*, in particular. Capital, faced with a strike by the IAM in 1958, convinced six airlines to agree to the initial Mutual Aid Pact which is a form of strike insurance.

The provisions of the MAP included recovery by the struck carrier of "windfall" revenues to other carriers if the strike resulted first from union demands in excess of those recommended by the Emergency Board, second a strike called prior to the exhaustion of prestrike procedures under the RLA, or third an otherwise unlawful strike. The phrase *windfall revenue* refers to returning money to the struck carriers by the amount of increased revenue of the Pact carriers attributable to the strike less the added expense of carrying the additional traffic. The carrier struck, in return, was to make every reasonable effort to provide the public with information concerning air service offered by other carriers in the Pact.

The unions naturally opposed the agreement on the grounds that the Pact implies collective bargaining in the lack of good faith by bringing carriers not party to the dispute into it, and that the agreement represented an attempt to force the unions to accept the recommendations of the Emergency Board. The real issue in the case was the union's belief that the Pact would interfere with prompt settlement of the disputes. The CAB rejected this issue on the grounds that there were other important factors that would stop the carrier from prolonging the strike. The CAB cited such factors as the long-term losses (due to the costs of resuming service), loss in market identity, and the fact that payments received by the struck carrier under the Pact did not cover the entire cost of the strike. However, the CAB did decide that the provisions on rerouting passengers as stated in the Pact were not in the public interest. Finally the CAB stated that although carriers receiving subsidy (local service carriers) were not members of the Pact, it would not allow subsidy funds to be used towards strike payments should subsidized carriers become members of this Pact.

A number of amendments were made to the MAP between 1958 and 1964, and in 1964 it was completely investigated by the CAB. The main purpose of the investigation was to pass judgment on the proposed supplemental payments to be made by the Pact members to the struck carrier if the windfall payments did not amount to 25 percent of the struck carrier's normal operating expense. The supplemental payments were to be made by all carriers in the Pact, whereas the windfall payments were to be made only by those carriers that actually competed with the struck carrier. Two conditions were attached to this supplemental payment proposal. First, the liability of any one carrier was limited to one-half of one percent of the carrier's operating revenue in the previous year. Second, the proposal did not involve the subsidized carriers.

During the investigation, the Bureau of Operating Rights of the CAB stated that the supplemental payments provision of the Pact was not in the public interest on the grounds that the Pact "obligates carriers who may not compete with a struck airline and who may have no direct interest in its labor problems to make substantial payments to the struck carrier even though the paying carrier receives no direct benefits from its payments or from the strike."[8] The Bureau further stated that the supplemental payments provision would strengthen the carriers' position to the point of inducing the unions to respond with similar multi-union bargaining. The carriers rejected the idea that supplemental payments would provide the struck carrier with sufficient funds to prolong the strike due to the existence of other costs during a strike not covered by the strike payments. In support of their arguments, the carriers presented evidence such as that shown in Table 8-1, showing that of the estimated $74 million incurred by the member carriers due to strikes, only $32 million was recovered from the Pact payments.

Despite the objection of the Bureau of Operating Rights the CAB approved the supplemental payments provisions of the Pact. Furthermore, in 1970 the CAB approved two additional amendments to the supplemental payments provisions. First, the level of the supplemental payments was increased to 50 percent of the normal operating expenses on a sliding scale going down to 35 percent. During the first two weeks the struck carrier was to receive 50 percent of the normal operating expense, and then for the third through fifth weeks, the supplemental payments would be limited to one percent of its previous year's revenues. In addition to these amendments, the carriers proposed that local-service carriers be allowed to join the Pact.

Table 8-1
Strike Losses Experienced by Mutual Aid Pact Members, 1958-1962
(In Thousands)

Year	Carrier	Union	Strike Period Loss	Lost Profits Strike Period	Mutual Aid Received	Net Strike Loss
1958	CA	IAM	$ 3,616	$1,332	$ 2,619	$ 997
1958	TW	IAM	5,094	493	2,372	2,722
1958	EA	IAM/FEIA	6,886	(727)	1,060	5,826
1959	AA	ALPA	11,398	1,750	3,372	8,026
1960	EA	ALPA	6,500	824	951	5,549
1961	NW	IAM	5,259	(342)	3,601	1,658
1961	AA	FEIA	1,466	(562)	1,059	407
1961	EA	FEIA	3,913	1,135	198	3,715
1961	PA	FEIA	3,001	(32)	121	2,880
1961	TW	FEIA	2,403	(807)	699	1,704
1962	EA	FEIA	25,224	2,765	15,788	9,436
Totals			$74,760	$5,829	$31,840	$42,920

Source: U.S. Civil Aeronautics Board, Reports 40 CAB 615.

During the third investigation in 1973, the CAB approved the previous amendments as well as the proposal to include the local service carriers, with the proviso that no Pact payments could be included as an expense in determining the subsidy need. The CAB restated its previous position that the Pact did not shift the bargaining power in favor of the carriers due to the nature of the air transport industry. This is evident from the investigation of airline employees' wages, which experienced faster increases and are higher than wages in other industries, including other transportation industries. The CAB pointed out that for the period 1967-1970, airline employment costs increased by about 33 percent, while the consumer price index increased only 17 percent. In particular, the employment costs increased by 13.3 percent in 1970 when the mutual aid payments were first increased. This increase was larger than any increase of the previous 3 years. Thus stated the CAB, "the facts do not show that the increased level of payments deprived employees of effective bargaining power."[9]

Certain allegations were made during the 1973 investigation that the increased strike payments resulted in short-term profits. For example, it was cited that National for the strike period from January 31, 1970 to May 26, 1970 experienced a net profit of $810,000, having received $28 million in mutual aid. However, the CAB pointed out that had "full" losses from the strike been taken into account, National would have reported a net loss of $19.4 million. This figure was derived from a total loss of $47.4 million consisting of $6 million loss of normal profits, $27.2 million strike-period loss, and $14.2 million post strike loss, against $28 million received from mutual aid.[10] Therefore National recovered less than 60 percent of its total strike losses in strike payments. The CAB also rejected the argument that the increased mutual aid payments have an adverse financial impact on the nonstruck carriers, on the grounds that a carrier may only contribute 1 percent of its operating revenue from the previous year. Investigation of the actual financial data for the period January 1, 1970 to June 30, 1971 shows that the contributions made by various carriers in the supplemental payments category were less than or equal to one-half of one percent of their revenues. Furthermore, as Table 8-2 shows, the supplemental payments as a percentage of total revenue represented only about 0.04 percent for each of the local-service carriers in the Pact.

From the above it is clear that the Pact is just a form of strike insurance that considerably increases airline management's bargaining power. It should be noted that the Pact is a step in the direction of industry-wide bargaining on the part of management. However, it should be kept in mind that it is only a step. Due to the highly competitive nature of the industry, it is unlikely that the carriers will get together to present a united front to the unions, even if the unions do agree to multicarrier bargaining. The CAB is in favor of the Pact as evidenced by the three investigations with consistent decisions. Besides balancing the bargaining power in favor of the carriers, the Pact is supposed to keep fares down by keeping costs down, and that is certainly in the public interest.

Table 8-2
Percent of Mutual Aid Payments to Carrier Revenues, 1970 to June 1971

Carriers[a]	Revenues ($000)	Payments ($000)			Percent of Payments to Revenues		
		Windfall	Supplemental	Total	Windfall	Supplemental	Total
Trunk-line							
American	1,701,893	3,136	7,880	11,016	.18	.46	.65
Braniff	485,139	175	2,407	2,582	.04	.50	.53
Continental	439,508	1,047	1,913	2,960	.24	.44	.67
Eastern	1,498,282	13,440	6,571	20,011	.90	.44	1.34
Pan American	1,661,428	2,286	7,937	10,223	.14	.48	.62
TWA	1,716,770	1,310	7,962	9,272	.08	.46	.54
United	2,213,133	10,967	10,961	21,928	.50	.50	.99
Local-service							
Frontier	138,384	—	59	59	—	.04	.04
Hughes Air West	113,635	—	50	50	—	.04	.04
North Central	139,554	—	43	43	—	.03	.03
Ozark	107,851	—	42	42	—	.04	.04
Piedmont	108,925	—	41	41	—	.04	.04

[a]Not included are National, Northwest, and Mohawk, whose revenues are substantially affected by lengthy strikes during the period, and Western which did not become a Mutual Aid party until October 3, 1970.

Source: C.A.B. Order No. 73-2-110, Issued February 27, 1973, page 30.

The other regulatory agency that has some impact on airline labor relations is the Federal Aviation Administration. Although the FAA's primary concern is with safety, it is involved indirectly with labor-management relations. The flight deck crew requires FAA licenses before it can operate the aircraft. Similarly the mechanics must also be checked and licensed. This requirement implies restriction of entry into their craft and classes and increases the bargaining power of their respective unions. In addition to this certification procedure, the FAA has certain crew requirements for both the cockpit and the passenger cabin. For example, the minimum flight deck crew requirement for a Boeing 727 is three persons. Likewise, an aircraft with twenty or more passenger seats must operate with one cabin attendant, and for each additional 40 seats or part thereof, an additional cabin attendant must be present. The net effect of these requirements is in favor of the unions.

Summary

Most of the provisions of the Railway Labor Act apply to the air carriers as a result of Title II, which was passed in 1936. This Act is based upon craft or class, each of which has the right to select a union to represent the group without any interference from the carriers. The Act, however, fails to define the term craft or class, except to state that in cases of dispute over representation of a craft, the National Mediation Board will determine the collective bargaining representative. Although the National Mediation Board serves a number of functions, its major functions are to settle representation disputes and to mediate on major and minor labor-management disputes. Although the Railway Labor Act has established certain guidelines to be followed in negotiating the settlement of labor disputes, these guidelines are quite vague in their interpretation and application and therefore have often created numerous problems.

Labor-management relations in the air carrier industry have been significantly influenced by both the Railway Labor Act and the regulation by the CAB and FAA. As shown in this chapter, it appears that the applications of the procedures in the Railway Labor Act as well as certain regulatory aspects have tended to increase the bargaining power of the unions. One exception to this generalization is the airline Mutual Aid Pact, which was designed to increase the bargaining power of airline management by increasing the ability of a carrier to withstand a strike.

Techniques for Forecasting Air Passenger Traffic

Forecasting Methods

An essential element in airline market planning is the process of obtaining accurate and realistic forecasts of the expected traffic volumes. Although the planning process involves more than just a forecast of the future traffic statistics, these statistics provide an essential quantitative dimension for the planning process. Forecasts of expected traffic are, therefore, an essential prerequisite to both short- and long-range planning. The first part of this chapter describes the basic techniques of forecasting both air passengers and cargo traffic. The differences among the various forecasting methods are due to the degree of formalization of the forecasting procedure. Each technique has its special use, and the selection of an appropriate technique depends upon a number of factors, such as particular application, available data, projection period, desired accuracy, and the cost of producing the forecast. The second part of this chapter describes the major sources of data used in the air transportation planning process.

Before discussing the various techniques or models for forecasting air traffic, it is necessary to define the time period for which forecasts are required. In general, there are two groups of time frames. The first group consists of short-, medium-, and long-range forecasts. The second group consists of special time frames, such as annual budgets. *Short-term forecasts* are normally used for planning current policy, evaluating current developments, and in general are concerned with such day-to-day operations as scheduling. The time frame can range from 1 month to 1 year. *Medium-term forecasts* normally cover a period of 2 to 5 years and are generally used for market planning. *Long-term forecasts* normally cover a period of 5 to 15 years. They are generally used for fleet planning and route planning. Budget forecasts normally refer to a fiscal year and are used for establishing basic operating and financial requirements, such as determining cash flow and adjusting station employee requirements in line with seasonal movements in traffic. The time frame for a forecast will influence the selection of a particular technique. For example, a long-range forecast of traffic for fleet planning requires a different technique than a forecast of the system traffic for producing next year's financial budget.

Judgmental Methods

Using the judgmental or subjective method, the analyst makes an educated guess of the travel demand for the forecast period based upon past experience of

131

traffic volume and intuition of the future. Although the analysts do not use any special travel demand models, they intuitively take into account the factors that influence the demand for air travel and weigh these factors according to their judgment. This method is especially useful in cases where the data sample is small or nonexistent, as may be the case when a traffic forecast is required on a new market or when market acceptance of a new type of aircraft must be forecast. Although the judgmental method has the dual advantages of low cost and ease of operation, it is limited to short-term forecasting. This approach has little merit in long-term forecasting since it is natural, although perhaps unintentional, for analysts to place greater weight on more recent developments.

The judgmental forecast can be produced by a single analyst or by a committee. One weakness of the committee approach is that it can be biased by the persuasiveness of individual members who may or may not have valid arguments. To overcome such psychological interferences that tend to reduce the value of forecasts reached by the group, Olaf Helmer at the Rand Corporation developed the Delphi Technique.[1] The aim of the Delphi Technique is to develop a carefully designed program for sequential individual interrogations, usually conducted by questionnaires, interspersed with information and judgment feedback derived from the consensus of the earlier parts. The idea is that through successive trials, the spread of forecasts can be reduced.

The Delphi Technique has been used a number of times in air transportation demand analysis. At the present time the economic staff of IATA is using this method to determine the traffic growth on major international sectors. In 1970 the technique was used by a major airframe manufacturer to forecast future air transportation developments. In a survey of air transportation developments, a questionnaire was sent to over 300 experts representing the decision-making levels of management from four major segments in the air transportation industry. Using the Delphi Technique, each participant was asked to make an anonymous forecast of future air transportation developments and to indicate when each event in question would happen. The participants were given a composite feedback based upon the analysis of the tabulated forecast. Based upon this feedback, the same experts were then asked to make a second and final forecast. They could either reaffirm their original opinions or revise them. More than one-half of the participants revised their forecasts based upon the feedback.[a]

Time-Series Methods

The time-series analysis method assumes that the air passenger traffic will follow its established pattern of growth. This means that the future travel demand is a

---

[a]The areas covered in the survey were advances in air transportation technology, development of air cargo, passenger preference for air transportation, seat capacities of future aircraft, and new markets for air transportation usage.

time function of the past experience. The time-series analysis, therefore, assumes very little causation. The method can be useful for broad long-term projections, especially in cases where there is very little knowledge of the cause for growth. On the other hand, the method has little merit for forecasting detailed long-term patterns. Since the assumption that the future is a direct function of the past is more likely to be true in the case of short-term, the trend method can be very useful for producing detailed forecasts on the short-term basis.

The application of time-series analysis varies from the simple extrapolation of historical trends to the use of complex mathematical growth curves, such as the Logistic and Gompertz curves. These models are known as *intrinsic models*; that is, time is taken to be the only predictor variable, reflecting the interplay of economic, industry, and government activities. Based upon the actual historical data on volume of traffic, a mathematical growth curve is selected to fit the data base. The difficulty lies in accurately determining the appropriate trend curve. Empirical and theoretical considerations can be used to narrow the selection of the growth curve. For example, the very long-term forecast of the air passenger traffic in the United States may be estimated by an asymptotic trend, such as a Gompertz curve, since there are good reasons to place an upper limit on the level of traffic.

The simple extrapolation involves a projection of past observed trends through visual inspection. Although such a method will suffice for certain applications, direct extrapolation, in general, is not considered a satisfactory method of forecasting, especially for cases involving turning points. The method merely indicates that parameters exist that have influenced the demand in the past at a rate that is a function of time. It is therefore difficult to project the demand based upon time alone, unless one knows these time-based parameters and the extent of their influence. It is also difficult to forecast the time that these influences may cease to operate or that their effects will change. For example, it is well-known that the sea traffic on the North Atlantic has been declining steadily. A direct mechanical extrapolation of this trend will produce a total disappearance of the sea traffic on this route after a certain amount of time. A reasonable forecast, on the other hand, would set a minimum level on the passenger market patronizing the water mode.

For annual budget forecasts the analyst is usually interested in forecasting monthly traffic that can fluctuate because of trend, cyclical, and seasonal factors. In addition, the traffic pattern may contain random noises. The long-term trend is usually the result of technical improvements and a steady and continuous growth in population. The cyclical fluctuations are generally the result of movements in the economy or business cycles and do not usually conform to a set pattern. The seasonal effects occur at a given time in the year and are usually the result of the season or custom. The random noise is the irregular or residual part of the pattern. The time-series forecasting model attempts to project the value of the first three components of the series and add the results to get the forecast value of the traffic. It is usually impossible to forecast the random noise component.

Various time-series statistical models are available to analyze and forecast values of a fluctuating pattern. Smoothing techniques are the most common means of investigating time-series components. These techniques attempt to cancel out the random effects by using averages. The normal smoothing schemes are the moving-average type and exponential smoothing. The former scheme calculates averages over a fixed base time period, while the latter scheme calculates an average using all past values of the series. The weight given to the individual value of the series is determined by the smoothing constant.

The accuracy of this method depends upon the behavior of the traffic pattern. A well-behaved pattern with small random variation will be relatively easy to forecast compared to one containing a significant random pattern. Normally the historical raw time-series data are adjusted and massaged to eliminate known distortions caused by ad hoc factors, such as strikes, introduction of new aircraft, bad weather, and extraordinary large-scale promotions. The time-series model can then be used on the clean data to produce a forecast of the seasonal traffic pattern. The experienced analyst would then apply to the predetermined forecast intuitive factors like expected changes in competitor's traffic, introduction of excursion fares, or movements in the economy to obtain a more realistic traffic forecast for budget purposes.

Trend extrapolation is often thought of as a simple and rough method of producing a forecast. The analyst is cautioned against this type of thinking. The image of simplicity is far from the truth. Recent applications include sophisticated methods, such as adaptive filtering techniques.[2] In the past the most common means of handling fluctuating patterns have been the simple and exponential smoothing techniques. However, improved results can be obtained by using time-varying (adaptive) smoothing constants. An example of an adaptive analysis is the Box-Jenkins method.[3] Another sophisticated time-series technique that has been applied to airline traffic data is known as *spectral analysis*. Again the technique is too complex to describe here. Basically, the assumption is that any stationary series (one with unchanging mean and variance) can be decomposed into a series of sine waves of various frequencies and phase. Thus given enough sine waves, any time-series can be "fit" accurately.[4]

Market Research Methods

The market analysis method relates the travel patterns of a given segment of the population to its demographic and economic characteristics. The Port Authority of New York and New Jersey has investigated the use of this method based upon a series of national household surveys conducted over a period of 20 years.[5] The results of these surveys indicate a strong relationship between the travel pattern of a group of people and such characteristics as income and occupation. One of the main purposes of the survey is to determine whether a person is a "flier" or not, and if a flier, how many trips are taken each year. Trends and growth rates are established for the number of trips per 1000 fliers in each cell.

The Port Authority model divides the air travel market into a large number of travel cells for personal and business travel. The personal travel cells are classified by age, occupation, education, and income; the business travel cells are by industry, occupation, and income. A typical matrix of personal travel has 134 individual cells showing the population in each cell. Forecasts are made by first estimating population growth in each of the cells and then calculating the expected number of trips by multiplying the number of people in the population, percent of fliers, and the trips per 1000 fliers. The estimates from each cell are summed and adjusted for elements not covered in the survey to produce totals for the future years.

There are three critical assumptions regarding the validity of this method. First, an assumption has to be made regarding the stability of the relationship between travel patterns and the socio-economic characteristics. Second, a realistic assumption is needed on the projected growth of the traffic group within an individual cell. Third, the model should take into account any expected changes in the socio-economic structure of the population and segments of the population that are not included in the surveys.

Market analysis can be an extremely useful tool in identifying those segments of the population that generated most of the air activity and those that are good future potentials. The weakness of the method is that it does not consider service characteristics such as fare and trip time. The market analysis method, for example, will not be able to relate the changes in the demand for air travel to changes in the average fare level or introduction of new fares established to attract a certain market.

Market surveys can be taken from actual travelers or from households with potential travelers. In the latter case consumers are asked about their travel intentions and the responses are subject to many "errors." The most common of these results from misinterpretation and lack of ability to quantify subjective responses. The common limitations of these surveys are that the respondents may not be the ultimate decision-makers or that they may be unable to accurately state their travel plans. In any case, the plans can change because of family circumstances and general economic conditions.[6]

Econometric Methods

The econometric method attempts to relate the variation in traffic to the movement of logically relevant economic variables such as income, demographic variables such as population, and service variables such as fare and trip time. This method explores and analyzes parameters that have affected the historical travel demand pattern and that may influence the future travel demand. An econometric demand model shows, through one or more equations, an economic relationship between demand and a number of predictor variables that can be classified as exogenous or endogenous. The endogenous variables are determined within the model itself while the exogenous variables are predetermined. It should be noted that although time can enter the relationship as a predictor variable, it cannot be the sole predictor variable. It should also be noted that statistical correlation does not always imply cause and effect. In many cases the relationship is empirical or logical at best.

Figure 9-1 shows the basic steps involved in the procedure for developing an econometric model and forecasting the air passenger traffic. Although the steps represent an oversimplified schematic procedure, they are nevertheless sufficient to outline the framework in which traffic forecasts are produced. The initial step in producing any forecast of air passenger traffic is to review the past year-to-year travel trends. This will provide the analyst with a reasonable indication of the general characteristics for the forecasting model. If, for example, the historical growth trend has been extremely stable, it may be sufficient to have time as the sole predictor variable in the model. On the other hand, periodic distortions in the basic trend may be identified through disturbances like the introduction of jet aircraft, strikes, and/or fare changes.

The next step is to identify factors such as populations, incomes, and fares that have influenced the travel pattern in the past and those that are likely to exert influence in the future. In modeling a complex socio-economic system, it is feasible to consider only a subset of all the factors. The selection of the variables is usually determined by the availability of empirical data, judged on the basis of quantification, consistency, reliability, the size of the base, and availability of projected values for a future time period.

Factors contributing to the changes in the travel demand can be grouped into two broad categories—socio-economic and transport-related. Socio-economic variables are those related to the general economic, geographic, social, and political environment. Transport-related variables, on the other hand, are those inherent in the transport mode, that is, cost, travel time, comfort, safety, and convenience. The volume of passenger traffic is influenced by a complex interaction of one or more of these variables.

The choice of the general form of the demand model will depend primarily upon such factors as the historical traffic trends, data considerations, the time period of the forecast, and certain desired properties of the demand function, such as constant or variable price elasticity of demand. The common forms of demand models are the linear form, the multiplicative or log-linear form, the exponential or semilogarithmic model, the nonlinear form, the difference model, or some combination of these basic forms. The choice between a linear and multiplicative form, for example, involves an analysis of the manner in which the selected predictor variables interact in the model. The linear additive form is

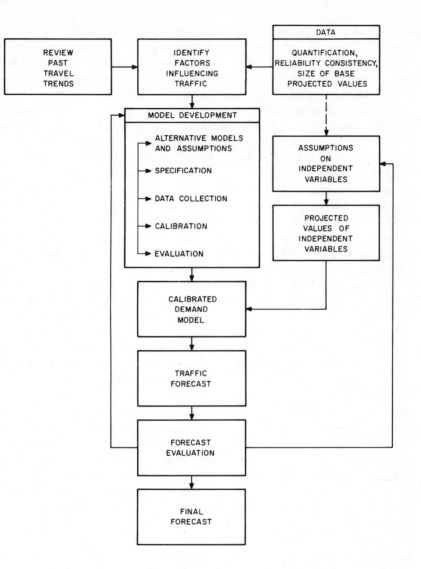

Figure 9-1. Econometric Model Development and Forecasting Procedure.

more suitable if the predictor variables are expected to be independent. Conversely, if there is a strong interaction among the predictor variables, then a multiplicative form may be justified. Similarly, a choice between the multiplicative and exponential form may be determined from an analysis of the desired properties of the elasticity of demand. Whereas in the multiplicative model the desired property is that the exponents represent partial elasticities, one elasticity coefficient for each factor that may be regarded as an average value over the range of data, the exponential formulation indicates that the price elasticity of demand is a function of the price itself. The difference models are normally used in cases where multicollinearity may represent a problem.[b]

The aggregate model (such as total travel over the North Atlantic) assumes that the demand for air travel is a homogenous unit, such as revenue passenger miles or revenue ton miles, and that the volume of passenger traffic is related to the same parameters in all markets. This implies that the travel demand on one route, such as New York-Lisbon, can be characterized by the same parameters as another route, such as New York-London. The aggregate travel demand model does not stratify traffic by mode, class of service, or purpose of trip. In the past, forecasters working with aggregate demand models have generally not included a supply parameter. The exclusion of supply has been justified on the grounds that the airlines usually operate with considerably less than full capacity, and therefore it is not necessary to include a supply variable. Second, monopolistic routes on the North Atlantic are almost nonexistent, and insufficient capacity is unlikely due to the market forces. The standard criticisms of excluding the supply factor are first that there may be some routes with very high load factors, and second that an increase in supply may increase demand.

There are three fundamental assumptions underlying the econometric approach. First, it is assumed that most of the variation in the dependent variable can be explained by using a few selected independent variables. This is a necessary assumption due to the fact that the data are limited. Furthermore, in many cases it is difficult, if not impossible, to quantify all the variables, even though the forecaster is aware that these variables have influenced the travel demand in the past and will continue to do so in the future. The second assumption is that it is easier and more accurate to forecast the independent variables than dependent variable. This is a very critical assumption, since the forecast of traffic cannot be better than the forecast of the independent variables. The third assumption is that the functional relationship will remain valid throughout the forecast period.

The specification phase consists of formulating a set of testable hypotheses showing the relationship between traffic volumes and factors related to the market and the trip. The selection of variables is based upon available empirical data, economic theory, statistical techniques, and computational advantages. The hypotheses concerning the above relationship are translated into precise mathematical equations by stipulating such characteristics as the structural form, the direction of marginal influence of each variable, and the manner in which the influences are jointly exerted.

The specification of the model should be dynamic, in that it should fully

---

[b]The problem of multicollinearity exists where there is a relationship between two or more of the independent variables.

reflect the time difference between a change in the independent variable and the accompanying response in the dependent variable. The application of this property is desired in differentiating between the short-term and long-term effects in the demand response when changes are made in the fare. This result can be achieved by using the technique developed by Marc Nerlove for estimating long-term elasticities from time-series data based upon assumptions with regard to the elasticity of adjustment of quantity demanded to changes in price.[7]

The next step involves the collection of statistical data on the selected independent variables for use in deriving the appropriate historical functional relationship between the dependent and the independent variables. The format of the independent variables is related to the availability of historical and projected values for the data. For example, there are at least three forms of income that can be entered into demand equations: national income, disposable income, and discretionary income. Although the latter would be a more logical predictor variable of air travel, its use is constrained because of its subjective value, the difficulty in quantification, and the unavailability of consistent data. The major sources of statistical data on traffic volumes are the airline trade agencies, government agencies, and civil air transport agencies. Traffic data sources are discussed at some length in the next section.

The calibration stage involves the empirical manipulation of various functional relationships for a base period. The object is to find the relationship that gives the least discrepancy between the computed demand and the actual observed demand. The calibration of the model, that is, the estimation of the demand coefficients, is normally performed by employing multiple regression analysis. The coefficients in a standard single equation can be estimated using ordinary least squares.[c] Multi-equation or simultaneous-equation models, on the other hand, require a more sophisticated calibration process. In general, the coefficients can be estimated using techniques such as the reduced form, two-stage least squares, and maximum likelihood.[d]

Sometimes calibration is performed through *conditional regression analysis*. This refers to the calibration process in which one of the independent variables in the equation is given a fixed value, while the remaining coefficients are derived through the normal process. Conditional regression is normally used when multicollinearity is a serious problem, or when prior knowledge indicates a particular value of a given parameter. For example, if one has prior information

[c]Readers not familiar with this technique are referred to an excellent article by John G. Myers, "Statistical and Econometric Methods Used in Business Forecasting," in *Methods and Techniques of Business Forecasting*, eds. William Butler, Robert Kavesh, and Robert Platt (Englewood Cliffs, N.J.: Prentice-Hall, Inc., 1974).

[d]Due to the introductory nature of this book, it is not feasible to discuss the details of simultaneous-equation models or their statistical problems. The advanced analyst is referred to the many excellent texts available on the subject, such as: Henri Theil, *Principles of Econometrics* (New York: John Wiley and Sons, 1971) and J. Johnston, *Econometric Methods* (New York: McGraw-Hill Book Company, 1972).

on price and/or income elasticity of demand, then the analyst can impose upper and lower bounds on the values of one or both of these parameters.

The final step in model development is evaluation in terms of its effectiveness to explain and forecast travel demand. This step may lead to reformulation of the model and hence to the repetition of the previous steps. The selection of a particular specification depends upon the purpose of investigation, the validity, the simplicity, the accuracy, the cost of operation and maintenance, and perhaps the personal preference of the forecaster. The following are a number of factors that can be used as guidelines for model selection and evaluation. The list is not exclusive, and criteria not discussed may be just as important, or even more so, than those included.

In evaluating any model, econometric or otherwise, the investigator must be very clear about the purpose of the investigation. For example, if the main object of the investigation were to estimate the true numerical value of demand elasticities upon which to base pricing and marketing strategies, the unbiased estimation of the particular demand elasticity should be the criteria for model specification and evaluation. On the other hand, if the main object of the study were to forecast the traffic volumes, the criteria for the specification of the model should be based upon the forecasting ability of the model or the accuracy of the forecast. In this case, the model selected should be the one that produces the smallest standard error of estimate and standard error of the demand coefficients. Similarly, if the purpose of the model were to produce a long-term forecast, the choice of a cross-sectional model may not be best, since the parameters in a cross-sectional model are estimated from a sample of observations at a given point in time.

The validity of a model can be investigated in four parts: the theoretical foundations of the model, the underlying assumptions, the statistical validation, and the empirical calibration data (in the case of an econometric model). All models should be based upon a fundamental theory. For instance, the analyst can relate the demand for pleasure travel to consumer utility theory, or business travel to the theory of the firm. (The gravity model for instance is derived from the gravitational law of physics.) Equally important in selecting a model are the basic assumptions incorporated in the model. One cannot justify using an aggregate demand model with constant price elasticity for forecasting the demand on a highly priced elastic route. Neither can the analyst use a model calibrated using subsonic aircraft data to forecast the potential with supersonic aircraft. In each case it is critical to investigate the fundamental assumptions on which the model is based.

The next area of evaluation refers to the statistical validity of the econometric model. These models may be subject to statistical problems, such as multicollinearity, autocorrelation, heteroscedasticity, and identification. In each case, if a statistical problem exists, chances are that the estimated parameters would be unreliable and the predictive ability of the model subject to errors. The existence of more than one type of statistical problem complicates the matter further, and evaluation of the model becomes even more difficult. There are a number of statistics that can be used to determine the existence and in some cases the extent of the problem. Statistics such as standard error of coefficient, multiple correlation coefficient, the F-statistics, the Durbin-Watson, the Von Neumann Ratio, and the Chow Test are often provided in the output from computerized statistical packages and can be used to determine the statistical validity of the model.[e]

The general validity of the calibration data is also very important. In selecting and evaluating a particular model one should investigate the calibration data that are used to estimate the demand parameters. The data should be analyzed for adequacy, consistency, and reliability. The analyst should carefully examine the data to make certain that each data point was measured in the same manner, the sample size was adequate, and the data were relatively free of significant errors. Furthermore the data should be analyzed to determine if the standard assumptions on which the least square estimation technique is based are violated.

The next set of selection criteria are somewhat interrelated. Simplicity is tied to the ease of operation and maintenance, on the one hand, and cost, accuracy, and personal preference of the investigator, on the other. An historical trend analysis may be simple, cheap, and easy to perform but may not be accurate enough to forecast the demand for travel in a time period that may have supersonic aircraft, subsonic mass transportation, or hypersonic aircraft. Equally important is the weight of the marginal predictive accuracy against the marginal cost of formulating a sophisticated model. In this context, cost is used in a general sense. It includes such components as the time required to produce a forecast, the need for computer facilities, the additional cost of acquiring more suitable data, and the cost of error in the forecast. A sophisticated model may not necessarily be more accurate than a simple one, and yet for the sophisticated model the collection and manipulation of the input data may be very expensive.

The final step in the forecasting procedure is to produce the traffic forecast itself. Forecasts are produced by using the calibrated demand model and projections of the independent variables. Traffic forecasts are then evaluated in a manner similar to that described for the demand model. Erroneous forecasts are usually the result of inaccurate data, inaccurate compilation, invalid model, or incorrect application of a valid model. There are two options available if the forecast does not meet the requirements set by the analyst. The initial reaction should be to re-examine the values and assumptions regarding the independent variables. The second option is to re-examine the various phases of the model development.

[e]For full explanation of these statistical problems the reader is referred to such standard texts as: J. Johnston, *Econometric Methods* (New York: McGraw-Hill Book Company, 1972) and Ronald J. and Thomas H. Wonnacott, *Econometrics* (New York: John Wiley and Co., Inc., 1970).

Modal Split Models

A modal split model determines the functional relationship between the share of traffic attracted to a particular mode over a route. The most common form of the modal split model assumes that total trip time and total cost are the two most significant factors that the traveling public will use in making the choice of a mode of travel. The mathematical formulation of one form of a modal split model is given in Figure 9-2. The total trip time includes the times for access, egress, passenger processing, and wait for the next line-haul service. These factors account for the conveniences aspect of the system. The model does not contain factors on comfort, safety, and reliability. In this figure the time to wait for next service T_w depends upon daily frequency. Again the total trip cost consists of trip fare and the cost of access and egress.

$$MS_{ijm} = \frac{c_{ijm}^{\alpha} \cdot T_{ijm}^{\beta}}{\sum\limits_{m-1, m} c_{ijm}^{\alpha} \cdot T_{ijm}^{\beta}}$$

WHERE MS_{ijm} = SHARE OF TRAFFIC BETWEEN i AND j TRAVELLING ON MODE m

C_{ijm} = TOTAL TRIP COST = ACCESS + EGRESS + TRIP FARE

T_{ijm} = TOTAL TRIP TIME

$= T_a + T_p + T_w + T_b + T_e$

T_a, T_e = TIME FOR ACCESS, EGRESS

T_p = TIME TO PROCESS PASSENGER AT STATION

T_w = TIME TO WAIT FOR NEXT SERVICE $= \dfrac{TD/2}{f_{ijm}}$

T_b = BLOCK TIME ON MODE m

TD = DAILY HOURS OF OPERATION FOR MODE m

f_{ijm} = DAILY FREQUENCY OF SERVICE FOR MODE m

α = TRIP COST ELASTICITY

β = TRIP TIME ELASTICITY

Source: Flight Transportation Laboratory, *Concept Studies for Future Intercity Air Transportation Systems*, MIT-FTL Report R-70, 1970, p. 55.

Figure 9-2. Modal Split Model.

Airline Market Share Models

A market share model shows the relationship between the share of the passenger traffic for an airline in a given competitive market and the factors that describe the quality of service offered in the market by the carrier. Since service factors, such as fares and the type of aircraft, are similar on all major U.S. domestic routes for all competitors, the market share becomes a function of factors such as frequency of service, departure and arrival times, and the image of the carrier.

Research in the area of market share estimation in the airline industry has indicated that the most significant explanatory variable of market share is frequency share. More precisely, empirical evidence shows that market share is an S-shaped curve, and its location is a function of the number of carriers in the market. This concept is illustrated in Figure 9-3. The effects of multistop service and preference for various types of aircraft are best accounted for by assigning weighted values to the daily frequency. Although these weights used by various investigators have been highly criticized for their numerical and relative value, it should be pointed out that the values of the various weights are not extremely critical, since services on competitive markets tend to be very similar.

In almost every investigation undertaken, the dominant variable explaining market share was the share of frequency. Until recently the rule of thumb has been that market share is equal to frequency share. However, the existence of the S-shaped curve shown in Figure 9-3 indicates that an airline with greater share of frequency than its competitor receives a more than proportional share of the traffic. Furthermore, the data also seems to indicate that the S-shaped curve is a function of the number of competitors in the market. The implication of the S-shaped curve can be explained in the following way. Suppose there are two carriers in a market, both offering equal frequency and both receiving equal market share. If one competitor increased its frequency, its market share would increase more than proportionately. If the other competitor maintained status quo, the average load factor of the aggressive carrier would increase, while the load of the other would decrease. On the other hand, if the second carrier decided to match the frequency by increasing its own frequency, the market share would remain the same, but the average load factor would decline for both carriers. Thus the aggressive carrier recognizes gains only when the competitor decides to maintain status quo; otherwise, in terms of load factors, both carriers will lose.

More recent research by Robert W. Simpson at MIT indicates that a carrier's image, both overall and local, plays a significant role in airline market share analysis. Denoting an average carrier's system image by 1.0, a carrier with a system image 1.2 will, in general, obtain 20 percent more traffic than the average carrier, all other things being equal. Using data for the first quarter of 1967 in his analysis of the top 25 domestic markets, Simpson obtained the following

144

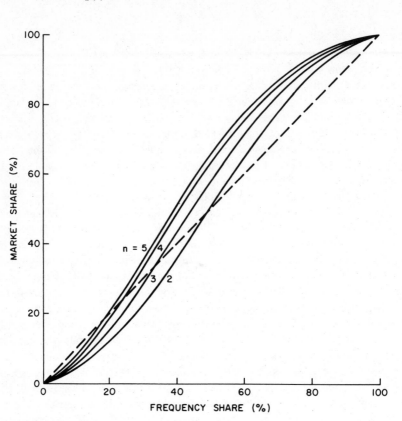

Note: n = Number of competitors in the market.

Figure 9-3. Market Share versus Frequency Share Curves.

systems image factors for six trunk-line carriers (Table 9-1). The market share of a particular carrier would therefore depend upon the identity of its competitor. Thus, if Continental competed with Western on a particular route, Continental's market share would be 60 percent. If, on the other hand, Continental were to compete with American, Continental's market share would be 54 percent. This example assumes that both competitors have equal local image factors.

Air Carrier Industry Data

Relative to the other modes of transportation, the airline industry provides large quantities of data that can be used extensively in the analysis and planning of

Table 9-1
System Image Factors

Airline	System Image Factor, 1967
American	1.11
Continental	1.32
Eastern	0.72
Trans World	1.00
United	0.93
Western	0.85

Source: Simpson, Robert W., *Airline Market Share Analysis*, class notes for 16.74, M.I.T., Cambridge, Massachusetts.

airline operations. Although most of this data are collected, edited, summarized, and published by the CAB, airport authorities and other agencies, such as the Department of Transportation (in particular the FAA), the Department of Justice (Immigration and Naturalization Service), the Bureau of Census, the International Civil Aviation Organization, the International Air Transport Association, and the Air Transport Association of America, also provide substantial quantities of data.

The purpose of this section is to describe the major sources of data used in the air transportation planning process. In describing the various data sources, the focus has been on the U.S. domestic certificated route air carriers. Readers with interests wider than this group of carriers are referred to a report entitled *Air Transportation Data Sources*, published by the Flight Transportation Laboratory at MIT.[8] This publication contains a comprehensive description of the data sources discussed in this section as well as many other domestic and international data sources. Readers particularly interested in the Board's publications are referred to a CAB report entitled *Statistical Programs*.[9]

The CAB Data Bank

Most of the data published by the Board are supplied by the U.S. certificated route air carriers on Form 41. These carriers are required to submit both financial and traffic data on a regular basis. In addition, limited data are also supplied by the U.S. certificated supplemental air carriers, commuter air carriers, the U.S. certificated route air carriers conducting international services, and the U.S. Air Freight Forwarders. Although some of the data are considered confidential for a certain time period, most of the data published by the Board are public information.

Financial Statistics. From the data collected on Form 41, the Board, on a quarterly basis, publishes *Air Carrier Financial Statistics* with information on revenues, assets, liabilities, stockholder equity, and expenses and income. This publication covers operations of certificated route air carriers in all of its issues and, in some issues, aggregate financial information on supplemental carriers. This report, commonly known as "The Yellow Book," provides financial data for the industry as well as for individual airlines by quarter and by calendar year. These data are then incorporated into the Board's *Handbook of Airline Statistics*; this report is published every 2 years and provides the historical data for the prior 10 years. *Air Carrier Financial Statistics* has been published by the Board since 1952. In addition to this basic source of financial data, the Board also publishes the following reports. (Initiation dates are given in parentheses.)

1. *Quarterly Airline Industry Economic Report* (1968)
2. *Quarterly Interim Report* (1973)
3. *Interim Report of Selected Profit and Loss Indicators for the Month* (1971)
4. *Projected Financial Commitments of Airlines* (1972)
5. *Sources and Application of Funds for Airlines* (1972)
6. *Causes of Change in Carrier Net Income* (1972)
7. *Air Freight Statistics, Certificated Route Air Carriers, Scheduled and Non-Scheduled Service of U.S. Passenger/Cargo and All-Cargo Carriers: Revenues and Yields Data* (1967)

Until recently air freight forwarders did not report financial data based upon the uniform accounting practices prescribed by the Board for the direct route air carriers. Some of the large air freight forwarders had developed a sophisticated accounting system. However, the smaller forwarders were still supplying data in the aggregate form that made the evaluation of forwarder rates extremely difficult. In light of this difficulty, the Board is now requiring air freight forwarders whose gross annual revenues exceed $3 million to establish and maintain the prescribed uniform system of accounts.

Another category of new data presently being collected by the Board concerns the use of fuel; these data are reported in Schedule P-12, entitled *Fuel Inventories and Consumption*, and in Schedule P-12(a), *Fuel Consumption by Type of Service and Specific Operational Markets*. On Schedule P-12, the carriers submit information on inventory and consumption by type of fuel, bonded, nonbonded, or foreign. *Bonded fuel* is fuel that is produced outside the United States, held under U.S. customs authority, and is to be used outside of U.S. territory. *Foreign fuel* is fuel loaded on the aircraft outside of U.S. territory and consumed in flight operations outside of the U.S. territory.

The Board has also recently begun to collect data on air cargo, which are published in a report entitled *Quarterly Cargo Review*. This report includes information on scheduled air freight and air mail revenue, air freight and air mail revenue ton miles, freight ton miles in all-cargo aircraft, and the relative magnitude of scheduled revenue freight ton miles compared to nonscheduled operations. The data are provided for each group of air carriers.

In spite of the vast quantities of financial data collected by the Board, the reader is cautioned on the limitations of these data due to their aggregate nature. The financial data in their aggregate form do not allow an airline analyst to analyze costs by type of service, such as first class, coach class, and passenger service versus freight and mail service. Furthermore, the aggregate financial reporting system prevents the analyst from analyzing in detail the operating profit and loss of different segments, flights, and markets. In order to perform this type of analysis, one needs detailed revenues and expenses by segment, flight, and market. While the Board is presently collecting traffic data by segment, it is also necessary to collect revenue and expense data by segment.

Statistics of Costs and Performance. The second major publication of the Board deals with costs and performance and is entitled *Aircraft Operating Cost and Performance Report*. Also known as "The Red Book," it contains aircraft operating expenses and performance characteristics of all aircraft types operated by U.S. certificated route and supplemental carriers. All data items for both the certificated route and supplemental carriers are given in three levels of aggregation: by equipment group and carrier group (Part I), by equipment type and carrier group (Part II), and by equipment type by individual carrier (Part III). This report is widely used by aircraft and engine companies, investment houses, research institutions, airlines, and universities. The Red Book has been published annually since 1966. In addition to this book, there are nine other reports dealing with cost and performance statistics.

1. *Trends in Airline Unit Costs* (1973)
2. *Trends in Airline Cost Elements* (1973)
3. *Domestic Jet Trends* (1972)
4. *Supplemental Carrier Jet Trends* (1972)
5. *Turbine Aircraft Operating Cost and Performance Report for Fiscal Years, Supplemental Carriers* (1968)
6. *Wide-Body Jet Aircraft Operating Cost and Performance Report* (1970)
7. *Trends in Scheduled All-Cargo Service* (1969)
8. *Operating Results of Scheduled All-Cargo Service* (1963)
9. *Schedule Arrival Performance in the Top 100 Markets, by Carrier* (1968)

Recently the Board began publishing a report entitled *Productivity and Cost of Employment* for trunk-line carriers and local-service carriers. These reports compare the productivity among various carriers with respect to the following categories:

1. Average number of employees
2. Total labor cost as a percent of total operating expense
3. Average labor cost per employee
4. Revenue and available ton miles per employee
5. Average labor cost per revenue and available ton mile
6. Labor cost categories
7. Yield and unit labor costs
8. Operating revenues and expenses per employee

Traffic Statistics. There are two major data sources (available through the Board) related to airline traffic. The first one is entitled *Origin-Destination Survey of Airline Passenger Traffic*. The Board, in cooperation with the carriers and the Air Transport Association of America, conducts a recurrent passenger survey of travel on scheduled carriers. The data are collected on passenger trip origin, destination, and volume of traffic by routing in terms of carriers and transfer points. More specifically this source provides market-type information, such as the distribution of traffic in each market, by carrier. The survey does not contain demographic information on passengers, such as trip purpose, occupation, and age. These data are extremely useful in route and rate investigation, fleet planning and scheduling, and market analysis, research, and traffic forecasting.

The domestic portion of the survey dates back to November 1939 with a break during the World War II years. The participating carriers collect the data on the basis of a continuous 10 percent sample of passenger tickets in accordance with the Board's instructions. The 10 percent sample is taken by lifting flight coupons with serial number ending in the digit zero. Group tickets for eleven or more passengers are sampled on a 100 percent basis. Eastern's tickets on the Boston-New York and New York-Washington air shuttle service are also sampled on a 100 percent basis. The Board processes and tabulates the reported survey data, which can be purchased from the Air Transport Association in either printed book or microfilm. The domestic survey contains eleven tables. The first eight tables are published in printed, bound volumes; the remaining three are on microfilm.

There are basically four types of data books established from the raw survey data. The first set provides information on ticket origination and destination with respect to the carriers and connecting points in the entire passenger ticket in sequential order from the point of origin to the final point of ticketed destination. The second set provides directional origin and destination with respect to the first and last points. The third set provides on-line origin and destination with respect to the points at which a passenger enters and leaves the system of one airline excluding intermediate points of intraline transfer. The final set provides information on coupon origin and destination with respect to the point of deplanement covered by one flight coupon. At present the domestic survey provides traffic data for more than 700 cities and over 59,000 city-pairs.

Similar to the domestic passenger origin and destination survey, the Board also collects data on the international operations of the U.S. carriers. The international survey began in March 1947. These data are restricted because the foreign flag carriers can use it to identify traffic sensitive to competitive diversion. Special permission has to be obtained from the Board before the international data can be released. The survey results are contained in three tables very similar to the eleven tables for the domestic operations.

The reader is cautioned on the use of traffic data. First, numerous changes have been incorporated with respect to sampling methods. However, since January 1968 the survey has been conducted in a consistent format. Second, passengers ticketed entirely on air taxis, commuter carriers, and helicopter carriers are not included. Third, passengers using intrastate carriers, such as Southwest Airlines (Texas) and PSA (California), are not counted. Fourth, traffic carried entirely by foreign flag carriers is not included.

The second major data bank containing traffic statistics is known as the *Service Segment Data*. These data are established on the basis of the operation of an aircraft from a point of take-off to the next point of landing. Thus the Boston-Chicago-Denver-San Francisco flight has three segments. The service segment data are on a 100 percent sample basis for the scheduled operations of the certificated route air carriers. The program was first initiated in 1970. Although the carriers collect information on every single flight operated, data are reported only on a monthly basis by service segment on traffic enplaned, transported, deplaned, and capacity available. The information is further separated by individual flight number, type of aircraft, and class of service. However, for each flight the data are aggregated for the entire month.

The service segment data are particularly useful for performing profitability analysis by individual segment and route in light of such information as load factor by class of service and the contribution to revenue of mail, express, and freight for each segment. Because of the competitive nature of the service segment data, the availability of these data is controlled by the Board in terms of when the data can be released after the carriers have submitted the data. The domestic portion of the data can be purchased 2 years after the time they are reported. The international portion of the data, as the origin and destination survey data discussed earlier, is restricted at all times.

One useful source of aggregate traffic data is the recurrent report entitled *Air Carrier Traffic Statistics*, published since 1954. This book is also known as "The Green Book" and contains information on traffic, capacity, and performance for all regulated air carriers and carrier groups. The traffic data are separated for domestic and international operations, and for scheduled and nonscheduled operations.

In addition to these data sources on traffic, the Board also produces the following five reports:

1. *Passenger Traffic Report, Scheduled Services* (1969)

2. *Adjusted Revenue Passenger-Miles, Available Seat-Miles and Passenger Load Factors, Domestic Trunks, Scheduled Services* (1963)
3. *Cargo Traffic Report, Scheduled Service* (1969)
4. *Air Freight Statistics, Certificated Route Air Carriers, Scheduled and Non-Scheduled Services of U.S. Passenger/Cargo Carriers, Traffic Data* (1967)
5. *Airport Activity Statistics of Certificated Route Air Carriers* (1958)

The last publication, *Airport Activity Statistics*, is published jointly by the Board and the FAA. This annual report contains data on the volume of revenue passenger, freight, express, and mail traffic handled by the U.S. certificated route air carriers at each airport served by these carriers. In addition the report shows the number of aircraft departures including details on aircraft type for total departures performed in scheduled, nonscheduled, and all services. The data are summarized in seven tables.

Special Purpose Reports. In addition to the financial, traffic, costs, and performance data reports, the Board has also published numerous special purpose reports. A partial list of these reports follows:

1. *Book and Regulatory Depreciation of Flight Equipment* (1972)
2. *Airline Property Obtained under Long-Term Leases* (1972)
3. *Aircraft Inventory Report* (1960)
4. *Summary of Airline Taxes* (1973)
5. *Belly Cargo Load Factors on Wide-Bodied Aircraft* (1973)
6. *Airline Investment in Ground Property and Equipment* (1972)
7. *Air Carrier Investments* (1971)
8. *Sale of Regular-Bodied Four Engine Jet Aircraft* (1972)
9. *Holders of Air Carrier Debt* (1965)
10. *Air Freight Loss and Damage Claims* (1972)
11. *Comparative Selected Data for Local Service Carriers* (1958)

Non-CAB Sources

In addition to the above data available through the Board, there are many other government agencies, trade associations, and industry publications that provide the airline analyst with useful data to analyze the industry and perform planning studies. Although it is not feasible to describe all the sources, the following six sources are particularly useful: IATA's *World Air Transport Statistics*, ICAO's *Traffic Flow and Financial Statistics*, Justice Department's *Immigration and Naturalization Traffic Data*, Port Authority of New York and New Jersey's *Traffic Survey Results*, Reuben H. Donnelley's *Official Airline Guides*, and Standard and Poor's *Air Transport Industry Surveys*.

The International Air Transport Association publishes annually the *World Air Transport Statistics*. This publication gives statistics on IATA members' traffic on both scheduled and nonscheduled operations. The data, organized by carrier, consist of aircraft departures, hours flown, passengers carried, revenue passenger kilometers, available seat kilometers, passenger load factor, weight load factor, length of route network, number of employees, composition of aircraft fleet, and daily utilization. Aggregate information is also given for specific areas such as the North, South, and Mid-Atlantic; the information is categorized by types of service, types of operations, and direction. Although the report is published annually, much of the aggregate data are available on a monthly basis.

The International Civil Aviation Organization publishes vast quantities of financial, traffic, and cost data. *Traffic Flow Statistics*, *Financial Statistics*, and *Traffic Statistics* are of particular interest to airline analysts. The financial statistics (F series) give balance sheet and profit and loss statements for the ICAO member carriers. The traffic flow statistics (TF series) provide by airline and country, city-pair traffic data on mail, passengers, and freights. The traffic statistics (T series) contain monthly and yearly traffic statistics for reporting scheduled airlines. These data include aircraft kilometers, departures, revenue passenger hours, and freight ton kilometers for the individual carriers for both scheduled and nonscheduled operations. Both domestic and international data are available. Recently IACO has begun to publish a special digest of statistics entitled *Non-Scheduled Air Transport*. This provides traffic and financial statistics of nonscheduled operators for the ICAO contracting states.

The Immigration and Naturalization Service of the Justice Department publishes statistics by country of origin or destination on passengers arriving in and departing from the United States by air or sea. These data have to be treated carefully because certain types of passengers are not included. For example, U.S. military personnel using commercial and military transports are not included, although civilians on military transport aircraft are counted. Despite these difficulties, the data are extremely useful for performing cross-sectional analysis for international routes.

The Port Authority of New York and New Jersey has been conducting in-flight surveys on flights out of the New York region since November 1955. Surveys on overseas flights have been conducted since 1956. In recent years the overseas surveys for transatlantic flights have been expanded to include flights out of Boston, Chicago, Washington-Dulles, and Philadelphia. Information is collected on trip purpose, trip length, local origin and destination, frequency of travel, family income, age, sex, occupation, marital status, and if traveling in a group, group composition. As well as being very useful in airport planning, the results of these surveys are also valuable for market analysis, since they provide information on passengers and their characteristics.[f]

---

[f]For an excellent description of the surveys with respect to content and methodology, the reader is referred to Fred Hurst, "Survey Programs at Port Authority Airports," in *Airport Economic Planning*, ed. George P. Howard (Cambridge, Massachusetts: Massachusetts Institute of Technology Press, 1974).

The *Official Airline Guide*, both domestic and international editions, are invaluable sources of data for airline market analysis. These guides provide the analyst with the carriers' planned schedules. The historical issues can be used to analyze the supply side of the equation in terms of a carrier's frequency, type of service, type of aircraft, and departure and arrival times. This source is particularly useful for performing airline market share analysis, since it has already been established earlier that market share is strongly influenced by frequency share. Reuben H. Donnelley, the publisher of the *Official Airline Guide*, also provides data on processed magnetic tapes. The information, which is extracted from the airline guides, consists of total frequency by city-pair, carrier, and type of service (nonstop, multistop, and type of aircraft). The analyst can also request total seats by city-pair and share of seats by carrier.

Finally, in its various industry surveys, Standard and Poor has been publishing a basic analysis of the air transport industry since June 11, 1947. Each time a new analysis is performed, it supersedes the prior analysis. The latest in the series was published on April 17, 1975. These surveys discuss the financial, regulatory, and economic aspects of the industry. In addition, they generally provide a very interesting section on "the outlook" for the industry. Although a voluminous amount of statistical data are presented, the market data with respect to airline stock prices, dividends, and price/earning ratios are particularly useful. This information is provided by carrier and usually contains the historical statistics for the prior 10-year period.

Summary

Passenger traffic forecasts are an essential element of both short- and long-range airline planning. Although there are a number of techniques for forecasting air passenger traffic, the differences among the various forecasting methods are due to the degree of formalization of the forecasting procedure. The techniques can generally be classified into judgmental methods, time-series analysis, market research methods, and econometric methods. Each technique has its special use, and the selection of an appropriate technique depends upon a number of factors, such as particular application, available data, projection period, desired accuracy, and the cost of producing the forecast.

During the past two decades the use of econometric methods has been widespread. In the econometric model the forecaster attempts to relate the variation in traffic to the movement of logically relevant economic, demographic, and service-related variables. Typically these models are calibrated through the use of regression analysis. Among the various sources of air transportation data, the CAB collects, edits, summarizes, and publishes enormous volumes of statistics that can be used extensively in developing econometric models to forecast the demand for air transportation.

10 The Regulatory Aspects of Airline Route Development: Domestic and International

It has often been said that a sound route structure is perhaps the most essential element of airline success. The routes of an airline are important not only for normal business operations but also as valuable assets because of the nature of their permanent and protected certificate rights. The economic regulations incorporated into the Federal Aviation Act prohibit an air carrier from offering scheduled service to the public without obtaining a certificate of public convenience and necessity issued by the CAB. It is possible neither for a new carrier to enter the industry on its own decision nor an existing carrier to modify its routes. While entry is controlled, it is not closed at the market level. The extent to which entry is controlled is not in any way fixed by law but rather is subject to the discretion of the Board.

The purpose of this chapter is to highlight the procedure, policy, and discretion of the Board in determining the need and extent of service on a route and the carrier or carriers most suitable to provide this service. It should be clear at the outset that there are no hard and fast rules or critical tests that are used by the Board in route proceedings. Each case is handled on its own merits. The Federal Aviation Act of 1958 (and its predecessor, the Civil Aeronautics Act of 1938) charges the Board to decide on route cases and to ensure that the air transportation system properly meets the public needs and promotes the growth and development of the airline industry. This broad statement of objectives has led the Board over the years to develop its own policy standards in deciding what is in the public interest and good for the industry. The attempt in this chapter is to focus on these general policy standards. The main part of the chapter is developed through an analysis of the decisions in various route cases. Extraction of the Board's policy standards from the various route cases (a difficult task in itself) will not necessarily give clear indications as to the way decisions may go in the future, due to the fact that the Board, using the same policy criteria, has sometimes arrived at very different decisions in cases involving similar routes and similar situations. The existence of inconsistent decisions in a number of cases is not a criticism of the Board's decision-making process but rather an illustration of the many trade-offs that can be made in similar cases. Because there is no mathematical formula, the Board is forced to decide the weight to be attached to each consideration for each particular case. However, an analysis of past decisions does highlight the important factors in route cases, regardless of the verdict of the decision.

Domestic Routes

Factors Considered in Route Cases

Before any carrier or group of carriers can be selected to offer service, the Board has to establish the public's need for such service. The need for service is usually established by analyzing the past traffic carried between the points under consideration, the operating performance of the existing carriers if the service is not new (for example, frequency and load factor), and the potential growth in traffic. The exact points considered and the weight attached to each point depend upon whether the service is new, or whether additional service is being considered. For example, the addition of another carrier on a route may be considered in light of the stimulation in traffic growth by the added service. A general policy of the Board appears to be that if a route shows significant growth potential, then the market will be developed to the greatest extent by the authorization of competitive services.

The selection of a carrier to serve a particular route depends upon a number of factors. The first consideration is usually the determination of the fitness of the applicant to provide the service. This task is conducted through an investigation of the carrier's size, financial resources, flight equipment, strategy for conducting the proposed operations, and its past performance with respect to conforming to the various legal regulations of the certificated operations. With respect to the size of the carrier, the Board has used this consideration both in favor of the carrier as well as against the carrier. For example, a carrier's application may be rejected because it is too small and too weak to provide the service. On the other hand, the same small and weak carrier may be awarded a lucrative route because of the route's impact on the future financial position of the carrier. With respect to the strategy for providing the service, the Board is generally interested in the frequency, schedule, and flight equipment that the carrier intends to use, to determine how economically the carrier can offer the service.

Once the fitness of a particular carrier has been established, the Board then considers the impact of the selected carrier on the carriers already in the market, or on those who are applying for the route. The diversionary effect (that is, the loss of existing carrier's or carriers' traffic) is usually weighted fairly heavily. It should be noted that the extent of diversionary effect depends upon the choice of a carrier. The impact on carriers B and C of awarding the route to A may be different than awarding it to carrier D. Thus the route is more likely to be awarded to the carrier that will result in minimum diversion from the existing carriers. In addition to the question of diversion, consideration is also given to the historical interest of the applicant in the route under consideration. For example, an applicant is more likely to be awarded a route if it is already operating in that market with a long-haul restriction or with connecting service. A carrier's participation in a market is normally looked upon quite favorably.

The appropriateness of the route with respect to the overall route system of the applicant is perhaps the most crucial issue under investigation. If a carrier can demonstrate the logical integration of the route in its system, the applicant will increase its chances of being awarded the route. Route-strengthening is usually achieved through the so-called tying-in factor. This factor indicates that the route should be given to the carrier whose overall route structure would be strengthened, resulting in improved service to the public. The appropriateness of a route can be illustrated by such measures as the ability to provide single carrier service, the existence of back-up traffic, reduction in peaking due to seasonality, and more efficient utilization of an existing fleet. Very often the relative size of the carriers enters the discussion at this point. The Board in the past has made decisions in favor of a particular carrier in order to reduce the disparity in the size of various competitors.

There is a tendancy on the part of the Board to consider domestic routes separately from international routes and trunk-line service separately from the local-carrier service. International route awards involve both the Department of State and the President of the United States (this issue will be discussed in Chapter 14). Sometimes there is a dispute as to whether a particular service can be better provided by a local-service carrier or by a trunk-line carrier. In such cases, the local-service carriers will argue that if they are allowed to operate the route, the total level of federal subsidy will be reduced, thereby reducing the burden on the taxpayer. The trunk-line carriers in return will argue that if the route is self-sufficient (thus requiring no subsidy), it should then be serviced by that part of the industry (trunk-line) that is established to offer such service and is not dependent upon subsidy requirements of the other routes. If the route authority under consideration is clearly the local-service type, selection of the carrier may be based solely upon cost (subsidy) considerations.

Once the Board has authorized a carrier (or a number of carriers) to provide the required service, the Board in theory has very little direct control over the extent of the actual operation, that is, schedules, type of flight equipment, and accommodations. However, the Board does exercise a significant amount of indirect control. The *Transpacific* case illustrates the power of the Board to dictate the type of equipment. The ruling of the Board in Phase 6(A) and (B) of the *Domestic Passenger Fare Investigation* (Chapter 11) is an example of the Board's power with respect to accommodations and schedule frequency. Under the adequacy of service requirements, the Board has the power to force carriers to offer minimum service on authorized routes. If the level of traffic changes on the authorized routes, the Board has the power to alter, amend, modify, or even suspend the authorized service. However, suspension is usually temporary.

In those cases where the Board wishes to limit the degree to which a new competitor can serve a specified route, restrictions are often included in the operating authority of the carrier. The two most common types of route restrictions are: first, the new carrier must make one or more intermediate stops between two points; and second, the new carrier must make one or more stops beyond the cities in the pair under investigation. The first type of restriction limits the new carrier's ability to compete with a nonstop carrier. The second type of restriction prevents the new carrier from offering turn-around service and obtaining a substantial part of the lucrative market. A good example of this is the restriction placed on TWA's operating authority in the *Transpacific* case. For the carrier's service between the U.S. West Coast and Hawaii, the flights were required to continue on to at least Guam. This action blocked TWA's efforts to operate a shuttle service and become an effective competitor in the West Coast-Hawaii market.

Over the years the Board has received more route applications than it can process, given its resources. In such cases the Board has used discretion in acting on these applications, based upon such factors as the time it would take to decide the case, total time the case has been pending, the impact of further delay, the time that has elapsed since the Board considered the service need of the geographic areas involved, the available resources of the Board with respect to its staff.

There are fairly precise administrative procedures used by the Board in formal route proceedings. While it is not necessary, the applications are usually initiated by the carriers. This is followed by a notice of a prehearing conference, where an examiner defines the scope of the proceedings, clarifies the issues, and sets tentative procedural dates. The examiner's findings are written in a report on the prehearing conference, and a notice is issued to all parties on objections and exceptions to the report. Applications for route authority are usually consolidated for simultaneous consideration if they have any bearing on one another, for example, if the grant of one such application would lead to the denial of another application or would seriously prejudice its consideration. This condition in the past has led to some rather lengthy route proceedings that have included a substantial number of parties (carriers and communities) and have encompassed broad geographic regions.

The public hearings usually consist of presentation of oral testimony and cross-examination of the exhibits, which are normally prepared prior to the hearings. At the end of these hearings there is an opportunity to file briefs to the examiner, who then issues a notice of completion to all parties and prepares his initial decision and recommendations to the Board. Once again there is an opportunity to file exceptions and briefs to the examiner's initial decision or recommendation. In the event of no exceptions, his decision is final. If, on the other hand, exceptions and briefs are filed, oral argument can then be presented before the Board, which is now ready to make the final decision. Finally there are means available for reconsideration, in which case there will be supplemental opinions and orders on the reconsideration. Routes involving international operations are subject to Presidential approval for foreign policy considerations.

The Board controls entry both into the industry as well as into individual markets in order to protect the existing carriers from unfair and destructive practices that may not be in the public interest. In short, the Board attempts to discourage the industry from taking on the uneconomic conditions that existed prior to its establishment. Presumably, it is feared that the carriers would practice cut-throat competition, leading to unsafe operations, or that the carriers would offer service only on the profitable routes. This would lead to the reasoning that if the federal government must pay subsidy to ensure service on marginal and unprofitable routes, there is, then, justification for controlling entry.

The grandfather routes have formed the basis of the current domestic trunk-line air transportation system. While no new domestic trunk-line carrier has been authorized since 1938, the Board has significantly expanded the routes of all of the original grandfather carriers. As a result of mergers, the number of trunk-line carriers on the domestic routes is considerably fewer. Since its establishment, the Board has denied the policy of closed entry into the industry. In 1940 it supported this position by pointing to the certification of two new airlines, one for international service and the other for mail.[1] However, in 1941 the Board stated that the number of air carriers then operating were sufficient to ensure against monopoly.[2] Nevertheless it should be pointed out that while new categories of carriers (local-service, all-freight, etc.) have been authorized, no new trunk-line carriers have been certified.

The Board therefore has controlled the extent of competition by expanding the routes of the existing carriers rather than authorizing new carriers. On any given route there are generally two, three, or four effective carriers. Strictly speaking, one could look in the *Official Airline Guide* and find as many as twelve carriers in some markets. However, for all practical purposes there are typically only two to four effective competitive carriers. There is no set number of carriers in any one market, and the Board's policy has been to certificate enough carriers to achieve the effectiveness of competition. However, while Congress authorized the Board to exercise firm control over the expansion of the routes, it did not lay down any definite rule or formula for determining the measure of competition. As noted in Chapter 1, the Declaration of Policy in the Act (Section 102) sets forth a series of general guidelines, such as:

. . . competition to the extent necessary to insure the sound development of an air transportation system properly adapted to the needs of the foreign and domestic commerce of the United States, of the Postal Service, and of the national defense.

While the amount and timing of competition is at the discretion of the Board, the level of traffic has always been viewed by the Board as an important criterion in arriving at that decision. From an important case in 1943:

While no convenient formula of general applicability may be available as a substitute for the Board's discretionary judgement, it would seem to be a sound principle that, since competition in itself presents an incentive to improved service and technological development, there would be a strong, although not conclusive, presumption in favor of competition on any route which offered sufficient traffic to support competing services without unreasonable increase of total operating cost. How that competition would be provided must depend upon the facts and circumstances of each particular case.[3]

The above statement that when there is sufficient traffic, there is a strong, although not conclusive, presumption in favor of competition is known as the "presumption doctrine." The relative importance of presumption in favor of competition as against the "specific facts and circumstances" in individual cases, is one of the aspects of the Board's philosophy that has undergone considerable variation in the years since the 1943 decision. Often the Board has been accused of favoring competition for competition's sake. The Board has denied this by stating that it considers numerous factors in each case, such as volume of potential traffic, total operating costs, benefits to the public in the form of improved service, and the financial conditions of the carrier. However, in 1944 the Board reversed its opinion and stated:

The mere fact that a particular route develops a large volume of traffic does not of itself afford sufficient justification for finding that the public convenience and necessity require establishment of an additional service exactly duplicating an existing operation. The public interest which must be served can only be determined after consideration of all the factors and circumstances surrounding each case.[4]

The argument that the Board has authorized too much competition that has not been in the public interest is based partly upon the contention that when two carriers operate over the same route by splitting the traffic between them, each carrier, in effect, is serving a lower density route. Since load factor is related to density, it also generally declines. Low load factors raise the cost of providing the service, which in turn leads to higher fares. However, the issue regarding the amount of competition is more complex. While a higher level of competition will lower load factors, less competition will result in high load factors, which in turn will lead to greater inconvenience to passengers. Thus it is quite possible that the increased inconvenience may deter some passengers from travelling, even if the fares were to be reduced. In any case, the contention that greater competition will result in lower load factors assumes little or no traffic generation effect from the increased number of schedules.

The critical issue is not the need for competition but the extent of competition. For example, too much competition can be worse than none. In the long-haul markets with light traffic flow, splitting the traffic in too many parts may produce poor results for all carriers, and the public may in fact receive worse service. The introduction of superior aircraft is a result of competition, but excessive competition may and has produced the effect of letting the carriers acquire the latest equipment prematurely, thereby jeopardizing their financial stability. Finally, the question of internal cross-subsidy must not be overlooked. Since carriers support their weak routes with the lucrative ones, excessive competition should not automatically cause these good routes to become marginal or unprofitable. The lucrative routes cannot be considered to be extra profitable if they are supporting some other weak routes.

Analysis of Selected Route Cases

West Coast Case. Some of the points raised so far were brought out in the two *West Coast* cases, 6 CAB 961 (1946) and 8 CAB 14 (1947). In the first *West Coast* case, American requested an extension of its route from Los Angeles to San Francisco on the basis that this would provide single-carrier service to and from San Francisco to passengers originating or terminating at points on its system. At the time, the route was served by three carriers: TWA, United, and Western. TWA provided services on this route as an extension of one of its routes, subject to the condition that service between San Francisco and Los Angeles would be limited to flights originating or terminating at points east of Albuquerque. United served the market on its route extending between San Diego and Vancouver. Western provided local service on the route. American's justification of a single-carrier service to its transcontinental passengers was further supported by the carrier's contention that San Francisco, one of the most important cities on the West Coast, needed service by three transcontinental carriers. These arguments were supported by the volume of traffic between Los Angeles and San Francisco and the number of San Francisco passengers, originating or terminating on American's system, forced to change planes at Los Angeles. In rejecting American's application the Board stated that the existing level of service was adequate to meet the public need. Furthermore, if American had been granted the route, not only would there be significant diversion of local traffic from TWA, United, and Western, but both TWA and United would experience a significant loss of their transcontinental traffic.

In its application TWA requested the removal of the restriction that prevented the carrier from conducting a shuttle type of service. TWA supported its request with traffic statistics (from September 1, 1943 to September 1, 1944) showing that almost 50 percent of the passengers carried by it were local passengers. In addition to this, the carrier stated that it was turning away 50 percent as much business as it carried between Los Angeles and San Francisco. The Board rejected the application on two counts. First, the traffic statistics cited by TWA were taken during war time and did not reflect peace-time traffic conditions. Second, the removal of the operating restriction would have harmful competitive effects on United and Western.

Western, in its application, requested authority to operate from San Francisco to Seattle (with intermediate stops) on the one hand, and between San Francisco and Portland, on the other. At the time, United was the only carrier providing similar service. Western's application was rejected for the following reasons. First, the record did not indicate the need for service to the intermediate points. Of all the intermediate points listed in Western's route application, only one lacked the needed air service, and the Board was willing to add that point to United's route due both to its substantial community of interest with San Francisco and Portland and to the difficulties in surface transportation to those cities. Second, there was no evidence of the need for a second carrier to compete with United between San Francisco, Portland, and Seattle. The Board stated that competition was not justified for competition's sake.

The Civil Aeronautics Act did not make competition mandatory but rather left the question to the Board's discretion. The Board will authorize additional service if the traffic potential exists, and if there is no financial impairment to the existing carrier. The Board may also introduce new service on a route if such service would improve some long-haul service connected to the route under investigation. In this case, it would be considered a route extension. If a route extension results in competition, then competition must be considered incidental and not the justification for the extension itself. In Western's application, neither of these conditions was met. There was no evidence of traffic potential, and the extension of Western's route to include San Francisco-Seattle would not have improved long-haul service. Finally, the Board reiterated that the present decision was based solely upon existing conditions, and that it was "not required to act now, or forever refrain from authorizing a new service on this route."

At the request of American and Western, the *West Coast* case was reopened in 1947. This time American submitted an application for service to San Francisco through various points east of Los Angeles, such as Phoenix. The Board approved the application to offer direct service between Phoenix and San Francisco/Oakland, subject to the restriction that all flights serving San Francisco/Oakland must stop at Tulsa, Dallas, or a point west thereof, other than San Francisco/Oakland. This decision was based upon the following considerations. First, San Francisco supposedly had a special need for convenient long-haul transportation due to its geographic location on the West Coast. Second, the average trip length of San Francisco passengers was relatively higher than for other cities, such as Boston, Detroit, and Washington. Third, the number of passengers affected by American's one-carrier service had increased significantly. Fourth, there had been significant industrial growth in the areas from which American could provide transportation to San Francisco. The restriction was placed so as to provide TWA and United with a significant mileage advantage to cities commonly served by American and either one of the other two carriers. Thus this restriction would prevent significant diversion from both TWA and United.

Western was allowed to extend its route to Seattle via Portland, subject to the condition that flights between Portland and Seattle originate or terminate at San Francisco/Oakland or a point south thereof. The question, then, is why did the Board reject the application in 1946 and then approve it in 1947? Two justifications were offered. First, new estimates of traffic potential (postwar) were higher than those previously available. Second, in the *Latin American* case the Board had authorized Western to serve the Mexico City-Los Angeles route; consequently, the San Francisco-Seattle route would now be treated as an extension resulting in a single-carrier service from Mexico City to Seattle. Thus this reversal in the Board's decision was explained by "a reappraisal of the record in the light of the added factors." This case also illustrates the fact that the weight given to each factor is subject to change. In 1946 the advantage of a single-carrier service was outweighed by the deterioration in the strength of the existing carrier. But just one year later top consideration was given to single-carrier service as being very much in the public interest.

Southern Service to the West Coast Case. Another important case that highlights the Board's reasoning in route cases is the *Southern Service to the West Coast* case, 12 CAB 519 (1959). Like the previous case, this one was also decided twice. The first investigation examined the need for through-service between various southeastern and southern points in the United States and points on the West Coast. Six carriers were party to the case. Existing service was conducted by connecting services at Dallas between Delta (east of Dallas) and American (west of Dallas). Applications for new authorization by American, Braniff, Continental, Delta, Eastern, and National contained proposals to provide single-carrier service, which would greatly expand the domestic air transportation system.

The Board studied the traffic estimates provided by each carrier and concluded that the traffic would not support more than one carrier. In fact the Board's analysis indicated that a single daily round trip with a DC-6 would accommodate all the existing traffic between the southeast, central, south, and west. New service was not needed for the local traffic. Since the traffic required only one carrier, the problem was obvious. No one applicant had more historic interest in the market than another. None of the applicants was established at both end points. The award of this route to any carrier would have had significant impact on the selected carrier's historic share of the market and significant diversionary effects on the others. The rejection of all applications, on the other hand, would have denied single-carrier service to the public. The issue was resolved by the Board's approval of appropriate interchange operations between connecting carriers. Interchange service authority was granted to National, Delta, and American for through-service between Miami, New Orleans, Dallas, and points west thereof. Similarly, interchange service was granted to Braniff, Continental, and American for through-service between Houston, San Antonio, El Paso, and points west thereof.

Ten years later the southern transcontinental route again came up for consideration, this time in the *Southern Transcontinental Service* case, 33 CAB 701 (1961). And once again the Board set out to determine the need for improved transcontinental and interregional air transportation in the southern tier of the United States, extending from Florida and Georgia to California, including Alabama, Mississippi, Louisiana, Texas, New Mexico, and Nevada. In addition to the original six carriers, applications were also received from TWA and Western. In light of a substantial increase in population and industrial development, the Board decided that a need existed for new and additional single-carrier service across the southern tier of the states, and that the transsouthern interchange agreements should be replaced with direct one-carrier transcontinental service. The basic issues to be resolved were the number of southern transcontinental carriers, the points to be included on the new transcontinental routes, and the selection of carriers that would provide this new service.

The examiner in this case described, at great length, the rationale behind his choice of carriers to serve individual routes. The first and foremost point highlighted by the examiner was the doctrine of strengthening the weaker carriers. Despite this policy of the Board, the dominance of the Big Four on all domestic routes had decreased only slightly, from 75 percent in 1955 to 71 percent in 1958. While the share of total domestic traffic ranged from 15 to 20 percent for three of the Big Four carriers party to this case, the share of the other carriers party to this case ranged from 1.7 to 5.7 percent. The next argument made in favor of selecting Braniff, Continental, Delta, National, and Western over American, Eastern, and TWA was the smaller carriers' need for access to city-pair segments of long stage lengths in order to justify the economic use of jet aircraft. National was singled out to show its need for longer haul segments, since its existing long-haul routes were concentrated in Florida markets, which were affected both by seasonality and unpredictable declines in traffic due to occasionally adverse weather conditions in Florida during the vacation season and varying economic conditions in the North.

The selection of a carrier was not an easy task in this case. On the one hand, only the larger carriers—American, Eastern, and TWA—had the equipment, resources, and connecting service patterns to assure satisfactory service to the public. On the other hand, the smaller carriers needed more mileage, markets, and traffic to assure their survival in the jet age. In any event, it was not feasible to authorize just one carrier (big or small) to provide all the services that the record demonstrated were required for the public convenience and necessity. More precisely, the selection of just one carrier was rejected on two counts. First, route authority of such magnitude would have made it impossible to ever achieve a reasonable degree of competitive balance in the southern transcontinental area. Second, the award of all routes to one carrier would have had a significant effect on the carriers not selected, since all had been serving parts of the area in question.

The final decision was to award individual routes to five carriers, three small and two large. The smaller carriers received significant route authority. National received authority to serve Houston-West Coast nonstop. Delta received authority to serve Dallas-West Coast nonstop. Eastern was awarded the route from Dallas to Miami. American and Continental were granted additional authority throughout the interior points in the West. The main points for individual selections of smaller carriers are best illustrated by the National airline situation: historic interest, need for route strengthening, good integration into the existing route system, reduction in seasonality problems, single-carrier service to the West Coast, and minimal diversionary impact. American was particularly distressed about the award of Dallas-West Coast to Delta due to the diversionary impact. The Board tried to console American by stating that it was recently awarded participation in the lucrative New York-San Francisco market (worth about $12 million annually in gross revenue), which should offset most of the loss due to diversion in the present case. With regard to service from Texas to Florida, the examiner recommended that Braniff serve Fort Worth-Dallas-Houston-New Orleans-Tampa-St. Petersburg/Clearwater-Miami/Fort Lauderdale. The Board, on the other hand, selected Eastern to serve Fort Worth-Dallas-New Orleans-Tampa-St. Petersburg/Clearwater-Miami/Fort Lauderdale. According to policy cited earlier regarding relative size of carrier, the choice should have been Braniff. However, Braniff's proposed single-carrier service to points beyond Dallas was not considered attractive. On the other hand, the Dallas-Florida route integrated well with Eastern's share of the route system.

Next, a number of route cases decided in 1955 and 1956 will be examined, since each one of these illustrates a significant point. Each of the cases is described in sufficient detail to highlight the relevant point only.[a]

New York-Chicago Service Case. In the *New York-Chicago Service* case, 22 CAB 973 (1955), several airlines applied for authorization to provide new or additional services in the general area bounded on the east by New York, on the west by Chicago, on the north by Rochester, and on the south by Pittsburgh. Having established the need for competitive service, both Capital and Northwest were awarded the significant routes based upon the integration of these routes into their systems and on the needs of these two carriers. The choice of Capital was made because the public would benefit most from having regional services provided by a regional carrier. Whereas Capital was interested in developing the short-haul routes under consideration, other applicants were most interested in improving their long-haul interregional or transcontinental services by using the routes applied for in this case as extensions. Furthermore, Capital's interest in developing the coach service was clear from its record, and the grant of the route authority under consideration would further stimulate the development of coach service in this area. It is interesting to note the Board's comment regarding

[a]Interested readers should refer to the actual text, which usually runs into several hundred pages.

Colonial, which did not get the route authorization but which did show the need for route strengthening. Although Colonial was badly in need of route strengthening, this carrier's application was denied because the Board felt that Colonial would be able neither to provide the required service on the New York-Chicago route nor compete actively with other carriers on the route.

The other significant point in this case was the application of a noncertificated carrier. North American Airlines, a group of six very small noncertificated airlines, applied for a certificate to conduct coach-only operations on a route between New York and Chicago via Philadelphia, Pittsburgh, Cleveland, and Detroit. North American did not apply for authority to carry mail but was willing to do so without subsidy and at rates agreeable to the Post Office Department, if this was a necessary condition to obtaining the grant of a certificate of public convenience and necessity. The carrier stated that it was in the public interest to certificate a nonsubsidized carrier that would provide an incentive for the development of coach traffic and, at the same time, provide the Board with a yardstick to measure the success of the subsidized carriers. North American was aware of the fact that in industries that require a large investment, such as public utilities, competition would be wasteful and not in the public interest. However, this did not apply to the airline industry. The carrier argues that in 1951 the ratio of investment to revenue was 390 percent for electric utilities, 268 percent for natural gas, 302 percent for telephone companies, 189 percent for railroads, and only 36 percent for the domestic trunk-line industry. The carrier claimed that based upon actual data, there was no evidence of economies of scale. Furthermore, existing carriers should not be allowed to earn excessive profits on heavy traffic routes in order to subsidize service to smaller communities. Finally the carrier produced extensive evidence showing that sufficient traffic existed on this route to prevent any carrier from suffering financially. The Board rejected all of these arguments and in addition stated that the carrier was not fit, willing, or able to comply with the Act, and that "the central figures in North American have a long history of association with flagrant violations of the Act and are not sufficiently reliable to be entrusted with the operation of the proposed certificated routes."

Denver Service Case. In the *Denver Service* case, 22 CAB 1178 (1955), six carriers applied for new or additional east-west service for Denver, Kansas City, Salt Lake City, and Reno, in the area between Chicago, on the one hand, and San Francisco/Oakland and Los Angeles, on the other. Further, this case involved determining whether any need existed for additional through-service via equipment interchange between the points west of Chicago listed above and points east of the Chicago and Kansas City gateways. The central issue in this case was the determination of the necessity for competitive east-west service and the selection of carriers to provide this service. This route authority between Chicago and California, while limited in geographic area, comprised almost two-thirds the width of the country. In addition, the area between Chicago and the East Coast was involved to some extent.

The first order of business was to establish the need for additional service. The new carriers applying for authority presented substantial evidence indicating the need for additional service. The evidence included data that demonstrated the lag in air traffic growth relative to economic growth in the area and the inferiority of the existing service as evidenced by under-scheduling high load factors, lack of equipment, and the underdevelopment of coach services. The existing carriers rejected these arguments with substantial traffic and service data. The Board analyzed the data and decided that existing service was indeed inadequate. Having resolved this issue, the Board was faced with the decision of selecting one or more carriers to provide the needed service. Again, each carrier opposed the proposals of all others, either as defense against new competition or due to the rivalry between applicants.

For reasons cited in earlier cases—the carriers' needs argument and the route strengthening argument—the examiner ruled in favor of two small carriers, Continental and Western. The examiner recommended first that Continental's route be extended from Denver to Los Angeles and from Kansas City to Chicago, and second that Western extend its route from Denver to San Francisco/Oakland via Salt Lake City and Reno. Third, he recommended that a Continental-Capital interchange at Chicago provide additional through-service to and from Denver and Kansas City. The first two recommendations were made to strengthen the two regional carriers. The third recommendation was made to meet Denver's need for additional long-haul services and at the same time minimize the diversion from Continental and avoid diversion from Western.

The Board basically agreed with the examiner's decision regarding Continental's route from Denver to Los Angeles and Kansas City to Chicago and Western's route from Denver to San Francisco. However, the Board rejected the Continental-Capital interchange at Chicago on two counts. First, the interchange was inferior to a single-carrier transcontinental service. In the Board's opinion Denver's needs justified service by a second transcontinental carrier. The interchange service, as proposed, could not compete effectively with United's service to the East. Second, an additional transcontinental carrier was needed to serve Denver because of the impact it would have on Denver's coach service. United's coach service, particularly to New York and Washington, was considered inadequate.

The Board selected TWA to provide this competitive service for Denver. While American was also a party to the case, the Board selected TWA for a number of reasons. First, TWA had a sales office in Denver for the previous 9 years and in 1953 alone had sold three-quarters of a million dollars worth of travel. Second, TWA was already a significant participant in the Denver traffic to the cities to which the carrier proposed new one-carrier service. Third, TWA provided coach service more aggressively than American. In order to protect the small carriers from the diversionary effect, the Board prevented TWA from serving Denver with Kansas City or St. Louis on the same flight and placed a long-haul restriction on its service between Denver and Los Angeles and San Francisco. Finally, the Board granted American the authority to serve Chicago-San Francisco nonstop and gave United the authority to serve Kansas City-West Coast markets.

New York-Florida Case. Another case worthy of investigation is the *New York-Florida* case, 24 CAB 94 (1956), and the related *New York-Florida Renewal* case. This case shows how the Board may change its decision, and the arguments used to defend its change in policy. In 1956 the Board extended Northeast's route beyond New York to Miami via Philadelphia, Baltimore, Washington, and Tampa on a temporary basis for a period of 5 years. At the time, the same markets were served by both National and Eastern with permanent certificates. Northeast had been providing local service on short-haul routes within the New England area on a subsidized basis. The carrier had been losing money heavily and needed strengthening by participation in a long-haul, high-density market. East Coast-Florida markets were experiencing high traffic growth rates that were expected to continue into the future. This route would be profitable for Northeast, and the general feeling was that the route would enable the carrier to become self-sufficient. Northeast was receiving government subsidy totalling about $1.5 million per year that it was willing to forego if it were awarded the route to Miami. The Board believed that New England would benefit for two reasons: first, by one-carrier service to points in the south and second, by the improved service in the New England area itself.

The route came up for renewal in 1961, and after two years of investigation the Board denied Northeast's application for renewal of the East Coast-Florida route. The matter was taken to court, and the case was reopened. The basic issue in the case was whether public convenience and necessity required the renewal of Northeast's temporary authority to operate New York-Miami service via intermediate points. The Court asked the Board to provide its rationale for the decision to deny the renewal application. Was the decision justified on grounds that there was no need for a third carrier on this route or was it that Northeast's application was not in the public interest?

In its reply to the Court, the Board stated that a standard issue in any proceeding under Section 401 is whether the applicant's proposed service could be offered economically. In the Board's opinion, the service could not be operated economically and therefore the request for renewal was denied. In addition to this, consideration is also given to subsidiary issues such as:

1. Whether the new service will serve a useful purpose, responsive to a public need.
2. Whether this purpose can and will be served as well by existing carriers.

3. Whether it can be served by the applicant with the new service without impairing the operations of existing carriers contrary to the public interest.
4. Whether any cost of the proposed service to the government will be outweighed by the benefit that will accrue to the public from the new service.

Subsidy is usually not an issue in cases involving trunk-line carriers; instead, high priority is given to making the carrier self-sufficient through a more rational route structure. Therefore, according to the Board, the main issue was not whether the service on this route was in the public interest, but whether Northeast was the appropriate carrier to provide this service. A service may be in the public interest if offered by one carrier, and not, if offered by another carrier.

The Board went on to justify its decision by stating that the circumstances had changed since its initial decision in 1956. At that time it had been in the public interest to award the route to Northeast; 5 years later this was no longer the case. In any case, even at the time of the initial award, the Board was not sure of its action, which is why the route award was made on a temporary rather than permanent basis. The carrier was supposed to integrate the route into its structure and become self-sufficient. Instead the carrier let its New England routes deteriorate, resulting in the continuation of its financial problems. Due to the lack of expected traffic growth, the carrier went from a small profit of approximately $800,000 in 1956 to a retained loss of almost $44 million in 1962, posting a negative stockholder's equity. Most of Northeast's difficulties were due to the lack of anticipated traffic growth in the East Coast-Florida markets, lack of other long-haul routes to provide traffic during off-peak months, and disparity of flight equipment requirements between the carrier's short-haul local routes in New England and its relatively long-haul route to Florida.

With regard to the issue of need for a third carrier on the route, the Board reversed its opinion between the time of the initial award and the time for its renewal. In 1956 there was a need for a third carrier, since both Eastern and National were unable to meet traffic demands at peak periods. Both of these carriers focused their attention on the lucrative New York-Miami market. On the other hand, with the introduction of jet aircraft with higher productivity, these two carriers were able to provide sufficient capacity to meet the traffic demands. The Board's analysis of traffic data for the peak period 1962-1963 indicated quite clearly that had Northeast not been in existence, Eastern and National could have accommodated, with the exception of the Boston-Miami traffic, the total traffic needs of the major Florida nonstop markets without additional capacity, and one additional daily round trip would have been sufficient to handle the Boston-Miami traffic. Northeast attempted to convince the Board by pointing out other markets that had less traffic with three competitors and by citing the benefits to the public of additional frequency and capacity. The Board rejected both of these arguments. First, since each case is handled on its own merits, a decision in one market cannot be taken as a standard for another market. Second, due to the costs of additional flight equipment and station costs, the benefits of extra capacity and frequency are not free. In rejecting the application for a third carrier on the market, the Board also cited Eastern's financial losses in the period from 1960 to 1963.

The Board's decision was once again appealed to the courts, but the decision was still the same. Northeast protested the decision on the grounds of improper use of data submitted to the Board. The carrier attempted to offer further data supporting its case, but the Board refused to hear this new evidence. The Court took sides with Northeast and ordered the Board to provide the carrier with an opportunity to explain its case. In 1965 the Board reopened the entire case for a complete review of the issues. During this investigation the Board's position changed. Three factors were cited for the reversal in the Board's position. First, the expected growth in traffic was more favorable. Second, Eastern's financial status was no longer of concern. Third, investment in Northeast by the Storer Broadcasting Company completely changed the capital structure of the carrier. Accordingly the Board found that Northeast should be selected as the third carrier to provide East Coast-Florida service and renewed its certificate on a permanent basis. The other applicants to the case did not challenge the final decision.

New York-San Francisco Case. In the *New York-San Francisco Nonstop Service* case, 29 CAB 811 (1959), American and Northwest applied for nonstop service from New York/Newark to San Francisco/Oakland to compete with TWA and United. Prior to this application, both TWA and United were authorized to provide nonstop service, and American was authorized to provide one-stop service through Chicago. The need for a third carrier on the market was based upon the economic importance of the two cities, the traffic growth, the existing limited nonstop schedules of TWA and United, the small number of coach seats available in comparison to the number of through passengers in the market, the unduly high load factors experienced by TWA and United, the inconveniences caused by the inability to obtain the desired space and departure time on nonstop flights during the peak months in 1957, and the availability of jet aircraft. While significant diversionary effects were evident, the Board believed that the benefits to the public of a fully competitive service in this market outweighed the loss in revenue due to diversion. In any case, according to the Board, expected traffic growth in the market was sufficient to offset traffic lost by the existing carriers. Ironically enough, it is the carriers most concerned about diversion in their own markets who press for additional competition in markets in which they are not authorized to operate.

Having established the need for additional service, the selection of a carrier was not an easy matter. Both American and Northwest were fit, willing, and able to provide the service. The Board selected American over Northwest on the grounds that American was already in the market as a restricted carrier and had been a substantial participant in the New York-San Francisco traffic. The carrier had an established identity in the market, and this would be instrumental in stimulating the new nonstop service. Northwest, on the other hand, had never been certificated to serve San Francisco and, for all practical purposes, was a newcomer to the New York-San Francisco market. Northwest pointed to the Board's policy in the *Denver Service* case favoring the strengthening of small carriers in order to achieve a better competitive balance. The Board stated that while these factors were important and were in Northwest's favor, other factors, such as historic interest, market identity, and route structure, were considered more important in this particular case. It is interesting to note that the major consideration favoring American was the carrier's existing participation in the market. However, it was the Board's decision in the *Denver Service* case that authorized American to serve Chicago-San Francisco in the first place.

Detroit-California Case. The *Detroit-California Nonstop Service Investigation*, 43 CAB 557 (1966), illustrates another precedent in domestic route awards. In this case, the problem was to determine whether the public convenience and necessity required modification of the certificates of American, TWA, and United, which allowed them to operate nonstop and turn-around services between Detroit and Los Angeles and between Detroit and San Francisco. All three carriers were previously servicing these markets with restrictive authority. The basic issue was the selection of the carrier. Since all three carriers were fit, willing, and able, with strong financial positions and roughly equal potential benefit with respect to route structure, the choice of the carrier was not clear. One thing that was clear was that if only one carrier were selected, the other two would suffer significant diversionary effects.

With such little differentiation among the three applicants, the Board empowered all of them to provide the nonstop service. This decision, made in 1966, was based upon a precedent set in 1955 in the *Louisville-New York Nonstop Investigation*, 21 CAB 794 (1955). In that investigation the Board needed to select a carrier to serve nonstop the Louisville-New York market. All three carriers party to the case—American, Eastern, and TWA—were serving the market with operating restrictions. All three were granted nonstop authority based upon two arguments. First, operating restrictions had outlived their usefulness and were now inhibiting improved service to the public. Second, the award of nonstop authority to only one carrier would destroy the existing competitive balance among the carriers. While the two cases are similar, it is interesting to note that the *Louisville-New York* decision was made in 1955—ten years prior to the *Detroit-California* decision—when the equipment operated by the carriers had much less capacity than the jets.

International Routes

The North Atlantic Route Cases

Prior to the establishment of the CAB, Pan American was the only United States carrier offering service from the United States to other foreign points. The Board was in favor of introducing competition for such obvious reasons as improved service through improved equipment, improved operating techniques, and promotion. In addition, the establishment of a competitor for Pan American would provide the Board with some means of comparing performance. With the policy of favoring competition, the Board authorized American Export Airlines [2 CAB 16 (1940)] to provide service between New York and Lisbon via the Azores. The Board justified its decision on the grounds that Pan American's monopoly was not in the public interest.

In 1945 the Board expanded service by U.S. flag carriers on the North Atlantic [6 CAB 319 (1945)] by giving new authorization to three U.S. carriers for a period of 7 years. Pan American's routes were extended beyond London, through Central Europe and the Near East, to Calcutta. TWA was awarded routes from the United States through Southern Europe to Bombay via Cairo and certain North African countries. American Export was authorized to serve Northern Europe, including the Scandinavian countries and Leningrad and Moscow. Again the decision was made to increase competition. In addition, the Board stated that the traditional division between domestic and international carriers, based upon the differences between landplane and flying-boat operations, was no longer valid. American Export was required to sever itself from its parent, the shipping company. In 1945, American Airlines purchased American Export, made it the North Atlantic division of the company, and changed its name to American Overseas Airlines. Pan American was selected because of its experience in the international field. TWA was selected because of its excellent record of operating efficiency in domestic service, sound financial position, and international experience gained during the war in flying for the armed forces. American Export was selected because of its experience and its newly acquired strength from the merger with American Airlines.

Pan American argued against the certification of additional U.S. carriers on the North Atlantic. First, it was inevitable that some foreign flag carriers would be authorized to compete on the North Atlantic. This proved to be very true. From 1946 to 1949 the Board granted authority to twenty-four foreign flag carriers to serve the United States and its possessions. Second, proper development of the North Atlantic would require the establishment of low-cost service using new, large, high-speed flight equipment, which would not be feasible if the available traffic were divided among several U.S. flag carriers. The Board rejected these arguments. Pan American, realizing that it could no longer keep other carriers away, changed its strategy. First, Pan American protested the distribution of routes among the carriers, with the result that its certificate was amended to provide service to the Azores, Bermuda, and Newfoundland, including Dublin as an intermediate point between Brussels and Prague, and eliminating New Brunswick as an intermediate point. In 1950 Pan American requested permission to buy and transfer all assets (including routes) of American Overseas, as well as approval for certain changes in the route pattern. The merger between American Overseas and Pan American was approved with the result that Pan American and TWA had approximately the same opportunity to serve the major European capitals, such as Frankfurt, London, Paris, and Rome. TWA's route authority on the Atlantic was expanded to connect with Northwest's authority on the Pacific, resulting in a second round-the-world U.S. carrier service.

The authorization issued in 1945 on the North Atlantic expired in 1952. In the first *North Atlantic Route Transfer* case, 15 CAB 1053 (1952), both Pan American and TWA's transatlantic route authority was renewed until July 4, 1959 with some changes. TWA was granted a permanent route from New York to Paris and Rome via Newfoundland, Ireland, or the Azores. Pan American was authorized to serve Nice and Lisbon via the Azores. In the second *Transatlantic Renewal* case in 1959 the above certificates were further renewed until 1966. The third *Transatlantic Route Renewal* case was heard in 1966 [44 CAB 9 (1966)], when significant amendments were made to the route pattern. These modifications reflected the growth of the U.S. West Coast. There were now two groups of coterminals: one in the East and Midwest consisting of Boston, New York, Philadelphia, Washington, D.C., Detroit, and Chicago; and one in the West consisting of Los Angeles, San Francisco, Portland (Oregon) and Seattle. Pan American requested that its East and West Coast coterminals be converted into one set of coterminals. In this application, Pan American was essentially requesting stop-over privileges at New York for passengers travelling between the West Coast and Europe on transcontinental flights. The examiner estimated this benefit to be worth $2 million to Pan American. The President asked the Board to consider the effect of this action, as it would place the U.S. air carriers on a comparable basis with foreign carriers, such as Qantas and BOAC, and any other Pacific carrier (Japan Air Lines, no doubt) authorized to serve New York and beyond to Europe. In addition, Seaboard was authorized to provide property and mail transportation between major capitals in Western Europe and Boston, New York, Philadelphia, and Baltimore.

The other significant policy issue in the third *Transatlantic Route Renewal* case was related to the area concept of route awards. The Board rejected this concept in this investigation as well as in the *Transpacific* case in 1969 [51 CAB 161 (1969)]. From 1940 to 1945 the Board had followed a policy of point-to-point competition. Between 1945 and 1950 the policy was to authorize service by exclusive areas.[b] The Board's decision to use the area concept was

---

[b]The reader is reminded that American Overseas was given the northern route via Scandinavia to Russia; Pan American was given the central route via England and Germany to northern India; and TWA was given the southern route via France and Iberia to southern India.

based upon the belief that indirect competition among U.S. carriers serving competing destinations was more appropriate than the point-to-point competition, given the uncertainties of traffic potential and the significant participation by the foreign flag carriers. Furthermore, it was easier to negotiate bilateral agreements if there was only one U.S. flag carrier designated in each market. However, in 1950 the policy was reversed again—this time in favor of point-to-point competition, when Pan American (having merged with American Overseas) and TWA were authorized to compete in four major European destinations: Frankfurt, London, Paris, and Rome. This policy was still in force during the *Transatlantic Route Renewal* case in 1966.

The *Transatlantic Route Renewal* case was once again investigated in 1967 to resolve two issues. The first issue was with reference to U.S. service to Dublin [46 CAB 64 (1967)]. The President asked the Board to select one U.S. carrier to serve Dublin. The Board selected Pan American due to its greater historical interest, greater traffic participation, earlier use of jets; and furthermore the service to Dublin seemed to integrate well into Pan American's transatlantic schedule. TWA was rejected by the Board because, in its opinion, the carrier did not require Dublin service in light of its excellent financial condition, its sound route structure, and its steadily increasing participation in the transatlantic market. Seaboard was eliminated since it was not in the public interest to designate an all-cargo carrier as the only carrier to serve Dublin. The second issue was with respect to Pan American's application to convert East Coast, Midwest, and West coterminals into one set of coterminals. The Board had denied this request the previous year. However, in the reopened case [46 CAB 75 (1966)] the Board reversed its previous decision. In the previous decision, the authority requested was denied on the grounds that it was not needed to place Pan American on an equal footing with Qantas and BOAC, due to the fact that Pan American's West Coast routes could be operated via polar routes. However, the reverse decision a year later was justified on the grounds that the service on the polar routes was different than service via New York.

In 1969 the Board authorized National to serve the Miami-London route [51 CAB 1007 (1969)]. Unlike the previous transatlantic cases, this case involved the certification of a new carrier on the Atlantic. The examiner had recommended that Pan American serve this route for several reasons: (1) Pan American's anticipated ability to promote the new service and develop traffic potential to its maximum extent, and (2) there was a need for a complimentary route structure beyond London. The Board selected National over Pan American because of the strength that the route would provide for the carrier. The Board cited the importance of traffic at the source, rather than at the destination, as a significant factor in the choice of National. This is directly consistent with the Board's choice of Western over Hawaiian in the *Transpacific* case. National's well developed identity in Florida and the back-up traffic from numerous U.S. cities were also cited as factors influencing the Board's choice. The fact that National did not possess any routes beyond London was of no consequence, since London was an established major connecting point. The fact that National had no international experience was even more reason for the carrier to develop this market more extensively than Pan American. As National would have just one major international route, it was expected that the carrier would conscientiously and vigorously develop this market, whereas Pan American would treat this as just another route in its system. Finally, the fact that National did not possess the appropriate aircraft was overlooked by the Board in light of National's commitment to purchase such equipment in time to inaugurate service.[c]

In 1973 the temporary transatlantic authority of the U.S. flag carriers had expired once again, and on September 21, 1973 the Board instituted the *Transatlantic Route Proceedings* to consider: (1) if the temporary authority of National, Pan American, Seaboard, and TWA should be renewed, and to what extent; (2) if additional domestic coterminals should be certificated, and which carriers should be selected; and (3) if the temporary certificates of the six supplemental air carriers should be renewed.

At present there are four U.S. carriers holding permanent and/or temporary certificates to offer scheduled service between the United States and Europe. For these carriers the permanent U.S. coterminals are shown in Table 10-1. Within Europe, each of the three combination carriers has permanent authority at different points. The permanent points for Pan American are the Azores, Shannon, and London. For TWA the permanent points are Ireland (with the

Table 10-1
Permanent U.S. Coterminals of U.S. International Carriers Operating on the North Atlantic

Baltimore/Washington	Pan American, TWA, Seaboard
Boston	Pan American, TWA, Seaboard
Chicago	Pan American, TWA, Seaboard
Cleveland	Seaboard
Detroit	Pan American, TWA, Seaboard
Los Angeles	Pan American, TWA, Seaboard
Miami	National
New York	Pan American, TWA, Seaboard
Philadelphia	Pan American, TWA, Seaboard
Portland	Pan American
San Francisco	Pan American, TWA, Seaboard
Seattle	Pan American

Source: U.S. Civil Aeronautics Board, *Transatlantic Route Investigation*, (Docket 25908), Examiner's initial decision, Washington, D.C., January 1975, pp. 9-10.

[c]Compare this with selection of Western over Hawaiian in the *Transpacific* case because Western possessed the appropriate jet aircraft and Hawaiian did not.

exception of Dublin) and Paris. For National the permanent and only point is London.[d] The remaining points on these carriers' routes are on a temporary basis. Table 10-2 shows the various applications of the combination carriers.

During the investigation, the Board's Bureau of Operating Rights recommended that Braniff, Delta, and Northwest be certificated to compete with National, Pan American, and TWA on the North Atlantic. The city-pairs were selected in such a manner that head-to-head competition was eliminated. The Bureau pointed out that this would reduce excess capacity and encourage the carriers to provide improved service. It was proposed that Braniff serve London and Paris from Houston, and that Delta serve the Atlanta-London market. Northwest was recommended to serve Copenhagen from Chicago, Detroit, Los Angeles, Minneapolis, and New York and to provide service on the New York-Oslo/Bergen-Helsinki-Stockholm route. Finally, it was proposed that National's authority be expanded to include Amsterdam and Paris from Miami and London and Paris from Houston.

The administrative law judge (the hearing examiner) took exception to the Bureau's proposal and stated:

The solution of these problems which has been offered by BOR and other proponents of the various realigned proposals is to remove and reduce head-to-head competition and thus eliminate excess capacity and uneconomic operations. . . . On the contrary, there is no solid evidence either in terms of traffic or cost data, upon which any major transatlantic route restructuring can be based at the present time. It would be unwise to destroy the present transatlantic route structure which has been laboriously built up by the Board and the carriers over the past 25 years on the basis of short-term evidence consisting largely of today's fast moving and unpredictable events . . . which can justify a diminuation in transatlantic head-to-head U.S. flag competition.[5]

The administrative law judge then went on to make his recommendation by stating:

The proceeding comes at a time when the transatlantic market is engulfed in a crisis of unprecedented proportions—a crisis brought about by astronomical prices being charged for airline fuel, by sharp escalation of costs other than fuel, by a general decline in transatlantic traffic. We are not dealing with a typical route case which is usually decided against a background of traffic growth and profitable carrier operations. Instead we have a situation where traffic is lagging and two major incumbent carriers are in extensive financial difficulty in their transatlantic operations.[6]

Fully aware of the importance attached to the back-up traffic in the previous cases, the administrative law judge went on to say,

[d]This information relates to Pan American's Part I for Route 132, to TWA's Segment I for Route 147, and to National's Route 168.

In deciding whether to certificate new carriers in the transatlantic market or to expand the incumbent transatlantic carriers it is necessary to carefully evaluate the proposals of the domestic carriers in light of the current economic situation in the transatlantic market. Obviously a domestic carrier has much to offer. All of the domestic carriers can show substantial public benefits by feeding on live traffic from their systems to the gateway terminal points. [However] ... the economic problems facing our transatlantic carriers are substantial. Nevertheless, the Board should do what it can to strengthen our international air transportation system and not to expose the existing transatlantic carriers to massive diversion. .... There is no way to certificate a new carrier for transatlantic service in this proceeding without inflicting substantial diversion upon PAA and TWA.[7]

Having stated his evaluation of the case, the administrative law judge concluded that no additional carriers should be authorized on the North Atlantic because of the diversionary impact on both Pan American and TWA. Instead the judge recommended that Pan American's authority be expanded to include Houston, Dallas/Fort Worth, and Atlanta as coterminals; and that TWA's coterminals include Cleveland, Pittsburgh, St. Louis, Denver, Kansas City, and Minneapolis. Finally, Tampa and New Orleans should be added as coterminals to National's route. It was recommended that all other applications be denied. In the final analysis the administrative law judge supported the head-to-head concept of competition but argued that the service should be provided by the incumbent carriers. The case now awaits final decision by the Board and Presidential approval.

The Transpacific Route Case

During the 1959-1960 period, the transpacific route was investigated in depth in order to determine the need for greater competition on the U.S. Mainland-Hawaii, United States-Orient, and United States-South Pacific routes [32 CAB 928 (1961)]. The justification of the need for added competition was based upon the existence of high traffic growth, high load factors, high fares, and excessive competition from foreign flag carriers. Evidence of the need for additional competition was clear from the investigation of load factors. For the month of August 1958, Pan American experienced a load factor in excess of 75 percent on its 130 flights between Los Angeles and Honolulu. Eighty-eight of these flights had a load factor of over 90 percent, and twenty-three flights were almost completely full. Similarly, the existence of high fares or the lack of fare experimentation on the part of the scheduled carriers was clear from the substantial number of passengers travelling on supplemental carriers.

The U.S. Mainland-Hawaii market was the first segment of the Pacific to be investigated. Of the four applicants—Continental, Northwest, Hawaiian, and Western—the examiner selected Hawaiian Airlines due to its relationship with the

Table 10-2
Proposed United States-Europe Service by U.S. Flag Combination Carriers

Braniff		Continental	
Dallas	– Amsterdam	Dallas	– Frankfurt
	– Frankfurt		– London
	– London	Houston	– Frankfurt
	– Paris		– London
	– Rome		– Madrid
	– Zurich		– Rome
		Los Angeles	– London
			– Madrid
			– Rome
National		Miami	– Madrid
Atlanta	– London		– Rome
	– Paris	Phoenix	– Frankfurt
Dallas	– London		– London
	– Paris		– Madrid
Houston	– Amsterdam		– Rome
	– Frankfurt		
	– London	**Northwest**	
	– Paris	Chicago	– Copenhagen
	– Madrid	Detroit	– Copenhagen
	– Rome	Los Angeles	– Copenhagen
Las Vegas	– Amsterdam	Minneapolis	– Copenhagen
	– Frankfurt	New York	– Bergen
	– London		– Copenhagen
Miami	– Amsterdam		– Glasgow
	– Frankfurt		– Helsinki
	– London		– Moscow
	– Luxembourg		– Stockholm
	– Madrid		– Warsaw
	– Paris	Seattle	– Copenhagen
	– Rome	Washington	– Copenhagen
New Orleans	– London		– Moscow
Tampa	– London		
		Delta	
		Atlanta	– London

Eastern	
Atlanta	– Frankfurt
	– London
	– Paris
Dallas	– Frankfurt
	– London
	– Paris
Houston	– Frankfurt
	– London
	– Paris
New Orleans	– Frankfurt
	– London
San Juan	– London
Tampa	– London

Table 10-2 (cont.)

Pan American

Atlanta	– London
Baltimore	– London
Boston	– Athens
	– Frankfurt
	– Lisbon
	– London
	– Madrid
	– Paris
	– Rome
	– Santa Maria
Chicago	– Athens
	– Lisbon
	– Madrid
	– Rome
	– Santa Maria
Cleveland	– London
Dallas	– London
Detroit	– London
Houston	– London
Los Angeles	– London
	– Paris
Miami	– Athens
	– Lisbon
	– Madrid
	– Rome
New York	– Amsterdam
	– Bergen
	– Copenhagen
	– Glasgow
	– Moscow
	– Oslo
	– Stockholm
	– Warsaw
	– Athens
	– Barcelona
	– Brussels
	– Frankfurt
	– Lisbon
	– London
	– Madrid
	– Munich
	– Nice
	– Paris
	– Rome
	– Vienna

Pan American

San Juan	– Athens
	– Lisbon
	– Madrid
	– Rome
Seattle	– London
Tampa	– Athens
	– Lisbon
	– Madrid
	– Rome
Washington	– Athens
	– Frankfurt
	– London
	– Paris
	– Rome
Philadelphia	– London
	– Rome
Portland	– London
San Francisco	– London
	– Paris

TWA

Atlanta	– Frankfurt
	– London
Baltimore	– Milan
	– Paris
Boston	– Lisbon
	– London
	– Paris
	– Rome
	– Santa Maria
	– Shannon
Chicago	– Athens
	– London
	– Paris
	– Rome
	– Shannon
Cincinnati	– London
Cleveland	– London
	– Paris
	– Rome
Dallas	– Frankfurt
	– London
	– Paris
Denver	– London
	– Paris
Detroit	– Dublin
	– Paris
	– Rome
	– Shannon

TWA

Indianapolis	– Athens
	– Rome
	– Tel Aviv
Kansas City	– Frankfurt
	– London
Las Vegas	– London
Los Angeles	– Athens
	– Frankfurt
	– Lisbon
	– London
	– Madrid
	– Paris
	– Rome
	– Tel Aviv
Minneapolis	– Athens
	– Paris
	– Rome
	– Amsterdam
	– Copenhagen
	– Athens
	– Dublin
New York	– Frankfurt
	– Geneva
	– Lisbon
	– London
	– Madrid
	– Milan
	– Munich
	– Paris
	– Rome
	– Santa Maria
	– Shannon
	– Vienna
	– Zurich
	– Athens
Philadelphia	– London
	– Rome
	– London
Phoenix	– London
Pittsburgh	– Milan
	– Frankfurt
St. Louis	– London
	– Frankfurt
San Francisco	– London
	– Milan
	– Paris

Table 10-2 (cont.)

TWA (cont.)

Hartford	– Copenhagen	Washington	– Athens
	– Frankfurt		– Frankfurt
	– London		– London
Houston	– Frankfurt		– Paris
	– London		– Rome
	– Paris		

Source: U.S. Civil Aeronautics Board, *Transatlantic Route Proceedings*, (Docket 25908), Rebuttal Exhibits of the Bureau of Operating Rights, Washington, D.C., May 28, 1974.

Hawaiian community, the need to strengthen the carrier, and the possibility of reduction in subsidy. The Board rejected the selection of Hawaiian because the carrier was too small to compete with Pan American and United, had no jet aircraft, and lacked the back-up traffic support on the West Coast. The Board selected Western on the basis of its policy to award new routes to smaller carriers in order to strengthen their route structure and make them more viable competitors with the larger carriers. Furthermore Western had the necessary jet experience and an identity and facilities on the West Coast. Although the Board is not supposed to regulate the choice of flight equipment, the selection of Western over Hawaiian (both small and relatively weak carriers) was indeed partially based upon flight equipment. With respect to the identity issue, the Board was more concerned with identity at the source of traffic rather than at the destination.

The international phase of the investigation dealt mainly with the expansion of Pan American's and Northwest's certificates to balance competition between U.S. flag carriers on an area basis, on the one hand, and to compete more effectively with the foreign flags, on the other. New York was authorized as a coterminal for Pan American on a route via Fairbanks to Tokyo, and on a Central Pacific route via Los Angeles/San Francisco and the Orient. Northwest was authorized to offer service from Boston, New York, Philadelphia, Washington, D.C., Detroit, and Chicago to Japan via Honolulu. Northwest was not authorized to serve between the West Coast and Hawaii. TWA's route over the North Atlantic was extended to Hong Kong to connect with Northwest's transpacific route to provide competition on the round-the-world service between the U.S. flag carriers. While the Board had made an extensive investigation, its recommendations in the international phase were disapproved by the President in light of foreign policy considerations. The Board, on the other hand, could not determine a rational route pattern in the U.S. Mainland-Hawaii market without knowledge of the foreign route pattern beyond Hawaii. Consequently none of the Board's recommendations were made effective.

For the reasons cited earlier, such as high traffic growth, high load factors, and high fares, the *Transpacific* case was reopened in February 1966. This time almost every domestic carrier was a party to the case. Eighteen carriers had made application for almost every major route on the Pacific. After a year-long hearing the examiner made his recommendations. Both Northwest and Pan American lost their monopolies over the Central Pacific and the North Pacific to each other. Eastern was recommended for routes between a number of U.S. eastern points and all points in the South Pacific, including Hawaii. TWA was recommended for the Central Pacific and North Pacific routes. United was given access from numerous mainland cities to Hawaii. Western was once again given its route to Hawaii.

The Board made a number of changes in the examiner's recommended route pattern. Of these changes, the most noteworthy were the replacement of Eastern by American to Japan and the elimination of TWA's route over the North Pacific. The result of the Board's decision was an establishment of eight carriers on the Mainland-Hawaii route, six with turn-around authority and two with long-haul restrictions. The Board's goal was to strengthen the routes of the smaller and weaker carriers. Whereas some of the large carriers had extensive unused potential for growth, the smaller carriers could only grow through new route awards. Thus the strong, successful carriers were criticized for lack of initiative and were provided with competition from small carriers with lucrative, long-haul routes. It is interesting to note that the transpacific routes were given to some carriers to strengthen their route structure and become successful. At the same time, carriers that were already successful on the Pacific were given added competition.

The Board submitted its recommendation to President Johnson for approval for the international portion of the decision. President Johnson concluded that the addition of a third U.S. flag combination carrier was not in the national interest. In light of this decision by the President, the Board changed its recommendations and cancelled American's authority to Japan but retained American's award from mainland to Hawaii. The Board gave three reasons for this decision. First, American was expected to contribute positively to the level of competition in the overall market. Second, the elimination of American's domestic award would reduce the level of competitive service in the overall Mainland-Hawaii markets, which the Board found necessary. Third, the desired competitive service could only be provided by American, Eastern, or TWA. The Board selected American because of its needs. Thus American was eliminated from the route authorizations to serve Japan.

The final route approved by President Johnson had not become effective when President Nixon's term began in 1969. Pending further review, the President postponed his decision. Since Mainland-Hawaii routes were tied to the foreign routes beyond Hawaii, the whole package was held up once again. Having reviewed the case, the President also made extensive changes to the package. In essence he recommended that the second carrier route to the South Pacific bypass the California gateway. Therefore he asked the Board to recommend a carrier to serve the U.S. East Coast and Midcoast coterminals. With this set of guidelines, the Board recommended Continental to serve between Washington, Chicago, Kansas City, Denver, and Phoenix and the intermediate points Hawaii, Samoa, Fiji, New Caledonia, New Zealand, and Australia. The selection of Continental was based upon its aggressive competitiveness with respect to low fare policy and the development of tourism.

The Board's recommendation was once again rejected. The President outlined further guidelines with respect to additional coterminals and the selection of the carrier. With respect to the last point, the South Pacific route was to be awarded to a carrier that did not, and would not, hold (as a result of the *Transpacific Route Investigation*) California-Hawaii domestic authority. This guideline left the choice between American and Eastern, since the Board argued that American's award between California and Hawaii was not necessary and could therefore be eliminated. The decision went in favor of American because of its financial strength (relative to Eastern), route characteristics, and potential ability to promote the South Pacific route. On the latter point American did not possess any significant foreign vacation destinations and could therefore be expected to fully exploit the new route. This decision was approved by President Nixon.

This is a very brief overview of the *Transpacific* case. During its 10-year course, one notes both the shift in the Board's policy from area to direct competition and the extent of the President's power in making the final decision. While at first it appears that American and TWA received extensive route authority, the financial results since the route awards tell another story. Based upon the expectations of high traffic growth, the new routes were supposed to strengthen the new carriers and stimulate Pan American into providing better service. Instead Pan American suffered extensive financial losses, and both American and TWA lost millions of dollars in their Pacific operations. In order to correct the situation, American and TWA agreed to abandon their Pacific routes as discussed in the following section.

The Pan American-TWA Exchange Agreement

In recent years both Pan American and TWA had been experiencing substantial losses in their transatlantic operations. For example, for the year ending September 30, 1974 the two carriers posted a pretax loss of $59.6 million. In light of these heavy losses, decline in transatlantic traffic, tremendous increases in fuel prices, and excessive competition, the two carriers began to investigate their route structure with the possibility of consolidating and suspending certain services. President Ford asked the Department of Transportation (DOT) to develop a plan to ease the financial problems of international U.S. flag carriers. In response to this request, the DOT produced the "Federal Action Plan for Improved Profitability in International Air Carrier Operations." The plan called for the following seven points: compensatory fare structure, reduction of excess capacity, tariff enforcement, a "Fly U.S. Flag" program, compensatory mail rates, elimination of discriminatory practices, and rationalized route structures. With respect to the last point, DOT urged Pan American and TWA to reach an agreement on a route exchange. Basically the agreement called for both the withdrawal of one U.S. carrier on certain routes that were previously served by both carriers and the substitution of one carrier for the other at selected points. It was estimated that the agreement between the two carriers would provide an operating profit of $16 million to $25 million for each carrier during the first year alone.

The agreement called for Pan American to suspend service on its Route 132 at Santa Maria, Lisbon, Barcelona, Nice, and Rome on Part I, Segment 1, and at Vienna on Part II, Segment 2, and at Paris on Part II, Segment 3; on its Route 133 Pan American was to suspend service at Santa Maria, Lisbon, Madrid, and Casablanca. The carrier would cease single-plane service in the Los Angeles-Chicago-Philadelphia-London markets. On the Pacific, Pan American's Route 130 would now allow the carrier to operate Los Angeles-Hawaii-Guam-Okinawa-Taipai-Hong Kong-Bankok-Colombo-Bombay service. In return TWA would suspend service on Route 147, Segment 1 at Frankfurt, Bombay, Colombo, Bangkok, and Hong Kong. The carrier would also cease single-plane service in the Washington-London market. Finally, the carrier was now authorized to serve Vienna on its Route 147, Segment 1, and Casablanca, Barcelona, and Nice on Segment 2.

The agreement was approved for a period of 2 years by the Board despite the objections of the U.S. Department of Justice with regard to its impact on competition. The carriers replied to the competitive issue by stating that each will provide service comparable to that which was previously offered. In any case, while head-to-head U.S. flag competition is being eliminated in certain markets, each U.S. carrier will still face direct competition from foreign flag carriers. The DOT argued that in most of the markets where competition will be reduced from three to two carriers, the level of traffic is too small to justify U.S. flag point-to-point competition. While the reduction of competition in the French and German markets is significant, the disadvantages are outweighed by the expected financial improvements. The Board did not submit the agreement to the President for his approval, as is usually the case in international route cases, on the grounds that the service suspensions did not change the certificate authority. Thus Section 801 was not applicable in this case. However, the President asked the Board to submit the agreement for his approval because of its broad impact upon international air traffic.

As stated earlier, the normal procedure in a route case is to hold extensive hearings. However, in this case the Board decided not to hold a hearing, in order to remedy, without further delay, the deteriorating financial position of the carriers involved. The Board has the power to suspend services temporarily under Section 401(j) of the Act as long as the Board's action is in the public interest. Under Section 416(b) of the Act, the Board also has exemption power to grant carriers the authority to serve new points. Finally, Section 416 of the Act authorizes the Board to relieve the carriers from the Federal Antitrust Laws. Although there are no statutory requirements for a formal hearing under Section 412, some parties argued that the Board should have held these hearings due to the anticompetitive aspects and the impacts on public interest of these agreements.[e]

The agreement was expected to provide cost savings in a number of areas. First, the reduction in duplicate operations will reduce fuel requirements. The two carriers estimated that these savings in 1975 would be about $59 million, based upon a fuel price of 37 cents per gallon. Second, the agreement will reduce labor costs through the elimination of some duplicate jobs. While the two carriers estimated a layoff of approximately 3,000 persons, the savings from this source will not be very significant due to the Board's labor protective provisions. Third, most of the expenses directly related to the services to be suspended will be eliminated. There will naturally be financial penalties for breaking certain lease agreements. Fourth, there could presumably be a reduction in promotional expenses due to the reduction of U.S. flag point-to-point competition. Part of these savings will naturally be offset by the usual start-up cost of inaugurating service.

In addition to the savings cited above, other benefits expected from the agreement include higher load factors on certain markets and possible improvement in back-up traffic on certain flights. On the double-tracked routes, the load factor should show a significant improvement for the other U.S. flag carrier. For example, with TWA's departure from the United States-Frankfurt market, Pan American's load factor should improve from the higher traffic density, assuming that Pan American does not increase its capacity on a seat-per-seat basis. As a direct result of this agreement, both Pan American and TWA expected to show an operating profit of nearly $25 million. Unfortunately, the DOT analysis found these estimates high. The Department's estimates are $17.1 million for Pan American and $16.2 million for TWA. The discrepancy between Pan American's estimate and the DOT's estimate is due to the conflicting views Pan American and the DOT hold on Pan American's deletion of London-Los Angeles service. With respect to TWA, the disagreement stems from the impact of Pan American's suspension of service at Paris. These are the major areas of disagreement; there are also some minor discrepancies.

[e]The Board's decision not to hold hearings has been practiced in a number of cases prior to this agreement. A recent example of such a decision involved the capacity agreement between American, TWA, and United.

The Pan American-American Route Exchange Agreement

The decision in the *Transpacific* case resulted in substantial operative losses for American, Pan American, and TWA. This was due to intense competition between U.S. flag carriers and among U.S. flag carriers and foreign flag carriers, lower than expected traffic growth, and the route restrictions placed upon American and TWA. During the first 3 years of operation, American's losses were over $30 million. Almost two-thirds of this loss was experienced in operations between the Mainland and Hawaii. American's management placed a good part of the blame on their inability to operate turn-around service to Honolulu. In addition, the carrier was required to maintain connections between the Mainland-Hawaii service and the South Pacific service. This resulted in scheduling difficulties and also placed the carrier at a substantial competitive disadvantage with both U.S. flag carriers and foreign flag carriers.

Interestingly enough, it was the lack of competition that was the central issue in the *Transpacific* case. However, after the route awards it was the additional competition that was given as the cause of poor financial results. It is true that American placed heavy emphasis on route restrictions, but the elimination of those restrictions would have created even more competition and excess capacity, resulting in a further reduction of the profit potential for all carriers. The U.S. flag carriers and the Board cited intense competition from the foreign flag carriers in the Pacific. However, it was not the competition itself that troubled the U.S. flag carriers; rather, it was the type of foreign competition that was bothersome. For example, it was cited that the foreign carriers received back-up traffic support from government-owned domestic carriers and from pooling arrangements with respect to schedules and joint promotion.

In order to strengthen Pan American in the Pacific and American in the Caribbean, the Board has recently approved a route swap between the two carriers. This is similar to the route exchange between Pan American and TWA discussed above. In realigning their route structure, Pan American received all but one of American's Pacific routes. American kept the route from Boston and St. Louis to Hawaii on which the carrier had unlimited turn-around rights. In return, American received nonstop rights from Boston and New York to Bermuda, from New York to Barbados, and from New York to Santo Domingo. This route exchange is supposed to improve the financial position of both carriers. American, for example, estimated that based upon the 1973 results the route exchange would have produced a net benefit of about $8 million.

The route exchanges between Pan American and TWA and between Pan American and American were made, primarily, to improve these carrier's financial positions. Both agreements are also indicative of the Board's shift in emphasis from the point-to-point competition created so carefully in the *Transatlantic* and *Transpacific* cases. A number of industry analysts feel that the Board is just undoing what it did, for example, in the *Transpacific* case. The implication, undoubtedly, is that the Board created too much competition. This view cannot be taken at face value, in that it was the carriers themselves who applied for the route authority in the first place. Recall the massive applications that were filed in the *Transpacific* case; virtually every trunk-line carrier requested routes on the Pacific. As R.E.G. Davies points out, American's application for new routes on the Pacific was so extensive that its domestic route system looked like a feeder network.[8] Even Northeast, which only served short-haul markets in the Northeast, initially applied for transpacific routes. A similar situation is taking place in the current *Transatlantic Route Investigation* (see Table 10-2). Thus the situation should be carefully analyzed before placing all the blame on the Board.

The Latin American Routes

Prior to 1946 Pan American enjoyed a virtual monopoly in Latin America, which for the purposes of this discussion includes Mexico, Central America, South America, the Caribbean, and Bermuda. However, in 1946, for reasons of inadequacy of service (and perhaps due to the U.S. foreign policy), the Board extensively expanded the route system of a number of U.S. carriers to provide additional service to Latin America. In the *Additional Service to Latin America* case, 6 CAB 857 (1946), ten airlines and four steamship lines applied for routes to Latin America. The extensive interest shown by numerous applications may have been the result of the Board's encouragement, the carriers' desires to share in the high mail payments made to Pan American, American's successful temporary route award to Mexico during the war years, and the encouragement given to American Export in its attempts to conduct services on the North Atlantic.

The decision to provide competition for Pan American was not a recent issue. For many years there had been a strong debate with respect to Pan American's monopoly. One group (those against Pan American's monopoly) pointed to the carrier's inadequate service with respect to low frequencies, day-time only operations, and prolonged transit times as compared to domestic services. Pan American defended itself on grounds of low traffic density on many routes and the inadequacy of ground facilities in many of the Latin American countries. The second group (those who favored Pan American's monopoly) believed in a "chosen instrument," with the idea that there was enough competition from the foreign flag carriers. This group argued that having only one international carrier led to savings in overhead expenses, higher load factors, cross-subsidization, and the ability to shift equipment to meet seasonal demands. The Board rejected most of these arguments and decided to end Pan American's monopoly.

The majority of the applicants were domestic carriers with very little experience on international routes. However, these domestic carriers possessed a significant advantage resulting from their network of domestic routes to the gateways and thus strong possibilities of one-carrier service from a number of points in the country. The steamship companies argued their case on the basis of their long experience in trading with Latin America, resulting in substantial goodwill that would facilitate the promotion of air transport in the area. Furthermore, there were some operating advantages in combining air and sea operations under the same ownership and management. While the Board agreed with this line of reasoning, it was afraid that in the event of a conflict of interest, "the air transportation may find itself a captive of the surface transportation interest." Furthermore, Section 408(b) of the Federal Aviation Act prohibits the Board from approving the acquisition of an air carrier by a surface carrier unless it is in the public interest. In light of this, the Board rejected the applications of the steamship companies.

The selection of routes, gateways, and carriers was somewhat interrelated. The southern gateways were Brownsville, El Paso, San Antonio, Fort Worth, Dallas, Laredo, and Houston in Texas; New Orleans in Louisiana; and Tampa and Miami in Florida. The western gateways were San Diego and Los Angeles. The most important consideration in selecting gateways was the existence of, or potential for, traffic in relation to the foreign terminal. Particular emphasis was placed upon the volume of the catchment area's trade with the Latin American city at the other end of the route. As a part of traffic considerations, attention was also focused upon connecting services from other U.S. cities. While traffic was the most important factor in the selection of gateways, consideration was also given to factors such as community of interest, geographic location (border or coastal), the city's hotels, and other passenger facilities.

The Board made its recommendations to the President; in general, the plan diluted Pan American's monopoly in Latin America. However, the President was not satisfied with these recommendations and made further changes that completely put an end to Pan American's monopoly. For example, he added Braniff to South America as far south as Rio de Janeiro and Buenos Aires, Eastern to San Juan, Colonial to Bermuda, and Western to Mexico City, and he justified his changes in the interest of "the broad national welfare." The final route awards follow: American was certificated to serve Mexico City from El Paso and from Fort Worth/Dallas, both via Monterrey, Mexico; Braniff was certificated to serve Mexico City from San Antonio and Laredo, both via Monterrey; furthermore, Braniff was authorized to fly between Houston and Rio de Janeiro, on the one hand, and Buenos Aires, on the other;[f] Chicago and Southern was authorized to serve between the coterminal points, Houston and New Orleans and San Juan, on the one hand, and Caracas, on the other;[g] Colonial was authorized to serve Bermuda from New York and Washington,

[f]Both routes were to be served via Asuncion (Paraguay) and a number of other intermediate points.

[g]Again, both routes were to be flown via Havana and other intermediate points.

D.C.; National was awarded the Tampa/Miami-Havana route;[h] for service to the Virgin Islands, Trans Caribbean was awarded the route from New York due to its need for strengthening, while Eastern was selected for the route from Miami because of the large number of interior points that would receive single-carrier service; and Pan American was authorized to serve the Bahamas from New York to compete actively with foreign flag carriers, particularly BOAC (now British Airways).

As in the Caribbean case, the basic idea in the South American service was also to strengthen the weaker carrier, namely Braniff. The carrier was awarded routes from the East Coast of the United States to the East Coast of South America. In addition, Braniff was certificated from the West Coast of the United States to South America. This decision served to strengthen Braniff's system, which was overhauled in 1966 with the merger of Braniff and Pan American-Grace Airways (Panagra), which was owned jointly by Pan American and W.R. Grace [45 CAB 495 (1966)].

Summary

From the brief investigation of these few cases it appears that there are at least seven points considered by the Board in route proceedings: (1) the need for service, (2) fitness of the applicant, (3) diversionary effects, (4) historic interest of the applicant in the route, (5) integration of the proposed route in the applicant's route structure, (6) the need for carrier strengthening, and (7) fulfillment of carrier obligations. As can be seen from the individual cases cited, the Board does in fact justify its decisions on the basis of these criteria. The complexity of the decisions lies not so much in determining if the applicant satisfies these tests but in resolving trade-offs between the various tests. Thus the Board's major problem is to weigh properly and accurately the importance of each criterion. The controlling factor, that is, the importance attached to any one criterion, varies from case to case and is subject to such outside influences as the economic environment. Changes in the Board's policy reflect changes in the economy, traffic, growth, and technology rather than changes in the Board's basic philosophy. The overall objective of the Board is, and always has been, the public interest.

Although it is difficult to pinpoint exactly the Board's policy on international route awards, several general observations may be made based upon the cases. First, successful applicants were generally in need of route strengthening and could show a substantial back-up route network, such as National in the Miami-London case. Second, the acquisition of jet aircraft had an important influence on route decisions. In some cases, the applicant needed to show jet

---

[h]This decision was based upon route strengthening, local identity, and National's integral relationship with the Caribbean community.

experience. In others, it needed to show a commitment to buy them. Yet in still other cases, having purchased the jets, a need was created to apply for denser, longer-haul routes to take advantage of their productive capabilities. Third, it was essential to demonstrate that the existing carriers were providing inadequate service as evidenced by high load factors and lack of initiative regarding schedules and fares. Recall the criticisms against Pan American's service in the *Transpacific Route* case. Fourth, the share of traffic carried by the foreign flag carriers played an important role in the route awards. TWA's round-the-world certificate and the award to Pan American are examples of the Board's concern with the U.S. flag carriers' position relative to foreign flag carriers.

11

Domestic Passenger Fare and Freight Rate Policy Decisions

The pricing of any product or service is a complex task. In the case of air transportation the task is even more complex due to the nature of the business and the fact that the industry is regulated. For example, as discussed in Chapters 3 and 4, once an airline schedules a flight, the marginal costs of carrying an additional passenger are essentially zero. Coupled with the fact that the demand is stochastic, the pricing decision can become quite complex. Even if the carriers were able to determine the optimal fare level and structure, the final results must still be approved by the Board, which has its own ideas on how the fares should be calculated. The purpose of this chapter is to discuss this latter point. In the last two decades the Board has made two extensive attempts—each investigation lasted 4 years—to resolve the many difficult issues that arise in establishing standards and timing for determining fare level and structure that is in both the public and the carriers' interest. Both of these cases are discussed at some length, since they illustrate the substantive issues relating to standards for rate making.

The discussion in this chapter is limited to domestic operations. Since pricing of international services has its own peculiarities, the fare setting machinery for international operations is described separately in Chapter 14. However, for the domestic operations the discussion includes both passenger fares as well as freight rates. While the standards for passenger fares have already been established with the completion of the *Domestic Passenger Fare Investigation* in 1974, the standards for freight fares are still an issue. *The Domestic Air Freight Rate Investigation*, begun in 1970, is still in progress. The examiner has issued his decision and submitted it to the Board. Therefore the policy with respect to freight rates is discussed in light of the examiner's decision and should not be taken as the Board's official policy. In order to provide the reader with the broader understanding of the Board's policy, the passenger fare and freight rate cases are preceded by a review of the historical developments.

Domestic Passenger Fares

The average passenger fare per mile has declined almost 50 percent (in current prices) over the past 50 years on the U.S. domestic routes. In 1930 carriers made the first substantial fare reduction to stimulate traffic during the depression (see Table 11-1). In expectation of a lull in winter business, a number of carriers reduced the fares to compete with the first-class-rail-plus-Pullman levels, to

189

Table 11-1
Average Total Passenger Revenues per Revenue Passenger Mile, Scheduled Service
(In Cents)

Year	Domestic	International and Territorial	Year	Domestic	International and Territorial
1926	12.00	NA	1950	5.56	7.28
1927	10.60	NA	1951	5.61	7.10
1928	11.00	NA	1952	5.57	7.01
1929	12.00	NA	1953	5.46	6.84
1930	8.30	NA	1954	5.41	6.76
1931	6.70	NA	1955	5.36	6.66
1932	6.10	NA	1956	5.33	6.68
1933	6.10	NA	1957	5.31	6.55
1934	5.90	NA	1958	5.64	6.46
1935	5.70	NA	1959	5.88	6.29
1936	5.70	NA	1960	6.09	6.35
1937	5.60	8.63	1961	6.28	6.08
1938	5.18	8.34	1962	6.45	5.87
1939	5.10	8.57	1963	6.17	5.82
1940	5.07	8.83	1964	6.12	5.45
1941	5.04	8.61	1965	6.06	5.29
1942	5.27	8.86	1966	5.83	5.16
1943	5.35	7.94	1967	5.64	5.01
1944	5.34	7.83	1968	5.61	4.95
1945	4.95	8.68	1969	5.90	4.95
1946	4.63	8.31	1970	6.00[a]	5.01
1947	5.05	7.77	1971	6.33[a]	5.08
1948	5.76	8.01	1972	6.40[a]	4.98
1949	5.78	7.72	1973	6.63[a]	5.32
			1974	7.52[a]	6.39

[a]Data compiled on fifty state basis.

Source: U.S. Civil Aeronautics Board, *Handbook of Airline Statistics*, 1973 Edition, *Air Carrier Traffic Statistics*, and *Air Carrier Financial Statistics*, December 1974.

determine if high fare levels were a greater hindrance to the development of air passenger traffic than public fear. The experiment was successful, and the traffic increased from 100 percent to 500 percent for the major airlines. With this observation, the carriers continued to reduce the fares during the depression and even afterwards, through such mechanisms as a 10 percent discount on round trip tickets, a 15 percent fare discount through the use of script books, free flights for wives of air travelers, adoption of half-fare tariffs for children, 15 percent discounts allowed for U.S. Government official travel, and discounts for travel on older flight equipment. United, for example, cut rates for passenger service in 1940 on its Boeing 247s between San Francisco and Los Angeles to approximately 3.67 cents per mile with the slogan, "Cheaper than you can drive your automobile."

The average passenger fare continued to decline through 1940. The following year the travel costs increased by the introduction of a 5 percent federal transportation tax. This excise tax was raised to 10 percent in 1942 and to 15 percent in 1943. In addition, during World War II, faced with the problem of too much traffic for too little capacity, the carriers eliminated all special fares and discounts. This resulted in raising the average passenger yield as shown in Table 11-1. After the war, as a result of various CAB "show-cause" orders, the carriers began to reduce passenger fares and partially restore the prewar discounts.

Besides bringing back the old system of discounts, the carriers began to introduce innovations in their fare structure. First, the carriers began to compute fares on a uniform mileage rate, that is, passenger fares were computed by applying a fixed amount per passenger mile to the airport-to-airport mileage between local points. Second, the carriers experimented with the establishment of a no-show penalty that was 25 percent of the unused portion of the ticket or $2.50, whichever was greater. Third, the carriers introduced a family plan that gave a 50 percent discount to each member of a family, with the exception of one person who was required to pay the full fare. Fourth, under the influence of Capital, most carriers introduced the domestic-coach service. These coach fares were set at an average of 4 cents per mile, compared to almost 6 cents for regular first-class service. And fifth, on an experimental basis, Western introduced the "no meal tariff" by offering passengers a 5 percent discount by dropping unnecessary frills.

Adopted in 1946, the original no-show penalty allowed passengers to cancel their tickets any time up to the scheduled flight departure time. The minimum penalty was $5 or the value of the flight coupon if it was less. This penalty was dropped in 1955. Two years later the airlines once again adopted a $3 penalty for failing to reconfirm reservations at least 6 hours before departure. In 1962 the Board approved a modification of the no-show policy by also penalizing the carriers for overselling the seats. The domestic trunk-line carriers were required to pay a fine to overbooked passengers amounting to 50 percent of the fare, with a $5 minimum and $40 maximum. No-show passengers were subject to the same penalties as the airlines. This policy successfully reduced the number of no-shows and saved the carriers approximately $1 million in 3 months. However, since the local-service carriers did not participate in this plan, the trunk-line carriers discontinued the no-show experiment but continued the overbooking feature.

In 1952 the trunk-line carriers introduced a $1 ticket-fare increase. This fare increase was unique in that the rate of increase per mile decreased as the trip length increased. This modified fare structure has had significant impact in later years; it laid the foundations for the philosophy in later rate cases that fare per mile should decline with distance at a rate generally consistent with the behavior of unit costs. This concept is discussed in greater detail in a later section. Another modification introduced to the fare structure in 1952 was that the Board eliminated the cents per mile limits previously used in evaluating fares for coach services. Instead, the Board instituted a policy that coach fares should not exceed 75 percent of the corresponding first-class fares. The object of this policy was to encourage and extend the coach services.

General Passenger Fare Investigation (1956-1960)

The *General Passenger Fare Investigation* (GPFI) and the *Domestic Passenger Fare Investigation* (DPFI—described later) are discussed in detail since they illustrate the complexities of problems faced by the Civil Aeronautics Board in rate regulation. These investigations illustrate the many difficult issues that arise in determining standards and timing for setting fare levels and fare structures. The presentation of these two cases is limited to substantive issues relating to standards for rate making. Financial analysis and arguments of the various parties are presented only insofar as a vital point is illustrated. Finally, before reading the various rate cases summarized in this chapter, the reader may find it useful to review Sections 403 through 406 of Title IV and Section 1002(d) and, particularly, (e) of Title X of the Federal Aviation Act.

In the GPFI the Board decided to adopt the rate-making procedures used by the Interstate Commerce Commission and the public utilities. The objective was to provide the carriers with sufficient revenue to cover their operating costs, including an adequate rate of return on investment under honest, economical, and efficient management. While the concept had been widely accepted, controversies regarding what constitutes operating expenses, investments, and an adequate rate of return for the air carrier industry were far from settled, as evidenced by the lengthy hearings in both the GPFI and the DPFI; each investigation lasted 4 years. The complexity of the various issues can only be fully realized by reading all the evidence presented in the investigations. It is hoped that the very brief summaries contained in this chapter provide the reader with some appreciation of the very difficult decisions faced by the Board. While it is quite easy for the casual observer to criticize the Board's decisions during both investigations, this author believes that the Board should be commended both for its investigations and for the difficult decisions that it has had to make. Making decisions on controversial issues, no matter what the final outcome, always leaves somebody unhappy.

The developments leading to the institution of the GPFI in 1956 can be traced back to 1952, when the carriers proposed a flat increase of $1 in all one-way passenger fares. The elimination of round-trip discounts was also proposed. The carriers justified the proposed rate revisions on the grounds of rising costs and lowered revenues. The investigation of the $1 increase proposal raised two issues: the level and structure of rates, which relates to the tapering rate structure concept based upon distance, in contrast to the previous, relatively uniform rate structure. Carriers with short-haul routes favored such a rate structure since it would allow more revenue per mile for short trips. In addition to the rate level and structure issue, the Board needed to decide on an appropriate method of determining proper profit for formulating sound industry-wide fare policies; consequently, it ordered an investigation to determine whether the fares, either already on file or expected to be on file, were lawful. The $1 increase was approved, and the proposal to eliminate discounts was suspended, pending the investigation's outcome.

In 1952 the Board held hearings to redefine and clarify the issues in the investigation. The carriers withdrew the proposal to eliminate round-trip discounts. Furthermore, after successive clarification of various issues, with the vital issue being whether rates were too low or too high, the carriers in 1953 filed petitions for the dismissal of the investigation. With a number of changes in Board membership, the decision on whether to hold a formal rate investigation was tossed back and forth. However, under Congressional pressure (initiated by the Antitrust Subcommittee of the House Committee on the Judiciary, which conducted a study in 1956 on "Monopoly Problems in Regulated Industries"[1]), the Board in 1956 issued an order instituting a new passenger fare investigation.[a]

The formal hearings in the GPFI were concluded on August 1, 1958. The carriers, experiencing a decline in profits during the recession period of 1957-1958, were given an interim fare increase of 4 percent plus $1 in the domestic passenger rates. In addition, the Board agreed to provide additional revenue by reducing family-fare discounts from 50 percent to 33.3 percent and eliminating round-trip discounts and free stop-over privileges. In the meantime, the Board had limited the investigation strictly to the overall level of fares. The question of fare structure was not to be considered. Thus the focus of investigation was on what the airline industry should earn on its domestic operations. However, before this issue could be resolved, it was necessary to determine the standards of rate making that should be applied to the airline industry.

Basically the rate-making process involves investigation of three elements—income, cost, and fair return. It is the function of the regulatory agency to properly determine each of the elements and project them into the future. The income element involves such factors as fare levels and structure, the price

---

[a]A complete and thorough list of events leading to the order instituting the investigation can be found in Emmette S. Redford, *The Regulatory Process* (Austin, Texas: University of Texas Press, 1969).

elasticity of demand, and load factors. The expense component, on the other hand, encompasses such factors as depreciation, taxes, allocation of costs, and load factor. Finally, determination of fair return involves evaluation of alternative financial methods, such as margin of return and rate of return on total investment, including the rate base. In addition, the calculations involve cost of equity and debt concepts and the optimal capital structure for the firm.

The airline industry argued that the return should be set higher than that of standard utilities, since the industry did not resemble the traditional utilities. There was heavy competition within the industry, accompanied by high rate of equipment obsolescence and instability of earnings due to the high operating ratios (ratio of expenses to revenue). The industry was seeking return commensurate with the risk of manufacturing industries. The Bureau Counsel, though, was in favor of recommending rates that were based upon the cost of providing the passenger service, including a reasonable earning.

The Bureau Counsel recommended that the return for investors should be determined in terms of return on a rate base that represents fair value of properties or investments. The carriers' views varied. Some proposed to use a margin of return approach where the investor's return is calculated as a percentage of revenue. In general these carriers were associating the risk comparable to manufacturing, due to high operating expenses and volume of business, rather than with capitalized expenditures. Other carriers proposed the traditional rate of return approach in conjunction with the operating ratio technique. The Bureau Counsel argued that investors are interested in return on their investments and not on the volume of expenses, revenue, or capital turnover. In addition, the margin-of-return method would provide excessive profits for those carriers who lease a significant portion of their fleet. The rate-of-return method only takes into account aircraft that are owned by the carrier, whereas under the margin-of-return method, profits are calculated on sales volumes.

The rate-of-return method considers the fair rate of return and the rate base. The fair rate of return is based upon the cost of capital. A carrier's capital normally consists of long-term debt and stockholders' equity. The cost of capital therefore depends upon cost of long-term debt, cost of stockholders' equity, and the ratio of debt to equity in the capital structure. Normally, long-term debt (for example, through bonds) can be obtained at a lower rate than equity capital. Therefore, a high debt ratio would reduce the overall cost of capital. On the other hand, debt implies regular interest payments, whereas dividends on equity (common stock) are not mandatory. Consequently, a high debt ratio is accompanied by a reduction of financial operating safety. The calculation of cost of equity is a complex task and involves considerations of such ratios as earnings to price for existing stock, earnings per share, and relationship of book value to market price of stocks. One reason for the complexity arises from the instability of these ratios over a time period.

On the question of the appropriate rate base, the airlines proposed that deposits placed with manufacturers for new aircraft be included in the rate base. The Bureau Counsel, on the other hand, recommended that the investment consist of depreciated original cost of capital used and useful in the business, and that equipment deposit should not be used until such time as the equipment was placed in service. The equation for the rate of return also included determination of costs, which among other things are dependent upon the load factor. As the load factor increases, the cost per passenger decreases. Because of this relationship, the Board attempted to incorporate an optimal load factor for each carrier in the fare level. An average load factor of 63 percent was recommended for the trunk-line carriers in general, a position the carriers objected to on the grounds that they could not achieve this during the period for which the rates were to be set, and that their ability to achieve such high load factors was not completely within management control. To illustrate this, the carriers cited the Board's competitive route grants.

The examiner's decision, released on May 27, 1959, contained the following recommendations. Fair return on investment is a more appropriate measure of profit for the trunk-line carriers than operating ratio. The examiner considered a reasonable cost of debt to be 4.5 percent for the Big Four and 5.5 percent for the other eight accompanied with a cost of equity of 15 percent and 17 percent respectively. A debt ratio of 45-55 for the Big Four and 50-50 for the other eight was considered reasonable. Deposits for future equipment purchases were allowed to be included in the rate base. However, accumulated reserve for deferred taxes were excluded from the rate base. The examiner was against the use of an optimal load factor in calculating the fare level. Finally, the examiner accepted the historical method of estimating depreciation.[2]

On November 25, 1960 the Board issued its opinion on the *General Passenger Fare Investigation*. The Board accepted the examiner's decision except in the following points. The Board accepted the rate of return on investment as the appropriate method of rate determination. However, the Board modified the cost of various elements in the capital structure. The final standards that were adopted are shown in Table 11-2. The Board accepted the examiner's decision that equipment purchase deposits be included in the rate base but rejected the inclusion of investments and special funds not used or useful in the airline business, such as National's investment in a Miami television station.

CAB Staff Study on Air Fare Structure

In 1968 the Board published the results of an extensive study of the domestic air fare structure. The GPFI had not addressed this issue explicitly. While this study provided an in-depth analysis of the existing (September 1966) passenger fare structure and the associated costs of providing the service, the conclusions of the

Table 11-2
Overall Rates of Return

Industry Unit	Security	Capitalization (Percent)	Security Cost (Percent)	Weighted Cost of Capital (Percent)
Big Four				10.250
	Debt	50	4.5	2.250
	Equity	50	16.0	8.000
Other Eight				11.125
	Debt	55	5.5	3.025
	Equity	45	18.0	8.100
12 Trunks				10.500

Source: U.S. Civil Aeronautics Board, *General Passenger Fare Investigation*, 32 CAB 291 (1960), p. 291.

study were not the official views or policy of the Board. The fare structure was analyzed in a general way to develop patterns and relationships. Following is a summary of the findings and conclusions, many of which bear a strong resemblance to the decisions in Phase 9 of the DPFI discussed later.

Passenger fares were very closely related to distance travelled. A regression analysis of jet day-coach fare with distance for 895 markets produced a correlation coefficient of 0.994. The straight-line relationship produced a fixed charge of $6.44 and a variable charge of 5.7 cents per mile.[3] The fare structure therefore indicated a moderate taper; that is, fare per mile varied inversely with distance. There was also a distinct relationship in fare between the various classes of services. For example, first-class and night-coach fares were both related to the day-coach fares. The first-class fare was 131.0 percent of the jet day-coach fare for distances of 100 miles and declined to 116.4 percent for distances of 2,600 miles. Similarly, night coach varied from 94.4 percent for 100 miles to 83.5 percent for 2,600 miles. The difference between jet and propeller fares tended to increase with distance in coach-class service but tended to decrease with distance for the first-class service.

There was a distinct pattern of variation in fare with the level of competition in the market. Fares in the noncompetitive markets were generally higher than in the competitive markets. A market was classified as noncompetitive if a single carrier's market share was equal to or greater than 90 percent. Of 133 noncompetitive markets with more than 6 percent variation from the computed fare, 78 markets showed a plus 6 percent variation and 55 markets showed a minus 6 percent variation. In contrast to this, of 157 competitive markets with more than 6 percent variation from the computed fare, only 35 showed a plus 6 percent, while 122 showed a minus 6 percent variation. Thus the noncompetitive market fares showed more variation on the positive side, while the competitive market fares showed greater variation on the negative side.

Analysis similar to the above showed that fares varied with direction; that is, fares in the north-south markets were generally higher than the comparable east-west markets. Next, fares were analyzed according to market density (number of passengers). Markets with less than 36,000 passengers per year were classified as light; between 36,000 and 200,000, medium; and over 200,000, heavy. Fares tended to be high in the light markets and low in the heavy markets. This variation must be carefully interpreted, since variation with respect to density also reflects directional and competitive characteristics. While the study did not investigate the discount fares, it was pointed out that they did dilute the yield significantly. The dilution was most significant for jet coach travel and in the competitive east-west markets.

In the analysis of costs, unit costs per mile varied inversely with distance but to a greater extent than the fares. The costs per passenger mile for first-class service were significantly higher than for coach service, reflecting differences not only in service but also in flight equipment and load factors. There were wide variations for costs among the carriers, due to such factors as route structure, flight equipment, and management policies. Finally the cost analysis was heavily dependent upon the methodology used to develop the costs.

Domestic Passenger Fare Investigation (1970-1974)

In the GPFI the Board made two fundamental decisions. First, a reasonable rate of return on investment for the domestic trunk-line was set at 10.5 percent. Second, it was concluded that the fare level should reflect the cost of service provided by the carrier. While this second concept represents a major policy direction, no standards were set. For example, the decision to incorporate load factor standards in the regulation of rates was rejected. Ten years after the decision in the GPFI, the Board once again ordered a comprehensive inquiry into the passenger fares charged for scheduled services within the United States. This investigation, known as the *Domestic Passenger Fare Investigation* (DPFI), was divided into nine separate phases. The first three phases were handled by the Board's rule-making proceedings, while the other six were handled through the normal public hearings.

Phase 1. Treatment of Flight Equipment Depreciation and Residual Values for Rate Purposes

Phase 2. Treatment of Leased Aircraft for Rate Purposes

Phase 3. Deferred Federal Income Taxes

Phase 4. Joint Fares

Phase 5. Discount Fares

Phase 6. A. Seating Configurations
          B. Load Factor

Phase 7. Fare Level

Phase 8. Rate of Return

Phase 9. Fare Structure

Phase 1: Aircraft Depreciation. For rate making purposes, the Board decided that flight equipment depreciation would be based upon the conventional straight-line method of accrual, employing the service lives and residual values listed in Table 11-3 below. The depreciation rates were based upon the reported practices of the carriers, the terms of long-term leases, the realization of high value of equipment disposed of over the past decade, and the expected demand and supply of used aircraft.

In general, the carriers argued for shorter service lives on the grounds that

Table 11-3
Depreciation Standards

Equipment	Service Life in Years	Residual Value as Percent of Cost
Turbo-fan Equipment		
4-Engine	14	2
3-Engine	14	2
2-Engine	14	2
Turbo-jet Equipment		
4-Engine	10	5
2-Engine	10	5
Turbo-prop Equipment		
4-Engine	12	5
2-Engine	10	15
Wide-body Equipment		
4-Engine	14	10
3-Engine	16	10

Source: U.S. Civil Aeronautics Board, *Domestic Passenger Fare Investigation*, Phase 1: Treatment of Flight Equipment, Depreciation and Residual Values for Rate Purposes, April 9, 1971, p. 3.

while the Board based its decision on the industry's reported depreciation practices, it reflected the upper limit of service lives used by the carriers. Second, the carriers claimed that the Board had erroneously concluded that capital gains realized on the sale of aircraft during the past decade were indicative of their conservative depreciation policies. The carriers claimed that these gains, which exceeded $100 million, were overstated as a result of substantial writedowns of the value of certain equipment types. Third, the carriers argued that leases did not provide an indication of the useful life of aircraft, had no residual value, and were essentially financing arrangements in which the length of the lease was relevant to the term of payment rather than to the service life of the leased equipment. Fourth, the carriers argued that the replacement of current aircraft by wide-body aircraft on a two-for-one basis increased the pace of aircraft retirement. Fifth, the market for used aircraft, presumably local-service carriers, supplemental carriers, and a number of the smaller "emerging" foreign carriers, was diminishing, since they recently had been buying aircraft directly from the manufacturer. Finally, United argued that the Board should adopt separate standards for engines and airframes on the grounds that engines had a shorter economic life due to greater technological obsolescence.

The Board rejected most of these arguments and made the following additional clarification. To the argument that the term of the lease relates to financing considerations rather than service life, the Board argued that it is unlikely in a "secured transaction" that the lender would accept as security, equipment that would have a useful life significantly shorter than the term of payment. On the issue of separate depreciation schedules for engines, the Board argued that sufficient data did not exist to justify separate standards. On the question of a market for used aircraft, the Board cited the study submitted by Eastern, which listed a number of smaller foreign carriers operating largely with turbo-prop and piston equipment as indicative of the potential market for used aircraft.

Phase 2: Leased Aircraft. In the second phase of the DPFI the Board investigated the treatment of the cost for leased aircraft in connection with determining domestic rates and fares. The Board rejected both the approach involving leasehold capitalization and depreciation. Instead the Board adopted the approach of a recognition of rental expense plus a profit element in certain unusual circumstances. Some carriers objected to this decision on at least two counts. First, they claimed that Congress enacted the Investment Tax Credit to provide an incentive for the industry to modernize its equipment and not as a means for the regulatory agency to use the credit to reduce taxes for rate-making purposes. The existence of poor earnings led some carriers into lease agreements to obtain partial benefit of the ITC by sharing the tax savings between the lessee and the lessor. Thus the recognition of only the rental expenses, which are lower than they would be otherwise because of the sharing of the tax savings, would deprive carriers of the benefits Congress intended them to have. Second, they argued that the higher risks involved in the operation of leased aircraft should be taken into account in providing for an adequate rate of return.

The Board rejected the ITC argument, stating that the law does not require the Board to recognize amounts in excess of actual rental expense. Furthermore the Board stated that it compensated the carriers adequately for the risks involved in leased aircraft operations in Phase 8: Rate of Return. In unusual circumstances, reflecting the additional risks of operations with leased aircraft that are not compensated by the return on investment, the Board was willing to allow an additional reasonable profit element.

Phase 3: Deferred Federal Income Taxes. In this phase the Board investigated the treatment of deferred federal income taxes for rate making purposes. The Board decided that the federal income tax expense should be based upon the normal taxes that would be paid under the depreciation standards used for rate making purposes in Phase 1. Furthermore, the accumulated reserves for deferred taxes should be excluded from recognized capitalization for rate purposes.

Phase 4: Joint Fares. This proceeding was instituted by the Board to determine the lawfulness of both joint and combination fares for interline service and the division of joint fares. However, following the hearings, the Board could not resolve the question of the extent to which joint fares should be ultimately reduced in the absence of an examination of the structure for single-carrier fares, which was at issue in Phase 9 of the investigation. Furthermore, the Board concluded that the prescription of the cost divisions should await the more comprehensive cost data to be presented in Phase 9. However, prior to its decision in Phase 9, the Board issued an interim decision in which it found that, (1) joint fares for all basic classes of service should be required in all markets over all routings; (2) the joint fares should be set at a maximum of the sum of each carrier's local fare for its segment of the interline trip, minus $4 for each intercarrier connection; and (3) divisions of joint fares should be based upon the relative costs of the mileage flown by each carrier.

The first issue in the final decision related to the determination of the structure of interline fares relative to the fares charged for single-carrier trips. As the structure of the normal fares for single-carrier service is tapered, an interline connecting passenger paying a sum of the local fares would result in a considerably higher fare than the single-carrier fare for a trip of equivalent distance. The Board found that even assuming that the interline trip should be viewed as a number of separate trips on separate carriers, the interline fares should at least reflect the cost savings that accrue from the reduction in processing costs of two or more separate local passengers. The local-coach fare formula adopted in Phase 9 applies to on-line connections and multistop services as well as to nonstop or "best authority" operations.

The Board was in favor of reducing the joint fares in order to reduce the substantial disparities between the maximum joint fares and the single-carrier fares. The extent to which the joint fares should be reduced depends, however, upon the need for lower fares for all joint-fare passengers, on the one hand, and the extent of reasonable cross-subsidization of these passengers by other passengers, on the other. The Board concluded that the basic issue involves three subsidiary questions: (1) whether joint fares should be set to achieve complete parity with single-carrier fares; (2) whether the level of joint fares should be affected by the traffic density of markets or routings; and (3) whether the circuity of the routing taken by the passenger should affect his fare. The final decision in this issue was that in routings generating fifty or more passengers per year, the maximum joint fare shall be the sum of the local fares over the shortest authorized interline routing minus one tax-rounded coach terminal charge for each intercarrier connection. Additional rules exist for routings involving less than fifty passengers per year or if mileage over the routing flown is over 120 percent of the mileage over the shortest authorized interline routing.[4]

The second major issue in this phase referred to the reasonable and equitable division of joint fares. The Board decided that divisions should be based upon a cost prorate such that each carrier's share of the joint fare should be based upon the costs of performing its portion of the interline trip. This decision, in turn, involves two issues—the determination of costs on which the divisions should be based and the application of these costs to a division formula. The decision was made to base the divisions on the trunk-line costs adopted in Phase 9 and on the analogous local-service carrier costs, adjusted to reflect overall load factors of 55 percent and 49.2 percent, respectively. These costs are to be applied by using (1) a cost curve based upon trunk-line first-class costs for determining the costs of first-class segments and (2) a curve based upon a traffic-weighted average of trunk-coach and local-service carrier costs for costing all other segments.

Certain carriers contended that these costs should be adjusted upward to account for the revenue dilution from discount fares. The Board rejected this contention on the grounds that the existing discount fares were not cost-based under the long-term standards adopted in Phase 5. Furthermore, since in the long run the cost of carrying a discount-fare passenger is essentially no different than the cost of normal-fare traffic, dilution is essentially a phenomenon of revenues not costs, and dilution factors incorporated in the normal fares basically represent the subsidization of discount traffic by full-fare traffic. Thus a dilution adjustment has no validity in cost-based division of joint fares.

In computing the actual prescription of the division formula, the Board decided to use trunk-line first-class costs for costing trunk-line first-class movements, and to combine trunk-line coach and local-service carrier costs (weighted by relative revenue passenger miles) for costing all other movements. Least-square regressions of these two sets of costs resulted in the following cost curve:

| First Class: | $24.53 + 5.93 cents per mile |
| Coach and Local Service: | $17.52 + 3.58 cents per mile |

The distance to which the division curves should be applied is the carrier's shortest authorized mileage between the origin (or destination) and the point of intercarrier connection used by the passenger.

Phase 5: Discount Fares. In the discount fares phase of the DPFI, the Board focused upon two broad issues. First, is a differentiated fare structure (normal fares and promotional fares) reasonable from an economic standpoint? Second, are some of the promotional (discount) fares discriminatory and therefore unlawful? Three types of promotional fares were investigated by the Board in this particular phase: the youth fare (both standby and reservation); the family fare; and the Discover America fare. The examiner in the initial decision determined that all the discount fares at issue were unlawful as they existed in 1969 but could become lawful if modified to conform with certain prescribed levels and conditions.

The discount fares under investigation are relatively new. The family fares were first introduced in 1948, but they were applicable only in first-class service. With the introduction of coach class, the use of family fare declined until 1963, when they were made applicable to the coach-class service. Although the carriers have been experimenting with the youth fares since the early 1960s, the present youth and Discover America fares did not come into existence until 1966. The youth fare, available to passengers in the 12-21 age group in coach service only, offered a 33.3 percent discount on a space-available basis and a 20 percent discount on a reservation basis. In the family fare plan, available in both classes of service, the head of the family paid the full fare, the first member received a 25 percent discount, and other members received either a 25 percent discount (12-21 age group) or 33.3 percent discount (2-12 age group). All members were required to travel in a group as a single unit on at least one segment of the trip. In addition, there were some blackout periods. The Discover America round-trip excursion fares, available in coach service only, offered a 12.5 percent discount in markets over 1,500 miles. There were some blackout periods and the trip had to be completed between 7 and 30 days. In 1971, for domestic operations, the youth standby accounted for 3.5 percent of the revenue passenger miles, youth reservation 2.0 percent, family fare 1.9 percent, and Discover America 8.4 percent.

The first issue was the economic reasonableness of a differential fare structure.[b] Two justifications are given to support the differential fare structure: (1) development and promotional considerations; and (2) the efficiency of

bThe economic terms *discriminatory, multiple, preferential,* and *differential pricing* are used interchangeably in the industry and relate to charging different prices to different segments of the travelling public for essentially the same service.

operations. With respect to the first point, it is hypothesized that there are passengers who otherwise would not fly. The additional traffic enables carriers to expand route systems, support additional competitive services, use improved equipment, and broaden the availability of schedules and services for all users, including the normal fare passengers. As for the second point, its proponents claim that the larger traffic volumes generated by discount fares enable the carriers to operate larger and more economical aircraft, reduce their unit costs by reducing excess capacity (partially the result of seasonability), and in general spread the overhead costs to a larger group of passengers. Not only do discount fares not burden full fare passengers, but they also result in overall lower fares.

The opponents of differential fare structure disagree with the above and make the following three counter-arguments. First, the total amount of traffic generated through the differential fare structure is only minimally larger than the traffic that would exist if all fares were slightly lower. Second, while discount fares may generate additional traffic, they also divert a significant amount of traffic. Third, discount fares do not in the long run result in substantial cost savings: carriers add equipment based upon traffic carried on discount fares, in which case not only do discount fares not cover costs, but they must be subsidized by normal fare passengers.

The discount fares will increase profits during periods of excess capacity as long as the net additional revenues cover the incremental costs. While these fares burden normal fare passengers in the long run, they represent a reasonable marketing tool to deal with short-term problems of excess capacity. However, there are usually three conditions that must be fulfilled before discount fares can be beneficial. First, multiple demand elasticities must exist. Second, the carriers must be able to dissegregate the passengers by their price elasticity of demand. Third, the carriers must be able to stop the passengers from switching or downgrading. Differences in fare charges in the differential fare structure are more frequently due to differences in the demand than to differences in the cost of providing service. In determining the reasonableness of any discount fare it became necessary to investigate the cost of providing the service and the effect of the discount fare on the carrier's profit, measured by the profit-impact test. The profit-impact test considers a fare reasonable if it improves the net profit position of the carriers, even though it does not cover the fully allocated costs. Thus the promotional fare must recover the marginal costs as well as loss in revenue due to dilution. However, the profit-impact test assumes that promotional fares do not affect capacity. Although this test appears reasonable, the lack of adequate accounting data makes the task of applying this test quite complex.

With respect to the long-term impact of the discount fares, the discount traffic should bear some allocation of the capacity costs, since the carriers do obtain capacity based upon total traffic and not just the traffic carried on full fare. From an historical investigation of the growth of the discount fare traffic and the decline in load factor, it is quite clear that the carriers' purchase of equipment and scheduling policies did not just reflect the full-fare traffic. Thus in the long-run case the argument that discount traffic raises the load factor by filling empty seats is not justifiable, based upon carriers' actual operations.

From the above discussion it is clear that the Board had to resolve two conflicting issues with respect to discount fares. On the one hand, there is a legitimate need for discount fares to fill the excess capacity on the short-run basis. On the other hand, a particular discount fare cannot be allowed to become a permanent component of the fare structure on a long-run basis because the result is burdening to the general fare and normal fare traffic. The Board decided to evaluate the economic feasibility of discount fares first by carrying out the profit-impact test and second by not considering the impact of promotional fares in approving fare changes. With respect to the latter point, the Board decided to fix normal fare level on the basis of the revenue it will generate and the expenses incurred in the absence of promotional fares.

The second major issue under investigation was whether the discount fares were discriminatory and therefore unlawful. In the *Summer Excursion Fare* case the Board said that a fare is unjustly discriminatory if it meets three fundamental conditions. First, the services to which the reduced fares apply are like and contemporaneous with service to which standard fares apply. Second, the services pertain to transportation of like traffic. Third, the circumstances and conditions under which the reduced and standard fare services are rendered are substantially similar. Therefore, if the discount fares are tied to certain restrictions and inconveniences, the service can be considered "unlike." For example, travel either on particular days or on a standby basis is different from the service offered under the normal fare. Discover America fares are available to all, subject to some conditions. So they are not unjustly discriminatory. Youth and family fares are available to limited classes of people; the former is defined by age, the latter by social relationships. Therefore these fares are discriminatory.

Under the basic rule of equity of Section 404(b) of the Act, discount fares are considered discriminatory and are not allowed. However, over the years the Board has approved these fares because they provided significant development benefits. The use of the Air Travel Card Plan (1936) was probably the first promotional fare aimed at a specific identifiable market segment—the businessman. The carriers offered a 15 percent discount to travelers who spent at least $500 in any calendar year for air travel and made a deposit of $425. Although the family fare plan was formally in effect in 1948, its existence can be traced back to the mid-1930s when some carriers offered free transportation to wives accompanying their husbands. The object of the family fare was to stimulate traffic on off-peak days. Currently, however, the development benefits are questionable; thus it would appear that the discount fares burden the normal fare passengers in the long-run. If normal passenger fares actually do subsidize discount fares such as youth and family plan, their elimination would result in lower normal fares. Finally, the discount fares are supposed to reduce peaking through the blackout periods. However, some of the discount fares have created their own peaks, specifically, immediately preceding and immediately following the blackout periods.

In its final decision the Board stated that the youth standby, the youth reservation, and the family fares were unjustly discriminatory and should be cancelled. The Discover America fares were not found unjustly discriminatory. Carriers were allowed to offer discount fares subject to the condition that they are not unjustly discriminatory, satisfy the profit-impact test, and contain an expiration date not to exceed 18 months from the effective date. Finally, the fare levels are to be computed on a hypothetical full normal fare basis; that is, discount fares are not to be included as a part of the fare structure.

Phase 6A: Seating Configurations. In the seating configuration phase, the Board considered the issue of the appropriate seating configuration in both narrow-body and wide-body jet aircraft for both the trunk-line carriers and the local-service carriers. The basic issue in this phase was the appropriate differentiation in fares charged for various configurations rather than how the carriers should configure their aircraft. The narrow-body jet aircraft are typically configured with four seats in the first-class compartment and five or six in coach compartments. For six-abreast configurations the seat width is approximately 16.5 inches, while with a five-abreast configuration the seat width is approximately 18 inches. The seat pitch (distance from the forward edge of a seat to the forward edge of the seat directly in front thereof) varies from about 34 inches in economy configuration to over 40 inches in the first-class compartment.

The first question in the issue related to whether the Board had the legal power to set seating configuration standards in light of the prohibition in Section 401(e)(4) against certificate limitations on carrier accommodations. The Board decided it had the necessary power to set seat configuration standards because the rate-making powers extend not only to rates, fares, and charges but also to any classification, rule, regulation, or practice affecting such rate, fare, charge, or value of service thereunder (Section 1002(d)). Thus the Board stated that since a carrier's product is cubic feet of space, the price must be related to that product. In this case, the Board has the power to see that fares are reasonably related to the accommodations provided.

The Board adopted the following standards for seating configurations for rate making purposes. For narrow-body jet aircraft the coach-class standard was set at six abreast and 36-inch pitch. No more than 20 percent of the coach seats are allowed to be spaced to exceed that pitch for safety or structural reasons. Smaller jet aircraft not capable of accommodating six abreast were allowed to have five abreast. The seating pitch for economy class was set at 34 inches. The first-class configuration consisted of four abreast with a 40-inch pitch, and a maximum of 10 percent of the seats can exceed this pitch for safety and structural reasons. For standard, custom, or regional single-class service, where a premium over normal coach fares is charged, the pitch may exceed the standard for normal coach service but should be less than the prescribed standard for first-class service. The number of seats abreast should be the same as in normal coach service with comparable aircraft. For wide-body aircraft the standard was set at six abreast for first class and nine abreast for the Boeing 747 and eight abreast for L-1011 and DC-10.

The Board also decided that carriers wishing to offer five abreast service in narrow-body jet aircraft capable of accommodating six abreast must collect a surcharge of at least 8.5 percent over the standard coach fares. The local-service carriers were exempted from these coach seating configuration standards on the grounds that such standards would prevent them from charging coach fares in competitive markets for their regional single-class configurations. In addition, due to safety and structural reasons, Delta was granted an exemption for its Convair 880 aircraft to the extent that the seat pitch in such aircraft exceeded the prescribed standard for coach service.

The inquiry into the seating configuration for the trunk-line carriers was first instituted in 1959 with the *General Passenger Fare Investigation*. This inquiry was based upon the fact that the effective utilization of aircraft capacity has a significant influence on airline economics and in turn on the level of fares and development of traffic. However, the Board did not set any seating configurations standards due to the very small variation in seating configuration among the carriers on comparable aircraft. In 1962 Continental proposed to offer three classes of service in the Chicago-Los Angeles market: four abreast in the first class, five abreast jet business, and six abreast jet economy. The Board approved Continental's fare in consideration of the relationship of the fare to costs, the limits contained in the proposal with respect to time and area, and the benefit to the public. In 1964 the Board again approved Continental's five-abreast seating configuration on the grounds that the service could be operated economically. Similarly, in 1968 the Board approved Continental's five-abreast proposal on the ground that this reflected competitive action from which the public would benefit through improved services at no additional cost. Finally, in 1969 in once again approving Continental's five-abreast configuration, the Board rejected the argument that the action would impair the carrier's ability to handle peak travel volumes. Despite the approval of Continental's five abreast at three separate times, the Board in this phase of the DPFI rejected the five-abreast service without an additional charge of 8.5 percent.

There are a number of reasons for the Board's ruling on a six-abreast coach seating standard on the trunk-line industry. First, without a well-defined standard, there is a strong probability of a competitive seat war, resulting eventually in increased costs to be borne by the travelling public.[c] Second, the

<hr />

[c]Earlier, when Continental, United, Northwest, and Piedmont offered five-abreast seating, a seat war did not take place on an industry-wide basis because of the limited availability of this service.

Board rejected the notion that five-abreast service is required to compete actively with wide-body equipment. Very little was known at the time about the competitive effects of wide-body aircraft, and the Board decided to reconsider its decision, if necessary, at a later time. Third, the Board concluded that if the total trunk-line industry converted the narrow-body aircraft to five abreast, the cost per available coach seat mile would increase by 15.2 percent. Fourth, the conversion would result in an average reduction of approximately 16.6 percent in available capacity, resulting in considerable difficulty in coping with peaking problems. The argument that current load factors were too low to turn away passengers due to lack of capacity was totally rejected on the grounds, for example, that almost 24 percent of the flights in the carriers' top three markets experienced load factors in excess of 84 percent.

The Board's coach-class seating configuration standard for wide-body aircraft appears to be somewhat inconsistent with that of narrow-body aircraft. In its analysis, the Board pointed out that a comparable level of comfort to six abreast in the narrow-body would be a ten abreast in Boeing 747 and nine abreast in L-1011 and DC-10, resulting in a seat width of 18 inches compared to 16.5 inches for the six-abreast narrow-body. And so a passenger would have to pay a surcharge of 8.5 percent to get an 18-inch seat in a narrow-body, five-abreast configuration; but at no additional cost could get the same seat in a wide-body.

A number of parties had suggested that the fare differential between five and six abreast should be half way between existing coach- and first-class fares. At the existing fares this would have meant a surcharge of between 12.5 percent and 15 percent above the coach fare. The Board rejected this proposal and set the differential at 8.5 percent with the following reasoning. The first-class configuration offers 65 percent more space per passenger than coach service. The difference in space offered between five and six abreast is 20 percent. The existing fare differential between first and coach class was 25 to 30 percent. Thus the 8.5 percent fare differential between five and six abreast was based upon the relationship between first-class differential and extra space offered in the first class over coach.

Phase 6B: Load Factor. This phase of the DPFI was concerned with the establishment of passenger load factor standards for use in determining the reasonable fare level in the present investigation (Phase 7) and for future rate making purposes. Load factor has a critical impact on the cost of providing the service and the quality of service offered. According to the Board's investigation, approximately 65 percent of the airline costs are related to the operation of the aircraft and are independent of the number of passengers on the aircraft. Therefore a high load factor will allow the allocation of these costs over a large number of passengers resulting in overall lower fares. On the other hand, high load factors lead to less convenient service. Prior to this investigation, the carriers applied for fare changes based upon actual or forecast load factors. If load factors increased, fares were lowered. On the other hand, if load factors declined, proposals were made to raise fares. Consequently, fares fluctuated with load factors. Once a load factor standard is established, fares can be set at a level that would produce a reasonable rate of return on investment. In this case earnings rather than fares would fluctuate with load factor.

There were two basic reasons for establishing load factor standards. First, the Board concluded that fares based upon actual load factors lead to overcapacity and that the passenger must pay higher fares to compensate the carriers for the cost of operating excess capacity. This action results from the fact that carriers use capacity or, to be more precise, frequency as a competitive tool to increase market shares. If fares could not be raised, carriers would add capacity resulting in lower load factors toward the break-even point. However, if fares increase, the break-even load factor will be lowered, and carriers will undoubtedly add more capacity. Second, since market-share and frequency-share wars tend to take place on high-density routes, added schedules create overcapacity and also add to congestion, with severe effects on aircraft delays and air and noise pollution.

The Board illustrated its point of overcapacity first by showing the results of traffic increases, capacity increases, and the resulting load factor for the trunk-line carriers from 1960 to 1969; and second by showing the segment data on average flights per day, average seats per aircraft, total seats, total passengers, and load factor for nine city-pairs from 1967 through 1969. For the total operation of the trunk-line carriers, the average load factor dropped from 59.5 percent in 1960 to 50.0 percent in 1969. The nine city-pair analysis showed that for the period 1967-1969, while passenger traffic increased only 10.5 percent, capacity increased by 30.9 percent. The increase in capacity was the result of increases both in aircraft size and schedule frequencies. Higher fares to cover the costs of additional capacity have a negative effect on traffic, resulting in further decline in load factors. For example, the Board stated that in order to achieve a 10 percent increase in revenue to cover the added costs of capacity, it would be necessary to increase fares by 20 percent, which would reduce traffic and load factors even further. The Board therefore justified the need for load-factor standards based upon the inherent interrelationship between capacity, traffic, fares, and profits on the rate of return on investment.

The carriers opposing the establishment of load-factor standards pointed to their lack of control over load factors and the competitive environment. With respect to scheduling, the carriers claimed that certain flights are scheduled independent of load-factor considerations for the purposes of aircraft positioning, maintenance, and crew rotation. However, these flights are a small percentage of the total system operations. The arguments with respect to route structure centered on certificate requirements, length of haul, degree of fragmentation of markets, and seasonality. The Board rejected this line of argument on the grounds that these factors do not change significantly from one year to the other. The competitive environment argument was a direct attack on the Board's route certification policies. However, this was a weak argument. Consider, for example, the New York-Chicago market. In 1967 there were three competitors offering approximately 102 flights per day with an average load factor of 59.2 percent. Two years later, with no added competition, the same three carriers increased the schedule frequency to 130 (at the same time increasing average seats per aircraft from 98.7 in 1967 to 106.7 in 1969) resulting in a load factor of 46.8 percent. In any case, the load factor standards are not set to apply on a market or even carrier basis but rather on an overall industry basis. Finally, the carriers attempted to explain the deterioration in load factor by the large-scale equipment acquisitions. Once again the Board rejected this explanation on the grounds that this was a management decision and completely within the carriers' control. The costs of overcapacity due to premature acquisition of flight equipment should be borne by the stockholders rather than by the passengers.

As in the previous phase (seating configuration), issues were raised with respect to the Board's legal power to establish load-factor standards. The critical part of the Federal Aviation Act at issue here is Section 1002(e). The opponents claimed that Section 1002(e)(5) requires the Board, for rate making purposes, to accept the level of capacity offered by the carriers unless dishonesty, inefficiency, and uneconomical management can be clearly shown. The Board, on the other hand, used the same section of the Act to state that the carriers are not entitled to more revenue than is sufficient to provide capacity that is reasonable in relation to the traffic needs. Furthermore, Section 1002(e)(3) requires the Board to determine (for rate making purposes) the capacity needed (in the public interest) to carry traffic at the lowest cost consistent with the furnishing of adequate and efficient service. Therefore it is the function of the Board to determine the amount of capacity in the public interest. Once this capacity has been determined, then Section 1002(e)(5) requires the Board to set fares that provide sufficient revenue for the carriers to cover costs incurred under honest, economical, and efficient management.

Once the Board established its power to set load-factor standards, the following long-range load-factor standards were adopted for rate making purposes. A long-range passenger load factor was set at 55.0 percent for trunk-line carriers and 44.4 percent for the local-service carriers, resulting in 54.1 percent for the industry. These results were derived from a thorough analysis of the data collected during the investigation.[d] Since its original decision in 1971, the Board investigated the petitions for reconsideration of this decision and issued a supplemental opinion on March 18, 1974 (Order 74-3-81). In this later decision, the board kept its earlier load-factor standard of 55.0 for the trunk-line carriers but exempted the local-service carriers from any load-factor standards. This decision was based upon a number of reasons. First, the trunk-line carriers are by far the predominant industry group, accounting for more than 90 percent of the revenue passenger miles. Second, due to the subsidized nature of the local-service

---

[d]The reader interested in the actual methodology is referred to the actual decision of the Board issued on April 9, 1971 (Order 71-4-54).

carriers, fare level and fare structure had been based upon the trunk-line carriers' data. Third, the local carrier industry is still in a developmental stage and is undergoing a transformation with respect to flight equipment and service.

Phase 7: Fare Level. This phase of the DPFI was concerned with an evaluation of the reasonableness of the existing passenger fare level; and in case the existing fare level was found unreasonable, appropriate fare levels were then to be determined. In addition to these two basic issues, there were at least six subsidiary issues to be resolved in this phase of the fare investigation:

1. At the present fare level, what traffic, yield, and revenue should be forecast for the future period?
2. What are the future operating costs?
3. What is the used and useful future investment?
4. Should expenses and investment be further adjusted to reflect a standard load factor?
5. What is the effect on the movement of traffic of adjustment in the overall fare level?
6. How should the rate of return standards established in Phase 8 be implemented?

Each and every point in this list is quite complex and is discussed in detail in the Board's decision on Phase 7 handed down on August 10, 1972. The material presented here is kept very brief for two reasons. First, unless the issues are discussed in as much detail as contained in the Board's decision, they tend to lose their significance. Second, a substantial part of the discussion is related to the existing fare level (1970), the state of the economy at the time, and forecasts of traffic yield and expenses for the immediate future. All of this is past history and very little can be gained by in-depth analysis of the various positions taken during the investigation. Instead, the discussion is limited here to some important, specific points raised in this phase.

The first order of business during this part of the investigation was to agree on a traffic forecast for the trunk-line carriers for the period 1971-1972. The Board rejected the carriers' forecast and accepted the Bureau's forecast. The forecast was necessary to compute not only revenue but also expenses and the related investment. All material covered in other phases of the DPFI was brought into the calculation of the fare level. For instance, the computation of expenses requires knowledge of capacity, which depends upon load factors and seating configurations. The expenses were calculated in two steps, direct and indirect. The direct expenses, as submitted by the carriers, were modified to reflect the revised depreciation standards adopted in Phase 1 and the adoption of the rental expense treatment for leased aircraft in Phase 2. Although the Board decided in Phase 6B to set a long-term passenger load factor of 55.0 percent, for the purposes of its decision in this phase, the Board decided to use an interim standard of 52.5 percent so as to allow carriers a transitional period to bring their load factor close to the long-term standard. Available seat miles, on the other hand, were computed using actual seating configuration instead of the standards set in Phase 6A. Next, a forecast of passenger yield was made.

Two other issues had to be resolved before a computation could be made for revenue. First, a decision had to be made with respect to allocation of costs to combination services. Here the Board adopted the revenue offset approach for allocating costs between passenger and belly-cargo services. Using this approach, the total expenses of operating the combined services are reduced by the amount of revenue generated by cargo. The remaining expenses are allocated to the cost of providing passenger service. The second issue related to the impact of fare changes on demand, that is, price elasticity of demand. Having examined in detail numerous statistical studies, the Board decided to use the value of −0.7 to measure the impact on traffic of across-the-board changes in fare level.[e] Finally, the rate of return on investment as defined in Phase 8 was used to determine if the existing fare levels were unreasonable, and if so, what should be the reasonable fare level.

Based upon all the facts and considerations in the investigation, the Board decided that the existing overall level of fares for domestic passenger services was unjust, unreasonable, and therefore unlawful. Reasonable normal coach fares on domestic points should be higher than the existing level but no more than 9 percent above the fares that became effective on October 15, 1970. This ruling applied only to normal coach fares; it was not applicable to discount fares, which were dealt with extensively in Phase 5.

Phase 8: Rate of Return. This phase was concerned with determining the appropriate rate of return on investment that is adequate to compensate the carriers for their costs of capital, provide the equity owners with returns comparable to other investment of similar risk, and enable the carriers to attract the necessary capital. Unlike the *General Passenger Fare Investigation* where a separate rate of return was established for the Big Four and one of the other eight, in the present investigation a single rate of return was established for the whole trunk-line industry. In addition, a rate of return was also established for the local-service carriers. As in the case of GPFI in 1960, the technique employed to determine the cost of capital involved separate determination for the cost of debt capital, the cost of equity capital, and the capital structure, that is, the debt to equity ratio.

Although all the parties to the case accepted the overall methodology used in determining the rate of return, there were differences in opinion with respect to the values of the various components. The major difference in opinion among

[e]There is no single unique value of price elasticity of demand. It varies by market, season, direction, purpose of trip, length of haul and over time.

the parties was with respect to the capital structure. The issue is quite critical; with the cost of debt much lower than the cost of equity, the debt to equity ratio would have a very significant effect on the overall rate of return. The first basic issue to be resolved was whether to use actual debt to equity ratio or some optimum value. The Board decided to use the optimum ratio, consisting of 45 percent debt and 55 percent equity for the trunk-line carriers and 60 percent debt and 40 percent equity for the local-service carriers.

The decision by the Board to use the optimum debt to equity ratio in the DPFI is quite the opposite of its decision in the GPFI in 1960. Four reasons were given to support this decision. First, the existing capital structure of the industry was heavily weighted with debt and needed improvement if the carriers were to obtain additional capital at a reasonable cost. As of September 30, 1970, long-term debt represented 61.3 percent of the total capital for the domestic trunk-line carriers, excluding Pan American. Second, the use of actual debt to equity would further deteriorate the existing financial structure. Third, the use of the optimum debt to equity ratio is consistent with the normalized rate concepts adopted in Phase 7. Fourth, the use of optimum debt to equity ratio is more appropriate in dealing with carriers whose actual capital structure is both unsound and also significantly different from other carriers. The 61.3 percent debt and 38.7 percent equity cited earlier is for the total trunk-line carriers. The percent debt varied from a high of 73.9 for Eastern to a low of 32.9 for Northwest. Finally, due to the fact that the capital market was much lighter in 1970 than in 1960, it was considered more appropriate to use optimum debt to equity ratios. The Board was well aware of the fact that the use of a hypothetical ratio instead of the actual ratio could result in a windfall to the common shareholders of some carriers. However, the use of actual ratio would force and maintain the capital structures of most of the carriers in an unsound and undesirable position.

The witness representing American, Delta, Eastern, Northwest, TWA, and United had performed an in-depth analysis of the reasonable capital structure for the trunk-line carriers with respect to their fluctuations in revenue, expenses, and the fixed interest charges. Taking into account the Board's decision in Phase 2 with respect to the treatment of leased aircraft, he had recommended the use of 30 percent debt. This compared with debt ratios of 48 percent for natural gas distributors, 40 percent for AT&T, and 30 percent for Standard and Poor's 125 composite. The Board decided against the use of debt ratio as low as 30 percent due to the excessive returns it would provide for the equity holders if the actual industry average ratio remained as high as 60 percent. In light of this, the Board decided to use a ratio of 45 percent debt to 55 percent equity.

The Board estimated the cost of debt at 6.2 percent, based upon the actual costs as of December 31, 1969, and projected requirements for new debt in 1970 to be borrowed at 10 percent. The convertible debentures were treated as debt securities rather than equity, with the associated costs based upon their coupon rate, a decision justified on the grounds that there was no evidence of conversion in equity in the near future. The cost of debt for local-service carriers was set at 7.25 percent. For cost of equity, although a number of different techniques were utilized (such as discounted cash flow and opportunity cost of capital), estimates provided by the various parties were surprisingly close and ranged from 16 to 19 percent for the trunk-line carriers. The Board decided on 16.75 percent as the cost of equity for the trunk-line carriers. For the local-service carriers, the decision was 20 percent. Using all of the preceding data, the final rate of return on investment turned out to be 12.00 percent for the domestic trunk-line carriers and 12.35 percent for the local-service carriers.

Phase 9: Fare Structure. The reader will recall that the overall objective of the DPFI was to set rate-making standards with respect to the various elements underlying both the passenger fare level and the passenger fare structure. The first eight phases of the DPFI dealt with issues related to the passenger fare level, that is, determination on an industry basis of revenue sufficient to recover costs including a reasonable rate of return. Phase 9, on the other hand, was "concerned with the manner in which the total costs of operations should be distributed to, and recouped from, the myriad of passenger services operated by the domestic certificated carriers."[5] Based upon the Bureau's cost estimates, the Board decided that the coach fares should be based upon a multi-element formula consisting of a fixed terminal charge and a variable line-haul charge as shown in Table 11-4.

There were generally two types of objection to the new fare formula. First, some carriers did not agree with the degree of taper. This group argued that there would be an unduly adverse effect on short-haul traffic because of the low value of service. Further, besides the direct impact on short-haul traffic, the long-haul flights would also be affected, since they draw a significant amount from the short-haul feeder traffic. Also, since a substantial number of short-haul segments are operated on flights that are operated primarily to serve long-haul markets, the short-haul segment should not be burdened with the fully allocated

Table 11-4
Domestic Passenger Fare Structure

Terminal Charge	Line-Haul Charge (Cents per Mile)	Mileage
$12.56	7.06	0-500
	5.39	501-1,500
	5.18	1,501 and over

Source: U.S. Civil Aeronautics Board, *Domestic Passenger Fare Investigation*, Phase 9: Fare Structure, March 18, 1974, p. 181.

costs. Finally, even when short-haul routes do not cover fully allocated costs, they can make a net contribution to overhead if they cover out-of-pocket costs.

The second group did not object as much to the taper as the first group did; they were more concerned about the many factors unrelated to the length of haul that affect the costs of individual carriers. Thus the new fare structure based upon industry average costs by distance only does not adequately represent the cost structure. In particular, TWA outlined over a dozen other factors that account for variations in the profitability of individual carriers. Some other carriers, such as Delta, Continental, and American, as well as some third parties to the case, such as the Departments of Transportation and Justice, also presented similar views. With so many factors affecting the cost structure, it is clearly not possible to include them all in the fare formula. This being the case, these parties requested the Board to allow the carriers a certain fare flexibility around the standard day-coach fare.

Many arguments were presented for a range of reasonableness in the fare formula. The most important reasons were: first, to allow the carriers to alter fares to meet short-term changes in market and economic conditions. For example, price elasticity of demand varies from market to market, and management needs increased pricing discretion to react to marketing realities. Second, due to the imprecision of costing techniques, it is difficult to determine the exact cost structure. Third, there are geographical variances in cost. Fourth, each carrier experiences different degrees of intermodal competition, which also varies from market to market. Since the Board cannot realistically establish fares, market by market, carrier by carrier, fare flexibility will relieve the Board of this cumbersome task, avoid the regulatory lag, and enable the carrier management to determine the optimal price-quality relationship in each market. Thus the parties favoring a zone of reasonableness claim that the formula should not necessarily be cost-based; rather, it should be cost-related or cost-oriented while also accounting for marketing and value of service considerations.

In Phase 9 the Board rejected the request for fare flexibility on a number of points. The argument presented was that partial deregulation of fares would not be in the public interest. It was claimed that fare flexibility would inevitably lead to an irrational and inequitable fare structure and to an unwarranted escalation of the fare level. It was noted that the carriers have rarely filed for fare decreases. Furthermore, in Phase 7, when the Board did attempt to give some managerial discretion in the setting of the fare level, the carriers immediately raised their fares to the maximum level permitted. Thus the Board contended that if permitted, the carriers would again raise their fares to the maximum limit and use any extra profit to finance additional service competition. The other possibility is that if one carrier reduces its fares, all others would be forced to reduce theirs, with the result that all carriers would be operating at the lower fares. If this were to be the case, why would a carrier reduce the fare if such action would not increase its market share since all competitors in the market would have similarly reduced their fare? Therefore the public would be forced to accept whatever level of service that could be economically provided at the established fare.

While the Board was not in favor of a reasonable zone of fare for the trunk-line carriers, the decision with respect to the local-service carriers was quite the opposite. The local-service carriers were allowed to charge fares from 100 to 130 percent of the fares computed by the formula. This decision was justified on the grounds of encouraging the local-service carriers to experiment with fares designed to maximize revenues and reduce subsidy. Over the years the Board has followed a policy of encouraging the subsidized carriers to experiment with fares. Under this policy the local-service carriers have charged the public two fares. In markets where they compete with trunk-line carriers, the fares have been the same as those charged by the trunk-lines. However, in noncompetitive markets the local-service carriers have charged a 15 to 19 percent higher fare. These carriers were able to do this because they were allowed to calculate their fares based upon actual mileage operated instead of the authorized mileage, as in the case of the trunk-line carriers. Due to the significant amount of circuity in the local carriers' operations, their fares in noncompetitive markets have always been higher.

While the major thrust of the investigation in Phase 9 was on the passenger fares in coach service, fares for other classes of service were also discussed. First-class fares were also found to be unjust and unreasonable. In the past first-class fares were based upon a percentage relationship to basic coach fares. On the average first-class fares were 30 percent above the normal coach fares. In this phase the Board decided to set first-class fares on fully allocated costs, with the result that the first-class fare ranged from a 149.3 percent of the coach fare for a distance of 100 miles to 163.3 percent for a distance of 2,800 miles. Similar to the arguments presented in Phase 5, it is essential that in the long run each class of fare should be based upon appropriate costs. Neither discount fares nor first-class fares should be expected to be subsidized by the normal fare passengers. The first-class traffic places a significant burden on the normal coach passengers, since carriers generally offer more first-class capacity than is needed. For example, in 1972 the first-class traffic accounted for only 12.2 percent of the total traffic carried by trunk-line carriers, while the first-class capacity amounted to 18 percent. The Board gave the carriers 2 years to bring their first-class fares in line with the fully allocated costs of these fares.

The issue with respect to the night-coach fares was not settled in Phase 9. Traditionally carriers have offered night-coach service between the hours of 10 P.M. and 4 A.M. and at 80 percent of the normal coach fares. Because of the lack of data on cost differential between day-coach and night-coach service, the Board was unable to decide on an appropriate night-coach fare differential and the associated conditions of its applicability. It was decided that a new proceeding should be instituted to resolve this issue.

With respect to economy-class fares, the Board decided that economy service may be provided only on flight segments on which meal service is provided and the fare differential is $4. In the past, the significant difference between coach and economy service was that the coach passenger received a complimentary meal whereas the economy passenger had the option to purchase a meal. In its decision in Phase 6A, the Board added a further distinction, in that the economy service would have a maximum seat pitch of 34 inches compared to the coach service at 36 inches.

Finally, there were a number of other minor issues resolved in this phase with respect to the computation of coach fares. Following is a highlight of some of these issues. For those cities that are served by two or more airports, the mileage should be calculated from the geographic midpoint between the airports. For those markets where common fares are provided, the fare should be based upon the average mileage to and from all common-fared points, weighted by the number of passengers to and from such points. The coach fare for on-line passenger trips via routings other than those available at the basic point-to-point fare should be the sum of the local fares for the actual routing less one terminal charge for each local fare. For the trips involving stop-overs, the fare should be the sum of local fares.

Domestic Freight Rates

Air freight is one component of air cargo. The other two components are air express and air mail. In 1974 air freight accounted for 5.8 percent of the total operating revenue for the domestic trunk-line carriers. Air express and air mail represented 0.6 and 1.6 percent, respectively. For the U.S. international and territorial airlines, the local-service carriers, the all-cargo domestic airlines, and the all-cargo international airlines, air freight accounted for 11.5 percent, 3.8 percent, 87.5 percent, and 10.9 percent of total operating revenues, respectively. Thus air freight, while the largest component of air cargo, is still a very small portion of the business of combination carriers. Air freight refers to the transportation by air of property received directly from the shipper. Air express, on the other hand, generally refers to the property received through Railway Express Agency and transported under published air express tariffs filed with the Board. Air freight differs from air express with respect to the service offered as well as the rates charged. Until 1944 most of the air cargo consisted of mail and express. However, since 1944 air freight has become much more significant relative to the other two components. The discussion in this section is limited to air freight.

Within the United States the air freight rate structures of trunk-line air carriers and all-cargo carriers are quite similar, although there are no legal requirements that different carriers charge the same rate for the same services. In very broad terms this rate structure consists of general commodity rates, specific commodity rates, and container rates.

The general commodity airport-to-airport rates apply to all articles and commodities that are acceptable for carriage. The rate structure begins with a basic minimum charge per shipment; includes rates for shipments under 100 pounds; and has lower rates at 1,000, 2,000, 3,000 pounds and over. In a few markets additional weight breaks are offered. The highest rates per pound are for shipments under 100 pounds. The difference between rates at various weight breaks, called *volume spreads*, allows the consolidation of smaller shipments by forwarders. The current general commodity rates vary according to direction. The westbound and southbound rates are generally higher than in the opposite direction. Local-service carriers' rate structures are substantially the same as the trunk-line carriers except that they do not usually offer reduced rates in the higher range of weight breaks, due to the size of aircraft operated by these carriers.

The specific commodity airport-to-airport rates offered by trunk-line carriers, local-service carriers, and all-cargo carriers apply to the articles or commodities specifically named in the tariff and are designed primarily to encourage the use of air transportation for new or additional quantities of the designated commodities. These rates are generally lower than the general commodity rates and were for the most part established to increase the eastbound and north-bound (back-haul) traffic. The specific commodity rates are essentially published for the same shipment weights as general commodity rates, except that they are not normally quoted for shipments below 100 pounds.

Exception rates apply to individual commodities but are normally at a premium above general commodity rates. Under these rates, unusual articles or commodities such as live animals, human remains, and art works are assessed at 150, 175, or 200 percent, etc., of the normal general commodity rate. In addition to the above exception rates, very low general and specific commodity rates also exist in a few selected markets for export and import traffic.

Container rates were established to overcome the cargo density problem faced by the carriers with the introduction of jet aircraft. Whereas the piston-powered aircraft were weight limited, the jet aircraft were density limited; that is, they were space limited rather than weight limited. For example, in the early 1960s the optimum density of the Boeing 707 jet freighter was around 12 pounds per cubic foot. However, the average density of air freight carried at the time was only about 8 pounds per cubic foot. Thus the aircraft "cubed out" before it "weighed out," and the carriers could not utilize almost a third of the payload weight of the aircraft. The carriers therefore offer discounts for traffic having densities of 7 pounds or more per cubic foot. The greatest discounts are allowed on general commodity traffic having a density of over 10 pounds per cubic foot. The second reason for introducing container rates was to overcome the excessive ground handling costs by having the shipper fill the containers.

Currently the air freight rate structure is very controversial. First, there are substantial number of specific commodity rates that are considerably lower than the general commodity rates, and there are no standard criteria available to evaluate the specific commodity rates. Second, there are no standards available to determine the optimum volume spreads. Air freight forwarders or consolidators naturally favor the greater volume spreads between rates for shipments below 100 pounds and the 100 pound rates, on the one hand, and rates for larger shipments, on the other. Third, directional rates were established to develop traffic for the back-haul directions. However, despite the fact that at the present time there is very little directional imbalance, carriers claim that if eastbound rates were not lower than westbound, eastbound traffic would decline. Fourth, the level of rates for small shipments is a significant issue. Paperwork costs, for instance, do not change whether the shipment weighs 1 pound or 10,000 pounds. Fifth, the level of rates for all sizes of shipments for short hauls is very controversial due to the high ground handling costs. Sixth, the present air freight structure is considered irrational in that it bears very little relationship to the costs. These points are discussed at some length in the recent (still in progress) *Domestic Air Freight Investigation.* In order to provide a more complete understanding of the freight rates, a brief description of the *Air Freight Rate Investigation* of 1948 is also included.

Air Freight Rate Investigation (1948)

As stated earlier, prior to 1944 air freight tariffs did not exist. In 1944 American filed the first set of comprehensive air freight tariffs. The other certificated carriers followed American with similar tariffs. At the time the noncertificated carriers were not required to file tariffs, and as such, their tariffs were not fixed. Each noncertificated carrier negotiated its own terms with the individual shipper. In 1946 a number of these carriers filed for the certificate of public convenience and necessity. A year later the Board issued a decision authorizing scheduled freight service by any carrier operating on May 5, 1944 that had filed for an operating certificate. Having filed for a certificate of public convenience and necessity, the noncertificated carriers were also required to file tariffs. As a result, a number of tariffs were filed effective August 1, 1947.

The tariffs filed by the noncertificated carriers were, in general, lower than those filed by the certificated air carriers who in turn filed for even lower rates. The noncertificated carriers objected violently to this and requested that the Board take appropriate action. Since no particular rationale appeared to be behind the tariffs filed by either group, the Board instituted an investigation to determine if the tariffs were unlawful and, if so, to determine the lawful rates. In short, the purpose of the investigation was "to attempt to develop some rational principles for tariff making in air transportation as well as to enquire into the validity of the tariffs that have been filed."[6]

The resulting investigation, known as the *Air Freight Rate Investigation* [9 CAB 340 (1948)], was the most comprehensive inquiry (until the recent study) and formulated the following basic principles regarding the development of air freight rates.[7]

1. Rate levels must have a reasonable relationship to attainable cost levels.
2. The tests of reasonableness must include the recognition of variations in the ability of traffic to carry a full share of costs at different states in the development of that traffic, the effect of low rates in generating new traffic, and the resultant effect of increased volumes in unit costs.
3. Promotional rates must be fixed not only with due regard to the traffic they are expected to generate but also with sufficient consideration of attainable costs to assure that the rates will not have to be raised when the expected volume is reached.
4. The costs of the noncertificated carriers are the most usable guide to the determination of the reasonableness of the rates under investigation, because they constitute the only pure freight costs available.
5. Cost considerations are of primary importance in establishing minimum rates.
6. Value of service considerations are of importance in developing rate structure.
7. The scaling of rates with distance of shipment is sound.
8. The cost reduction that arises from increased weight of shipment may be recognized in the rate structure.
9. The maintenance of competitive balance, the development of air freight on a sound economic basis, and the need to avoid discretionary rates demand that no action be taken that affords a different treatment of the rates to be charged for a comparable service by any carrier as compared to another.

During the investigation the Board made an attempt to develop some rational principles for air freight tariff making. However, it was difficult, if not impossible, to determine rates based upon costs if the carriers did not know the appropriate costs of carrying the freight. Besides, the cost of carrying freight was different for the all-cargo carriers and the combination carriers who could offer lower rates based upon marginal costs. The Board leaned heavily toward the use of fully allocated costs and utilized the costs of all-cargo carriers as a standard, since their operations represented the actual cost of carrying freight. However, the Board did not possess sufficiently detailed cost data to be able to recommend a reasonable freight rate structure. Despite the lack of detailed cost data, the Board had to take some action to prevent unlimited rate cutting on a purely competitive basis. The Board resolved the issue by prescribing general minimum rates applicable to the entire industry. The minimum standards were set at 16 cents per ton mile for the first 1,000 ton miles of any shipment and 13 cents per ton mile for all ton miles in excess of 1,000 ton miles of any shipment. The carriers were allowed to set and file their own rates above this minimum.

Domestic Air Freight Rate Investigation

The minimum rate standards set in 1948 were revoked in 1961. The Board felt that there was no longer any threat of aggressive rate wars. In addition, with the introduction of jet aircraft with higher speeds and capacity, the Board felt that the carriers should have a greater flexibility in establishing rate proposals. Since then the Board did not investigate the freight rates until 1970 when it instituted the *Domestic Air Freight Rate Investigation* to study the lawfulness of existing rates. There were a number of reasons for instituting this investigation. First, while air freight had experienced significant growth, a number of carriers consistently reported that their all-cargo services were suffering operating losses. Second, apart from the investigation in 1948, the Board had not made any extensive study of the freight rates and felt the need to establish criteria for assessing freight rate filings similar to the criteria developed in the DPFI to evaluate passenger fares. Therefore the main goal of this investigation was to perform a detailed analysis of the domestic air freight level and structure. At the time of this writing the examiner had issued his initial decision, but the Board had not made its final decision. The following is a summary of the examiner's findings, conclusions, and recommendations.[8]

In Phase 7 of the DPFI the Board decided to use the revenue offset or by-product method of allocating costs. Using this method, the revenue derived from cargo services, less direct costs, is deducted from the total operating expenses, and the remaining expenses are allocated to the passenger services. There was a general feeling that if the rates were set based upon fully allocated costs, the resulting rates would be so high that much of the freight would no longer be carried by air. However, during the investigation substantial evidence was presented by Flying Tiger and United to show that the demand for air freight is inelastic. In light of this evidence, the examiner recommended that air freight rates be based upon fully allocated costs of the domestic trunk-line carriers (except Pan American), Airlift, and Flying Tiger.

The costs were divided into two categories, capacity costs and noncapacity costs. The *capacity costs* are related to the direct operations of the aircraft. The *noncapacity costs* refer to the ground costs. It was recommended that capacity costs be based exclusively upon the operations of all-cargo aircraft (freighters). In the DPFI the Board had tentatively decided to use the industry average costs, including the costs of both combination and freighter aircraft on the basis that almost 50 percent of all domestic air freight moves in the bellies of the combination aircraft. The examiner, on the other hand, decided to use the costs of freighters only for the following two reasons:

First, freighter aircraft are scheduled primarily to fulfill the needs of freight service; combination aircraft are purchased and operated chiefly to meet passenger demands. Second, the problems of allocating common costs exist to a much smaller degree with reference to all-cargo as compared to combination aircraft.[9]

For allocating capacity expenses among freight, express, and mail, it was recommended that the appropriate revenue ton miles for each category be converted into cubic foot miles using the following densities: 12.41 for priority mail; 18.86 for nonpriority mail; 7.60 for express; and 8.61 for freight. Each category is to be given the same priority in allocating common capacity costs.

During the load factor phase of the DPFI, the Board established a standard load factor to be used in the rate-making process. The reader will recall that this decision was made because the Board feared that without such standards the carriers would create overcapacity by adding flights on the basis of marginal profitability "in the expectation or hope that the Board would ultimately grant fare increases." In the present investigation the examiner decided not to use any load-factor standards for the following reasons. First, since the combination carriers are not obliged to offer all-cargo service, it is not known what they will do if such standards were incorporated into freight rates. Second, since freight is basically a one-way commodity, the impact of load-factor standards is not known. Third, the size and shape characteristics of "freight pieces foreclose 100 percent use of the lift capacity." Fourth, detailed data on freight movements comparable to the passenger traffic are not available at present. Most of the carriers, with the exception of Flying Tiger, advocated the use of actual load factor. Flying Tiger, on the other hand, proposed the use of a standard weight load factor of 51 percent in determining general commodity rate structure.

To allocate the noncapacity common costs, the examiner recommended the use of the results of an extensive study of freight terminal handling operations conducted by The Ralph M. Parsons Company. The objective of this study was:

... to ascertain and measure, through accepted industrial engineering techniques, the cost-causative elements involved in handling domestic air cargo (including air freight, mail, and express), and, on the basis of such analysis, develop cost factors or coefficients related to the number of shipments, number of pieces, weight, density, etc., reflecting special cost aspects of perishable, fragile, or valuable traffic.[10]

The Parsons' study concluded that weight was not the most significant cost-causative factor, and that there were other elements such as shipments, pieces, and volume. In light of these findings, the examiner recommended the use of the methodology of the Bureau of Economics (based upon the Parsons' study), which:

... allocated the labor and support elements of the traffic servicing function among baggage, freight, express, and mail on the basis of the Parsons' man-minutes. Facility costs, as they relate to cargo, were assigned wholly to freight. No reservation and sales or advertising and publicity expenses were allocated to express or mail. Some of these expenses were directly assigned to the passenger and freight cost pools. Common costs were distributed between the two cost pools on the basis of handling personnel and traffic solicitors in the case of reservation and sales expenses and on the basis of revenue as regards advertising and publicity expenses.[11]

The examiner also accepted the Board's decision on rate of return, aircraft depreciation, leased aircraft, and deferred federal income taxes as stated in the DPFI. Then, using all of the above recommendations, it was found that the existing domestic freight rates of 25.69 cents per freight revenue ton mile are unjust and unreasonable and should be increased on an average by 38.8 percent to 32.88 cents per freight revenue ton mile. The costs were calculated for the base year 1972 and then updated for the year ending September 30, 1974. The examiner recommended that the freight rates should be increased accordingly over a period of years with the increase in any one year not to exceed 12 percent.

Historically, the freight charges have been based upon weight and distance. In this investigation the examiner recommended the adoption of the freight rate structure proposed by the Bureau under which the bulk freight was divided into six categories: regular, small package, environmentally controlled and hazardous, valuable, live animals, and human remains. The container freight was divided into four groups according to size. The rate for each of these traffic types was based upon capacity charges per pound mile and a per hundred-weight. Line-haul charges per pound mile or capacity charges per hundred-weight are the same for all categories. Any variation in unit charges is related to the noncapacity costs. This structure is based upon the Parsons' study.

Minimum charges and weight breaks were found to be unnecessary and inappropriate in the rate formula. Minimum charges were developed to recover the fixed costs of processing a shipment regardless of its weight. Under the multi-element formula this is not necessary, since the formula is supposed to produce rates that recover all costs. The weight breaks were established to reflect savings in cost from shipping larger weights. The common weight breaks have been less than 100, 1,000, 2,000, and 3,000 pounds. As in the case of minimum charges, there is no longer justification for weight breaks, because the savings resulting from larger weights are already taken into account by the multi-element rate formula.

As in the case of passenger services, the carriers offer a variety of discount freight rates. The most common discount rates are the specific commodity rates, the directional general commodity rates, and the daylight container rates. The specific commodity rates were established to stimulate new traffic. The directional general commodity rates were established to offset the imbalance in the east-west and north-south directions. The daylight container rates were established to fill the unused space in belly compartments of wide-body aircraft. The examiner adopted the Board's decision in Phase 5 of the DPFI as it relates the freight rates. The arguments presented in the discount fares investigation will not be repeated here. However, it should be recalled that in the passenger investigation the Board did not reject discount fares in their entirety. Instead, the policy was to evaluate discount fares under the profit-impact test and the expiration date. Likewise, in the present case the examiner recommended that discount fares be "permitted only when there is space available to carry such traffic, the discount rate is necessary to attract the traffic to air transporation, and the rate, at a minimum, fully covers noncapacity costs and 50 percent of capacity costs." The expiration date of 18 months was also recommended. Only the specific commodity rates were considered lawful if they met the above requirements. The existing directional general commodity rates and the daylight container rates were ruled unlawful.

Finally, as in the case of passenger services, it was recommended that the local-service carriers be allowed to charge rates ranging from 100 to 130 percent of the applicable trunk-line rates. The Board's policy in the DPFI was based upon the theory that such policy would allow these carriers to maximize revenues and reduce subsidy. Presumably the same policy applies in the case of air freight services. Similarly the Board's arguments about mileage operated and low-density, high-cost operations in noncompetitive markets apply in this investigation.

Summary

The complexity of pricing air transportation services was highlighted in this chapter through a lengthy discussion of two passenger fare and one freight rate investigations. All three cases illustrate the substantive issues relating to standards for rate making.

Prior to 1952 the domestic passenger fare structure reflected a relatively uniform rate. In 1952 the trunk-line carriers introduced a $1 ticket fare increase that was unique in that it laid the foundations for the philosophy that fare per mile should decline with distance. Later in the *General Passenger Fare Investigation* the Board decided to adopt the rate-making procedures that would provide the carriers with sufficient revenue to cover their operating costs, including a rate of return on investment of 10.5 percent. However, while the Board established a general policy that the fare level should reflect the cost of service provided by the carriers, it did not set specific standards to achieve these objectives. For example, the decision to incorporate load-factor standards in determining the cost of service was rejected. In the Board's second comprehensive passenger fare investigation, the *Domestic Passenger Fare Investigation*, it established specific standards for setting fare level and structure. This investigation was divided into nine separate parts: the first three phases were handled by the Board's rule-making proceedings, while the other six were handled through the normal public hearings.

Similar to the passenger fare investigations, the freight rates have also been investigated twice in depth. First, in the 1948 *Air Freight Rate Investigation* the Board made an attempt to develop some rational principles for air freight tariff making. Due to the lack of detailed cost data the Board was unable to recommend a reasonable freight rate structure. However, in order to prevent unlimited rate cutting between the all-cargo and the combination carriers, the Board prescribed general minimum rates applicable to the entire industry. Twenty-two years later the Board instituted the *Domestic Air Freight Rate Investigation* to study the lawfulness of existing rates and to perform a detailed analysis of the air freight level and structure. Although the examiner has issued his initial decision, the Board has not made its decision.

12 Airline Subsidy

Since the early days of civil aviation, the federal government has provided financial assistance to air carriers to encourage the development of air transportation. The Federal Aviation Commission, in its report in 1935, recommended that the federal government provide whatever financial aid necessary to maintain and develop adequate transport services and that:

... the formulas under which aid is extended should be such as to encourage good management and technical progress, and to stimulate rapid evolution towards complete self support and independence of direct government aid.[1]

Thus there appears to be some indication of how long the federal government should provide the financial aid. However, the Civil Aeronautics Act of 1938 placed no statutory limits with respect to time or amount of this aid. According to the Board's deductions, it paid approximately $17.5 million in fiscal 1939 and about $73 million in fiscal 1974 as direct subsidy to:

... maintain and continue the development of air transportation to the extent and of the character and quality required for commerce of the United States, the Postal Service, and the national defense.[2]

The purpose of this chapter is to discuss the Board's policy towards subsidy to the air carriers during the last three decades, methods of administering subsidy, and its benefits and costs to the public.

In the past the carriers have received both direct and indirect subsidy. The *direct subsidy* represents cash payments, whereas *indirect subsidy* can take many forms, such as development and maintenance of airways infrastructure and the availability of weather service. In this chapter the discussion is limited to direct subsidy. Tables 12-1 and 12-2 show the amounts of direct subsidy paid to the air carriers since 1939. Prior to October 1953 the Board established the total mail compensation representing both subsidy and service mail pay. The total amount was paid by the Post Office Department, and no separation was made between subsidy and service mail payments. However, the data shown in Table 12-1 for the years of 1939 to 1953 represent the Board's best estimate of the subsidy portion of the total mail payments. Thus the data from 1939 to 1953 are based upon some administrative allocation by the Board and do not necessarily represent the carriers' actual subsidy need. Since 1954 the Board is responsible

Table 12-1
Summary of Allocated Subsidy Payments by Carrier Groups for Fiscal Years 1939-1953[a]

(In Thousands of Dollars)

Fiscal Year	Alaskan	Hawaiian	Helicopter[b]	Local-service	International	Domestic Trunk-line	Grand Total
1939	52	44	—	—	5,077	12,300	17,473
1940	51	44	—	—	7,865	13,807	21,767
1941	50	44	—	—	9,756	13,857	23,707
1942	51	43	—	—	7,477	13,881	21,452
1943	109	22	—	—	2,499	4,969	7,599
1944	212	—	—	—	1,349	2,007	3,568
1945	1,804	—	—	—	2,788	2,305	6,897
1946	2,176	—	—	1,081	13,709	4,082	21,048
1947	2,542	—	—	3,674	28,180	9,056	43,452
1948	3,004	—	—	9,411	31,015	21,574	65,004
1949	2,930	—	—	12,396	32,809	26,188	74,323
1950	2,851	18	—	14,848	37,472	26,749	81,938
1951	3,007	48	—	17,319	28,034	16,510	64,918
1952	5,368	715	—	18,990	31,442	6,607	63,122
1953	7,844	871	—	21,852	33,642	3,527	67,736

aThe amounts shown reflect the estimated subsidy portion of the total mail compensation. Therefore these amounts should not be construed as being necessarily representative of the carriers' actual subsidy need in the assigned periods.

bAlthough helicopter service began during fiscal year 1948, passenger service was not inaugurated until fiscal year 1954. Prior to that year all of the mail compensation was designated as service mail pay.

Source: U.S. Civil Aeronautics Board, *Subsidy for United States Certificated Air Carriers*, March 1974, Appendix I.

Table 12-2

Summary of Subsidy Accrued by Carrier Groups for Fiscal Years 1954-1974

(In Thousands of Dollars)

Fiscal Year	Alaskan	Hawaiian	Helicopter	Local-service	International	Domestic Trunk-lines[a]	Grand Total
1954	8,303	689	2,574	24,299	18,714	3,822	58,401
1955	7,902	293	2,656	22,358	3,757	2,773	39,739
1956	7,619	291	2,735	24,122	6,632	1,790	43,189
1957	7,707	216	3,771	28,444	6,903	1,572	48,613
1958	8,179	45	4,419	32,703	4,911	2,283	52,540
1959	7,337	168	4,860	36,450	—	1,201	50,016
1960	8,818	330	4,930	51,498	—	—	65,576
1961	9,313	505	5,538	56,300	—	—	71,856
1962	9,056	338	5,781	64,835	—	—	80,010
1963	9,690	520	5,000	67,700	—	—	82,910
1964	9,411	802	4,300	65,511	—	2,566	82,590
1965	8,163	995	3,358	61,453	—	3,475	77,534
1966	6,509	1,124	1,170	58,562	—	3,089	70,454
1967	5,939	567	—	54,966	—	2,477	63,949
1968	5,894	—	—	47,982	—	1,343	55,219
1969	5,421	789	—	40,513	—	—	46,723
1970	4,896	—	—	34,830	—	—	39,726
1971	4,499	—	—	55,940	—	—	60,439
1972	4,394	—	—	62,160	—	—	66,554
1973	4,365	—	—	60,206	—	—	64,571
1974 (Estm)	4,345	—	—	68,988	—	—	73,333

[a]Trunk-line accruals for 1964 through 1968 reflect local-service operations in the New England area.

Source: U.S. Civil Aeronautics Board, *Subsidy for United States Certificated Air Carriers*, March 1974, Appendix VII.

for payments of direct subsidy and the Post Office Department is responsible only for service mail payments.

For all practical purposes the trunk-line carriers (for both domestic and international operations) have been off subsidy since the late 1950s. The only exception to this was Northeast Airlines, which received subsidy from 1964 to 1968 for its operation in the New England area. With the withdrawal of trunk-line carriers from subsidy payments, the local-service carriers have been receiving the lion's share of the total subsidy. In fiscal 1974 the eight local-service carriers received $68.7 million out of a total of $73.0 million, or approximately 94 percent. The remaining 6 percent of the subsidy was received by the three Alaskan carriers. The $68.7 million paid in fiscal 1974 for subsidy to the local-service carriers represents a little over 5 percent of their total operating revenue. In return, the local-service carriers provided air transportation service to approximately 500 communities.

The local-service experiment was initiated in 1943 when numerous applications were filed for route authority to provide local and feeder service. Initially, the term *local* applied to air service between small towns, and the term *feeder* applied to the transportation of passengers from small communities to major terminals to connect with trunk-line service. However, this distinction no longer applies, and the two terms are often used interchangeably. In order to decide on these applications the Board instituted the *Investigation of Local, Feeder and Pick-Up Air Service* and held public hearings to determine the need to extend air service to communities to which this service did not appear to be warranted on economic grounds. The investigation was concluded in 1944 [6 CAB 1 (1946)], and the Board decided to establish local and feeder service on a temporary basis at points where there was at least an expectation of success. By 1949 the Board had authorized twenty carriers to provide local air transportation in different areas of the country. These decisions were made in the so-called area cases. In the Board's own words,

From these area cases evolved the original concept of what local and feeder transportation should be, although it was not specifically defined by the Board. The new class of carriers was to serve the smaller communities in their areas, and to feed passengers from them into the larger area hub cities, either for connections to continue their journeys, or to serve some interest in the hub city itself. In order to insure that these carriers would focus their attention on service to intermediate points on their routes, they were specifically required to serve each intermediate point on each flight provided. The condition became standard in the certificates of all local-service carriers.[3]

The Board had labelled the local-service carriers as a group of "specialists." One explanation of this concept was the reference to the use of small aircraft of these carriers. The trunk-line carriers were not interested in servicing small communities, because the type of equipment they had was more suitable for long-haul routes. Thus it was more reasonable to certificate local-service carriers to serve numerous small communities than to gradually extend trunk-line carriers to those small communities that could accommodate service by larger aircraft. Furthermore, the Board alleged that the management of local-service carriers were expected to show more ingenuity and initiative, since the bread and butter of these carriers was wholly dependent upon the successful development of traffic on these short-haul routes. Using this philosophy, whenever a trunk-line carrier and a local-service carrier filed for a short-haul route involving service to small communities or isolated, sparsely populated areas of this country, the local-service carrier was selected over the trunk-line carrier. In general, the Board was very careful not to create competition either between the local-service carriers and the trunk-line carriers or between the local-service carriers themselves.

As stated in Chapter 1, the Board has a dual role: both to regulate and to promote the air transportation industry. With respect to the promotion provisions, the Board is guided by Section 406(b) of the Act, which states:

In fixing and determining fair and reasonable rates of compensation . . . the Board . . . may fix different rates for different air carriers or classes of air carriers, and different classes of service. In determining the rate for each case, the Board shall take into consideration, among other factors, . . . the need of each such air carrier . . . for compensation . . . to insure the performance of such service, and, together with all other revenue of the air carrier, to enable each air carrier under honest, economical, and efficient management, to maintain and continue the development of air transportation to the extent and of the character and quality required for the commerce of the United States, the Postal Service, and the national defense. . . .

Thus Section 406(b) of the Act provides for the payment of whatever subsidy is needed, in addition to other revenue, to develop and maintain the air transportation system. Initially subsidy was required to cover the higher operating costs of local-service carriers due to such factors as light traffic density, short hops, high variability in traffic, greater intermodal competition, and inappropriate fleet. However, the Board was hopeful that the subsidy requirements would decrease, and it stated concerning the service in the *Rocky Mountain States Area:*

. . . the operation of any service receiving a certificate should be such as to justify an anticipation that commercial revenues will show a continued tendency to increase, with a subsequent progressive decrease in the degree of the carrier's dependency upon the Government for financial support.[4]

In 1953 the method of payment of subsidy was changed from the previous method of including it in the payments made by the Post Office Department for the transportation of mail.[5] There were basically two reasons for this action.

First, Congress and the public would be able to review the costs associated with developing the airlines. Second, separation of the subsidy element from the mail pay would provide a more representative cost of the postal services. Also in 1953 the President requested the Air Coordinating Committee (established in 1946) to produce a comprehensive review of the nation's aviation policy. One of the conclusions of the committee was that the future growth of air transportation should no longer be dependent upon federal subsidy. In particular the committee believed that the subsidy to local-service carriers should be phased out according to a schedule. Further, the committee recommended that carriers whose operations could not be sustained without subsidy should terminate their operations. The committee was not alone in this general desire to reduce and eventually eliminate subsidy. The Board, in the 1952 *Southwest Renewal-United Suspension* case [15 CAB 61 (1952)], had also expressed its concern with the problems of reducing subsidy for air service to small communities.

Steps were taken in the 1950s and 1960s to achieve this goal of reducing the level of subsidy. The local-service carriers had been experiencing substantial growth since their establishment in the mid-1940s. However, being an experiment, the Board had issued temporary certificates for their operations. In 1955 Congress enacted legislation to provide the local-service carriers with permanent certificates. This legislation was a monumental achievement on the part of the local-service carriers. Their temporary certificates had four fundamental drawbacks. First, the original certificates were for a period of 3 years, and the expense involved in their renewal was quite large. Second, the uncertainty associated with the renewal of their certificates made acquisition of capital not only difficult but more expensive. Third, the municipalities were hesitant to invest large amounts in airports and facilities due to the uncertainties of future operations by these carriers. Fourth, because of the temporary nature of the local-service carriers' operating certificates, the aircraft manufacturers were not inclined to develop a replacement for the DC-3, which, according to many of the local-service carriers, had become inefficient for their commercial operations. As a justification of the need for their service, the local-service carriers pointed to the 366 communities in 42 states that they served, with 216 communities receiving air service exclusively by the local-service carriers.

The Board had the power to issue permanent certificates, but it decided not to use it for three basic reasons. First, the Board felt that the subsidy would become permanent. Second, the certification of route authority on a permanent basis would reduce management's incentives to increase revenue and reduce costs. Third, the Board felt that the local-service carriers were not ready for permanent certification since subsidy still amounted to approximately 50 percent of their revenues. The local-service carriers, left with no other alternative, appealed to Congress. After extensive hearings, Congress required the Board to provide those carriers with permanent certificates and, if necessary, modify their certificates with respect to restrictions on intermediate stops. The Board, under the Congressional directive, decided to offer permanent certificates for points enplaning five or more passengers per day. Thirteen local-service carriers received permanent certificates.

As pointed out earlier, one of the main justifications for the permanent certification of the local-service carriers was to facilitate the acquisition of capital to purchase new aircraft. In addition to certification on a permanent basis, Congress, in 1957, enacted the Government Guaranty of Equipment Loans Act to authorize the Board to guarantee loans to aid the local-service carriers (and some other groups) to modernize their equipment. Furthermore in 1958 the original 1938 Act was amended to allow these carriers to retain any profits realized in the sale of aircraft, provided the profits were used to acquire new aircraft. Prior to this new provision in the Act any profits realized from selling aircraft were classified by the Board as operating profit and were used to offset subsidy.

The encouragement from Congress induced many communities and carriers to request new and additional service. In addition, the trunk-line carriers began to request the Board's approval to suspend service at many of the small communities. Because of the voluminous nature of these requests, the Board decided to institute "regional proceedings" beginning with the *Seven States Area Investigation* [28 CAB 680 (1958)], encompassing Illinois, Iowa, Minnesota, Nebraska, North Dakota, South Dakota, and Wisconsin. This investigation began in 1956 and concluded in 1958. The Board authorized three local-service carriers to serve this region and eliminated service by trunk-line carriers at twelve points with a cost of the new service estimated at $5.7 million. Due to the high cost of subsidy, the Board adopted its "use-it-or-lose-it" policy. This policy established two requirements for service to be offered to small communities. First, each city was required to enplane an average of at least five passengers per day. Second, for new routes, it was necessary to have at least five passengers on board per flight. If these conditions were not met, the carrier could either drop the service or take action to institute a formal proceeding. The purpose of this policy was that if a carrier or a community felt the need for service, then either or both parties had to make an effort to develop the minimal traffic to meet these tests. In applying these tests, the Board often took into consideration such external conditions as poor ground transporation or isolation of the city.

Another factor that strengthened the local-service carriers in the late 1950s was the Board's liberalized policy with respect to serving intermediate points.[a] Occasionally, a carrier applied for an exemption and the Board approved, with certain conditions, this skip-stop authority. However, in the *Seven States Area Investigation* [28 CAB 680 (1958)], decided in 1958, the Board liberalized its policy and stated that the carriers could skip certain intermediate stops as long as each intermediate point received two daily round trips. Once this condition

[a]The reader is reminded that when these carriers were first authorized, they were required to stop at all intermediate points on each scheduled flight.

was satisfied, the carriers could offer nonstop service on noncompetitive routes and one-stop service on competitive routes. This policy was established to provide adequate service to the public on all segments and, at the same time, to allow management to conduct more economical operations with better service to the public on routes where traffic was more than the bare minimum. The one-stop restriction on competitive routes not only limited competition with the trunk-line carriers but restricted the local-service carriers from conducting competitive service on routes that, in the Board's opinion, were not ripe for competitive service.

At this point it may be useful to discuss the method of calculating the amount of subsidy to be paid to the carriers. As stated earlier, prior to 1953 the subsidy and service mail pay were calculated together. In essence, the total air mail compensation to a carrier was determined by estimating the total cost of providing the service including a rate of return on investment used and useful in conducting the services. From this figure the anticipated revenue from passengers and any cargo that may have been carried was deducted. The difference between the expenses and revenue represented the carrier's need and the amount to be paid by the Post Office Department for carrying air mail. This process was a tailor-made method of determining the subsidy requirements for individual carriers and provided the Board with a certain amount of control over each carrier's profit. However, because of the uncertainties of knowing expenses and revenue in advance, management was unable to determine the actual level of subsidy until the Board had made all necessary adjustments. In addition, this method of subsidy payments took away management's incentives for maximizing efficiency, which in turn placed a heavy burden on the Board's staff to investigate the carrier's operations more thoroughly.

Payment of subsidy based upon future operations had the obvious problems. The subsidy was either not enough or too much. Either way, the amount of subsidy had to be reassessed. However, there was the option of setting subsidy rates after the fact. Under this scheme, the carriers were to be paid subsidy on their past actual operations. This scheme also had its problems. Most important of all, a carrier did not know how much subsidy it would receive. The carrier knew how much it would claim based upon its operations. However, this is not to say that the Board would actually pay this amount. The Board had to examine all the expenses, revenues, and the investment base; and it often questioned some of these elements. The cost component in particular was always debatable: Was management efficient? Was management using the most appropriate equipment? Was management scheduling excessive flights? Therefore the Board was heavily involved in managerial decisions, which really was not its proper function. Furthermore, this method of calculating subsidy created a significant time lag between the carriers' claim and the time they actually received the payment.

In order to overcome some of these difficulties, the Board instituted the

Local-service Class Subsidy Rate Investigation in 1958 and adopted a new policy in 1961. Prior to this, each carrier had its own subsidy rate; but under the new policy, the Board established a single schedule of subsidy rates (based upon the average costs of the local-service carriers) for all thirteen local-service carriers. The rate schedule (Class Rate I) consisted of a scale of rates based upon volume of operations per station (the density factor), that is, total plane miles flown divided by the average number of stations serviced per day. Initially, the rate was set at 3.11. cents per available seat mile for density factors of 600. No additional subsidy was given for operations in excess of 600 plane miles per station per day. This class rate also contained a profit sharing formula under which a carrier was to refund 50 percent of the profit between a fair rate of return and a rate of return of 15 percent and 75 percent of the profit in excess of a return of 15 percent on investment. This rule was accompanied by a 2-year carry forward clause, under which earning deficiencies were allowed to be offset against any future excess earnings.

The subsidy payments based upon the class rate formula were thought to be more efficient than the individualized method of determining subsidy. To begin with, the new method provided for greater incentive to efficiency. Second, the class rate subsidy concept significantly reduced the open rate situation. Third, it substantially reduced the Board's workload in determining the level of subsidy to be paid to the carriers. The class subsidy rate formula has been refined a number of times to adapt to the changing needs of the industry, to increase managerial incentive to efficiency, and to provide improved service to the public at a lower cost. For example, the profit sharing scheme was replaced by the "need adjustment" factor. Later, the concept of revenue-sharing was introduced. This revision automatically reduced the subsidy as the passenger revenues increased regardless of the impact of the reduction of subsidy on the carrier's financial condition. The Board is presently using Class Rate VII formula to calculate the subsidy payments.

It was not until the late 1950s that the Board began to make some tentative statements about reducing and eventually eliminating subsidy to local-service carriers. In the Board's 1958 and 1959 annual reports some reference was made to the reduction and eventually elimination of subsidy, but no formal policy was adopted. The class rate concept, initiated in 1958, was perhaps a move in this direction. In 1959 the local-service carriers received a total of $36.5 million in subsidy. This increased to $51.5 million in 1960 and $56.3 million in 1961. In 1962 President Kennedy sent a special message to Congress recommending the reduction and eventual elimination of subsidy to the various groups of air carriers. The rationale for this decision was based upon the desire to establish an efficient air transportation system, and this could simply not be achieved by subsidized operations. Therefore the President asked the Board to develop, within a year, a step-by-step program to reduce the level of subsidy.

In its reply to the President's request the Board outlined its plan for the reduction of subsidy. The Board anticipated, for a number of reasons, a considerable reduction in subsidy. First, it was expected that revenues would increase faster than costs. Second, subsidy would be reduced gradually with the introduction of high density routes in the carriers' networks. Third, consolidation of airports for two or more cities would reduce operating costs and, in turn, subsidy. Fourth, the Board would continue to employ its use-it-or-lose-it policy. While the Board made this general policy clear, the methods of achieving the desired results were not clear until several years later.

In 1965 the Board began to strengthen the route structure of the local-service carriers. This route strengthening was achieved by removing many operating restrictions and by adding the authority to serve higher density, short- and medium-haul markets on a subsidy-ineligible basis. In many cases this policy resulted in competition between the local-service and the trunk-line carriers. This policy was a reversal of the Board's previous policy of avoiding direct competition between the local carriers and the trunk-line carriers. The Board justified its decision on the grounds that the trunk-line carriers were too strong in size and financial condition to suffer any significant impairment on account of competition from the local-service carriers. Incidentally, the new policy was also inconsistent with the Board's initial statement that the local-service carriers were established only to provide service to small communities.

The basic objective of route strengthening was to allow the local-service carriers to internally cross-subsidize the weak routes with excessive profit from the lucrative routes thereby reducing subsidy. However, it is not clear that the route strengthening program was the appropriate method to achieve the goal of subsidy reduction. For example, since the local-service carriers were to compete with the trunk-line carriers, it is unlikely that they could have realized excessive profits. Only on those routes where local carriers had a monopoly and the traffic density was high could this objective have been achieved. Thus the extent to which local-service carriers could provide subsidized service depended upon the level of profits in the new and additional markets. In any case, this philosophy did not really reduce subsidy; rather, it just shifted the subsidy from the federal government (all taxpayers) to individual passengers traveling on the high-density routes. Finally, if there are excessive profits on a given route, it is possible that the level of fares may be too high, in which case the policy of route strengthening was promoting travel on low-density routes at the expense of diminishing demand on the denser routes due to the existence of higher fares.

In 1966 the Chairman of the Board, in hearings on *Review of the Local Air Carrier Industry*, indicated that subsidy could be reduced by the introduction of more efficient jet aircraft, which would reduce costs and increase revenue through stimulation of traffic.[6] The introduction of jet aircraft, coupled with the authority to serve more lucrative routes, was supposed to increase the earnings and thus reduce subsidy. The Chairman also indicated that there may be significant economic advantages to local carrier mergers. Despite any formal policy of the Board to reduce subsidy through mergers, three mergers have been approved since the mid-1960s involving local-service carriers. In 1967 a merger was approved between Frontier and Central. A year later a merger was approved between Bonanza, Pacific, and West Coast. Finally, in 1972 a merger was approved between Allegheny and Mohawk. In each case the possibility of a reduction in subsidy influenced the Board to approve the mergers. The influence of subsidy reduction on merger decisions is discussed at some length in the next chapter.

The issue of elimination of subsidy must still be resolved. From 1939 to 1974 a total of $1.9 billion in direct federal subsidy had been received by the U.S. commercial airline industry. Local-service carriers received nearly 60 percent of this amount, and during the last 5 years they received almost 93 percent of the total subsidy. It was estimated in a 1969 Board staff study that the subsidy needs per passenger on marginal routes of Air West, Allegheny, Frontier, and Texas International amounted to $21.23 to $23.92 per passenger.[7] For individual cities such as Martinsburg, Virginia, the subsidy per passenger ran as high as $206.13.[8] A marginal route included services to one or more points at which the carrier originated less than forty passengers per day. While the small communities have received substantial benefits over the years through the availability of air services and/or lower fares, it is debatable whether the benefits outweigh the costs.

It is sometimes forgotten that the Board has an obligation to support the local-service carriers. First, despite the Board's reluctance, Congress did certificate the local-service carriers' routes on a permanent basis. Second, the Federal Aviation Act required the Board to fulfill the "need" of each certificated carrier. In addition, there is always pressure from the communities to continue air service for such reasons as community pride, economic development, and isolation and urban-rural equity.[9] Thus the issue is not whether to have air service for small communities, but what is the most economical method of achieving the desired service. The question of a more efficient mechanism for dispersing subsidy has been investigated extensively by the Board's staff, and the following three alternatives have been suggested.[10]

First, points that do not require subsidy support should be retained by the local-service carriers. Those points that require subsidy support should be gradually transferred to commuter carriers, who in turn should be certificated just like the local-service carriers.

The second alternative is to extend the "flow-through" concept whereby a local-service carrier makes arrangements with a commuter carrier to provide service to small communitites. This concept was first approved in 1973 as a 2-year experiment to provide better service to small communities at a lower cost to the government. Under this concept, Frontier has ceased service at Dodge City, Great Bend, and Hutchinson, Kansas and has turned over the operations to Air Midwest, a local commuter carrier. Frontier, instead of subsidizing its own services at these three points, pays Air Midwest out of the subsidy it receives from the Board. While this form of "subcontracting" appears to be beneficial in terms of better service and lower subsidy costs, there are some legal questions. The basic problem is that the flow-through concept allows a private carrier to control entry, exit, and market behavior of another private carrier. Another problem with this method is that subsidy cannot be provided to a commuter carrier to conduct service to an uncertificated point.

The third alternative suggested is to award contracts through a competitive bidding system for those points that cannot generate sufficient traffic but, nevertheless, are in need of air service. In 1972 the Board proposed this system to Congress as a 2-year experimental program. Under this concept, the contract would be awarded to the lowest bidder on the understanding that it may not be renegotiated. This proposal was abandoned, since Congress did not take any action on it.

These alternatives are considered more efficient than the past methods of subsidizing the local-service carriers. In his book, *The Local Service Airline Experiment*, George C. Eads concludes that the quality of air service provided by the local-service carriers to small communities has been poor and the associated cost higher than necessary.[11] It is a paradox that on numerous occasions the local-service carriers have placed the blame for poor service to a community on the lack of traffic generated by the community, while the community naturally cited the lack of service as the cause of lack of traffic. This chicken-and-the-egg dilemma was clearly demonstrated in the case involving Frontier's service to Pueblo, Colorado.[12]

Until 1967 Pueblo was served by Continental and Frontier. Continental abandoned the service and Frontier provided nonstop or one-stop service to seven cities. Service to Denver was provided with four nonstops and two one-stops. By 1970 the service was reduced both in frequency and quality. At the same time the passenger traffic in and out of Pueblo had also declined. According to a market survey, poor service was found to be the main reason for the declining traffic. One way of improving service was to introduce jet service to Pueblo, which according to Frontier's analysis would lose $48,000 every year. The city decided to subsidize Frontier's operation with $4,000 a month for a period of 6 months. The monies were to be taken from the airport funds. Both Frontier and Pueblo's Chamber of Commerce began an extensive advertising and public relations campaign based upon the use-it-or-lose-it philosophy. The improvement in service as a result of jet aircraft and joint and through fares, combined with honest support from the community, resulted in a substantial increase in both passenger and freight traffic. By the end of the 6-month experiment traffic had increased sufficiently, and Frontier was willing to operate the service without subsidy. This example clearly shows that both sides must make a serious effort. If a carrier's service is considered poor, it may not always be the fault of the carrier.

The other reasons for declining service to small communities are the increasing competition from the automobile and the relatively low growth of population of the rural areas relative to metropolitan areas. The competition from the automobile is the result both of the significant development of the interstate highway system and of a greater widespread ownership of the automobile. The development of the interstate highway system is expected by 1978 to reach 92 percent of the cities with a population of 50,000 or more.[13] The greater use of the automobile is the result of various improvements in cars (such as air conditioning), more cars per family, and the greater availability of rental cars. With respect to growth in population, the metropolitan areas have been growing at a rate almost 3 times faster than the nonmetropolitan areas. This rate is not to imply that the central cities have been growing at this rate. The growth in metropolitan areas, as discussed here, includes the growth of suburban areas. Thus the decline in air service to small communities is also the result of intermodal competition and demographic changes.

Thus far very little has been said with regard to subsidy to other carrier groups. As of 1974 most of the subsidy had been received by the local-service carriers. The only other group receiving subsidy are the three Alaskan carriers for service within Alaska, where air service is essentially the only means of travel. Subsidy to this group of carriers is perhaps the only real example of the role of subsidy in the national interest. Subsidy was terminated in 1959 to trunk-line carriers (except Northeast) and in 1966 to the helicopter and Hawaiian carriers. The U.S. international carriers have been operating without subsidy since 1959.

In April 1974 both Pan American and TWA applied for subsidy to offset the substantial increase in fuel costs. Both carriers filed for a subsidy mail rate under Section 406(b) of the Act to adequately compensate the carriers so as to insure the continued performance of their services. Pan American requested an annual subsidy of $194 million. This consisted of a break-even need of $85.4 million and a return on investment of $108.6 million. The carrier pleaded its case by stating that the subsidy was needed to "protect a national asset." The carrier went on to explain that by stating:

1. Pan American is the standby provider of more CRAF long-range aircraft available on call by military authorities in the event of any national emergency than *any* other airline—a capability which could be of crucial importance if the need arises for instant movement of troops, personnel, and equipment to far places. Pan American currently has assigned 63 aircraft to CRAF, exceeding the next highest (Northwest) by 36, and exceeding all supplemental carriers put together.

2. Pan American is by far the largest international U.S.-flag air carrier of mail, passengers, and cargo throughout the world, thus promoting our national interests in this advancement and facilitation of trade and commerce. It would be unthinkable for the United States to permit foreign air carriers to increase their already substantial participation in the carriage of U.S. originating traffic. Further, as opposed to domestic travel, where there is viable alternative travel

(bus, truck, rail, barge, automobile), the *only* surface transportation alternative to U.S.-flag air transportation over the world is slow surface shipping. This would be an utterly unacceptable mode of transportation and there are large areas of the world where passenger ships (except for cruise ships) no longer operate.

3. Pan American is an instrument of national policy (where the U.S. government desires it to be such), as, for example, in its service to Moscow and other eastern European countries. Today, Pan Am is the *only* U.S.-flag presence in 40 foreign countries.

4. Pan American is a substantial earner of dollars and foreign currency, thus materially assisting in the balance of payments problem. The international air transportation is one of the principal contributors to our favorable balance of payments.

5. Pan American is the nucleus of a worldwide organization with know-how which is capable of rapid expansion in the event of a national emergency need, as contrasted to the years it takes to start up a new organization. The existing skilled personnel and the maintenance, communications, and other facilities of Pan American are invaluable to this country.[14]

Since the Board's decision to this application would have taken considerable time, the carrier requested in August 1974 an immediate temporary payment of $10 million per month. In September 1974 the Administration indicated that the U.S. taxpayers should not be required to support U.S. flag carriers offering international service. The Board, on the other hand, did not flatly reject the subsidy request. While the temporary subsidy request was rejected, the Board indicated that it might be necessary to subsidize a few routes considered to be in the national interest. In any case, the Board made a strong point of suggesting the restructuring of routes to reduce the financial problems.

Similar to Pan American's request, TWA also filed for subsidy in April of 1974. The arguments presented in TWA's case were very similar to those in the application of Pan American. The carrier stated that, ". . . unless substantial relief is afforded, TWA's international operations in 1974 will suffer losses that would make it impossible for it to maintain anything approaching adequate service between the United States and foreign countries." In his remarks before the Travel Research Association on April 16, 1974, TWA's senior Vice President of Marketing cited numerous industries, such as the railroad industry, the maritime industry, and the agricultural industry, that were receiving government subsidy. The request for subsidy by the U.S. flag carriers was quite small relative to the subsidy paid to other transportation industries. TWA's Vice President cited, for example, that a bill authorizing more than $2 billion in subsidy for the railroads of northeastern states was passed with relatively little resistance compared with the Lockheed loan guarantee which aroused the whole country even though it involved tax funds that were an order of magnitude smaller.

Similarly the TWA executive expected that the Pan American and TWA's subsidy requests would attract substantial public attention.[15]

TWA also filed for temporary subsidy in August 1974. However, the carrier's chances were substantially reduced when the Department of Transportation indicated that the request was not justified, due to the carrier's relatively good domestic operations. The Board denied the request in September 1974 on the basis that TWA had failed to provide sufficient information on its domestic operations. TWA refiled its application in October requesting $61.6 million, of which $31.4 million was to break even and the remaining $30.2 million was to provide for adequate return on investment. Presently the carrier has accused the federal government of discriminating against it with respect to fuel matters and has, therefore, asked for compensation (in terms of subsidy) for higher fuel prices.

Although the Board has instituted an investigation to determine Pan American's and TWA's need for subsidy, it is doubtful that direct subsidy will be granted for at least two reasons. First, historically the Board's policy has been to reduce subsidy not increase it. This was demonstrated in the case of local-service carriers. Second, the Board's tendency is to improve the routes rather than provide direct subsidy. This was illustrated in the case of new routes in the Caribbean for TCA and Caribair and more recently by the route exchanges between Pan American and TWA, and between Pan American and American.

Summary

From 1939 to 1974 the U.S. commercial airline industry received almost $2 billion in direct federal subsidy to maintain and continue the development of air transportation. The local-service carriers have received nearly 60 percent of the total subsidy; and during the last 5 years they received almost 93 percent of the total subsidy. For all practical purposes, the trunk-line carriers (for both domestic and international operations) have been off subsidy since the late 1950s.

During the mid-1940s the Board established local and feeder service on a temporary basis at points where service did not appear to be warranted on economic grounds, but where, nevertheless, there was at least an expectation of success. The Board was very careful not to create competition either between the newly established local-service carriers and the trunk-line carriers or among the local-service carriers themselves. In 1955 Congress enacted legislation to provide the local-service carriers with permanent certificates, and the Board took a number of steps to reduce and eventually eliminate the subsidy. These steps included the Board's use-it-or-lose-it policy, its liberalized policy with respect to serving intermediate points, establishment of Class Rates Structure for determining subsidy requirements, route strengthening, allowing mergers to take place among the local-service carriers, and the flow-through concept.

A number of industry analysts have concluded that the quality of air service provided by the local-service carriers to small communities has been poor and the associated cost higher than necessary. The carriers have placed the blame for poor service on the community, due to the lack of traffic generated by the community, while the community cited the lack of service as the cause of less traffic. However, additional explanations of this phenomenon of declining service to small communities may be the increasing competition from the automobile and the relatively low growth of population of the rural areas relative to the metropolitan areas.

13 Airline Mergers

Why do two air carriers decide to merge? What is the Civil Aeronautics Board's policy concerning mergers? What is the Department of Justice's policy on airline mergers? What is the role of the Department of Transportation in airline mergers? These questions are by no means easy to answer due to the complexity of airline mergers.

The purpose of this chapter is to attempt to provide the reader with some insight into the subject of airline mergers. Unlike the chapter on airline routes, the material on mergers is not developed through particular cases but rather in light of the questions posed above. However, extensive reference will be made to various consummated, proposed, or rejected mergers.

Air Carriers' Interest

First, the mergers are investigated from the viewpoint of the carriers. The analysis of airline mergers is a complex task, since the reasons for merging vary from one airline to another. For example, the main object of one carrier may be to become more efficient (advantages of economies of scale and the ability to spread overhead costs over a large volume) and serve its markets more effectively. Second, the objective may be the wholesale purchase of a network of routes instead of applying for one route at a time through the lengthy proceedings discussed in Chapter 10. Third, the reason for a merger may be to eliminate the possibility of bankruptcy. Fourth, a merger may be one way of eliminating competition on certain segments of a route network. Fifth, a merger may provide an opportunity to diversify. Sixth, a merger may provide an opportunity to reduce critical seasonality problems. These are just a few of the many reasons for two carriers to propose a merger.

Naturally, there is another side to mergers. While mergers may provide benefits to the two partners, the public and the employees may be adversely affected. First, since mergers could eliminate competitors, the public may be deprived of the benefits of competition. Second, it is the inevitable that certain employees will be shortchanged, either because their jobs will be eliminated or because they will be dominated by another group. Thus there are conflicting objectives, and it is the function of the Board to weigh the pros and cons in making a decision. To put these pros and cons in a little more perspective, it may be beneficial to discuss some of these points in light of three merger cases:

241

Northeast-Delta (and the previous proposal between Northeast and Northwest), Allegheny-Mohawk and Allegheny-Lake Central, and American-Western.

Northeast-Northwest and Northeast-Delta

At the beginning of this decade when it was clear that airline profits were rapidly declining, a number of merger proposals were announced. Competition in the 1970s, as a result of recent route awards, was far more extensive than that which existed in the 1960s. The carriers had originally applied for these newly acquired routes at a time when traffic growth was very high. However, at the time the routes were actually awarded, the traffic had declined significantly. One of the first proposals was between Northeast, a weak New England carrier with some long-haul routes to Florida, the Bahamas, and Bermuda, and Northwest, a strong transcontinental and transpacific carrier. Why did Northwest want to merge with Northeast? Although it is impossible to determine the exact reasons, one can see a couple of obvious reasons. Financially this appeared to be a sound investment. The agreement was to exchange one share of Northwest stock (with a market value at the time of $35) for five shares of Northeast stock (with a market value at the time of $14). Storer Broadcasting Company, which owned about 86 percent of the Northeast stock, was willing to accept this offer. Thus Northwest would have acquired Northeast assets (basically, its fleet) at a reasonable price, and it also would have picked up a $17 million tax loss carry forward.

Besides the financial advantages, the merger with Northeast would have provided some good routes for Northwest, whose domestic routes were basically east-west across the northern tier of the country. Northwest would have acquired eastern seaboard routes from Montreal to Miami, including all major cities in between. Since east-west traffic peaks occurred in the spring and fall and eastern seaboard peaks occurred in the winter, Northeast's routes would have provided a seasonal balance to Northwest's routes. One route, in particular, was extremely attractive to Northwest; namely, Northeast's recently acquired Miami-Los Angeles route.[1] This route would have provided Northwest with authority to offer direct service from Florida to Hawaii and the Orient through the Los Angeles gateway. Furthermore, since the Board had recently recommended approval for Northwest's application to serve Seattle through San Francisco and Los Angeles, the merger would have resulted in service around the entire periphery of the United States. Finally, the Miami-Los Angeles route would have been quite suitable for Northwest's long-range jet aircraft.

The merger between Northeast and Northwest was approved by the Board and by President Nixon, whose approval was needed because the merger involved some international routes. However, there was one condition attached to this approval. The Board decided that the recently awarded Miami-Los Angeles route would not be included in the package. If Northwest wanted this route, it would need to apply after the merger for this route, just like any other route application. This condition was totally unacceptable to Northwest, since it valued this route at 15 to 20 percent of Northeast's value in terms of revenue potential. There was a feeling in many circles that Northeast had obtained the Miami-Los Angeles route prior to its proposals to merge in order to make itself more attractive to prospective buyers. The Board had granted the route to Northeast based upon the route strengthening doctrine and without any prior knowledge of Northeast's intentions to merge. Early in 1971 Northwest appealed to the Board to reconsider the attached conditions. But the Board upheld its ruling and Northwest withdrew its merger proposal.[a]

In 1971 Delta announced its interest to merge with Northeast. As in the case of Northwest, financial and route considerations were the reasons for Delta's interest in Northeast. Delta was large enough to be able to absorb Northeast without biting off more than it could chew. Yet the company was small enough to benefit from the addition of Northeast's routes in its future growth plans. Delta's offer was to exchange one of its share for ten of Northeast's share. Based upon the existing market value, the total value of Delta's stock to be exchanged was approximately $30 million. With regard to the Miami-Los Angeles route, there was no escape clause as was the case with Northwest. Thus if the Board and the President were to approve the merger without the Miami-Los Angeles route, Delta would be obliged to accept the agreement.

Now the reader should realize that even though a merger agreement is approved, it does not necessarily mean that all the problems are over. To the contrary, there are many issues that must be resolved before the merger is a working reality with completely integrated routes and operational service. One of the most important issues to be resolved concerns the employees of the merged carrier. The problems in this area are not related so much to any large scale dismissals; rather they are related to moving (in Northeast's case from Boston to Atlanta), working under different conditions, being in a different union structure, and dealing with the integration of seniority. In the case of the Northeast-Delta merger, the agreement stipulated that none of Northeast's employees be dismissed. However, a good many of the Northeast employees were required to move to Atlanta.

Another problem is usually the organization structure. Although a pilot is a pilot before and after the merger, the problem here is the job status of the airline's management personnel; this is quite a complex issue to resolve. In the case of Northeast-Delta there was another problem. Whereas Northeast was a heavily unionized carrier, only pilots and dispatchers belonged to unions at Delta. Therefore most of Northeast's union contracts were not binding on Delta, which only recognized Northeast's pilots' union. Northeast went all the way to

[a]Strangely enough, TCA was also awarded some lucrative routes prior to its merger with American. However, the merger approval was not conditional upon any route restrictions similar to the Miami-Los Angeles restrictions in the *Northeast-Northwest* case.

the Supreme Court but lost its case. Delta returned the union dues paid by Northeast employees while at Northeast and also gave each of them an across-the-board pay increase.

Besides the problems of merging employees, there are problems related to the merging of technical systems (such as reservations), physical facilities (office buildings and hangars), and scheduling. With regard to flight equipment, the problems relate both to qualifying the pilots on new equipment and resolving the issues related to the mechanical differences in the aircraft itself. These two matters are time consuming and costly, since the pilots as well as the aircraft must meet standards set by the Federal Aviation Administration. The problems of combining reservation systems and scheduling must not be underestimated. Quite often the computer system handles reservations as well as payroll and general accounting. Speed and accuracy are essential in moving the computer system from one city to another. Finally, on account of the many new routes, aircraft, and crew that are added, the scheduling process takes a long time to stabilize. The intricacies of scheduling were discussed in Chapter 7.

Allegheny-Mohawk and Allegheny-Lake Central

The basic reason for the mergers of Allegheny-Mohawk and Allegheny-Lake Central was related to the improvement of route structure. Prior to the mergers with Lake Central and Mohawk, Allegheny's operations were confined to the Middle Atlantic States, with Boston and Washington, D.C. on the east; and Pittsburgh, Cleveland, and Detroit on the west. This route structure was limited with respect to the potential of jet operations as well as route restrictions with respect to competition with trunk-line carriers. The merger with Lake Central provided Allegheny with access to major cities west of its route system, such as Cincinnati, Columbus, Dayton, Indianapolis, Louisville, Chicago, and St. Louis. In addition to new points, management is also usually interested in the common points. In the case of Lake Central and Allegheny, the common points included Baltimore, Buffalo, Cleveland, Detroit, Pittsburgh, and Washington, D.C. Lake Central's routes contained relatively few nonstop authorizations. The authority of most of its routes was restricted, requiring intermediate stops between most of its larger cities. After its merger with Lake Central, Allegheny took advantage of the Board's route strengthening policy and applied for permission to eliminate the restrictions. This action was quite successful in improving Allegheny's route system.

The merger with Mohawk was also based upon reasons related to route structure. The two carriers had nineteen points in common. The new points for Allegheny included Minneapolis, Montreal, Rochester, and Syracuse. On account of the two mergers with Lake Central and Mohawk, Allegheny expanded its markets from being the tenth largest carrier of domestic passengers in 1967 to the sixth in 1973. Although classified as a local-service carrier, Allegheny carried more domestic passengers in 1973 than five trunk-line carriers—Braniff, Continental, National, Northwest, and Western. In fact, out of a total of 32.5 million domestic passengers carried by the eight local-service carriers in 1973, Allegheny carried 10.8 million, a market share of 33.3 percent. Mohawk's interest, on the other hand, was purely financial (as in the case of Northeast); Mohawk was almost bankrupt.

American-Western

In 1970 American proposed to merge with Western. For 4 consecutive years the net operating income of the domestic trunk-lines had continued to decline from $454 million in 1966 to a low of $17 million in 1970. The Big Four posted an operating loss of $105 million for their domestic operations in 1970. American's operating loss on its domestic operations totaled $19 million. On its international and territorial operations the carrier showed an operating profit of $4 million. Reduction in business travel was the main reason for the operating loss. American, a carrier with a large percentage of revenue derived from business travelers, suffered more than those carriers who primarily handled the personal and pleasure markets. American's proposed solution to the problem was to merge. The situation was very similar to its proposal to merge with Eastern in 1962, when the trunk-line carriers were showing a deficit due to the slowdown in the economy and the overcapacity as a result of the introduction of jet aircraft. Western, on the other hand, had shown a small profit in 1970 but was facing difficulties in financing the $200 million purchase of wide-body equipment.

The merger with Western (if it had been approved) would have strengthened American's route system significantly. Mergers such as Allegheny-Lake Central and American-Western are known as "end-to-end" mergers. This type of merger ties together the routes of two carriers at the common points without significant duplication of route segments. The real advantage arises if the common points are either large connecting cities such as Chicago, Atlanta, and Los Angeles or geographically strategically located cities such as Los Angeles for the Hawaii market. Both of these conditions existed in the American-Western proposal. Western's routes were very compatible with those of American. For example, American's transcontinental routes terminated at the same three West Coast cities where Western's routes to Hawaii originated—San Francisco, Los Angeles, and San Diego. Also, American's route to Salt Lake City from the East integrated well with Western's route from Salt Lake City to the West Coast. Throughout their system, there were only three markets where both American and Western competed: Los Angeles-Phoenix, Los Angeles-San Diego, and Phoenix-San Diego. In the Phoenix-San Francisco market, Western could not be considered an effective competitor of American, since it did not have nonstop authority. The two carriers had fourteen points in common, including important cities such as Honolulu, San Diego, Los Angeles, San Francisco, Salt Lake City, Phoenix, and Mexico City. Thus, in addition to providing American with new points, such as Las Vegas and Denver, the merger would have allowed one-carrier service in almost 100 markets.

As in the Northeast-Northwest proposal with respect to the Miami-Los Angeles route, there was one market of particular interest to American in its proposal to merge with Western, namely, the West Coast-Hawaii market. While American could operate on this route as a result of the transpacific decision, its authority from the California gateways to Hawaii was limited by its frequencies from the East beyond Hawaii to the South Pacific. Thus the merger with Western would have provided American with unrestricted authority to serve Hawaii from the West Coast. Furthermore, since American had nonstop authority from numerous points to California, the merger would have allowed American to offer one-stop service to Hawaii via California from such major cities as Boston, New York, Detroit, Washington, and Chicago. Finally, while American was not allowed to serve the South Pacific from the California gateways, the merger would have allowed single-plane service from the West Coast to the South Pacific with a stop at Honolulu.

The Board's Policy

The Federal Aviation Act of 1958 requires both the CAB and the President to approve any mergers involving international operations. The Board, in deciding a merger case, carefully examines the issues of competition, diversion of traffic from other carriers, level of service, industry structure, and market conduct. Section 408(b) of the Act requires that the Board not approve a merger that would create a monopoly, restrain competition, or jeopardize another carrier not party to the merger proposal. However, there is a way of getting around the antimonopoly provisions of Section 408(b). The Board can and has approved mergers that resulted in a reduction of competition under the so-called failing business doctrine. It should be made clear that a carrier does not have to prove that it is failing in order to receive the Board's approval to merge. The doctrine allows a merger without having to prove public benefits. In other words, the Board will approve a merger even if some of the conditions in Section 408(b) are not satisfied, providing the carrier is failing. Finally, in recent years the Board has begun to approve mergers in order to improve the financial position of one or more of the participant carriers. The approval of mergers in these cases was based upon the notion of promoting public interest rather than under the failing business doctrine.

In the years following its establishment in 1938, the Board's policy in merger cases was in favor of competition. The fear that the surviving carrier would become too powerful (in relative size), resulting in elimination of competition, played a major role in the decision to disapprove merger applications. This policy was brought out clearly in 1940 in the proposal of United to merge with Western [1 CAB 739 (1940)] and again in 1946 in American's proposal to merge with Mid-Continent [7 CAB 365 (1946)]. The Board's objection with respect to the size of the surviving carrier related to its impact on competition and not so much to any diseconomies of scale that may, or may not, have existed. The mergers that did receive the approval of the Board did not eliminate competition to any significant extent.

During the few years following the end of World War II, the industry's financial position was fairly weak. Excessive capacity and excessive competition both within the scheduled industry and between the scheduled and charter carriers were the chief causes of the deteriorating financial position. In its "Economic Program for 1949" the Board made strong suggestions for mergers as a means of improving the financial position of the industry. Thus the Board was quite willing to entertain merger proposals from carriers whose routes would integrate logically, resulting in the elimination of unnecessary duplication of services, greater benefit to the public, and lower rates for the transportation of mail.

In about half a dozen years following this encouragement from the Board, several mergers were approved between the local-service carriers, between trunk-line carriers, and between a local-service and a trunk-line carrier. These mergers were approved based upon the projected savings in total overhead costs, improvement in utilization of flight equipment, and a substantial reduction in subsidy payments. For all practical purposes, none of these mergers resulted in the elimination of point-to-point competition with the exception of one route, Kansas City to Houston, where competition was eliminated by the merger of Braniff and Mid-Continent. Several applications from local-service carriers to merge with one another were disapproved on the grounds that the surviving carriers would have ended up with a route system that was outside the scope of local-service operations.

Whereas the mergers approved prior to 1961 did not eliminate point-to-point competition, Capital's merger with United [33 CAB 307 (1961)] was another case. This merger, approved in 1961, eliminated competition in nineteen city-pair markets including New York-Cleveland and Cleveland-Chicago. Utilizing the failing business doctrine, the Board approved this merger despite the resultant reduction in competition. Capital desperately needed funds to modernize its fleet but, in light of its financial losses in recent years, was unable to obtain these funds. Since Capital was a trunk-line carrier, the possibility of a subsidy, especially of the amount needed, was slim. In short, the carrier was about to declare bankruptcy. Since the Board is responsible for maintaining sound economic conditions in the air transportation industry and since the

Board is supposed to accommodate the needs of the carriers, it was decided that the demise of Capital would not be in the public interest. Thus the Board approved the merger between United and Capital. It should be emphasized that it was the failing business doctrine that enabled this merger to receive approval, despite the unfavorable impacts on competition that was the reason merger proposals between American and Eastern and between Pan American and TWA were rejected. It is interesting to note that after reducing competition in four major markets by approving the United-Capital merger, the Board, in the *United Air Lines Competitive Service Investigation*, concluded that the public interest required that competition be restored in the same four markets. American was selected to provide service on the New York-Cleveland route and Northwest was selected to provide service on the other three routes.

The mergers between local-service carriers in the 1960s were the direct result of the Board's policy (under advisement from President Kennedy) to reduce the level of subsidy. As stated in the previous chapter, mergers were one way of reducing the level of subsidy. In light of this policy, the Board approved mergers between Frontier and Central; between Bonanza, Pacific, and West Coast; and between Allegheny and Lake Central. Although these merger approvals did not significantly reduce point-to-point competition, they did result in route systems that were clearly outside of the definitional scope of local-service operations. It is pointed out that two merger proposals, Southwest-West Coast [14 CAB 356 (1951)] and North Central-Lake Central [25 CAB 156 (1957)], had been rejected earlier on these grounds. The Bonanza-Pacific-West Coast merger (surviving carrier known as Air West) resulted in a route system bounded on the north by Los Angeles, Seattle, and Calgary; on the south by San Diego, Yuma, and Phoenix; and extending from the West Coast to Great Falls, Idaho Falls, and Salt Lake City. Such extensive route structures were clearly not the intent of local-service operations when they were first authorized. Similarly, large extensions in routes resulted from the Frontier-Central and Allegheny-Lake Central mergers. However, the Board felt that the advantage of subsidy reduction outweighed the disadvantages of any reduction in competition in the respective areas.

In the early 1970s the Board once again adopted its policy of the failing business doctrine and approved the mergers between American and TCA, between Northeast and Delta, and between Allegheny and Mohawk. The merger between Eastern and Caribair (although still approved within the scope of the failing business doctrine) took a different slant. Late in 1970 the Board approved a management agreement between Eastern and Caribair, whereby Eastern was to supply the needed financial support to Caribair. In 1971 the examiner recommended a full-fledged merger between the two. In 1972 the Board rejected the proposal on the grounds that the merger would have diverted substantial revenue from Pan American, which was experiencing large losses in its Caribbean operations. The President, wanting to maintain service by U.S. flag carriers to non-U.S. points in the Caribbean, requested the Board to reconsider the case with the view of placing operating restrictions on the routes of the surviving carrier (Eastern), such that the diversionary losses from Pan American would be minimized. This concept proved to be quite important and played a significant role in the Northeast-Delta merger case with respect to the Miami-Los Angeles route.

There are a couple of other interesting points regarding the approval of the mergers in the early 1970s. First, Northeast's merger proposal was approved on the grounds that service in New England was needed and the bankruptcy of the carrier would not have been in the public interest, especially for people living in New England. Thus it was assumed that the surviving carrier (Delta) would continue to provide this service. However, Delta, soon after the merger approval, filed an application for permission to delete service at approximately two-thirds of the points in New England that previously were served by Northeast. One member of the Board wanted to reopen the whole case in light of this new application, particularly when Eastern indicated that it was willing to provide the service under consideration. This issue had not been resolved when, in the meantime, the Board approved the merger between Allegheny and Mohawk, which affected some of the points in New England. The issue was finally resolved in 1975 in the *New England Service Investigation* when the Board issued a certificate of public convenience and necessity to a commuter carrier, Air New England, to conduct local-service operations in the New England area. Some of the points requested by Delta for suspension of service were transferred to Air New England, and service on some other points was terminated.

The second point of interest relates to the Board's labor protective provisions in merger cases. The landmark decision on this matter was made in 1961 in the United-Capital merger. In this case the Board gave extensive consideration to the labor protective provisions that were adopted in subsequent merger cases. Basically the Board provided protection for labor in merger cases with respect to integration of seniority lists, displacement allowances, dismissal allowances, traveling and moving expenses, protection of real estate investments, and exceptions for employees earning more than a certain amount. In the Allegheny-Mohawk decision, the adequacy of the standard provisions adopted in 1961 was questioned, and it was further questioned if the previously established standards needed revision. The decision was made to use the existing standards and deal with any required changes on a case-by-case basis. The decision to deal on an ad hoc basis was not new. For example, in the American-TCA proposal, the Board rejected the clause stipulating that American employ TCA's largest shareholder at a given salary.

While most of the mergers approved in the early 1970s were based upon the failing business doctrine, it should be made clear that this doctrine does not mean that two healthy carriers cannot merge. If a merger between two healthy carriers does not disrupt the size and balance relationship between the trunk-line carriers, does not adversely restrain competition, does not jeopardize other carriers not parties to the case, and is not inconsistent with the public interest, such a merger will get the Board's approval. The American-Western merger proposal, however, did not meet these conditions. The main problem in this case was not the size of the surviving carrier (American); rather, the chief concern was with the diversionary effect on the existing carriers serving the Mainland-Hawaiian market, particularly Pan American and United. Continental estimated that approximately $35 million in revenue would be diverted from existing carriers in 1973 in the Hawaiian market: United, $13.4 million; Pan American, $6.5 million; Continental, $6.4 million; Northwest, $4.4 million; Braniff, $3.1 million; and TWA, $1.4 million. On the South Pacific market, Pan American estimated a diversion of $10 million in 1973. Air West, Alaskan, and Frontier also pointed to the diversion from their markets; this was particularly important since these carriers were receiving subsidy. Continental's final analysis (including diversion from the foreign flag carriers) showed that, as a result of the merger, total diversion in revenue would amount to $148 million in 1973. In addition Continental pointed to the diversion of $71 million as a result of new routes awarded to American and Western in 1970.

In the American-Western merger proposal, the two carriers leaned heavily on the wording of Section 408(b) of the Act. According to this Section, a merger proposed by two carriers should be approved by the Board unless the Board finds, after a proper hearing, that such a merger either would be inconsistent with the public interest or would result in a monopoly. Therefore, since it was not established that the merger would result in a monopoly, the Board must approve the merger unless it could be shown that it was inconsistent with the public interest. In this particular case, there was no strong evidence of either benefit or disbenefit to the public. American and Western felt that according to the language of Section 408(b), the "burden of proof" of public benefit did not lie with them. Therefore, unless the Board could prove inconsistency with the public interest, it must approve the proposal. The examiner based his case (as not being in the public interest) on the disruption in "size and balance relationship" among the trunk-line carriers.

Department of Transportation's Policy

The Department of Transportation (DOT) is an executive department that was established to exercise general leadership in the identification and solution of transportation problems. As such it has the responsibility to provide leadership in the development of national transportation policies and programs. Within these broad objectives, the DOT participates extensively in the Board's proceedings, some of which deal with the subject of mergers. Since, under Section 801 of the Federal Aviation Act, the President reviews all merger cases involving international routes, the DOT, being an Executive Branch agency, is an active participant in the various merger cases. As seen in the *Transpacific* case, the President's review of cases that involve international routes is far more complex than a cursory review and perfunctory rubber stamp. This is also true in merger cases; the reader will recall that when the majority of the Board rejected the proposed Eastern-Caribair merger, the President agreed with the minority opinion (based upon his foreign aviation policy) and sent the Board's decision back for review.

In 1971 DOT developed a set of criteria for evaluating domestic airline merger proposals. The purpose of these criteria was to assist the Executive Branch agencies first in determining whether to intervene in an airline merger proposal before the Board and second in deciding if, and what, any recommendations should be made to the Board. In developing these criteria a number of people at DOT felt that the tests for evaluating mergers in the regulated industry should be different from those used in the unregulated industries. Thus the standard criteria used by the Department of Justice (such as the market share tests developed under the Clayton Act) were inadequate to perform a thorough evaluation of mergers in the airline industry. In the end, the DOT developed the following seven guidelines that can be used in evaluating airline merger proposals:

1. A merger should not result in either the elimination of effective competition, or an excessive market share for the surviving firm, in significant city-pair, regional, or national markets for airline services.

2. A merger should not result in undue concentration within the air carrier industry.

3. A merger should not be likely to lead to extensive reactions and defensive merger proposals by competitive carriers so that the end result will be a restructuring of the industry and excessive concentration in a few firms.

4. A merger should not result in substantial foreclosure of competition for interchange traffic or other excessive injury to other carriers.

5. A merger should bring about substantial operational, service, or organizational benefits for the surviving firm so that the public will receive significant benefits such as greater efficiency and better service, and the size of the airline resulting from the merger should not be such as to produce significant diseconomies.

6. In the case of a merger of a relatively effective carrier and one that is marginal, or in the case of two marginal carriers, the resulting benefits of the surviving firm should be corrective of the original difficulty of the weaker merger partner. Alternative solutions to the problems of a marginal merging carrier should be shown to be considerably less effective than merger.

7. The protection afforded labor in the merging firms should be in accordance with the present policies of the Board.[2]

The first criterion refers to competition in major markets. Of 58,000 city-pair markets that receive scheduled air service, the top 135 city-pair markets accounted for almost 50 percent of the total domestic market. Thus the elimination of an effective competitor (one having at least 10 percent of the market) from a major market should not be allowed. It appears that a merger involving carriers that compete in about 12 of the top 135 city-pairs would not pass this test. Thus a merger between any two of the Big Four would not go through. On the other hand, Northeast and Northwest competed in only three markets and consequently passed this test. While carriers generally compete on a city-pair basis, the effect of a merger on competition should also be considered in terms of regional and national markets. For example, while Northwest and National are not authorized to serve the New York-Los Angeles market, each still participates in that market since a certain number of passengers fly from New York to Los Angeles via Minneapolis on Northwest, and via Miami on National.

The second guideline refers to the concentration in the airline industry. In establishing the guidelines, it was felt that even the largest airline is too small relative to the rest of the economy to ever entertain the possibility of economic dominance outside of the industry itself. It is, however, important to consider relative size within the industry. Even then, size should not be the only, or even the major, factor in evaluating mergers. The critical test is to determine the impact of the merger on the market share by market. Should this share be found excessive, benefits resulting from the merger must be weighed against the anticompetitive impacts. Although no precise figures are given, it is possible that United's share of the total market may provide a bench mark with respect to concentration.

The third guideline suggests that a merger should not be approved if it would breed or trigger other mergers. This action may result in the following manner. An approval of one merger may be taken as an indication of the Board's willingness to approve other mergers. More important, the approval of one merger may create a situation in which other carriers may be forced to merge. For example, if the merger between American and Western had been approved, Continental might have felt that it could not survive in the new environment and would have to merge with another carrier. Since there are only limited merger possibilities for any one carrier, a carrier must look for the most appropriate partner before it is too late. So, whatever the reason, if the approval of one merger triggers off other mergers, it should be rejected, since the series of mergers may destroy the desired competitive structure.

The fourth guideline states that a merger between two carriers should not severely injure a third carrier. An example of direct injury would be the loss of competitive or connecting traffic due to the increase in market power of the surviving carrier in a merger. An example of indirect injury would be that the third carrier may not be in a position to acquire the appropriate flight equipment to compete with the more powerful surviving carrier in a merger. A merger may also provide city dominance at some of the common points. The result of city dominance is that a passenger is more likely to call up the dominant carrier in a city, even when the dominant carrier does not offer service to the passenger's destination.

The fifth guideline states that the merger should result in greater efficiency for the surviving carrier and better service for the public. The merger should result in long-term improvements and developments in the industry rather than provide solutions for the short-term conditions. Thus mergers should not, for example, be used as vehicles to reduce excess capacity problems. Since there is a need for continued operational adjustment in the industry, only those mergers that can meet this need should be approved. In short, mergers should take into account the long-term needs instead of just the short-term considerations.

The sixth guideline states that if a weak carrier is allowed to merge with a strong carrier, the problems of the weak carrier must not simply be transferred to the strong carrier with the subsequent result of making the strong carrier weak. Unless a merger clearly corrects the problem(s) of either one or both partners, it should not be approved. The last guideline refers to the impact of mergers on employees and has been discussed in the last section.

The issue of economies of scale, which is important in analyzing mergers, was not discussed to any extent in the set of criteria issued by the DOT. This exclusion may be due to the fact that the issue is far from settled. It is not clear that the traditional economic relationship between unit costs and size of the firm (U-shaped curve) is applicable to the airline industry. As discussed in Chapter 3, the unit cost is not just a function of the size but also a function of route density, average stage length, type, size, and mix of aircraft, and management policies. Over the years, a number of analysts have come to the conclusion that there are no economies of scale for airlines the size of American, Eastern, Delta, Pan American, TWA, and United. A more elaborate discussion of this was presented in Chapter 3. However, relative to the discussion here, this conclusion, that is, unit costs are independent of sheer size, would support the argument that potential changes in size per se should not influence the decision in a merger proposal. Thus it would be more useful to analyze the impact of a particular merger on industry performance rather than the sheer size of the surviving carrier.

The other factor not adequately considered in the DOT's list of criteria is the effect of a merger on innovation. There is a feeling among certain economists that increased concentration can have adverse effects on innovation. In analyzing various industries other than the air transport industry, a number of analysts have shown that small- and medium-sized firms may be more innovative than the large firms.[3] This conclusion appears to be true within the airline industry, particularly with respect to marketing innovations. To cite a few examples, coach service was first introduced by Capital in 1948. The summer excursion fares on the New York-Florida market were first introduced by National in 1949. Later Continental was the big promoter of economy class and Western was the first to space its seats further apart to give more leg room. More recently National was the first to introduce the no-frill fares to Florida at rates comparable to those charged by surface modes. One possible explanation for why the larger carriers are less innovative may be related to the fact that the industry is heavily dependent upon consumer appeal and is quite sensitive to economic fluctuations. This dependence would mean that airline management must react quickly, an action that is usually difficult to undertake in larger companies. Thus, if the assumption that small- and medium-sized airlines tend to be more innovative is realistic, the elimination of small carriers is not justifiable, particularly if there are no savings in unit costs for large carriers. The argument is strengthened even more if there are diseconomies of scale.

Department of Justice's Policy

Like the DOT, the Department of Justice (DOJ) may intervene and participate in airline merger proceedings to urge upon the Board basic legal points concerning the anticompetitive effects and to recommend that the merger be rejected if it would create a substantial monopoly. The DOJ also relies upon Section 408(b), which states:

Any person seeking approval of a . . . merger . . . shall present an application to the Board, and thereupon the Board shall notify the persons involved in the . . . merger . . . , and other persons known to have substantial interest in the proceedings, of the time and place of a public hearing. Unless, after such hearing, the Board finds that the . . . merger . . . will not be consistent with the public interest or that the conditions of this section will not be fulfilled, it shall by order approve such . . . merger . . . : Provided, that the Board shall not approve any . . . merger . . . which would result in creating a monopoly or monopolies and thereby restrain competition or jeopardize another air carrier not party to the . . . merger. . . .

It should be noted that the antimonopoly proviso indicates a flat rejection of the merger proposal. Unlike the public interest proviso, which can be a balancing process, the anticompetitive proviso is not flexible enough to allow the Board any discretion.

The Federal Aviation Act emphasizes competition, both in general and also with respect to mergers. According to the Act, the purpose of economic regulation is to promote public interest. However, under Section 408(b), in order to approve a merger, the Board is not required to prove that it would be in the public interest. On the contrary, unless it can be shown that the merger is not in the public interest, or if there is any doubt regarding the public interest, then the Board is required to approve the merger. Thus it is left to a merger's opponents to show that the merger will not be in the public interest. Similarly, Section 401(h) also relates to mergers and states: "No certificate may be transferred unless such transfer is approved by the Board on being consistent with the public interest." However, under Section 401(h) the Board normally requests that the applicants establish consistency with the public interest. This requirement is evident in numerous cases decided by the Board. The applicants attempt to bypass this section on the belief that it does not apply to merger cases and that the public convenience and necessity test for transfer of route authority is somewhat different from the public interest in merger applications. From this view point it would appear that a transfer of a route through merger is easier than without a merger.

The Department of Justice is usually interested in seeing that the Board does not overlook the antitrust laws and that the Board can employ the appropriate analytical techniques developed and used by the courts in merger cases (Section 7 of the Clayton Act). The Board is, however, not required to make sure that the provisions of Section 7 of the Clayton Act are upheld. It can use this law to determine the antitrust implications and use the results in conjunction with other public interest considerations.

The Justice Department, in short, investigates the antitrust and anticompetitive effects of mergers. For example, the DOJ recommended that the American-Western merger be rejected because it felt that the anticompetitive effects outweighed any public benefits that might have resulted. This conclusion was based upon the analysis of American's postmerger share of the domestic trunk-line market. The Justice Department could not see any significant public benefits and, furthermore, argued that Western was neither a marginal nor ineffective carrier that needed to be saved by a merger.

Summary

As shown in this chapter, there are many reasons for two air carriers to propose a merger. These include economic efficiency, wholesale purchase of a network of routes, elimination of the possibility of bankruptcy, elimination of competition, and an opportunity to reduce seasonality problems. However, while mergers may provide benefits to the partners, the public and the employees may be adversely affected. In the years following the Board's establishment in 1938, its policy in merger cases was in favor of competition. However, during the few years following the end of World War II, the Board was quite willing to entertain merger proposals if they improved the financial position of the industry, which was quite weak due to excessive capacity and excessive competition. During the sixties The Board's policy was to approve the mergers under the failing business doctrine and in the case of local-service carriers, mergers were approved as a means of reducing the level of subsidy.

From time to time the Department of Transportation and the Department of Justice have also become active participants in merger cases. In 1971 DOT developed a set of criteria for evaluating domestic airline merger proposals. The purpose of these criteria was to assist the agency in determining whether to intervene in particular airline merger proposals and to decide if and what recommendations should be made before the Board. The Department of Justice, on the other hand, may participate in an airline merger proceeding if it feels that there is a need to urge upon the Board basic legal points concerning the antitrust and anticompetitive effects of mergers.

14 International Aviation

Commercial airlines of the free world carried 95 million passengers in international operations during 1973. Of this, U.S. flag carriers transported 27 million passengers between the United States and foreign countries. The diversity of the U.S. flag carriers can be illustrated by the fact that in 1973 the U.S. certificated route carriers provided scheduled passenger service from the United States to 136 foreign cities in 89 countries, and the U.S. supplemental airlines also provided worldwide services. In addition, the U.S. all-cargo airlines provided scheduled service to 32 foreign cities in 22 countries. This magnitude and diversity of the U.S. flag international air carrier system contributed more than $3 billion in gross balance of payments benefit in foreign exchange in 1973, promoted foreign sales of U.S. aircraft, promoted travel by foreigners to the United States, and constituted a major portion of the Civil Reserve Air Fleet available in a national emergency to the Department of Defense.[1]

The purpose of this chapter is to examine the development and operation of the international air transportation system in general and the U.S. system in particular. The first section discusses the development of international routes and the negotiation of bilateral agreements. The second section contains a discussion on the passenger fare and cargo rate-setting machinery of the International Air Transport Association (IATA). This section also includes a discussion on whether or not IATA is a cartel. Other functions of IATA are discussed in the third section. The fourth section presents a brief description of the role of the International Civil Aviation Organization (ICAO) in international aviation. The fifth section introduces the topic of government interests in the airline industry. The final section discusses the various types of interline agreements in the international airline industry.

International Route Development

Since international air transportation involves crossing national frontiers, a need arose as early as 1919 for establishing some principles of international law regulating aerial navigation and a state's sovereignty over its airspace. The Aeronautical Commission of the Peace Conference held in Paris in 1919 established the basic rule of international law regarding commercial aviation. This law stated that every nation has complete and exclusive sovereignty over the airspace above its territory. The Paris Convention instituted the International Commission for

Air Navigation to resolve any technical problems arising between countries. The nontechnical issues were to be resolved by the International Court of the Justice of the League of Nations. Although the United States did not ratify this convention, the Pan American Convention signed in Havana in 1928 agreed to most of the principles of the Paris Convention. Also in 1919 six European nations—Denmark, England, Germany, Holland, Norway, and Sweden—jointly created an organization called the International Air Traffic Association. The initial functions of this organization were to clarify international aviation law and to standardize aviation technology. The main aim of the member airlines was to standardize the conditions and facilities of air travel between countries.

The Chicago Convention

Prior to World War II the negotiation of international routes was left to the initiative of the American carriers themselves. The U.S. government did not take an active part in such negotiations. For example, as discussed in Chapter 1, Pan American in the early days negotiated a number of private agreements with foreign nations for landing rights. However, toward the end of World War II many nations were interested in formulating a universal international air transport policy with regard to commercial air rights and in establishing rules governing technical and navigational aspects. In 1944, at the invitation of the United States, more than fifty nations sent their representatives to the Chicago Conference to formulate universal international air transport policy for international travel and commerce.

Due to the conflicting interests of the various nations present, agreement was not reached on providing a means for exchanging commercial rights to fly in and out of independent nations. Basically, there were two conflicting views. The United States wanted relatively complete competitive freedom; it had the necessary aircraft, experience, and finances to dominate such a state of affairs. Most of the other nations, suffering from a poor economic state following World War II and fearing a U.S. dominance from which they might never escape, wanted heavily regulated operations. The United Kingdom and other Commonwealth countries wanted to set up an international agency to control capacity, frequency, and fares. The routes were to be assigned through bilateral agreements. The Americans in the end agreed that the routes should still be negotiated through bilateral agreements but felt that the international agency should perform a consultative function only with respect to economic regulation and should control the technical side of air transportation.

The final outcome of the Chicago Conference was "The Chicago Convention" and in particular:[a]

---

[a]The first part of the Convention contains forty-two articles of rules for civil aviation, and the second part contains fifty-four articles governing the creation of an international agency.

1. International Air Services Transit Agreement. This agreement allowed the signatories to (a) fly across another nation's (if the nation was a participant to the agreement) territory without landing, and (b) land for noncommercial purposes.

2. Provisional International Civil Aviation Organization (PICAO). The function of this organization was to coordinate the activities of the nations that signed any agreement made at the Chicago Conference. PICAO was also to act as an arbitrator in case of conflicts between the various member states. The organization, however, did not possess any economic powers to be applied to the international air transport industry.

In 1945 the International Air Transport Association (IATA) was formally established at Havana, Cuba. This organization superseded the original one formed in 1919. Unlike the old organization, the principal function of the new IATA was to set up mechanisms for setting rates on international routes. There were no provisions for controlling capacity or frequency. The extent of capacity was to be negotiated in the bilateral agreements. In addition, some of the functions of the old IATA were still to be performed by the new IATA. The three most important provisions in the functioning of IATA with regard to establishing fares are: (1) a proposed tariff has to be approved unanimously by all the members; (2) the approved tariff is still subject to the approval of the aeronautical agency of each of the member nations that would be affected by the proposed tariff; and (3) the fare machinery cannot be used for intercarrier allocation of production. Initially IATA was given the power to recommend fares and rates for a trial period of 1 year; this authority was extended and in 1955 made permanent. The fare setting machinery of IATA is discussed in greater detail in subsequent sections.

The Bermuda Agreement

Since the Chicago Conference did not result in a multilateral solution to the problems of deciding on a means of exchanging commercial rights, it became necessary for countries desiring air service between their territories to agree to exchange commercial air rights through bilateral negotiations. Representatives from Great Britain and the United States met in Bermuda in 1946 to exchange operating rights between the two nations. The Bermuda Agreement resulted in the famous "five freedoms" of the air discussed in Chapter 1.

The first two freedoms were essentially agreed upon at the Chicago Confer-

Articles 1 and 6 represent the major decisions reached at the Convention. Article 1 states that each of the contracting states has a complete and exclusive sovereignty over the airspace above its territory. Article 6 implies that a carrier wishing to operate international air service over, into, or out of a contracting state's territory must obtain specific permission from that state.

ence, and the last three were the result of the Bermuda Agreement. With regard to the frequency of service, there were no constraints as far as the third and the fourth freedoms are concerned. However, with respect to the fifth freedom, traffic, the capacity was restricted to a "reasonable" level. Although reasonable level was not defined, it was generally accepted that a reasonable level of capacity should reflect the level of potential traffic. The language on capacity restrictions is quite vague. For example, the Bermuda Agreement states that the capacity should be related first, to traffic requirements between the country of origin and countries of destination; second, to the requirements of through airline operations; and third, to the traffic requirements of the area through which the airline passes after taking account of local and regional services.

According to the above language there is no clear way of determining the amount of capacity each carrier is allowed to offer. The best interpretation of the above appears to be that on a route such as New York-Frankfurt-Rome-Athens-Tel Aviv-Bombay, the appropriate U.S. carriers are allowed to offer capacity on each leg of the route sufficient to carry passengers from the United States bound for the country concerned and vice versa. The Bermuda Agreement also contained a provision for an *ex post facto* review of capacity, which authorized either party to the agreement to review capacity levels if this party considered the level to be unreasonable. In this case PICAO would be called upon to settle the differences.

The essence of the Bermuda Agreement was that the United States gave up its ideas for seeking unrestricted air transport policy and accepted fifth freedom rights with capacity constraints. The United States also accepted the IATA machinery for setting fares.[b] Great Britain, in return, gave up the idea of capacity and frequency control on the third and fourth freedom traffic. Another attempt to achieve a multilateral agreement was made in 1947 at the Geneva Conference. Again, due to wide differences in opinion, no solution was reached.

The importance of the Bermuda Agreement should not be underestimated. Most of the bilateral agreements in existence at the present time resemble the original Bermuda Agreement, signed by the United States and Great Britain in 1946. On the other hand, the general trend with respect to capacity regulation is away from the relatively liberal Bermuda system and toward more protectionism. For example, even the United States, which has been fairly liberal in the past, has tended to be more cautious in recent years. In 1955 the United States gave significant fifth freedom rights to Lufthansa by allowing the German carrier to conduct service on New York-Caribbean routes to all points in the South American route. In return, the U.S. carriers received relatively minor fifth

[b]There appears to be an inconsistency in the policy with respect to control of fares. The United States favored freedom from control of fares on the international routes, and complete control of fares by the CAB on the domestic routes.

freedom rights beyond West Germany. However, the views of the United States began to change in the next decade. For instance, for a number of years the United States denied Japan Air Lines the authority to offer service to New York and points in Europe. It was not until 1965 that in exchange for U.S. landing rights in Osaka, the United States allowed Japan Air Lines into New York and beyond to points on the North Atlantic.

The attitude of various nations with respect to protectionism versus free trade is quite different. This difference in attitude results from factors such as the political environment, the need for air transport services, the bargaining strength of a particular nation, its geographic location, and its traffic-generating potential. For instance, the Scandinavian countries have supported free trade due to their relatively low traffic-generating potential, their reliance on fifth freedom traffic, and their geographic location. This is easily seen in the traffic carried on the North Atlantic by SAS via Copenhagen originating in New York with ultimate destinations beyond Denmark. On the other hand, certain nations have tended to protect their carriers through restrictive capacity regulation.

Route Evaluation

The major issue in any bilateral negotiation is the determination of a fair route exchange. But how does one evaluate route exchanges? Although there is no scientific method of doing this, a number of criteria have been developed over the years to answer these questions. In general, no single criterion is sufficient by itself. One must investigate the various points together. In the evaluation of a route exchange, negotiators normally consider aviation one bargaining chip in their overall foreign economic trading activity. For instance, a country may exchange a route for relaxation of export-import restrictions.

There are basically three groups of methods for exchanging routes. The first group consists of two types. One common basis for bilateral route exchanges is known as *visual reciprocity* or *double tracking*. In such an exchange, two nations agree to the same routes. For example, New York-Paris-Athens would be served by both TWA and Olympic. In this type of exchange, the U.S. carrier cannot serve, for example, Boston-Paris, unless Air France can also fly Paris-Boston.

Another common basis for route exchange is known as *mirror reciprocity*. This phrase should be interpreted more conceptually than literally. On this basis the routes granted to each country are mirror images. For example, the U.S. carrier would obtain a route to Rome via Paris and beyond to Athens. In return the Italian carrier would obtain a route to New York via Paris and beyond to Mexico City.

The second group also consists of two types of route exchanges. The first method in this group is known as the *most favored nations approach.*[2] Under this method, France would, for example, negotiate for Air France routes equivalent to those that the United States has granted to West Germany, assuming that France considers itself similar to West Germany relative to the United States. Unfortunately the similarities considered are usually with respect to size or population and not so much with respect to geography and tourist attractiveness.

The second method in this group is known as the *lost opportunity approach.* Under this approach, an attempt is made to measure what the airlines of one country would lose if they did not obtain the routes under consideration. Suppose a bilateral agreement did not exist between the United States and Spain. The U.S. carriers could still carry passengers from New York to Lisbon, for example, but would lose the traffic from Lisbon to Madrid. However, Iberia, on the other hand, could carry traffic from Madrid to Lisbon but would lose transatlantic revenue from Lisbon to New York.

The third group consists of methods known as *bargaining strength* and the *exploitation approach.* Under this method, a nation will try to get the best deal, using all possible leverage. This kind of route exchange negotiation was quite common after World War II, especially by nations with strategic geographical locations, such as Iceland, Ireland, and Portugal.

The United States has generally favored yet another route exchange method known as *access approach.*[3] With this method, each side gets routes and rights that provide each side with access to equivalent market value, notwithstanding the amount of traffic. Thus both sides receive equivalent economic benefit regardless of the number of passengers carried. This approach involves estimating, for the routes involved, third, fourth, fifth, and sixth freedom traffic for each nation.[c] This traffic is then converted into potential revenue. Under this method, fifth and sixth freedom traffic play a much more dominant role in the evaluation of route exchanges relative to third and fourth freedom traffic. For example, in the United States-India bilateral agreement, the fifth freedom route London-New York is much more important to Air India than the third freedom Delhi-New York.

International Fares and Rates

The reader should recall that no agreement was reached on international fares and rates at the Chicago Conference. However, it was generally agreed among the carriers that fares and rates between the same points should be uniform, and those between comparable points should bear a fixed ratio to each other. In October 1945 the International Air Transport Association adopted a resolution

[c]The sixth freedom traffic is defined as traffic carried between two foreign countries via a carrier's home country.

entitled "Provisions for the Regulation and Conduct of Traffic Conferences of International Air Transport Association," which allows carriers to negotiate international air fares, cargo rates, and conditions of service. While procedures have been revised over the years to meet changing circumstances, the basic mechanisms developed 30 years ago still provide the necessary foundations for making agreements on a worldwide network of fares and rates. The framework in which the fare-setting negotiations take place is not to be taken lightly. It is extremely complex; negotiations involve the profit motive, social considerations, national policies, and to some extent, international politics. An attempt is made in this section to describe three things: (1) the intricate machinery of setting international fares and rates; (2) the pattern of international fares and rates; and (3) the arguments for and against the accusations that IATA is a cartel.

The Traffic Conference Machinery

Since World War II the IATA member airlines have negotiated international fares and rates with the associated conditions of applicability through the IATA Traffic Conferences. Prior to this the rules and regulations of international fares were set by the airlines through the predecessor of the present IATA—International Air Traffic Association—which was confined virtually to airlines based in Europe. After World War II the pattern of the conference machinery set up nine different regional conferences with the idea that their activities should be coordinated. These conferences were:

North Atlantic Traffic Conference
European Traffic Conference
Middle East Traffic Conference
African Traffic Conference
Europe-South America Route Traffic Conference
Pacific Route Traffic Conference
Asiatic Traffic Conference
Australasian Traffic Conference
Western Traffic Conference

In general terms, the purpose of the traffic conferences is two-fold. First, these conferences deal with the subject of fares and rates to be charged for international air transport. Second, the conferences are concerned with facilitating interline traffic; namely the movement of passengers and cargo that uses the routes of more than one airline from its origin to destination. With the establishment of nine conferences, the coordination process (based upon the premise that all fares and rates—since they are interrelated—should be set at one time) became impractical.

Thus in 1947 the system of conferences was rearranged by establishing three conference areas. These areas are referred to as TC1, TC2, and TC3. In addition to these three conferences, each of which refers to matters that concern its area, there are joint conferences to allow for action on matters that affect more than one area. Thus Joint Traffic Conference JT12 deals with matters affecting both TC1 and TC2.

Traffic Conference One. TC1 includes all of the North and South American continents, and the adjacent islands, Greenland, Bermuda, the West Indies and the Caribbean Islands, the Hawaiian Islands including Midway and Palmyra.

Traffic Conference Two. TC2 includes Europe, including that part of the USSR in Europe, the adjacent islands, Iceland, the Azores, Africa and the adjacent islands, Ascension Island and that part of Asia lying west of and including Iran.

Traffic Conference Three. TC3 includes Asia, and the adjacent islands except that portion included in TC2, the East Indies, Australia, New Zealand and the adjacent islands, the islands of the Pacific Ocean, except those included in TC1.

While the traffic conference system still functions according to the original concept, the divisions between the three areas are quite arbitrary in that the major international carriers operate services that affect more than one conference. These divisions were more meaningful at the time of their establishment, since many carriers remained completely within a single conference area. Although each conference can act independently, all conferences generally meet simultaneously (Composite Conference) to discuss matters that need to be resolved on a worldwide basis. The fares and rates are handled through individual and joint conferences. In 1964 it was agreed that separate composite conferences should be arranged to deal with passenger fares and cargo rates; these topics are discussed in alternate years at these annual conferences. Passenger fare conferences normally take place in the fall; the new fares become effective in the following year on April 1st and remain in force for a period of 2 years. Cargo rate conferences normally take place in May and the rates become effective on October 1st of the same year.

While international fares and rates are agreed upon at the conferences, procedural matters are handled by a series of dozens of special committees and working groups under the Traffic Advisory Committee, which concerns itself in a policy advisory capacity with all traffic and sales matters connected with international air transport. This committee has appointed numerous other permanent committees to consider and take action on forms, procedures, administrative, and other matters, excluding fares, rates, and levels of commissions. Examples of these are the Cost Committee, Passenger Agency Committee, Cargo Agency Committee, Passenger Traffic Procedures Committee, Cargo Traffic Procedures Committee, and Reservations Committee. The Passenger Agency Committee, for instance, reviews and develops recommendations concerning IATA policy with respect to passenger aspects of airline/agent relationships (excluding commission levels). Each permanent committee has, in turn, established subcommittees, working groups, task forces, and other administrative bodies to consider specific assignments.

The basic purpose of the conferences is to work out recommendations for fares and rates to be charged on international services. The final recommendations must be unanimously approved, with each active carrier member of IATA having one equal vote. But before a particular set of recommendations becomes effective, the carriers' own governments must review and approve the recommendations. Carriers not only have a vote in each of the conferences of which they are a member, but they can also vote on resolutions that deal with operations between that conference and another. Thus all TC1 and all TC2 members may vote on the North Atlantic fares. While this provision is essential for the effective transportation of interline traffic from the origin to the final destination, it can, and sometimes does, lead to abuses.

As previously mentioned, the fares and rates finally negotiated at the conference are subject to government approval for each carrier. While reasons for government approval vary from country to country, the two primary reasons are first, to protect the public from extraordinarily high fares, and second, to make sure that competitive price cutting does not lead the carriers to lower their safety standards. In addition, there are two secondary reasons. First, each government will protect the commercial existence of its flag carrier due to its dependency on the carrier for commercial and military transportation. Second, the government is often interested in the negotiated fare of the carrier if the carrier is receiving government subsidy. The extent of government involvement in international fares varies from country to country. In the United States, for example, the Civil Aeronautics Board is not authorized to set fares on international routes. The Board has power only to disapprove those fares that it considers discriminatory.

Reaching an acceptable agreement on 60,000 routes is a difficult task in normal times, let alone in times of great technological, economic, and political change. Two good illustrations of the power held by governments in international fares and of the problems encountered at the traffic conferences are the Honolulu crisis in 1959 and the Chandler controversy in 1962. At the traffic conference in Honolulu in 1959, the British, under strong pressure from their government, proposed lower fares between Europe and Africa and Europe and the Far East. Ordinarily the situation might have been resolved through some compromise. However, in this case it was difficult for the carriers to compromise, since a British Minister in Parliament warned that unless the British carriers' demands were met, they would set their own fares. This threat placed the British carriers in an awkward position, with no possible compromise. Six months later, following a change in British Ministers after an election, the problems were resolved at a conference in Paris.

The Chandler controversy was also related to fares. In 1962 the introduction of jet aircraft over the most important routes of the world had created the problem of overcapacity. Some carriers believed that fares should be increased in order to improve their financial position. Other carriers felt the solution was to lower fares to increase traffic with the result that increased load factors would improve their financial position. The CAB was in favor of lowering fares, or at least maintaining status quo. The carriers reached an agreement to increase fares by lowering the discount for round trips from 10 percent to 5 percent. As required, this agreement was filed by the appropriate U.S. flag carriers with the CAB; but the Board disapproved the recommendation, not because of the reduction of the round trip discount per se, but because of the unreasonableness of the resulting fare. The Board stated that the existing fares were adequate to produce fair return on investment at reasonable load factors, and that a fare increase to offset the low load factors was unfair. However, having disapproved the fares, the Board had no power to set the appropriate fares, whereas the British and other European countries did have such power.

The Board supported its position by pointing out that both Pan American and Northwest had achieved a 15 percent return on total investment in 1962 on the transpacific routes. Such a return, substantially above the recommended 10.125 percent for the domestic carriers in the *General Passenger Fare Investigation*, was not indicative of a need for higher fares on the Pacific. On the transatlantic routes, the return on investment was low due to the temporary problem of overcapacity. The problem was considered temporary since it was expected that the high traffic growth prevalent at the time would resolve the problem. On the other hand, fare increases would further exacerbate the problem of low load factors and poor financial results. The situation of the South American routes was quite different. Here, the poor financial condition of the carriers was due not to low load factors but to the low level of average passenger yields. On these routes the Board was willing to approve the increase in fares by reducing round-trip discounts.

Certain IATA member carriers urged the Board to reconsider its position on the following grounds. First, the Board's disapproval of one part of the whole package (consisting of a variety of promotional fares) would mean disapproval of the whole package, since achievement of unanimity required compromises on many issues. The U.S. carriers (Pan American and Northwest) pointed out, for example, that it was necessary for the sake of uniformity in tariff publication and fare construction for the Board to agree to reductions in round-trip discounts on a worldwide basis. Second, some carriers requested the Board's approval not so much of the discount issue per se but of the entire package in order to improve the financial situation of most of the world's airlines. These parties pointed to the need of higher revenue to maintain a level of growth in the industry commensurate with technological advances. The Board in an order dated March 18, 1963 rejected the comments of those carriers and disapproved the Chandler Resolutions. The dates are important in this case, since the previous agreement was not valid after March 31, 1963. If a new agreement was not in force by this date, the carriers would have faced an open rate situation in which each carrier could set its own rates. However, the effective date was postponed.

In a meeting between the appropriate British and American authorities, an attempt was made to resolve the issue. The U.S. State Department sent letters to fourteen countries informing them of the CAB's disapproval of the Chandler package as required under the terms of the bilateral agreements. The delegates from the European countries and the chairman of CAB met in London but again an agreement was not reached. The effective date was now postponed to May 12, 1963. In the meantime the British government warned that unless the U.S. flag carriers agreed to the new fares by mid-May, the U.S. carriers would not be allowed to land at British airports. Other European countries also urged the U.S. flag carriers to adopt the new fares by May 12. However, the CAB advised Pan American and TWA that they should maintain the status quo by charging the old fares.[d]

It appears that the dispute was between the European governments and the CAB and not among the airlines, since both Pan American and TWA were willing to charge the higher fares. The British Ministry of Aviation threatened to detain U.S. aircraft if the U.S. carriers did not comply with their request to charge higher fares. On the other hand, it is not clear what steps the United States could have taken to enforce its point of view if the British carried out their threat. It seems unlikely that the United States would have retaliated in a similar manner.

The British were interested in the approval of the Chandler package since it contained a number of new cheap promotional and group fares designed to increase the market outside the North American area. Such fare packages would have had a significant impact on such markets as United Kingdom to Australia. However, these lower promotional fares were partially offset by the increase in the normal economy fare brought about by the reduction in the round-trip discount. The British, therefore, had definite and clear reasons for wanting the Chandler fare package approved. Nevertheless they were willing to renegotiate the Chandler package at a later date in order to avoid the heated controversy that would inevitably erupt if the CAB were to disapprove the whole package at that time. The Board still maintained its earlier position.

There was some feeling that the CAB, having made a decision, could not now back out. The Board consulted the Department of State for advice regarding the

[d]Senator Warren Magnuson (D-Washington), chairman of the Senate Commerce Committee, and several other members of the U.S. Congress supported the CAB in its policy to favor lower fares.

fare dispute. The Department of State advised the Board to authorize the U.S. flag carriers to modify their fares and comply with the foreign laws and regulations. This advice was based upon the grounds that neither the U.S. Government nor the CAB had the legislative authority to regulate rates in international air transportation. This ended the dispute, and the U.S. flag carriers began to charge the higher fares. The State Department pointed out the need for legislation giving the Board authority over international fares, an authority that foreign aeronautical agencies similar to the CAB do possess.

Pattern of Passenger Fares

There are basically two types of fares—normal fares and special fares. The *normal fares*, both first class and economy class, are the standard fares available all year with no restrictions. There is apparently no standard percentage differential between the first and economy class of fares. The first-class markup varies from market to market. In addition to the normal fares, there are a variety of *special fares* designed to attract special categories of passengers. Most of these are promotional type of fares and carry certain restrictions with respect to time of origin, direction of travel, length of stay, number in a group, and personal characteristics, such as age, military status, or airline employee. Most of the restrictions are with respect to origin, direction, and length of stay.

The normal fares are constructed in two steps. First, a comprehensive pattern of specified fares are agreed upon at the traffic conferences in either U.S. dollars or British pounds. The second step is to calculate a large number of additional fares based upon the set of specified fares. These fares are calculated after the traffic conference by the carriers themselves according to defined and agreed rules. Since there are about half a million fares available to the public on a worldwide basis, it becomes necessary to have the individual carriers calculate and publish their own fares according to the construction rules agreed upon at the conference. The construction rules are extremely complicated. These are described in IATA's Resolution O14a. The basic objective of the construction principles is two-fold. First, it should not be possible to construct fares that undercut the specified fare structure. Second, the final fares must be similar for all carriers.

In very broad terms, the pattern of normal first-class and economy-class fares agreed upon at the traffic conferences are based upon distance flown in *relative*, rather than absolute, terms. Unlike the case of U.S. domestic services, the specified fares are not based solely upon mileage. This is due to the different conditions in different traffic areas. The specified fares are normally linked to the shortest mileage operated. However, while the specified fares are based upon the shortest mileage operated, deviations up to 20 percent above this mileage are allowed without any additional charge. The calculated fares then apply whether the trip is made by a single carrier between two points or by a combination of carriers. The total fare is eventually shared between the carriers according to the agreed rules. The circuitous concept was originally developed because frequency of direct services between many points was either small or nonexistent. However, the concept is still in existence, since it is attractive to tourists who can thus visit other cities between the point of origin and ultimate destination.

A major objective in the settlement of specified fares is to reach a compromise on the desired regional fare and its relationship to the rest of the specified fares on a worldwide basis. For example, fares on the North Atlantic should bear a reasonable relationship to fares in Europe, the United States, Canada, and over the South and mid-Atlantic. Similarly, eastbound fares (over the Atlantic) and westbound fares (over the Pacific) from New York to New Delhi cannot be out of line with each other. Fares on polar routes from Europe to the U.S. West Coast must be in line with fares from Europe to the U.S. East Coast and with U.S. transcontinental fares. Thus every possible attempt is made to produce a network of fares that holds together and minimizes the possibility of undercutting the specified fares. The final agreed fares reflect a compromise between the airlines based upon their cost structures, route characteristics (density, length of haul, seasonality, etc.), and the desires of the governments with respect to tourism. Thus while it is mathematically possible to base all fares on a uniform rate per passenger mile, this concept, from a practical point of view, would never be agreed upon due to the conflicting requirements of individual airlines and their governments.

The special or promotional fares are introduced by carriers to meet the needs of certain categories of passenger traffic moving within specified regions or over certain routes. For example, in 1973 there were eight special fares available in Traffic Conference 1, twenty-seven in Traffic Conference 2, and ten in Traffic Conference 3. Thus there are many special fares—enough to attract almost any kind of traffic. Now while it is true that some promotional fares are very desirable and even necessary to meet the needs of passengers, airlines, and governments, the number of fares in effect in 1973 was so large as to be counterproductive. Since special fares are designed to attract special types of passengers, they carry a number of conditions and restrictions. These conditions vary from region to region but in general apply to geographic limits, times of origin, length of stay, and personal characteristics of the traveller. Originally, the promotional fares were introduced to fill excess capacity, reduce seasonality problems, and compete actively with the nonscheduled carriers. Since these fares are not based upon fully allocated costs (not to imply, though, that the normal fares are) but rather on marginal costs, the associated conditions are necessary to achieve such desirable results as increased load factors in highly seasonal markets during the off-peak periods. The conditions are two-fold; they must attract new passengers but, at the same time, must not give the normal fare passenger the right to a special fare.

Table 14-1 shows the level of both normal and special fares available during the year 1973-1974 over sixteen worldwide geographic groups. The data are split over the period 1973-1974 because IATA fares normally come into effect on April 1st and remain in effect for at least 1 year. The data describe two types of normal fares—first class and economy—and the average level of certain defined categories of special fares that show how they relate to the normal fares. Rather than show all types of special fare levels and their associated conditions, the spread of fare levels is shown for selected categories. This spread covers differences due to season and other conditions. The table also shows the mean sector length of each of the sixteen route groups to provide a yardstick to compare fare levels.

Table 14-1
International Passenger Fare Levels, 1973-1974

| | First Class (U.S. Cents /RPK) | Low Class (U.S. Cents/Revenue Passenger Km) | | | | Mean Sector Length (km) |
| | | Economy Class | Excursion | Group Fares | | |
				Public	GIT	
North Atlantic	7.3	4.1-5.2	2.1-3.7	1.9-2.6	2.1-2.8	7,571
Mid Atlantic	7.3	5.0	3.2-3.5	2.9	2.6-2.9	8,358
South Atlantic	7.6	4.9	3.6	–	–	10,914
North America-South America	6.8	4.8	3.5-3.7	3.1	2.8-3.1	6,329
North America-Central America	7.4	5.5	3.9-4.0	–	2.9	3,009
Local South America	8.0	5.6	4.3	3.8	–	2,541
Local Europe	12.5	8.9	5.4-5.8	–	4.4-4.8	1,546
Europe-Northern Africa	10.0	6.8	5.1	–	4.2	4,503
Europe-Southern Africa	10.3	6.5	4.1	–	3.7	6,774
Local Africa[a]	9.2	6.6	4.8	4.0	3.6-3.7	3,850
Europe-Middle East	10.2	7.2	–	–	–	3,578
Europe-Far East/Australasia	9.2	5.7	2.5-2.6	–	2.6-3.7	12,566
Local Far East/Australasia	8.8	6.4	5.1	–	–	2,705
North and Mid-Pacific	8.3	5.2	4.4	3.0-3.9	2.9-4.3	10,392
South Pacific	7.6	5.6	3.4-4.0	2.8	2.9-3.3	10,525
Africa-Far East/Australasia	7.8	5.6	–	–	3.8	12,351

[a]Data for 1972/1973.

Source: International Air Transport Association, *Agreeing Fares and Rates*, June 1974.

The North Atlantic is perhaps the most significant route group in Table 14-1 and has had the most innovative fares. In 1952 tourist class was introduced on this route, and this was replaced by an even lower economy-class fare in 1956. The normal economy-class fares are set at three levels: high season, shoulder months, and off season. The first-class fares remain unchanged through the year. In addition, there are the excursion and group fares. Figure 14-1 shows the increase in the use of low promotional fares from 1963 to 1973. Figure 14-2 shows the typical distribution of revenue passengers by fare category for Pan American and TWA's transatlantic operations in 1972. Almost 80 percent of the transatlantic passengers carried by these two carriers in 1972 utilized the low fares. Figure 14-3 shows the typical distribution of transatlantic passengers by fare type and by month. The largest use of low fares is made during the peak summer months. Finally, an examination of the long-haul fares (May 1975) on both IATA and non-IATA carriers and U.S. domestic operations shows that the high season economy fare is 11.1 cents per mile for IATA carriers, 8.2 for Icelandic (New York-London) and 7.0 for U.S. domestic operations (Boston-San Francisco). High season excursion fares were noted to be 8.6 cents per mile for IATA, 6.2 for Icelandic, and 5.6 for U.S. domestic carriers.

It is fairly clear from Table 14-1 that the lowest passenger fares exist on the North Atlantic while the highest fares exist on local European routes. One reason for the high fares in Europe is the relatively short length of haul. Another reason is perhaps the lack of competition due to excessive pooling arrangements between carriers. Examination of the fare level for selected city-pairs in the 200-250 mile range shows that the highest fares per mile exist on the London-Paris and Oslo-Stockholm routes, while fares tend to be lower in the U.S. and Canadian markets. The lowest fares available were found to be on the Eastern European routes. Similar analysis of long-haul routes shows that the lowest fares are on the U.S. domestic routes.

Pattern of Cargo Rates

As previously mentioned, cargo includes freight, express, and mail, with freight the largest component. International air freight rates are based upon gross weight or volume shipped between airports, and the price per mile depends upon distance, type of commodity, and the point of origin and destination. The international freight rates are even more complex than the passenger fares. Like the passenger fares, there are basically two types: general commodity rates and specific commodity rates. The *general commodity rates* apply to general merchandise. The *specific commodity rates* apply to the transportation of specific commodities. They are similar to the special or promotional passenger fares and are designed to meet specific requirements and develop new traffic. Both types of rates vary, depending upon direction, weight, or volume of shipment.

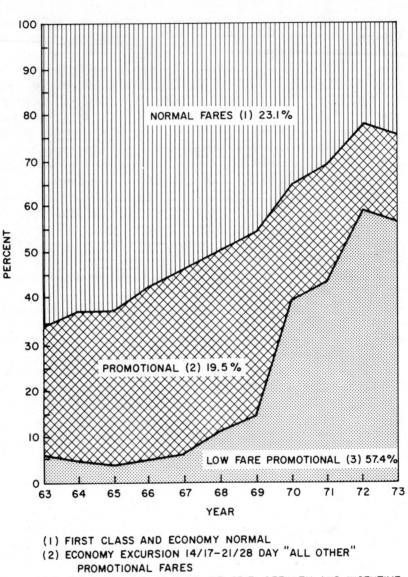

Figure 14-1. Composition of North Atlantic Scheduled Traffic, 1963-1973.

(1) FIRST CLASS AND ECONOMY NORMAL
(2) ECONOMY EXCURSION 14/17−21/28 DAY "ALL OTHER"
    PROMOTIONAL FARES
(3) EXCURSION 29−45 DAYS, GIT, CBIT, AFFINITY AND INCENTIVE
    GROUP FARES

Source: International Air Transport Association, *Agreeing Fares and Rates*, June 1974, p. 239.

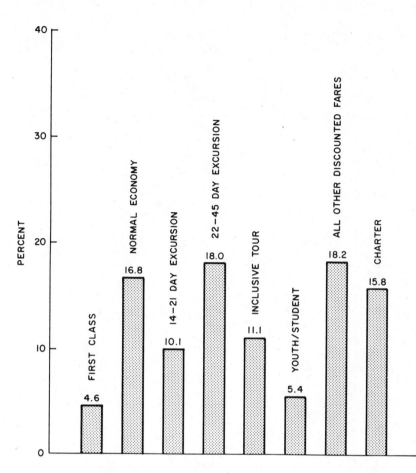

Source: U.S. CAB, *The Effect of Discount Fares and Charter Operations on Yields and Operating Revenues in Transatlantic Operations*, June 1973, p. 34.

Figure 14-2. Distribution of Revenue Passengers by Fare Category, Transatlantic Operations, Pan American and TWA, 1972.

The general commodity rates are lower on a per pound basis for larger shipments. For example, the rate per pound is lower for shipments of 100 pounds (45 kilograms) or more. In addition to this breakpoint, there are other weight breakpoints that offer an incentive to shippers to transport larger shipments. On the other end of the scale, there is a minimum rate no matter how small the shipment may be. This minimum rate is necessary due to the high documentation and other ground handling costs. The combination of the minimum freight rates and the availability of large discounts for large shipments

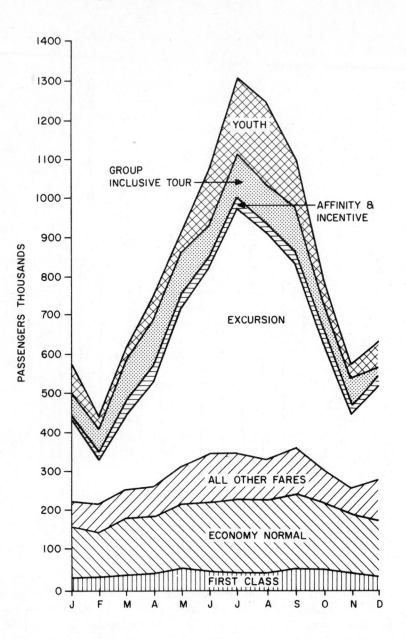

Source: International Air Transport Association, *Agreeing Fares and Rates*, June 1974, p. 240.

Figure 14-3. Monthly Distribution of Scheduled Passengers by Fare Type, 1970.

is basically the reason for the existence of consolidators or air freight forwarders, who receive and combine shipments from many shippers destined for a common point. The difference between the bulk rate that the consolidator receives and what the individual shipper would have to pay for small shipments is shared between the shipper and consolidator. Sometimes freight rates are based upon volume instead of weight. Due to the nature of the goods shipped at the present time (low density), the jet aircraft cubes out before it weighs out. Therefore goods that are bulky relative to their weight are charged by a different rate. This is one area where special rates have been established to encourage the transportation of high-density goods.

The specific commodity rates allow shippers to transport goods by air that may not be economically feasible at the general commodity rates. These rates depend upon factors such as the potential traffic, the cost of transportation both in the air and on the ground, the value of goods, competition from other modes, and the impact on general commodity rates. Like the general commodity rates, the specific commodity rates also have weight breakpoints. A special category of specific commodity rates is known as *class rates*. These rates apply to a specific class of commodities, such as newspapers, live animals, currency, and gold. Class rates generally are a percentage of the general commodity rates. For example, newspapers may be shipped at a 50 percent discount, whereas gold could be charged at a 100 percent surcharge. The percentage surcharge or reduction is supposedly related to the special ground handling costs.

Table 14-2 shows the international freight rate levels for 1973-1974 for selected worldwide route groups. Two weight breakpoints are shown for over 45 kilograms and over 500 kilograms. Generally speaking, a discount of 25 percent is allowed on shipments weighing 45 kilograms or more. Similar to passenger fares, freight rates are in general the lowest on the North Atlantic and the highest within Europe. However, unlike passenger travel, the seasonal imbalance

Table 14-2
International Freight Rate Levels, 1973-1974

| | Rate Levels (U.S. Cents/Ton km) | | | Mean Sector Length (km) |
| | General Cargo Rates | | Average Specific Commodity | |
	Over 45 Kilograms	Over 500 Kilograms		
North Atlantic	42	19	11	7,071
North and Mid-Pacific	37	23	18	10,392
Europe-Far East/Australasia	46	29	15	12,923
Europe-Southern Africa	53	40	12	6,774
Local Europe	90	67	32	1,565

Source: International Air Transport Association, *Agreeing Fares and Rates*, June 1974.

is less severe for freight transportation. For example, on the North Atlantic during 1973 the lowest month (January) accounted for approximately 40,000 tons; whereas the highest month (October) accounted for approximately 52,000 tons. Thus freight rates do not vary from month to month as much as passenger fares. Furthermore, unlike passenger movements, freight movements can vary depending upon direction and type of shipment. Eastbound and westbound movements in December 1973 were 26,000 and 22,000 tons respectively. Thus freight rates for one direction may be quite different from rates for an opposite direction. Finally, the nature of goods moving on the North Atlantic varies according to the direction. For example, eastbound commodities are more production and technology oriented with high value per pound, while westbound commodities tend to be more consumer oriented with lower values per pound. Therefore specific commodity rates are appropriate and necessary to balance this difference in the total trade flow.

Is IATA a Cartel?

Ever since its establishment, the issue as to whether IATA is a cartel has been fiercely debated by students of international aviation. While the issue is far from settled, the reader may find it helpful to compare various aspects of IATA's behavior and authority to selected attributes of cartel behavior. The major difficulty regarding classification of IATA as a cartel revolves around the uniqueness of the industry, on the one hand, and the lack of an explicit definition of a cartel, on the other. In numerous class discussions conducted by the author, the general consensus is that IATA is not a perfect cartel; however, it is not completely free of all cartelistic characteristics. A number of students leaned heavily towards the classification "imperfect cartel," an uncommon phrase, but one that has been used by some economists in the past.[4]

To begin with, there is no explicit definition of a cartel. Various standard dictionaries give slightly different definitions. For example, some contain the phrase "control of production and pricing," while others use the phrase "control of production or pricing." The difference is significant. If the conjunction *and* is used, as in the first definition, it would be difficult to prove that IATA is a cartel, since it does not control capacity. But when *or* is used, it may be possible to establish a case for a cartel, since there is a certain amount of control exercised on setting prices. Unfortunately this is just the beginning of the problem. Even if the issue of definition were settled, there are still many other controversial issues that must be resolved before it can be determined whether or not IATA is a cartel.

It is generally agreed that a cartel is a formal agreement among firms to limit competition in the market they serve. Supposedly this is achieved (behind closed doors) by dividing the market, controlling production, or fixing prices. However, as previously pointed out, the capacity and price decisions of an airline are controlled by forces that primarily are external to the carrier. The capacity produced by the carrier is at least partially the result of bilateral negotiations. In any case, leaving aside the recent fuel crisis, the average load factor has declined over the years, hardly the result of controlled production. However, it is only fair to remind the reader that while capacity per se is not discussed at the traffic conferences, there are no laws prohibiting the discussion of load factors. Thus it would be naive to assume that capacity is not discussed during traffic conferences. The prices to be charged by each carrier are negotiated by the member carriers through the machinery of IATA Traffic Conferences and are subject to government approval, which, as the Chandler controversy in 1962 attests to, is not guaranteed.

The critics of the IATA traffic machinery have often complained that it is the airlines that set the fares, since government approval is a mere formality. Therefore, if airlines get together to set fares, IATA must be a cartel. Furthermore, if government approval is just a formality, the government is not safeguarding the public interest. This reasoning is not quite correct. First, as stated earlier, capacity is not explicitly discussed at these meetings. Second, every carrier has one vote. Surely it is fairly obvious that the least-cost carriers will propose low fares, while high-cost carriers propose high fares. In this case, the low-cost carriers can vote against the high fares. Third, it is not correct to assume that government involvement is minimal and takes place only after the carriers have negotiated a fare package. Conversely, carriers must, and generally do, discuss the various fare proposals with their appropriate governmental agencies prior to the traffic conferences.

It should be kept in mind that membership in IATA is, with one exception, unrestricted; namely membership is limited to scheduled carriers; nonscheduled carriers are not admitted. Any certificated scheduled airline performing international transportation is eligible for full membership. Carriers not engaged in international transportation that want to be tied into the interline clearinghouse and technical services of IATA are eligible for associate membership. Thus, if the CAB were to authorize an additional U.S. carrier on the North Atlantic, this carrier would be eligible for full membership.

The competition is far from limited. Many people—in fact, often the same people who are attempting to prove that IATA is in fact a cartel—claim the market is too competitive. In addition to the aggressive competition among the members themselves, there is strong competition between the scheduled carriers and the nonscheduled carriers. Approximately twenty-four carriers operate on the North Atlantic; each market may be a duopoly if there are two dominant carriers in the market. The evidence with respect to competition between scheduled carriers and nonscheduled carriers is also quite clear. The share of the U.S. flag charter passenger traffic increased from 3.2 percent in 1963 to 15.7 percent in 1972, a gain of 12.5 percentage points. The existence of this competition has produced a continuous decline in passenger fares. The passenger yield for the U.S. scheduled carriers declined from 6.64 cents in 1963 to 4.76 cents in 1972; for the U.S. nonscheduled carriers, passenger yield declined from 3.06 cents to 2.35 cents during the same time period. Further evidence of competition on the North Atlantic between U.S. scheduled and nonscheduled carriers is clear from the continuous debate over the question of diversion of passenger traffic. Both Pan American and TWA have claimed that there has been a substantial diversion during the peak periods, and that traffic carried by the supplementals would have moved on the scheduled services had the supplementals not existed.

Standard definitions also contain two other ideas: the phrase "division of markets to maximize profits" and the requirement that the participants be private, or independent, or both. First of all, markets can hardly be classified as divided, at least on major international regions such as the North Atlantic, when the markets are controlled by the government. The carriers cannot offer service on an international market without prior permission from the respective governments. Furthermore, the object of maximizing profits through the division of markets can only be achieved if the interests of all carriers are the same, a condition unlikely to exist. The other aspect of the definition is also not justified in the case of international carriers. Most of the international carriers (except the U.S. flag carriers) are at least partially, directly, or indirectly owned by their governments. Thus the majority of the international carriers cannot be considered private or independent firms.

The theory of cartel pricing depends upon assumptions with respect to individual firm costs, product homogeneity, and the market demand curve. Thus the carriers will encounter difficulties in establishing a single cartel price required by product homogeneity, since they have different cost structures and because each carrier will determine a different optimal price from its own standpoint. A close examination of operating cost data for seventy-four international airlines for the year 1972 showed wide differences in total unit operating costs, ranging from 11.6 cents per available ton-kilometer to 54.2 cents. Thus it is very difficult to imagine a single price level that would maximize the profit for each carrier. Even if a single price level did exist, it is extremely doubtful that the carriers would unanimously agree to charge that particular price.

Assuming that a single cartel price could be determined to maximize joint profits, the allocation of capacity would be an extremely difficult task. On the surface it would appear that the cartel members can maximize profits through a profit pooling system. However, there would be little incentive for a carrier to become more efficient or improve the service offered if it could only receive a portion of the additional profits that it generated. On the other hand, a carrier would benefit more by competing for a higher market share, since it would then receive all the additional profits derived from improved service policies. However, this philosophy will temporarily raise costs (due to extra service provided) and result in excess capacity. But, while rising costs tend to raise fares, excess capacity will eventually force the fares down again.

It should be evident from the above discussion that it is difficult, if not impossible, to establish whether IATA is a cartel. Part of the difficulty arises from the uniqueness of the industry, and part from the lack of an explicit definition of a cartel. On the one hand, the secrecy of traffic conferences is a cartelistic characteristic. On the other hand, the secrecy may simply be a result of the lack of accurate information about what really goes on at a traffic conference. This forces the industry's investigators to make a subjective judgment based upon the information contained in the news media. And here, one must be careful. Not only is the reported information often inadequate and inaccurate, but one assumes—and not always correctly—that the reporter has a good knowledge of the fare-setting machinery and associated matters. In the final analysis, while IATA does show some characteristics of a cartel (joint determination of price and level of service behind closed doors), the final agreement is not effective unless approved by the governments. The end product of a traffic conference is nothing more than a set of recommendations submitted to the various governmental agencies for their approval. Thus, one wonders who really does set the prices: the carriers, or the governments?

IATA's Other Functions

In addition to the administration of its traffic conference machinery, IATA performs a number of other useful functions that benefit the member airlines. The most important and significant of these functions is the operation of the IATA Clearing House. Through this system the member airlines, as well as a group of non-members, clear their interline accounts. Established in 1946, the Clearing House today handles interline claims amounting to approximately $10 billion in nearly 50 currencies of the 168 currencies in which IATA members transact their business. Prior to the establishment of the Clearing House, the carriers restricted the number of currencies used in accounting between any two airlines to the national currencies of the two carriers in question. For example, a Swissair bill to KLM was charged in either Swiss francs or Dutch guilders. Similarly, a Swissair bill to Lufthansa was charged in either Swiss francs or German marks. Today the carriers may submit bills in many currencies, but the Clearing House makes settlements in only two major currencies, the U.S. dollar and the British pound. These two currencies are also the basic currencies in which IATA passenger fares and cargo rates are negotiated. The cost of the system, which used to be borne by the member airlines in proportion to their gross annual claims, is now virtually nothing, due to the investment management of short-term settlement funds flowing through the system.

There are basically two advantages of the Clearing House system. First, the carriers save administrative costs and bank charges associated with settling interline accounts. Second, the carriers can settle their accounts in days, instead of months. This avoids tying up hundreds of millions of dollars, which with today's short-term interest rates can cost the carriers millions of dollars. In addition to these two advantages, IATA is currently trying to establish a more stable basis for airline transactions in order to protect member airlines from losses through persistent currency fluctuations. At the present time there is some positive feeling toward adopting International Monetary Fund's Special Drawing Rights (SDR) as the new foundation for IATA's fares and rates structure. This system will reduce costs even further, ensure a more accurate sharing of revenue, and protect carriers' revenue despite fluctuating rates in the world markets. The SDR system has an international value base made up of sixteen major currencies and reflects a greater stability than any single currency.

Besides administering the traffic conference machinery and operating the Clearing House system, IATA performs many other useful services related to finance, legal issues, technical matters, economic statistics and research, traffic standardization procedures, and public relations. In the area of legal matters, IATA has worked with ICAO on actions related to charges by governments, security, and international conventions, such as the Guatemala Protocol. In technical matters, IATA has taken an active interest in representing their members with respect to Aeronautical Satellite System and airport activities. Finally the Association also provides valuable statistical, economic, and research services to members. These services are particularly useful at the traffic conferences.

International Civil Aviation Organization

As stated in Chapter 1, one of the outcomes of the Chicago Conference was the establishment of the International Civil Aviation Organization (ICAO). The aims and objectives of ICAO are "to develop the principles and techniques of international air navigation and to foster the planning and development of international air transport." Specifically, the objectives of ICAO are:

1. Insure the safe and orderly growth of international civil aviation throughout the world.
2. Encourage the arts of aircraft design and operation for peaceful purposes.
3. Encourage the development of airways, airports, and air navigation facilities for international civil aviation.
4. Meet the needs of the peoples of the world for safe, regular, efficient, and economical air transportation.
5. Prevent economic waste caused by unreasonable competition.
6. Insure that rights of contracting states are fully respected and that every contracting state has a fair opportunity to operate international airlines.

7. Avoid discrimination between contracting states.
8. Promote safety of flight in international air navigation.
9. Promote generally the development of all aspects of international civil aeronautics.

The Organization, which at the end of 1972 consisted of 124 states, became a special agency of the United Nations after the establishment of the United Nations. The Organization discharges its functions through the ICAO Assembly, Council, and various subsidiary bodies. Each member state is represented in the ICAO Assembly, which meets at least once every 3 years to review the entire work of the Organization in the technical, economic, and legal fields and to set general policy guidelines for the Organization. In addition, the Assembly elects the ICAO Council, which is a permanent body made up of twenty-seven contracting states elected for a 3-year term. The Council provides the legislative, judicial, and administrative direction for the Organization. The legislative functions include the adoption of various ICAO air navigation and air transport regulations. The judicial functions are illustrated by the Council's power to adjudicate disputes between contracting states relating to the interpretation and application of the Chicago Convention. The administrative functions include the usual activities, such as the appointment of the Secretary General, and the administration of the finances of the Organization. The Council is assisted by five committees and commissions: Air Navigation Commission, Air Transport Commission, Legal Committee, Committee on Joint Support of Air Navigation Services, and Finance Committee. These are closely tied to the five bureaus: Air Navigation Bureau, Air Transport Bureau, Legal Bureau, Technical Assistance Bureau, and Bureau of Administration and Services.

The Air Navigation Commission, consisting of twelve experts, has the responsibility of developing the international air navigation legislation. The Commission's recommendations for standards and practices of international air navigation are adopted by the ICAO Council as annexes to the convention on International Civil Aviation. The Commission deals with the technical standards and practices for all aspects of international civil aviation operations, including the operation of aircraft, aircraft worthiness, and the many facilities and services required in their support, such as airports, aviation medicine, telecommunications, navigational aids, meteorology, rules of air and air traffic services, search and rescue, environment, aeronautical information services, and aircraft noise and security measures. In conjunction with this Commission, the Committee on Joint Support of Air Navigation Services advises the Council on technical problems relating to air navigation facilities and services. The Committee also assists the ICAO Council with various issues related to the joint financing of certain air navigation facilities serving the North Atlantic air routes.

The Air Transport Committee advises the Council on the economic aspects of international air transport. In addition to this, the Air Transport Commission is also engaged in activities relating to the facilitation of air travel. These activities are aimed at eliminating the nonessential documentary requirements and simplifying and standardizing the clearance procedures at terminals. With respect to air transport economics, the Air Transport Bureau is actively studying the development of passenger and cargo transport in various regions of the world, joint financing of air navigation facilities, airport financing such as landing charges, and route facility costing. Recently the Bureau is examining the feasibility of undertaking studies on fares and rates in international air transport.

The Legal Committee studies various problems of private and public international air law affecting international civil aviation. Although this Committee has a number of items on its general work program, the attention recently has focused on hijacking. The Legal Committee has also been very active in the areas of international conventions.

An important function of ICAO is to provide technical assistance to developing countries. This technical assistance, normally requested by the individual countries, is provided with funds available through the United Nations Development Program (UNDP). The technical assistance program covers many activities, such as training courses and the provision of aviation experts. Although ICAO's technical assistance is generally of an advisory nature, the Organization has provided assistance of an operational nature such as the Associate Experts Program.

Most of the work described above is carried out through the five bureaus under the Secretary General. The Organization is headquartered in Montreal with a staff of almost 700 persons. In addition to its offices in Montreal, ICAO also maintains six regional offices in Bangkok, Cairo, Dakar, Lima, Mexico, and Paris.

Government Interests in the Airline Industry

Although the governments have always had an active interest in their airlines, the extent and type of interest varies from one nation to another. In Chapters 1 and 12 the reasons for the U.S. government involvement in the U.S. airline industry were cited. In this section an attempt is made to investigate the reasons for some of the foreign governments' interests in the developments of their international carriers. While the reasons for governmental involvement, such as impact of balance of payments, are common to all, the extent of government involvement varies significantly depending upon the type of ownership and the political, social, and economic outlook. This section will focus upon the fundamental reasons for establishing international carriers, and the influence of type of ownership on the economics and operations of their flag carriers. One point that must be kept in mind is that a nation's goals for establishing an international air carrier are not always based upon economic reasoning. Very often political and social reasons dominate the economics.

One of the basic economic reasons for establishing an international air carrier is its impact on the balance of payments. Favorable balance of payments effects are achieved by collecting fares from foreign travelers in the traveler's own currency and transporting its own nation's travelers. Obviously not all of the fares collected from foreign travelers get translated into favorable balance of payment effects, since there are also costs involved in foreign countries. For example, the U.S. international carriers have to pay airport costs (landing fees, fuel costs, etc.), salaries of foreign based employees, and promotional expenses in foreign currencies. Some years ago these costs were estimated to be about 25 percent of the fares collected in foreign currency. Furthermore, it is also necessary to deduct approximately the same amount to account for the funds that foreign carriers would pay in the United States if they had carried the passengers. Thus the net positive impact on the balance of payments is approximately 50 percent of the fares collected in foreign currency. Since the U.S. international carriers fly U.S. manufactured aircraft, there is no impact of this on the U.S. balance of payments. However, since the foreign carriers conduct a large portion of their operations with U.S. manufactured aircraft, they incur additional balance of payments costs. Over the years this advantage has been partially offset both by the decline in the U.S. share of the total traffic and because U.S. travelers have been spending more abroad relative to foreign travelers' expenditures in the United States.

Another major economic reason for the establishment of an international flag carrier is to promote trade, investment, and travel from other countries. For developing nations, an additional argument is frequently cited: international flag carriers aid the country's economic development through improved communications for trade, investment, and tourism. The merit of this justification is not clear, since these benefits can be achieved regardless of which airline provides the service. It is more likely that developing nations are interested in international flag carriers for reasons of national image and prestige rather than for economic and financial reasons. For some of the developed nations another major reason for establishing international flag carriers is the support of their domestic aircraft manufacturing industries; England and France are two good examples of this. In addition to these economic reasons, there are at least two political reasons for international flag carriers. First, the carriers can provide a relatively inexpensive strategic reserve of airlift capacity. Second, these carriers can serve various political routes, such as to and from former colonies.

Depending upon a nation's goal for an international air carrier, the government usually provides direct and indirect economic assistance if the carrier is economically unable to provide the service. This economic assistance can take the form of government provision of equity capital, loans from the government or government loan guarantees, special tax provisions, mail subsidy, provision of equipment, aid to flight and technical training, direct cash payments for operating losses, provision of goods and materials, and measures to channel nationals on their own flag carriers. The nature and extent of the government's economic assistance depends upon the control and ownership of the carriers by their respective governments.

The most direct form of economic assistance is the direct subsidy. For example, Air France recently received direct subsidy from the French government. In 1968 the carrier received over $40 million or roughly 10 percent of its revenue. The Belgian government provides an operating subsidy to its carrier, Sabena, equal to any deficits incurred. In addition to direct cash payments to cover operating losses, most of the foreign carriers receive equity capital from their governments. Receiving equity capital from a government is quite different from acquiring it on normal commercial markets. One major difference is the payment of dividends. Although some carriers do pay some dividends to their governments, a number of them are not required to do so; Iran Air, for example, is not required to pay dividends to its government. Japan Air Lines is another carrier exempted from paying dividends as long as the rate of dividends paid to the private shareholders is less than 8 percent.

The most significant form of indirect subsidy are government loans or government loan guarantees. These loans are usually at a much lower rate than loans available on commercial markets. The international airline of Israel, El Al, for example, is eligible for government loans at a rate of almost one-half the current commercial rate. In some cases the interest rate is very close to the public government borrowings. In addition to the actual loans, many governments guarantee loans from commercial sources or the U.S. Export-Import Bank for credit to purchase aircraft. Other forms of indirect subsidy have been cited earlier, but one that deserves special mention is the special tax treatment. A number of foreign carriers enjoy some very favorable tax exemptions. Several carriers are not required to pay any taxes at all. Air New Zealand can offset its tax liabilities with tourism promotional outlays. Japan Air Lines is allowed accelerated depreciation periods for its fleet.[5] It is interesting to note that in 1973 the U.S. carriers paid 18.5 cents per gallon of aviation fuel in Bombay. In 1974 the price was raised to $1.16, of which 31 percent represented the government surcharge, 23 percent the sales tax, and 46 percent the cost of fuel itself. While the foreign carriers were required to pay $1.16 per gallon, Air India was exempted from both the surcharge and the sales tax.[6]

Unlike the U.S. air carriers, which are all privately owned, most of the foreign carriers have some amount of government ownership, which can be direct or indirect. In a recent CAB study of fifty-five foreign air carriers, twenty-five were entirely owned by their governments; twenty-two had substantial government ownership, and only eight were wholly owned by private interests.[7] There are some international air carriers that are owned by the governments of more than one country. A description of two such carriers, East African Airways and SAS, is given in the next section. While it is cumbersome to describe the details of every carrier's ownership, the following examples provide some insight into the different approaches to ownership.

1. Air Canada is completely owned by the Canadian National Railway Company, which, in turn, is entirely owned by the Canadian government.
2. Air Afrique is owned by a consortium of eleven former French colonies and the Société pour le Développement du Transport Aerien en Afrique (SODETRAF). The eleven sponsoring member states control 72 percent of the shares while SODETRAF controls the remaining 28 percent.
3. British Airways is entirely owned by the British government.
4. Seventy percent of KLM is owned by the Dutch government. The remaining 30 percent is held by private investors and institutions, mostly in the United States. The carrier's stock is listed on the New York Stock Exchange.
5. Lufthansa's ownership is quite mixed. The Federal Republic of Germany owns 74.31 percent. The general public owns 17.84 percent. Land of Nordrhein-Westfalen (state of West Germany) owns 2.25 percent. The German banks own 3.00 percent. The German Post Office owns 1.75 percent, and the German Railroad owns the remaining 0.85 percent.
6. VARIG is almost entirely privately owned. Private investors own 96.11 percent of the stock; the State of Rio Grande Do Sul holds the remaining 3.89 percent. The Government of Brazil does not own any stock in the carrier.

Interline Agreements

Despite the intense competitive environment, there has been a substantial amount of cooperation and interaction among the international carriers. Over the years, interline agreements have ranged from ticketing to multinational airline organizations. There are at least three reasons for the extensive spread of interline agreements. First, as mentioned before, the airline industry possesses some unique characteristics, such as the inability to store capacity, restricted market areas, and localized competition. Thus it is quite possible to cooperate on one segment of the network and compete on another. Second, the establishment of an international airline represents a significant financial investment on a long-term basis. Interline agreements can increase the productivity of labor and equipment. Third, some interline agreements can increase the safety of operations. The importance of cooperation among the international carriers for economic and safety reasons is recognized by the governments, which in some cases have specifically exempted the negotiation of the agreements from the antitrust laws.

Leasing

Leasing agreements can take many different forms, ranging from the entire aircraft, including the crew, fuel, and maintenance, to blocking space on particular flights. The financial aspects of aircraft leasing were discussed in Chapter 5. In regard to operating features, there are two common forms of aircraft leases: *dry leases* and *wet leases*. In a dry lease the carrier takes possession of just the aircraft itself, in a wet lease the carrier obtains not only the aircraft but also the fuel, the crew, and the maintenance. The benefits of leasing, as discussed earlier, fulfill the temporary need of flight equipment. (In the United States the Board takes a particular interest in wet leases.)

The blocked space agreement is another form of leasing. In such agreements one carrier would rent a specific amount of space on another carrier's regularly scheduled flights. The payment is usually based upon the amount of space rented rather than on the amount of space actually utilized. For example, suppose a small European carrier obtained traffic rights into the United States but could not economically justify regularly scheduled service because of lack of traffic, even for one daily round trip. This is not unusual considering the low traffic density on many individual routes and the high capacity of long-range jet aircraft. In this case, the carrier could block, for example, 40 seats on every flight of another transatlantic carrier operating between the same points. Thus the small carrier could advertise regularly scheduled service and if necessary, arrange for the large carrier to handle the traffic with respect to reservations and ticketing in return for a fixed fee (for the entire space rented) plus a handling charge per passenger.

Management Agreements

Management agreements between airlines can range from management training programs to pooling agreements established to share revenues and capacity. In between these two categories are such agreements as maintenance contracts, agency arrangements, and crew interchange agreements. Management training programs are usually entered into between large, established carriers and small, newly established airlines. Under the agreement, the large experienced carriers usually provide management assistance and training in such areas as finance, flight operations, and scheduling. Ethiopian Air Lines has been working with TWA under this type of agreement since 1945. The large carriers provide these services for many reasons over and above the direct cash payments. For instance, the large carrier may benefit in terms of feeder traffic from the domestic routes of the small carrier if their systems should meet at certain points. Second, the large carrier may be able to sell some of its used aircraft to the smaller carrier. Third, helping the small carrier analyze the local routes may provide the large carrier with useful information regarding future route expansion possibilities.

Pooling arrangements, most common within Europe, represent another form of management agreements. The idea here is to offer the service jointly and share the traffic on specific routes. The most common form is to reach an agreement on capacity and frequency to be offered on a given route. Other arrangements can include the sharing of expenses, revenues, and even joint promotion. The advantages of pooling are quite obvious in markets where the traffic density is low, or where competition is intense. However, it is debatable whether the passengers actually benefit from the existence of pooling arrangements. The pooling partners often state that the passengers receive improved service. For example, thin markets are serviced on a daily basis and the competitive "bunching" of flights around the periods of peak demand are reduced. This in turn provides the passengers with a wider selection of flight departures. However, in opposition to this, a number of industry investigators maintain that the service deteriorates in the pooled markets. The most common explanation of this is the existence of high load factors accompanied by an increased probability of space unavailability.

Joint Ventures

Small countries sometimes face economic problems in developing international airlines. The main problem lies in the lack of sufficient traffic necessary to justify the establishment of the total infrastructure that is necessary to compete effectively. One strategy to overcome the economic problem is to form a consortium. However, while the formation of such consortia may help achieve the desired economies of scale, the existence of nationalism and incompatible political, military, economic, and industrial philosophies of the partner countries can represent real practical difficulties in implementation. Over the years a number of multinational airlines have tried to set up consortia. Only three consortia have been successfully implemented: East African Airways Corporation (EAAC), Air Afrique, and the Scandinavian Airlines System (SAS). Many others, such as the one in Malaysia and Singapore and the one in West Africa, have failed because of different philosophies in regard to nationalism and economic development.

The feeling that the formation of a multinational airline dilutes national prestige is perhaps the main barrier to the formation of an air union in Europe. As early as 1958 discussions were held between Air France, Alitalia, Lufthansa, and Sabena to determine the feasibility of joint airline operations. This never materialized, and these carriers later decided to form an organization known as ATLAS to cooperate on technical levels with respect to maintenance of wide-body equipment.[e] Iberia and KLM also joined the group, but KLM later left. The present members cooperate on maintenance programs on aircraft such as the Boeing 747 and the DC-10. However, there is interest among the members to expand the joint cooperative programs to include such functions as ground handling services, scheduling, and electronic data processing systems.

[e]In addition to ATLAS, there is another technical group known as the KSSU operated by KLM, Swissair, SAS, and UTA.

East African Airways Corporation (EAAC). East African Airways is a corporation jointly owned by the governments of Kenya, Uganda, and Tanzania. It was initially formed by the British in 1946 as a feeder system for British Overseas Airways Corporation's (BOAC) long-haul routes to and from East Africa. In 1957 the airline began service to London and Asia. The airline took on its present constitutional status under the East African Airways Corporation Act of 1967. As mentioned earlier the main reason for the formation of EAAC was to gain in economies of scale by avoiding duplication of aviation infrastructure, which none of the countries in the consortium could afford. In spite of the many crucial differences in the philosophies of the three states, the most important factor influencing the formation of EAAC has been economics.

In establishing the EAAC, East African Airways Act of 1967 has built-in provisions to balance the power of each state. The carrier is managed by a ten-member Board of Directors, two appointed by each of the partner states and four others. The East African Authority that makes the appointments is an institution of the East African community comprised of heads of state from the partner states. The bilaterals are negotiated by three East African Ministers, one appointed by each partner state and all appointed by the East African Authority. The bilaterals are negotiated in accordance with the criteria approved by the Communications Council, which is the executive organ of the community, and controlled by the Authority. Each state has an equal financial interest in the Corporation.

The Scandinavian Airlines System (SAS). The Scandinavian Airlines System is a multinational aviation consortium formed by three airlines from Sweden, Denmark, and Norway. The consortium was organized in 1946 to conduct operations on the North Atlantic. The corporation was originally restricted to the North Atlantic, while each of the three carriers continued to serve their domestic markets and the European markets independent of one another. In 1951 these three Nordic carriers combined all their operations and allowed the consortium to handle all intercontinental, European, and domestic routes. Even though there were differences of opinion with respect to the political nationalistic considerations between the three countries, the economic rationale was the overriding factor in the establishment of the consortium. For example, lack of sufficient traffic by each individual country to obtain the benefit of economies of scale with respect to larger aircraft and the boost in the bargaining power in negotiating Bermuda-type bilateral agreements played a key role in favor of a joint Scandinavian air venture. The three governments, which jointly have 50 percent ownership in the consortium, have given SAS exclusive rights to all Scandinavian international air transport. The domestic network is served on a contract basis with the three governments having authority to demand that SAS serve certain domestic markets that might, in fact, be uneconomical.

The SAS consortium is managed by an Assembly of Representatives, a Board of Directors, and a General Manager. The Assembly, which consists of the Board of Directors of the parent carriers that "merged" to form the consortium, elects the Board of Directors of SAS who, in turn, appoint a General Manager. From the outside, SAS resembles a typical national flag airline. However, the internal management system is quite complex with respect to the sharing of revenue, costs, profits, losses, ownership of aircraft, maintenance, and personnel. In spite of these difficulties, the consortium makes every effort to facilitate allocations in a reasonable way between the three countries. For example, SAS equipment and spare parts inventory is taxed only at the time of entry into Scandinavia; there is no multiple taxation. With regard to the negotiation of bilateral agreements, the "SAS" clause is almost always included; this clause allows aircraft licensed in one Scandinavian country to fly, for commercial purposes, into a country that has a bilateral agreement with a second Scandinavian country. The three countries do not have an equal financial interest in the consortium. Most of the allocations are based upon three parts for Sweden, two parts for Denmark, and two parts for Norway.

Summary

In this chapter an attempt was made to provide the reader with some insight into the development and operation of the international air transportation system. The two most important characteristics of international aviation are the negotiation of bilateral agreements and IATA's machinery for setting passenger fares and cargo rates—both of which involve reconciliation of conflicting views of many airlines and their governments. The negotiations of bilateral agreements have been performed in the framework established some 30 years ago at Chicago and Bermuda. Passenger fares and cargo rates are established through IATA's traffic conferences, which given all the constraints and despite all the criticisms, have provided a necessary forum for establishing over half a million different passenger fares and a quarter of a million different cargo rates on some 60,000 routes. In the administration of its traffic conference machinery, IATA has often been criticized for being a cartel. However, as pointed out in this chapter, there is no conclusive evidence for this classification. The major difficulty in proving cartelistic behavior centers first, around the uniqueness of the industry and second, due to the lack of an explicit definition of a cartel. In light of the various points raised in the chapter, IATA is perhaps best described as an "imperfect cartel."

In addition to its operation of the fare setting machinery, IATA performs a number of other useful functions ranging from intraindustry coordination and industry spokespersonship to cooperating with other international organizations, particularly the International Civil Aviation Organization. With respect to the latter point, IATA works closely with ICAO on matters dealing with airports, user charges, security, facilitation of travel, and more recently with respect to ICAO's undertaking of feasibility studies on fares and rates in international air transport.

A substantial portion of the world's airlines are directly, indirectly, wholly, or partly owned by their governments. The governments have, therefore, always had an active interest in their airlines. The extent of government involvement varies significantly among the airlines, depending upon the type of ownership and political, social, and economic outlook. However, in recent years the governments have been exercising a greater degree of influence over the industry, due partially to the increase in economic and political importance of air transportation. The increased participation by the governments accompanied by often conflicting national aviation policies is a significant reason for the present state of the international airline industry. Thus the future structure, performance, and profitability will depend not only upon economic factors such as world economy and fuel prices but also on the existence of a coordinated international government policy for civil aviation.

15 Policy Issues in Air Transportation

The purpose of this chapter is to identify some sensitive issues in air transportation. While only a few issues are discussed on a limited basis in this chapter, the reader is reminded that problems in other areas indeed do exist, such as general aviation, air traffic control, safety, liability of carriers for accidents in international flight, aircraft hijacking, carriage of hazardous materials by air, bilateral negotiation mechanisms, tourism, and user charges. The few issues highlighted in this chapter are only illustrative of the many issues that face the commercial airline industry.

The Deregulation Debate

Ever since the establishment of the Civil Aeronautics Board in 1938, the costs and benefits of regulation within the airline industry have been debated. It should be pointed out that in the past the debate has always centered on "economic" regulation with respect to freedom in pricing and barriers to entry and exit. However, in recent years, particularly since 1970, the deregulation debate has acquired a new emphasis. With recent publications by academic economists, active participation from consumer groups, support from the Department of Transportation, extensive lobbying from the supplemental carriers, and proposed legislation from the White House, the deregulation debate is more active than ever before.[1] Initially many observers believed that after a certain amount of early, intensive interest, this discussion would disappear. However, this event has not occurred. In February 1975 Senator Edward Kennedy held extensive hearings before the Subcommittee on Administrative Practice and Procedure of the Committee on the Judiciary, resulting in a report entitled *Practices and Procedures Used to Regulate Airlines*. In July 1975 the Board and the consulting firm of Harbridge House, Inc. issued a study entitled *A Proposed Means of Evaluating the Consequences of Changed Approaches to Economic Regulation of the Domestic Commercial Air Transportation System*, which outlined an experimental program to "assess the operation of the U.S. domestic air transport system under limited or no regulatory constraints." Also in July 1975 a special staff established by the Board issued an extensive study and a set of recommendations on regulatory reform.[2] Also in 1975 President Ford transmitted to Congress the Aviation Act of 1975, which is supposed to increase efficiency in the airline industry by removing "artificial and unnecessary regulatory constraints."

On July 7, 1975 the Board issued a press release related to the Harbridge House study that suggested that an experimental program be initiated to test the consequences of deregulation. The Board asked for comments from various groups on a proposed series of controlled experiments designed to test the effects of free entry and more freedom to set fares in selected markets. It was anticipated that the Board would allow the carriers in the selected markets to set fares within a "reasonable zone." The specific markets or city-pairs were to be selected after the Board had received comments on the proposed experiment.

There were three initial criteria:

1. Selection of two or more long-haul markets between major cities (over 750 miles) of high-density, and having characteristics of through or connecting service to nearby points and both business and pleasure traffic.
2. Selection of four or five short-haul city-pairs (under 750 miles) having a medium- or light-density traffic.
3. Possible service to satellite airports at selected high-density points.[3]

On July 22, 1975 the Board's special staff on regulatory reform issued its recommendations. The general conclusion of this study was that the present system of protected entry and exit and the public utility type of price regulation are not justified by the underlying cost and demand characteristics of the industry. This special staff recommended that the regulation of entry, exit, and price be eliminated within 3 to 5 years. The staff was in favor of keeping other controls that protect the public. Finally, the staff recommended that subsidized service to small communities be maintained by means of low-bid contracts awarded to operationally and financially qualified carriers. All interested readers are referred to the full text cited earlier.

As stated in Chapter 1, the Administration's Aviation Act of 1975 is claimed to increase efficiency in the airline industry and provide the public with improved air transportation services at a lower cost. Basically the objectives of the proposed legislation are first to introduce price competition in the industry and second to provide for entry of new airline firms into the industry. In a nutshell what the sponsors of the Act really are driving toward is lower fares. More specifically the sponsors believe that airline fares are too high, that there is not enough competition and that competition would bring lower fares.

In April 1976 hearings began before the Aviation Subcommittee of the Senate Committee on Commerce regarding the Aviation Act of 1975. The Board supported some legislative changes such as open entry into freight and charter markets, more pricing flexibility and expansion of the air taxi exemption to use aircraft up to a maximum capacity of 56 seats or 16,000 pounds of payload. In general while the Board was favorable to economic regulation by market forces, it felt that changes in airline regulation must be made gradually. Specifically the Board suggested the following twelve point legislative program.

1. Amend the congressional Declaration of Policy to place primary reliance on the natural forces of the marketplace, carrier efficiency and competition including the entry of new carriers into the industry.
2. Open entry, exit, and pricing in the domestic air freight industry.
3. Open entry, exit, and pricing in charter transportation and liberalization of charter requirements.
4. Statutory expansion of the unregulated air-taxi zone by removing entry, exit and pricing regulation over any air carrier using aircraft with a maximum passenger capacity of less than 56 seats or a maximum payload capacity of less than 16,000 pounds if the carrier meets financial responsibility requirements.
5. Congressional authorization to permit the Board to develop mechanisms which would allow the expansion of carrier domestic route systems, limited creation of new route systems, and removal of certificate restrictions under expedited procedures not requiring an evidentiary hearing.
6. Elimination of statutory proscriptions prohibiting charter carriers from holding certificates authorizing scheduled service and scheduled carriers from holding charter certificates.
7. Carriers would be free to terminate service at any point upon 90 days notice filed with the Board, and the affected communities, subject to the power of the Board to suspend termination up to nine months to allow arrangements for replacement service.
8. Elimination of subsidy eligibility for domestic trunk airlines or any carrier that has been on a subsidy-free basis for five consecutive years.
9. Support of a subsidy program to insure service to small communities under provisions for direct subsidy on the basis of services provided without regard to the kind of carrier operating the service.
10. Amendment of the rate-making provision of the present law so as to stress reliance on competition and carrier efficiency and to limit the Board's rate-making powers to the establishment of maximum fares and to the establishment of minimum fares to prevent fares which are predatory, discriminatory, and preferential pricing or fares which result in inadequate scheduled service (regulatory control expected to be phased out as freer entry becomes meaningful throughout the system).
11. Elimination of mandatory Board jurisdiction over mergers, consolidations and acquisitions of control in any unregulated sector of the air carrier industry (see numbers 2, 3, and 4 above), the Board retaining discretionary power to assert jurisdiction as required by the public interest.
12. The antitrust immunity powers of the Board to be limited to "transactions specifically approved by the Board, and those necessarily flowing therefrom" and the Board will be authorized to define and limit the scope of the immunity.

In light of the above twelve point plan it appears that the Board's program is similar to the Administration's proposal with the only difference in timing. The question now is not whether there should be changes but rather what type of changes and the time for deregulating the industry. The Board's plan however did not establish any specific time period for the proposed changes. The carriers are generally speaking, in favor of more pricing flexibility and changes in the Board's procedures but oppose most of the other provisions of the bill which they believe if adopted would bring chaos to the industry—a chaos which would be irreversible. United opposed the Act except for some of the provisions. However the carrier said that it "could be comfortable with total deregulation in contrast to what we have now."

The real issue is whether the proposed Act will enable the airline industry to provide more efficiency, responsive and less costly transportation service to the public. The proponents of economic deregulation claim the regulation of fares, entry and exit barriers, and air carrier agreements that control capacity produce an inefficient air transportation system. With fixed prices the carriers compete on service, particularly with respect to frequency. It is alleged that this results in overcapacity, low load factors, and fares that are about 30 percent higher than they would be if the carriers were not regulated. This belief is based to a large extent upon the operating result of two intrastate carriers, Southwest in Texas and PSA in California. Furthermore, it is believed that barriers to entry and exit increase the cost of air travel due to the protection given to the inefficiencies of the regulated carriers. In particular the present regulatory system encourages internal cross-subsidization; that is, passengers traveling on dense routes subsidize those traveling on thin routes.

With open entry and unrestricted fares, the desired equilibrium between price and service should be achieved through the market forces. According to this hypothesis the public "wants" low cost travel even at the expense of a lower quality of service. Deregulation would eliminate the monopoly held by the present carriers in certain markets, resulting in lower overall fares. There would be no internal cross-subsidization. Very thin density markets would be served by commuter carriers. The desired competitive situation would reduce overcapacity, raise load factors, and in general provide a more efficient air transportation system.

Before the reader accepts this theory, the arguments presented by the other side should also be considered. First of all, it must be emphasized that the opponents of economic deregulation do not imply that the present system of regulation cannot be improved upon. On the contrary, there are numerous flaws in the present system that can and should be corrected. However, those in favor of regulation maintain that the solution is not to throw away the entire system, which on the whole has worked fairly well. They state that present airline fares are still a bargain, considering the value of service provided. The existence of low fares relative to the service provided is probably the reason for the tremendous growth rates in the past years. The fares are established on a system average basis because of the dependent nature of the airline networks. This system averaging leads to a certain amount of internal cross-subsidization and protection of inefficient carriers. However, if anything, air fares are too low and are certainly lower than they would be if the industry were deregulated. If the fares were, in fact, unreasonably high, why has the industry repeatedly been unable to achieve the allowable rate of return on investment? The fact that the carriers have used the so called excess profit in additional service has only benefited the public in terms of higher quality of service. The U.S. passenger has received a higher quality of service at lower fares than any other passenger in the world. The opponents of deregulation also cite safety as one reason for regulation. It is widely believed that the existence of cut-throat competition would force the carriers, in order to reduce costs, to cut corners that would jeopardize safety.

Having briefly outlined the thinking of each group, it may be instructive to examine the crucial arguments in more detail. Basically, the proponents of deregulation assume that the textbook microeconomic theory would work if the carriers were deregulated. A number of analytical models have been developed that support their arguments. However, closer examination of these models shows that while there is nothing wrong with them per se, many of the assumptions incorporated into these models are too weak to justify the complete scrapping of the present regulatory framework. Given the present state of the art in modeling and the dynamics of the airline industry, it is difficult for the models to produce realistic answers. Just as an example, none of the models contains any socio-political inputs.

The second point to be considered is that the hypothesis of the proponents of deregulation is heavily justified on the operation of the intrastate carriers. This line of reasoning needs some amplification. First, there is no proof that the intrastate system of operation can be transferred to the interstate markets of varying densities, stage lengths, and seasonality. For example, Southwest is able to offer lower fares because, (1) it is a young carrier and its labor costs are less, (2) it effectively has a monopoly position, and (3) it only serves medium and high density markets. Second, even if the transfer could be made, who is to say that the general public would want this system. Only the markets that can show profit would be served. Fares might move up and down like a yo-yo. There might not be interline facilities to transfer baggage, for example, from one carrier to another. Third, although operations of intrastate carriers have historically been regulated to a limited extent by their states, who is to say that the extent of regulation would not increase? If this became the case, one can just imagine the chaos that would ensue from having fifty different regulatory agencies, one in each state.

The third point to consider is the financial stability of the carriers. With free entry and a free pricing system, each carrier would probably try to undercut its competitor's price. This process might continue until all the weak competitors were driven out. Once the weak competitors were out, the remaining carriers could then raise the prices. It is not realistic to assume that new carriers would again enter the market once the prices had been raised. First, one does not "give birth" to an airline overnight. Besides the millions of dollars in capital, one needs fully qualified crews, maintenance bases, reservation systems, and a full complement of ground crew and equipment. Banks and insurance companies can hardly be expected to give the necessary capital on a long-term basis to the transient operators. However those opposed to regulation believe that the carriers would have an easier time of getting money from the financial community because they would be more profitable with deregulation.

The fourth point to consider is the airport operator. A good many airports finance their operations through revenue bonds; operators acquire the necessary capital on the assumption that certain carriers are going to be operating flights in and out of their airports. Under the new system, an airport operator could not be assured of the existence of a particular carrier or even of having flights in and out of a particular airport. The expansion of existing airports and the development of new airports represent not only capital investments but also long-term projects. These projects cannot be undertaken unless the airport operator knows that there will be carriers using the services of an airport. Furthermore, carriers normally lease property and facilities at an airport on a long-term basis. The airport operator can hardly count on subleases let alone plan for future facility requirements. However, the other side of the argument is that, "it is the traffic generated by the carriers serving a community that is the basic guarantor of airport revenues." Thus greater efficiency will result in lower fares which in turn will increase the traffic that supports airport financing.

The fifth point to consider is the aircraft manufacturing industry. A number of the studies cited earlier assume that a new carrier can enter a market with as few as four aircraft. One can then imagine hundreds of airline operators with four to six aircraft, each being a so-called specialist, serving a particular type of market. If this were to be the case, it is difficult to envision the development of new commercial aircraft, since the minimum order point would be beyond the financial capability of any one carrier. The development of a truly new aircraft may cost the manufacturer as much as $1 billion, and the so-called specialist airline operators with four to six aircraft would hardly be in a position to back such a venture. It also appears unrealistic to assume that a group of carriers would join forces to agree on a common specification. Thus under the new system it is unlikely that the public would ever see a good V/STOL aircraft, a U.S. built SST, HST, or a fully dedicated freight aircraft. At present U.S. manufacturers have something like 80 percent of the world market for aircraft. One wonders what this share would have been had the domestic carriers not been regulated back in 1938.

The sixth point to consider is the possible elimination of scheduled air service on unprofitable routes. At present these routes are served by carriers on either an externally subsidized or an internally cross-subsidized basis. Under the deregulated framework there may be no certificated service to many small communities.[4] This argument assumes that there will be no federal subsidy within the deregulated framework. However, proponents of deregulation contend that markets found to be unprofitable by trunk-line carriers would be served by local-service carriers, and those found to be unprofitable by local-service carriers would be served by the commuter carriers. This assumption does not seem realistic for at least two reasons. First, throughout their history carriers have always expressed their desire to serve only the high-density, long-haul routes. The trunk-line carriers have abandoned the medium and small communities. The local-service carriers have also attempted to drop many of the small communities. That leaves the commuter and the supplemental carriers. While a number of commuter carriers are reliable and efficient, the overall record of their stability does not compare favorably with the scheduled carriers. In any case, it may become necessary to provide federal subsidy to commuter and air-taxi carriers to provide service to small communities. It is unlikely that the supplemental carriers would serve the unprofitable routes. Recall a recent application by World to offer scheduled service. The application was to serve transcontinental markets not puddle jumpers. Second, even if these markets were served, either the fare would be fairly high or the new carriers would be forced to cross-subsidize internally. It is almost impossible not to cross-subsidize. Even if a carrier only served one route, the fact that traffic varies by day, week, and month means that it would be impossible to have a fare for each passenger.

Leaving the smaller and medium-sized communities without scheduled air service is certainly not in the public interest. The lack of a reasonable amount of air service would have serious impact on the economies of these regions. For example, it is unlikely that many commercial companies would locate their businesses in remote places that do not have air service. Finally, without the "traffic feed" from local markets, many of the long-haul markets would also suffer. The traffic feed from short-haul operations is very important for some carriers for their high-density connecting services. Delta, for example, has been able to serve its small southeast markets only by feeding passengers and cargo from the short-haul flights into long-haul flights that are more profitable.

In summary the sponsors of the Act assume that there is not enough competition and that competition would bring lower fares. No one has proved conclusively that the proposed changes will result in improved service and lower fares. If labor and fuel costs increase, one way of lowering fares is to reduce the quality of service—less frequency, more seats per aircraft and higher load factor. This will make air travel less convenient and less comfortable. But it will be cheaper. However, not everyone is willing to sacrifice convenience and comfort for lower price.

These are just a few of the important questions that must be considered before the decision is made to scrap the entire present regulatory system. Remember if deregulation is tried and it does not provide the desired results, it would be very costly to reverse the situation. However, this argument does not imply that the present regulatory system is perfect; to the contrary, much can be improved. The Board's procedures for route awards and rate changes are certainly in need of a major overhaul. Basically the Board's procedures should be modified to reduce regulatory lag. There is also nothing wrong with experiments.[a] New concepts and innovations should be tried. For example, while the author is not convinced that the zone of reasonableness concept would achieve its desired results, it certainly deserves a trial on an experimental basis. While the regulatory system should not be totally abolished, it should certainly be made more flexible and efficient. Finally, it is interesting to note that some industry observers feel that the regulation of the air carrier industry can never be eliminated. Even if the Board were stripped of its economic powers, the regulatory function would merely shift to the Justice Department, the Department of Transportation, the State Department, and the airport authorities. If this were to be the case, the proponents of deregulation may take the system out of the frying pan and into the fire.

Fuel Costs

A major issue in the airline industry is related to the substantial increases in the cost of providing air service in recent years. While high operating costs due to the increased costs of goods and services purchased by the airlines are a general problem, the real issue at the present time is the cost of fuel. For domestic operations the carriers paid an average of 12 cents per gallon in 1973. In 1974 the price per gallon had increased to 22 cents. For international operations the price had increased from an average of 13 cents per gallon in 1973 to 34 cents in 1974. In 1974 the additional cost of fuel amounted to more than $1 billion, which is more than three times the total net profit of all the U.S. scheduled airlines. In addition, the higher fuel costs have further increased the costs of other goods and services purchased by the air carriers.

A number of steps have been taken by the carriers to reduce the impact of higher fuel costs. First, the carriers have sought and received higher fares. Second, the carriers have attempted to change their operating procedures both on the ground and in the air to reduce fuel consumption. Third, the carriers have grounded some of the fuel-inefficient aircraft as well as reduced capacity by selling a number of wide-body aircraft. Fourth, the carriers have reduced the level of service by reducing frequency and consolidating flights. Fifth, a number

---

[a]It was recently reported in *Aviation Week and Space Technology* (January 19, 1976) that a Board staff analysis concluded that it was not possible to design an experiment to produce meaningful data on the impact of deregulation on the basis of some small fraction of the domestic system.

of carriers, particularly in international operations, have realigned their route structure to reduce total operating costs. Sixth, a number of major carriers (Eastern, Pan American, and TWA) have applied for federal subsidy to reduce the impact of high fuel costs.

These are short-term actions. For the long-term solutions the federal government has taken two actions. First, a substantial amount of research has been undertaken to examine alternative fuels such as liquid hydrogen and atomic energy. However, the use of these alternative fuels is more than a decade away. Second, research is underway to improve engine and airframe designs for optimal fuel use. The economic benefits of new designs are already beginning to show. The European designed A300 with improved engine technology and wing design is supposedly 25 percent more fuel efficient.[5] On an even longer-term basis, advanced concepts in aircraft design are being studied, such as the use of the oblique wing.[b] It is believed that this would result in a quiet, fuel-economic aircraft capable of operating at a variety of speeds.[6]

At the request of the Senate Committee on Aeronautical and Space Sciences, NASA submitted a Task Force Report on September 10, 1975 outlining a challenging but realistic technology program that could result in conservation of fuel use in air transport. The NASA Task Force made a comprehensive review of possible advances in aeronautical technology and focused upon six major programs to conserve fuel. Three programs include improvements in propulsion and aerodynamics. The other three require different technology from that used by the present air transport aircraft—turbo-props, laminar flow control, and composite primary aircraft structures.[c] The total cost of the R&D program is estimated to be $670 million over the time period fiscal 1976-fiscal 1985.[7] According to a study prepared by Ultrasystems, Inc., implementation of the results of NASA's program will save about 2 billion barrels of oil from 1975 to 2005, and each dollar invested in the program will save between $7.50 and $26.00 in fuel purchase costs.[8]

Supersonic Transport

In 1962 the United Kingdom and France agreed to combine their supersonic air transport projects to develop a common aircraft known as the Concorde. The prototype aircraft was first flown in 1969. In January 1976 British Airways and Air France placed the Concorde in scheduled service between London and

---

[b]Basically this concept involves mounting a straight wing on top of the fuselage. The wing is pivoted so that it can be positioned at 90 degrees to the fuselage for take-offs and landings and at various oblique angles during the flight.

[c]Readers with sufficient background in aeronautical engineering can find a description of these programs in Frederick P. Povinelli, John M. Klineberg, and James J. Kramer, "Improving Aircraft Energy Efficiency," *Astronautics and Aeronautics*, American Institute of Aeronautics and Astronautics (February 1976), pp. 19-31.

Bahrain and between Paris and Rio de Janeiro, respectively. In February 1976 the U.S. Secretary of Transportation approved limited service to New York and Washington by British Airways and Air France on a 16 month trial basis. While scheduled service by supersonic aircraft has begun, many questions regarding environmental impact, economics of operations, and equity issues remain unanswered.

With respect to environmental impacts, a number of basic questions are at issue. On some factors data have been collected to show negative environmental impact, while on other factors there is no conclusive evidence. For example, data recorded on noise levels show that the noise characteristics of the Concorde are somewhat comparable to those of the narrow-body subsonic aircraft. There is no conclusive evidence that the Concorde will upset the stratosphere and harm life on the earth. Similarly, while sonic boom does exist at supersonic speeds, the majority of long-haul routes are either over oceans or remote areas. The aircraft is not intended to be flown at supersonic speeds over populous areas and is in fact prohibited from flying over the continental U.S. at supersonic speeds. There are also questions regarding the possibility of passengers being poisoned at high altitudes by ozone contamination in the cabin air and exposure to radiation. Again there are no hard facts to show that these dangers exist.

The major issue faced by airline management is in reference to economics of operations or profitability. From the numerous calculations performed by the manufacturers and the potential carriers, it appears that the Concorde can be economically viable at fares around 20 percent above the present first-class fares on the appropriate routes. The question of profitability then boils down to whether there are enough passengers willing to pay about 20 percent above the present first-class fares. On the North Atlantic the present first-class traffic is probably sufficient to make the Concorde economically viable. However, due to its limited range and the fact that it has to operate at subsonic speeds over land, carriers such as British Airways would find it difficult to provide significant time savings using the Concorde versus the Boeing 747SP on routes such as London-Australia. Thus given the current operating cost levels and the payload range characteristics of the Concorde, the only potential market appears to be the North Atlantic.

The other major issue is equity. The Concorde research and development program cost the British and French taxpayers approximately $3 billion.[d] Many people would argue that the money could have been spent on other more worthwhile social services instead of developing an aircraft that would benefit a few affluent travelers. Other people would argue that the total benefits will exceed the total cost. For example, besides large scale employment for many people and the significant contribution to European technology on many fronts, the Concorde could help the balance of payments of Great Britain and France.

---

[d]The U.S. SST program was cancelled in 1971 for environmental, social, economic, and political reasons. Approximately $1 billion had been spent on the program.

The export argument assumes that many more than the sixteen Concordes committed to production will be produced and sold to foreign carriers. Finally, the proponents argue that additional benefit can be derived in foreign trade by the increased productivity of overseas business travelers who fly the Concorde.

Whether you like it or not, the SST is here. The big question on the horizon is, how successful will the Concorde be? It is difficult to answer this question because there are so many factors involved. Assuming rapid recovery of the U.S. economy, stable fuel prices, little or no opposition from the Port Authority of New York and New Jersey, no significant pressure from environmental movements, and great passenger acceptance, the U.S. international carriers operating on the North Atlantic (most important international market in the world) may be forced into purchasing the Concorde for competitive reasons. Once the U.S. carriers order the Concorde, the other major international carriers operating on the North Atlantic may also be forced to buy the aircraft for competitive reasons. However, the probability of all these events occurring simultaneously is minimal. One fact is clear, however: unless the limited, carefully controlled experimental operation of the Concorde to the U.S. proposed by Secretary Coleman is allowed to proceed, the true answers to the numerous environmental, operational, and economic questions will never be known.

Although the U.S. SST program was cancelled officially in 1971, feasibility studies have been conducted continuously. Recently, the LTV Aerospace Corporation completed a study of an advanced technology supersonic cruise vehicle concept for the Supersonic Cruise Aircraft Research Office at NASA's Langley Research Center.[9] The basic design consisted of a vehicle capable of flying 4,000 nautical miles at a cruise speed of Mach 2.7 carrying 292 passengers. The Ames Research Center of NASA performed an economic sensitivity analysis of this aircraft with respect to its cost, production quantity, range, fuel cost, load factor, and fare level. The Ames study concluded that a 20 percent discounted cash flow return on investment would require "an aircraft unit cost less than $90 million or a production run of at least 200 vehicles, an average trip length of 3,000 miles or greater, a fuel cost of less than 38 cents per gallon, an average load factor greater than 47 percent, or a fare surcharge if any of these factors cannot be met."[10] The nominal fare was assumed to be $12 plus 6.58 cents per nautical mile. However, despite the encouraging recent studies in technology and economic viability, it would probably take the United States 10 years to develop and build an advanced SST.

V/STOL

In 1971 a month long workshop sponsored by the Office of Advanced Research and Technology of NASA and conducted by the Flight Transportation Laboratory of the Massachusetts Institute of Technology investigated the potential and the problems associated with short-haul air transportation. The workshop found,

... that future air systems hold great potential in satisfying society's needs for low noise, low landspace, high access, high speed, large network systems for public travel over distances between 5 and 500 miles.[11]

The workshop investigated in depth the institutional, socio-economic, operational, and technological problems and concluded that the community acceptance and passenger acceptance of new airport/metroport ground facilities were the critical issues for introducing new forms of short-haul air transportation. With respect to these issues, the following recommendations were made:

An extremely high priority must be assigned to the development of quiet aircraft for future short-haul systems, such that the environmental impact hearings can show net benefits from introducing the system.

Studies of community acceptance factors should be undertaken to collect information, and develop strategies for working with the community in the process of site selection and approval.

A national method for measuring community noise around airports and metroports should be developed. Local communities should be able to select standards for community noise using this method and to have a nonaviation agency monitor and ensure compliance.

All aircraft proposed for use in short-haul demonstration projects should be significantly quieter than present day jet transports even if their operations is at busy airports or small airports with no noise problems. Demonstration projects for short-haul air services pointed at obtaining research data should be carried out under the leadership of the Department of Transportation.[12]

From an airline's point of view, there is a critical need for market research on V/STOL service to determine the relative importance of fare frequency, trip time, accessibility, comfort, and ride quality to the passenger. This market research data can be partially obtained from a demonstration project. A good example of such a demonstration project is the Canadian STOL commuter service, Airtransit. In 1971 the Canadian government's Ministry of Transport set up a demonstration program to "investigate, define, and develop the technical, operational, and regulatory components" of a STOL air transport system.[13] A subsidiary of Air Canada was established, called Airtransit, which began to operate STOL service between Montreal and Ottawa in July, 1974, using the de Havilland of Canada's Twin Otters in competition with existing ground modes and conventional air services. Because of the special modifications on the DHC Twin Otters, the operations were subsidized by the government to maintain a competitive fare structure. Although passenger acceptance exceeded original expectations, it could not be self-supporting, and since sufficient technical data on the operations were obtained, the experiment is being terminated.

Airports

The most critical issues with respect to airport development relate to the environment, land-use planning, ground access, airport financing, and the importance of airport and aircraft compatibility. The environment is probably the most important single factor affecting the development of major airports not only in the United States but throughout the world. Within the environment category the most critical element delaying the implementation of airport master plans is noise. If airport development is to continue, then a solution has to be found in the near future to eliminate noise so that the airport can become a good neighbor. Part of the current noise problem would not have existed had proper land-use planning been considered around major airports in the earlier years. In recent years more attention is being paid to proper land-use planning. Dallas-Fort Worth airport (U.S.A.) and Charles de Gaulle airport (Paris, France) were developed with almost 18,000 acres each, which is adequate to prevent adverse environmental impacts. Similarly, the recently completed Mirabel airport (Montreal, Canada) contains approximately 68,000 acres within its boundaries.

Of the other issues cited with respect to airport development, an important one relates to airport and aircraft compatibility. Historically, the manufacturers developed the aircraft and the airport authorities modified the airport to fit the needs of the aircraft. However, there is now a need to go even beyond the aircraft/airport compatibility requirements. Professor John R. Wiley of the Massachusetts Institute of Technology and the former Director of Aviation for the Port Authority of New York explains:

We must go beyond just airport/aircraft system study and examine in depth the implications of airport/aircraft systems on regional and even national systems. What does this mean?

It means that it would do no good to design an airport that would handle large numbers of large aircraft and their large numbers of passengers if the city or the region served cannot support that large number of passengers (or the activities that generate them)—i.e., cannot provide housing, or electricity, or potable water or sewage disposal, or industry (jobs) or an acceptable quality of life (QOL) to support them and their generating activities.

It is not only airport construction that is being environmentally opposed today. New York City has power "brown outs" but cannot construct new power generating stations.

Perhaps there should be a limit on the size of cities. Perhaps expansion should come nationally by means of more, smaller cities with more smaller (though not necessarily small) airports, both planned from inception with the broadest participation in the planning process.[14]

Another issue of significant concern to the airlines, airports, passengers, and shippers is the Airport Development Aid Program. As stated in the first chapter, the Airport and Airway Development and Revenue Acts of 1970 provide for a capital improvement program with minimum annual funding of $250 million for airports and an equal amount for airway facilities. The funds are collected from special taxes and placed in a Trust Fund. During the first 5 years over $1 billion has been spent on improvement for airports, and about the same amount for improvements in air traffic control. In addition, almost a half a billion dollars has been spent on research, engineering, and development. Despite these large expenditures, there is a surplus of almost $700 million, which is expected to reach $4 billion by 1980.[15]

Specifically, there are two issues. First, a number of people feel that the operations of the Trust Fund should be reviewed and revised (for example, use Trust Fund for retrofit) in view of the community opposition to airport expansion, marginal and uncertain benefits of increased investment in air traffic control projects, lower expected traffic growth, and changing federal transportation policies.[16] Second, the airline industry feels that the taxes should be reduced in view of the surplus, an action it believes is not only in the public interest but would help the industry during the current inflationary and recessionary period.[17]

Air Cargo

For the past three decades the air transportation industry has focused primarily upon the movement of people. Air cargo has been given a secondary role, to fill available space in the bellies of passenger flights. Less than 10 percent of airline industry revenues are derived from air cargo. Approximately half of the volume moves in the belly-holds, and all-freighter service has shown minimal profits. Many forecasters are now considering that perhaps the passenger market has matured and more and more attention should be devoted to investigating the potentialities of air cargo. The more optimistic forecasters predict that air cargo revenue will surpass passenger revenue during the next 20 years. Others, while not so optimistic, still predict that the demand for air cargo will double in the next 20 years.

The growth of air cargo will depend upon a number of factors such as the rate structure, substantial change in industrial marketing and distribution processes, cooperative arrangement with truckers and freight forwarders, aircraft technology, automation of cargo terminals, environmental improvement costs, the state of the U.S. as well as world economy, greater knowledge of future industrial alignments, and a change in airline management attitude toward providing air cargo transportation services. Among the most important issues to be resolved are rate structure, aircraft technology, and airline management attitude.

As stated in Chapter 11, the CAB has initiated its first investigation to review air cargo rates since 1948 with the object of establishing a cost based set of tariffs. In the past cargo rates have been low and the rate structure unsatisfactory, particularly with respect to the multiplicity and often uneconomic nature of specific commodity rates. With respect to cargo aircraft, there are several options in terms of size, range, airframe, and propulsion technology. There is a need for a variety of sizes of dedicated freighters from the very small ones (feeder service) to vehicles up to four times the size of the Boeing 747F. Finally, there is a need for passenger airline managements to change their attitudes, since there are substantial differences between the operations of cargo and passenger services. For example, there are differences between the two services with respect to economics, logistics, and preferences of passengers and shippers.

Summary

This chapter has focused upon just a few of the many issues, challenges, and opportunities facing the air transportation industry in the coming years. For the last six decades the federal government has played a major role in the development of the industry. Since 1974 there have been strong pressures for regulatory reform to produce more competition and lower prices for the users of air transportation services. However, it is possible that the proposed regulatory reform may achieve quite the opposite results, namely higher prices and lower quality of air transportation services.

While the policies of the federal government will play a critical role in the future development of the air transportation industry, the initiatives taken by the airlines themselves in meeting challenges and exploiting new opportunities will also have a significant influence on the growth of the industry. In conclusion, the survival and structure of the U.S. airline industry will be influenced not only by the regulatory policies that relate to competition and fares but also by the ways in which airline managements react and adapt to the consequences of these regulatory policies through their marketing, scheduling, and operations functions. In view of the managerial practices discussed in this book, it will be necessary for the carriers to develop innovative methods of resisting wasteful competition, controlling their costs, and matching demand with the appropriate mix of capacity supplied. Only in these ways will the airline industry remain viable and profitable.

Notes

Notes

Chapter 1
A Review of the Historical Developments

1. U.S. Civil Aeronautics Board, *Handbook of Airline Statistics*, 1973 ed. (Washington, D.C.), p. 477.

2. Ibid., p. 510.

3. Committee of Inquiry into Civil Air Transport Report, *British Air Transport in the Seventies* (London: Her Majesty's Stationery Office, May 1969).

4. The Federal Aviation Act of 1958, Title X, Section 1002(e).

5. U.S. Civil Aeronautics Board, *The Civil Aeronautics Board* (Report prepared by the Office of Information, Washington, D.C.: 1968).

6. U.S. Civil Aeronautics Board, *General Passenger Fare Investigation*, 32 CAB 291 (1960).

7. Grant Miller Davies, *The Department of Transportation* (Lexington, Massachusetts: Lexington Books, D.C. Heath and Company, 1970).

8. Dudley F. Pegrum, *Transportation: Economics and Public Policy*, 3d ed. (Homewood, Illinois: Richard D. Irwin, Inc., 1973), p. 468.

Chapter 3
Airline Economics

1. U.S. Civil Aeronautics Board, Staff Report. *A Study of the Domestic Passenger Air Fare Structure* (Washington, D.C.: January 1968).

2. U.S. Civil Aeronautics Board, *Domestic Passenger Fare Investigation, Phase 9: Fare Structure* (March 18, 1974).

3. George W. Douglas and James C. Miller, III, *Economic Regulation of Domestic Air Transport: Theory and Practice* (Washington, D.C.: The Brookings Institution, 1974); William A. Jordan, *Airline Regulation in America: Effects and Imperfections* (Johns Hopkins Press, 1970); Theodore E. Keeler, "Resource Allocation in Intercity Passenger Transportation," Ph.D. Thesis, (Cambridge, Mass.: Massachusetts Institute of Technology, August 1971).

4. Robert W. Simpson, *A Theory for Domestic Airline Economics*, FTL Report R74-2 (Cambridge, Mass.: Massachusetts Institute of Technology, July 1974).

5. U.S. Civil Aeronautics Board, *Uniform System of Accounts and Reports for Certificated Air Carriers* (Washington, D.C.).

6. Robert W. Simpson and Y.P. Chan, *A Structure for Airline Operating Costs*, FTL Technical Memorandum 71-9 (Cambridge, Mass.: Massachusetts Institute of Technology, December 1971).

7. U.S. Civil Aeronautics Board, *Aircraft Operating Cost and Performance Reports* (Washington, D.C.).

8. Harold D. Koontz, "Domestic Airline Self-Sufficiency," *American Economic Review*, vol. 42 (1952).

9. Paul W. Cherington, *Airline Price Policy: A Study of Domestic Airline Fares* (Cambridge, Massachusetts: Harvard University Press, 1958), pp. 42-62.

10. Richard E. Caves, *Air Transport and Its Regulators* (Harvard University Press, 1962), pp. 58-62.

11. Mahlon Straszheim, *The International Airline Industry* (The Brookings Institution, 1969), p. 96.

12. G. Eads, M. Nerlove, and W. Raduchel, "A Long Run Cost Function for the Local Service Airline Industry," *Review of Economics and Statistics*, vol. 51 (August 1969), pp. 259-270.

13. Committee of Inquiry into Air Transport, *British Air Transport in the Seventies* (London: Her Majesty's Stationery Office, May 1969), pp. 65-66.

14. William A. Jordan, *Airline Regulation in America: Effects and Imperfections* (Baltimore, Maryland: The Johns Hopkins Press, 1970), p. 228.

15. James E. McMillen, "The Effect of Scale in the Airline Industry" M.S. Thesis, (Cambridge, Mass.: Massachusetts Institute of Technology, September 1971).

16. Ibid., p. 40.

17. Samuel R. Reid and James W. Mohrfeld, "Airline Size, Profitability, Mergers and Regulation," *Journal of Air Law and Commerce*, vol. 39 (1973).

18. Robert J. Gordon, "Airline Costs and Managerial Efficiency" in *Transportation Economics*. National Bureau of Economic Research (New York: Columbia University Press, 1965).

19. U.S. Civil Aeronautics Board, Order 69-6-124 (1969).

20. "CAB Reviews Capacity Pact Decision," *Aviation Week and Space Technology* (November 25, 1974), p. 30.

21. "Capacity Pact Disapproved," *Aviation Week and Space Technology* (July 28, 1975), p. 28.

Chapter 4
Marketing Air Transportation Services

1. Philip Kotler, *Marketing Management: Analysis, Planning and Control* (Englewood Cliffs, N.J.: Prentice-Hall, Inc., 1967), p. 266.

2. J.L. Grumbridge, *Marketing Management in Air Transport* (London: George Allen and Unwin Ltd., 1966).

3. Ibid., pp. 29-38.

4. European Travel Commission, An Industry/Consumer Study, *The One Week European Winter GIT* (New York), p. 14.

5. U.S. Civil Aeronautics Board, *Conditional Reservations Rule Proposed by Eastern Air Lines, Inc.*, Order No. 71-6-120 (June 24, 1971), p. 1.

6. The Port Authority of New York and New Jersey, *Transatlantic Air Travel "Fifteen Years in Review," 1956-1971* (New York: June 1975), p. 1.

7. Lawrence M. Hughes, "Airline Ads in Five Media Rise to $188.4 Million," *Air Transport World* (July 1975).

8. Randall L. Schultz, "Market Measurement and Planning with a Simultaneous-Equation Model," *Journal of Marketing Research*, vol. 8 (May 1971), pp. 153-164.

9. Kit G. Narodick, "What Motivates the Consumer's Choice of an Airline," *Journal of Retailing*, vol. 48, no. 1 (Spring 1972), pp. 30-38 and p. 96.

10. Lawrence M. Hughes, op. cit., p. 32.

11. "Getting Back to Basics," *Advertising Age* (October 24, 1972).

12. Kit G. Narodick, op. cit., p. 96.

Chapter 5
Financial Practices

1. Air Transport Association of America, *Air Transport 1975* (Washington, D.C., August 1975).

2. Robert Simmons, "Airline Financing Requirements" in *Proceedings of the Workshop: Air Transportation Demand and Systems Analysis*, FTL Report R75-8 (Cambridge, Mass.: Massachusetts Institute of Technology, August 1975), pp. 237-247.

3. Richard S. Bower, Frank C. Herringer, and J.P. Williamson, "Lease Evaluation," *Accounting Review*, 41 April 1966, pp. 257-265; Thomas H. Beechy, "Quasi-Debt Analysis of Financial Leases," *Accounting Review*, 44 April 1969, pp. 375-381; Harold E. Wyman, "Financial Lease Evaluation under Conditions of Uncertainty," *Accounting Review*, 48 July 1973, pp. 489-493; Robert W. Johnson and Wilbur G. Lewellen, "Analysis of the Lease-or-Buy Decision," *Journal of Finance*, 27 September 1972, pp. 815-824; Robert W. Johnson and Wilbur G. Lewellen, "Reply," *Journal of Finance*, 28 September 1973, pp. 1024-1028; Harold Bierman, Jr., "Analysis of the Lease-or-Buy Decision: Comment," *Journal of Finance*, 28 September 1973, pp. 1015-1016.

4. Robert W. Johnson and Wilbur G. Lewellen, "Analysis of Lease-or-Buy Decision," *Journal of Finance*, 27 September 1972, pp. 815-824.

Chapter 6
Aircraft Selection and Fleet Planning

1. Alan H. Stratford, *Air Transport Economics in the Supersonic Era*, 2d ed. (London: The Macmillan Press, Ltd., 1973), pp. 200-202.

2. Robert W. Simpson, "Technology for Design of Transport Aircraft" Lecture notes for Massachusetts Institute of Technology courses, Flight Transportation Laboratory (Cambridge, Mass.: Massachusetts Institute of Technology, July 1972).

3. J.E.D. Williams, *The Operation of Airliners* (London: Hutchinson and Company, Ltd., 1964), p. 241.

4. Robert W. Simpson, *Scheduling and Routing Models for Airline Systems*, FTL Report R68-3 (Cambridge, Mass.: Massachusetts Institute of Technology, December 1969); McDonnell Douglas Aircraft Co., *Computer Applications for Airline Progress and Profit*, Report Number 800-1159 (September 1969); N.S. Clerman, "An Airline Fleet Planning Model" M.S. Thesis (Cambridge, Mass.: Massachusetts Institute of Technology, August 1969); Henry Faulkner, "An Airline Fleet Planning Model with Financial Constraints" M.S. Thesis (Cambridge, Mass.: Massachusetts Institute of Technology, June 1970).

5. Raymond A. Ausrotas, et al., *Aircraft Requirements for Low/Medium Density Markets*, FTL Report R73-4 (Cambridge, Mass.: Massachusetts Institute of Technology, September 1973).

Chapter 7
Problems in Airline Scheduling

1. C.H. Glenn, "Factors to be Considered in Airline Scheduling," *Canadian Aeronautics and Space Journal* (June 1972), pp. 149-156.

Chapter 8
Airline Labor Relations

1. *Pan American World Airways, Inc., v. TWU*, 7 Av. Cas. 18, 428 (E.D.N.Y. 1972).

2. *Ruby v. American Airlines*, 329 F. 211.

3. James E. Annable, "The ICC, the IBT, and the Cartelization of the American Trucking Industry," *The Quarterly Review of Economics and Business* (Summer 1973).

4. U.S. Civil Aeronautics Board Reports, 36 CAB 430 (1962), p. 433.

5. U.S. Civil Aeronautics Board Reports, 11 CAB 701 (1950).

6. U.S. Civil Aeronautics Board Reports, 14 CAB 910 (1951).

7. U.S. Civil Aeronautics Board Reports, 33 CAB 307 (1961).

8. U.S. Civil Aeronautics Board Reports, 40 CAB 587 (1964).

9. U.S. Civil Aeronautics Board, Order 73-2-110, Issued February 27, 1973, p. 10.

10. Ibid., pp. 12-13.

Chapter 9
Techniques for Forecasting Air Passenger Traffic

1. Olaf Helmer, *Convergence of Expert Consensus through Feedback* (Santa Monica, California: RAND Corporation, September 1964), p. 2973.

2. Donald S. Garvett and Nawal K. Taneja, *New Directions for Forecasting Air Travel Passenger Demand*, FTL Report R74-3 (Cambridge, Mass.: Massachusetts Institute of Technology, July 1974).

3. George E.P. Box and Gwilym M. Jenkins, *Time Series Analysis: Forecasting and Control* (San Francisco: Holden-Day, Inc., 1970).

4. Robert C. Brown, *Smoothing, Forecasting and Prediction of Discreet Time-Series* (Englewood Cliffs, N.J.: Prentice-Hall, Inc., 1963).

5. J.G. Augustinus, *Air Traffic Forecasting at the Port Authority of New York and New Jersey*, Port Authority, Aviation Economics Divisions (July 1972).

6. Roger K. Chisholm and Gilbert R. Whitaker, Jr., *Forecasting Methods* (Homewood, Illinois: Richard D. Irwin, Inc., 1971).

7. Marc Nerlove, "Distributed Lags and Estimation of Long-Run Supply and Demand Elasticities: Theoretical Considerations," *Journal of Farm Economics*, vol. 40, no. 2 (May 1958).

8. Flight Transportation Laboratory, *Air Transportation Data Sources*, FTL Technical Memorandum 71-5-R3 (Cambridge, Mass.: Massachusetts Institute of Technology, January 1972).

9. U.S. Civil Aeronautics Board, *Statistical Programs: Publications and Reports: A Tabular Summary*, Bureau of Accounts and Statistics, 1973 Edition.

Chapter 10
The Regulatory Aspects of Airline Route
Development: Domestic and International

1. American Export Airlines, *Certificate of Public Convenience and Necessity*, 2 CAB 16 (1940) and All American Aviation, *Certificate of Public Convenience and Necessity*, 2 CAB 133 (1940).

2. Delta Air Corporation, et al., 2 CAB 447, 448 (1941).

3. Transcontinental and Western Air Inc., et al., *Additional North-South California Services*, 4 CAB 373, 375 (1943).

4. Northwest Air, et al., *Chicago-Milwaukee-New York Service*, 6 CAB 217, 228 (1944).

5. U.S. Civil Aeronautics Board, *Transatlantic Route Investigation* (Docket 25908), Examiner's Initial Decision (Washington, D.C., January 1975), pp. 29-30.

6. Ibid., p. 48.

7. Ibid., pp. 50-52.

8. R.E.G. Davies, *Airlines of the United States since 1914* (London: Putnam and Company, Ltd., 1972).

Chapter 11
Domestic Passenger Fare and Freight Rate
Policy Decisions

1. U.S. Congress, House, Hearings before the Antitrust Subcommittee, Committee on the Judiciary, *Monopoly Problems in Regulated Industries*, 84th Cong., 2d Sess., Airlines 1, 1956.

2. U.S. Civil Aeronautics Board, *General Passenger Fare Investigation* (Docket 8008), Examiner's Decision (Washington, D.C., May 27, 1959).

3. U.S. Civil Aeronautics Board, Staff Report. *A Study of the Domestic Passenger Air Fare Structure* (Washington, D.C., January 1968).

4. U.S. Civil Aeronautics Board, *Domestic Passenger Fare Investigation, Phase 4: Joint Fares* (March 18, 1974), p. 50.

5. U.S. Civil Aeronautics Board, *Domestic Passenger Fare Investigation, Phase 9: Fare Structure* (March 18, 1974), p. 2.

6. U.S. Civil Aeronautics Board, *Air Freight Forwarder Association et al.*, Motions, 8 CAB 469, 474 (1947).

7. U.S. Civil Aeronautics Board, *Domestic Air Freight Rate Investigation*, Initial Decision of Administrative Law Judge Arthur S. Present (Docket 22859, April 15, 1975), pp. 12-13.

8. U.S. Civil Aeronautics Board, *Domestic Air Freight Rate Investigation*, Initial Decision of Administrative Law Judge Arthur S. Present, (April 15, 1975).

9. Ibid., p. 37.

10. Ibid., p. 67.

11. Ibid., p. 66.

Chapter 12
Airline Subsidy

1. U.S. Congress, Senate, *Report on the Federal Aviation Commission*, Document No. 15, 74th Cong., 1st Sess. (1936), p. 10.

2. U.S. Civil Aeronautics Board, *Subsidy for United States Certificated Air Carriers* (Washington, D.C., March 1974).

3. U.S. Civil Aeronautics Board, *Annual Report of the CAB, Fiscal Year 1968* (Washington, D.C., 1968), p. 112.

4. *Service in the Rocky Mountain States Area*, 6 CAB 695 (1946), p. 730.

5. *Reorganization Plan No. 10 of 1953*, 63 Stat. 203 (1953).

6. U.S. Congress, Senate, Aviation Subcommittee of the Committee on Commerce, *Review of the Local Air Carrier Industry*, Hearings before Subcommittee, 89th Cong., 2nd Sess. (1966).

7. U.S. Civil Aeronautics Board, *Service to Small Communities*, A Staff Study of the Bureau of Operating Rights (Washington, D.C., March 1972).

8. Ibid.

9. Joseph F. Vittek, *Air Service to Small Communities, Directions for the Future*, FTL Report 73-5 (Cambridge, Mass.: Massachusetts Institute of Technology, February 1974).

10. U.S. Civil Aeronautics Board, *Service to Small Communities, op. cit.* Part III, p. 36.

11. George C. Eads, *The Local Service Airline Experiment* (Washington, D.C.: The Brookings Institution, 1972).

12. Raymond Ausrotas, et al., *Aircraft Requirements for Low/Medium Density Markets*, FTL Report R73-4 (Cambridge, Mass.: Massachusetts Institute of Technology, September 1973).

13. U.S. Civil Aeronautics Board, *Service to Small Communities, op. cit.*, p. 17.

14. Pan American World Airways, Inc., *Petition for Establishment of a Subsidy Mail Rate*, Before the U.S. Civil Aeronautics Board (Washington, D.C., April 3, 1974), pp. 3-4.

15. Blaine Cooke, "International Aviation Policy: Heretics at Home, Orthodox Abroad" (Remarks before the Travel Research Association, the Waldorf-Astoria, New York, April 16, 1974), p. 4.

Chapter 13
Airline Mergers

1. *Southern Tier Competitive Nonstop Investigation*, July 24, 1969.

2. U.S. Department of Transportation, *Executive Branch Criteria for Domestic Airline Merger Proposals* (August 31, 1971).

3. E. Mansfield, "Size of Firm, Market Structure, and Innovation," *Journal of Political Economy*, vol. 71, no. 6 (December 1963), pp. 556-576.

Chapter 14
International Aviation

1. U.S. Department of Commerce, *National Interest Aspects of the Private International Air Carrier Systems of the United States* Office of the Secretary: Office of Policy Development (September 1974).

2. Frank E. Loy, "Bilateral Air Transport Agreements: Some Problems of Finding a Fair Route Exchange," (Paper contained in *The Freedom of the Air*, ed. Edward McWhinney (Dobbesferry, N.J.: Oceana Publications, Inc., 1968).

3. Robert A. MacCallum, "A Systematic Approach to International Civil Aviation Route Exchange," M.S. Thesis, (Cambridge, Mass.: Massachusetts Institute of Technology, Department of Political Science, June 1971).

4. J. Bain, "Output Quotas in Imperfect Cartels," *Quarterly Journal of Economics*, vol. 62 (August 1948), pp. 617-622.

5. U.S. Civil Aeronautics Board, *Government Ownership, Subsidy and Economic Assistance in International Commercial Aviation* (Washington, D.C., May 1975).

6. Blaine Cooke, *International Aviation Policy: Heretics at Home, Orthodox Abroad, op. cit.*, p. 9.

7. U.S. Civil Aeronautics Board, *Government Ownership, op. cit.*, p. v.

Chapter 15
Policy Issues in Air Transportation

1. George C. Eads, *The Local Service Airline Experiment* (Washington, D.C.: The Brookings Institution, 1972); George W. Douglas and James C. Miller, III, *Economic Regulation of Domestic Air Transport: Theory and Policy* (Washington, D.C.: Brookings Institute, 1974); William A. Jordan, *Airline Regulation in America: Effects and Imperfections* (Baltimore, Maryland: The Johns Hopkins Press, 1970); Theodore E. Keeler, "Resource Allocation in Intercity Passenger Transportation," (Cambridge, Massachusetts: Massachusetts Institute of Technology, August 1971).

2. U.S. Civil Aeronautics Board, *Regulatory Reform: Report of the CAB Special Staff* (Washington, D.C., July 1975).

3. U.S. Civil Aeronautics Board, *CAB Suggests Experimental Program to Test Consequences of Deregulation*, A Press Briefing (July 7, 1975).

4. Air Transport Association of America, *Consequences of Deregulation of the Scheduled Air Transport Industry, An Analytical Approach* (Washington, D.C., April 1975).

5. Robert Blanchet, *Fuel Consumption and Environmental Needs: New Key Factors in New Airliner Design*, ICAO Bulletin (June 1975), pp. 18-20.

6. International Civil Aviation Organization, *International Civil Aviation in 1974*, ICAO Bulletin (May 1975), p. 51.

7. Craig Covault, "Study Backs Fuel-Saving Design," *Aviation Week and Space Technology* (November 3, 1975), p. 23.

8. Ultrasystems, Inc., *Examination of the Costs, Benefits and Energy Conservation Aspects of the NASA Aircraft Fuel Conservation Technology Program*, Report prepared for NASA (Contract No. NASW-2859), (Irvine, California: November 15, 1975), p. 41.

9. Hampton Technical Center, *Advanced Supersonic Technology Concept Study Reference Characteristics*, LTV Aerospace Corporation (NASA-CR-132374), (December 21, 1973).

10. Cynthia L. Smith and Louis J. Williams, *An Economic Study of an Advanced Technology Supersonic Cruise Vehicle*, NASA TMX-62,499, Ames Research Center, (Moffett Field, California, October 1975), p. 14.

11. Robert W. Simpson, *Summary and Recommendations NASA/MIT Workshop on Short-Haul Air Transportation*, FTL Report R71-4 (Cambridge, Mass.: Massachusetts Institute of Technology, October 1971), p. v.

12. Ibid., pp. 65-71.

13. Vic Davidson, *Canadian STOL-Commuter Service Demonstrates Early Success*, ICAO Bulletin, vol. 29, no. 12, (Montreal, December 1974), p. 14.

14. John R. Wiley, "Class Notes From Courses on Airport Planning," Flight Transportation Laboratory (Cambridge, Mass.: Massachusetts Institute of Technology, 1972).

15. Air Transport Association of America, *Air Transport 1975* (Washington, D.C., 1975), p. 8.

16. Robert W. Simpson, "Get Ready for the Great Debate on Transportation," *Astronautics and Aeronautics*, American Institute of Aeronautics and Astronautics (February 1976), p. 41.

17. *Air Transport 1975*, op. cit., p. 8.

Selected Bibliography

Selected Bibliography

U.S. Government Publications and Legal Documentations

U.S. Civil Aeronautics Board

*Air Carrier Financial Statistics
*Air Carrier Traffic Statistics
*Aircraft Operating Cost and Performance Report
*Airport Activity Statistics of Certificated Route Air Carriers
*Commuter Air Carrier Traffic Statistics
*Economic Cases of the Civil Aeronautics Board, Volumes 1 through 52
*Handbook of Airline Statistics
*Origin-Destination Survey of Airline Passenger Traffic
*Productivity and Cost of Employment—Local Service Carriers—Calendar Years 1972-1973
*Productivity and Cost of Employment—System Trunks—Calendar Years 1972-1973
*Quarterly Cargo Review
*Reports to the Congress
*Subsidy for United States Certificated Carriers
*Trends in Airline Cost Elements
*Trends in Unit Costs
*Uniform System of Accounts and Reports for Certificated Air Carriers
*Wide-Bodied Jet Aircraft Cost and Performance Report

Air Freight Forwarding: the Decade 1963-1972. September 1973.

A Study of the Domestic Passenger Air Fare Structure. A Staff Report. January 1968.

CAB Orders 71-4-54, 69-6-124, 71-6-120, 73-2-110.

CAB Suggests Experimental Program to Test Consequences of Deregulation. A Press Briefing. July 7, 1975.

Conditional Reservation's Rule Proposed by Eastern Air Lines, Inc. Order No. 71-6-120, June 24, 1971.

Domestic Passenger Fare Investigation. Docket 21866-9 Phases.

Domestic Air Freight Rate Investigation. Initial Decision of Administrative Law Judge Arthur S. Present. Docket 22859. April 15, 1975.

General Passenger Fare Investigation. Docket 8008.

---

*Recurring publications.

Government Ownership, Subsidy and Economic Assistance in International Commercial Aviation. May 1975.

Impact of the New Large Jets on the U.S. Air Transport System, 1970-1975. October 1973.

Pan American World Airways, Inc., *Petition for Establishment of a Subsidy Mail Rate.* Before the U.S. Civil Aeronautics Board. Washington, D.C.: April 3, 1974.

Regulatory Reform. Report of the CAB Special Staff. July 1975.

Service to Small Communities. A Staff Report Study of the Bureau of Operating Rights. March 1972.

Statistical Programs: Publications and Reports: A Tabular Summary. Bureau of Accounts and Statistics. 1973

Subsidy for United States Certificated Air Carriers. March 1974.

The Civil Aeronautics Board. Report prepared by the Office of Information. 1968

The Domestic Route System: Analysis and Policy Recommendations. A Staff Study by the Bureau of Operating Rights. October 1974.

The Effect of Discount Fares and Charter Operations on Yields and Operating Revenues in Transatlantic Operations. June 1973.

Transatlantic Route Investigation. Examiner's Initial Decision. Docket 25908. January 1975.

Pan American World Airways, Inc. v. TWU, 7 Av. Cas. 18, 428 (E.D.N.Y.) 1972.

Reorganization Plan No. 10 of 1953. 63 Stat. 203. 1953.

Ruby V. American Airlines. 329 F. 211.

U.S., Congress, Senate. Aviation Subcommittee of the Committee on Commerce. *Review of the Local Air Carrier Industry.* Hearings before Subcommittee, 89th Cong., 2d Sess., Washington, D.C., 1966.

U.S., Congress, House. *Monopoly Problems in Regulated Industries.* Hearings before the Anti-trust Subcommittee, 84th Cong., 2d Sess., Airlines I., 1956.

U.S., Congress, Senate. *Report on the Federal Aviation Commission.* Document No. 15, 74th Cong., 1st Sess., 1935.

U.S. Department of Commerce. *National Interest Aspects of the Private International Air Carrier System of the United States.* Office of the Secretary: Office of Policy Development. September 1974.

U.S. Department of Transportation. *Executive Branch Criteria for Domestic Airline Merger Proposals.* U.S. D.O.T. Washington, D.C.: August 31, 1971.

Books

Baitsell, John M. *Airline Industrial Relations: Pilots and Flight Engineers.* Boston, Massachusetts: Harvard University, Graduate School of Business Administration, 1966.

Barry, W.S. *Airline Management.* London: George Allen and Unwin, 1965.

Box, George E.P., and Jenkins, Gwilym M. *Time Series Analysis: Forecasting and Control.* San Francisco, California: Holden-Day Inc., 1970.

Brogden, Stanley. *Australia's Two-Airline Policy.* Melbourne, Australia: University Press, 1968.

Brooks, Peter W. *The Modern Airliner: Its Origins and Development.* London: Pitman, 1961.

Brown, Robert G. *Smoothing, Forecasting and Prediction of Discrete Time-Series.* Englewood Cliffs, New Jersey: Prentice-Hall, Inc., 1963.

Buergenthal, Thomas. *Lawmaking in the International Civil Aviation Organization.* Syracuse, New York: Syracuse University Press, 1969.

Burkhardt, Robert. *The Civil Aeronautics Board.* Dulles International Airport, Virginia: The Green Hills Publishing Company, Inc., 1974.

Butler, William; Kavesh, Robert; and Platt, Robert, eds. *Methods and Techniques of Business Forecasting.* Englewood Cliffs, New Jersey: Prentice-Hall, Inc., 1974.

Capron, William M., ed. *Technological Change in Regulated Industries.* Washington, D.C.: The Brookings Institution, 1971.

3 — Caves, Richard E. *Air Transport and Its Regulators.* Cambridge, Massachusetts: Harvard University Press, 1958. ×

Caves, Richard E., and Roberts, Marc J., eds. *Regulating the Product: Quality and Variety.* Cambridge, Massachusetts: Ballinger Publishing Company, 1975.

Cherington, P.W. *Airline Price Policy: A Study of Domestic Airline Fares.* Cambridge, Massachusetts: Harvard University Press, 1958.

Chisholm, Roger K., and Whitaker, Gilbert R., Jr. *Forecasting Methods.* Homewood, Illinois: Richard D. Irwin, Inc., 1971.

Corbett, D. *Politics and the Airlines.* London: George Allen and Unwin, 1965.

Davies, Grant Miller, ed. *Transportation Regulation: A Pragmatic Assessment.* Danville, Illinois: The Interstate Printers & Publishers, Inc., 1976.

Davies, Grant Miller. *The Department of Transportation.* Lexington, Massachusetts: Lexington Books, D.C. Heath and Company, 1970.

Davies, R.E.G. *A History of the World's Airlines.* Oxford, England: Oxford University Press, 1964.

Davies, R.E.G. *Airlines of the United States since 1914.* London: Putnam & Company Limited, 1972.

Douglas, George W., and Miller, James C., III. *Economic Regulation of Domestic Air Transport: Theory and Practice.* Washington, D.C.: The Brookings Institution, 1974.

Eads, George C. *The Local Service Airline Experiment.* Washington, D.C.: The Brookings Institution, 1972.

324

Faulks, R.W. *Elements of Transport*. London: Ian Allan, 1969.

Frederick, John H. *Commercial Air Transportation*. Homewood, Illinois: Richard D. Irwin, 1961.

Friedlaender, Ann. F. *The Dilemma of Freight Transport Regulation*. Washington, D.C.: The Brookings Institution, 1969.

Fruhan, William E., Jr. *The Fight for Competitive Advantage: A Study of the United States Domestic Trunk Air Carriers*. Boston, Massachusetts: Graduate School of Business-Administration, Harvard University, 1972.

Gill, Frederick, and Bates, Gilbert L. *Airline Competition*. Cambridge, Massachusetts: Harvard University Press, 1949.

Gordon, Robert J. "Airline Costs and Managerial Efficiency." In *Transportation Economics*, National Bureau of Economic Research. New York: Columbia University Press, 1965.

Gronau, Reuben. *The Value of Time in Passenger Transportation: The Demand for Air Travel*. New York: Columbia University Press, 1970.

Grumbridge, J.L. *Marketing Management in Air Transport*. London: George Allen and Unwin, 1966.

Hollander, S.C., ed. *Passenger Transportation: Readings Selected from Marketing Viewpoint*. East Lansing, Michigan: Business Studies, Michigan State University, 1968.

Hopkins, George E. *The Airline Pilots: A Study in Elite Unionization*. Cambridge, Massachusetts: Harvard University Press, 1971.

Howard, George P., ed. *Airport Economic Planning*. Cambridge, Massachusetts: Massachusetts Institute of Technology Press, 1974.

Hurst, Fred. "Survey Programs at Port Authority Airports." In *Airport Economic Planning*, George P. Howard, ed. Cambridge, Massachusetts: Massachusetts Institute of Technology Press, 1974.

Jackson, Paul, and Brackenridge, William. *Air Cargo Distribution*. London: A Gower Press Special Study, 1971.

Johnston, J. *Econometric Methods*. New York: McGraw-Hill Book Company, 1972.

Jones, William K. *Regulated Industries: Cases and Material*. Brooklyn, New York: The Foundation Press, Inc., 1967.

Jordan, William A. *Airline Regulation in America: Effects and Imperfections*. Baltimore, Maryland: The Johns Hopkins Press, 1970.

Kane, Robert M., and Vose, Allan D. *Air Transportation*. 4th ed. Dubuque, Iowa: Kendall/Hunt Publishing Company, 1974.

Keyes, Lucile Sheppard. *Federal Control of Entry into Air Transportation*. Cambridge, Massachusetts: Harvard University Press, 1951.

Kneafsey, James T. *The Economics of the Transportation Firm: Market Structure and Economic Performance in the Transportation Industries*. Lexington, Massachusetts: Lexington Books, D.C. Heath and Co., 1974.

Kneafsey, James T. *Transportation Economics Analysis*. Lexington, Massachusetts: Lexington Books, D.C. Heath and Co., 1975.

Kotler, Philip. *Marketing Management: Analysis, Planning and Control.* Englewood Cliffs, New Jersey: Prentice-Hall, Inc., 1967.

Lewellen, Wilbur G. *Cost of Capital.* Belmont, California: Wadsworth Publishing Company, 1969.

Locklin, Philip D. *Economics of Transportation.* 7th ed. Homewood, Illinois: Richard D. Irwin, Inc., 1972.

Lowenfeld, Andreas F. *Aviation Law: Cases and Material.* New York: Matthew Bender and Company, 1972.

Loy, Frank E. "Bilateral Air Transport Agreements: Some Problems of Finding a Fair Route Exchange." In *The Freedom of the Air.* Edward McWhinney, ed. Dobbesferry, New Jersey: Oceana Publications, Inc., 1968.

McWhinney, Edward, and Bradley, Martin, eds. *The Freedom of the Air.* Dobbesferry, New Jersey: Oceana Publications, Inc., 1968.

Meyer, J.R.; Peck, M.J.; Stenason, J.; and Zwick, C. *The Economics of Competition in the Transportation Industries.* Cambridge, Massachusetts: Harvard University Press, 1959.

Miller, R., and Sawers, D. *The Technical Development of Modern Aviation.* London: Routledge & Kegon Paul, 1968.

Miller, R. *Domestic Airline Efficiency.* Cambridge, Massachusetts: Massachusetts Institute of Technology Press, 1963.

Myers, John G. "Statistical and Econometric Methods Used in Business Forecasting." In *Methods and Techniques of Business Forecasting*, William Butler, Robert Kavesh, and Robert Platt, eds. Englewood Cliffs, New Jersey: Prentice-Hall, Inc., 1974.

National Bureau of Economic Research. *Transportation Economics.* New York: Columbia University Press, 1965.

O'Connor, William E. *Economic Regulation of the World's Airlines: A Political Analysis.* New York, New York: Praeger Publishers, Inc., 1971.

Pegrum, Dudley F. *Transportation: Economics and Public Policy.* 3d ed. Homewood, Illinois: Richard D. Irwin, Inc., 1973.

Pillai, K.G.J. *The Air Net: The Case against the World Aviation Cartel.* New York: Grossman Publishers, 1969.

Phillips, Almarin. *Technology and Market Structure: A Study of the Aircraft Industry.* Lexington, Massachusetts: Lexington Books, D.C. Heath and Co., 1971.

Quandt, R.E., ed. *The Demand for Travel: Theory and Measurement.* Lexington, Massachusetts: Lexington Books, D.C. Heath & Co., 1970.

Redford, Emmette S. *The Regulatory Process: With Illustrations from Commercial Aviation.* Austin, Texas: University of Texas Press, 1969.

Richmond, S. *Regulation and Competition in Air Transportation.* New York: Columbia University Press, 1962.

Rosenberg, A. *Air Travel Within Europe.* Stockholm: Swedish Consumer Council, 1970.

Schneider, Lewis M. *The Future of the U.S. Domestic Air Freight Industry: An*

Analysis of Management Strategies. Boston, Massachusetts: Graduate School of Business Administration, Harvard University, 1973.

Schriever, Bernard A., and Seifert, William W. *Air Transportation 1975 and Beyond—A Systems Approach.* Cambridge, Massachusetts: Massachusetts Institute of Technology Press, 1968.

Simon, Julian L. *The Management of Advertising.* Englewood, New Jersey: Prentice-Hall, Inc., 1971.

Stevenson, Gordon McKay. *The Politics of Airport Noise.* Belmont, California: Duxbury Press, 1972.

Straszheim, M. *The International Airline Industry.* Washington, D.C.: The Brookings Institution, 1969.

Stratford, A.H. *Air Transport Economics in the Supersonic Era.* 2d ed. London: The Macmillan Press, Ltd., 1973.

Thayer, Frederick C. *Air Transport Policy and National Security.* Chapel Hill, North Carolina: University of North Carolina Press, 1965.

Theil, Henri. *Principles of Econometrics.* New York: John Wiley and Sons, 1971.

Thornton, Robert L. *International Airlines and Politics.* Ann Arbor, Michigan: University of Michigan Press, 1970.

Warford, J.J. *Public Policy Toward General Aviation.* Washington, D.C.: The Brookings Institution, 1971.

Wassenbergh, H.A. *Aspects of Air Law and Civil Air Policy in the Seventies.* The Hague, Netherlands: Martinus Nijhoff, 1970.

Wonnacott, Ronald J., and Wonnacott, Thomas H. *Econometrics.* New York: John Wiley and Sons, Inc., 1970.

Reports

Air Transport Association of America. *Consequences of Deregulation of the Scheduled Air Transport Industry, An Analytical Approach.* Washington, D.C.: April 1975.

Air Transport Association of America. *U.S. Airline Industry Costs and Productivity 1967-1973.* Washington, D.C.: May 17, 1974.

Augustinus, J.G. *Air Traffic Forecasting at the Port Authority of New York and New Jersey.* Port Authority, Aviation Economics Division, July 1972.

Ausrotas, Raymond, et al. *Aircraft Requirements for Low/Medium Density Markets.* FTL Report R73-4. Cambridge, Massachusetts: Massachusetts Institute of Technology, September 1973.

Committee of Inquiry Into Civil Air Transport Report. *British Air Transport in the Seventies.* London: Her Majesty's Stationery Office, May 1969.

European Travel Commission. *The One Week Winter GIT Programs.* An Industry Consumer Study. New York.

Flight Transportation Laboratory. *Air Transportation Data Sources.* FTL Technical Memorandum 71-5-R3. Cambridge, Massachusetts: Massachusetts Institute of Technology, 1972.

Flight Transportation Laboratory. *Concept Studies for Future Intercity Air Transportation Systems.* FTL Report R-70. Cambridge, Massachusetts: Massachusetts Institute of Technology, 1970.

Flight Transportation Laboratory. *MIT/NASA Workshop: Airline Systems Analysis.* FTL Report 72-7, vols. I and II. Cambridge, Massachusetts: Massachusetts Institute of Technology, July 1972.

Flight Transportation Laboratory. *Proceedings of the Workshop: Air Transportation Demand and Systems Analysis.* FTL Report R75-8. Cambridge, Massachusetts: Massachusetts Institute of Technology, August 1975.

Garvett, Donald S., and Taneja, Nawal K. *New Directions for Forecasting Air Travel Passenger Demand.* FTL Report R74-3. Cambridge, Massachusetts: Massachusetts Institute of Technology, July 1974.

Glendinning, Iain D.C. *Non-Scheduled Passenger Air Transport: Its Characteristics and Issues.* FTL Technical Memorandum M73-4. Cambridge, Massachusetts: Massachusetts Institute of Technology, March 1973.

Hampton Technical Center. *Advanced Supersonic Technology Concept Study Reference Characteristics.* LTV Aerospace Corporation, NASA CR-132374. December 21, 1973.

Helmer, Olaf. *Convergence of Expert Consensus Through Feedback.* Santa Monica, California: RAND Corporation, September 1964.

International Air Transport Association. *Agreeing Fares and Rates.* Geneva, Switzerland, June 1974.

International Air Transport Association. *Consumer Perceptions and Evaluations of Transatlantic Air Fares.* Prepared by Robinson Associates, Inc. Bryn Mawr, Pennsylvania, November 1974.

McDonnell Douglas Aircraft Co. *Computer Applications for Airline Progress and Profit.* Report Number 800-1159, September 1969.

Simpson, Robert W. *A Market Share Model for U.S. Domestic Airline Competitive Markets.* FTL Technical Memorandum M70-5. Cambridge, Massachusetts: Massachusetts Institute of Technology, May 1970.

Simpson, Robert W., and Chan, Y.P. *A Structure for Airline Operating Costs.* FTL Technical Memorandum 71-9. Cambridge, Massachusetts: Massachusetts Institute of Technology, December 1971.

Simpson, Robert W. *A Theory for Domestic Airline Economics.* FTL Report R74-2. Cambridge, Massachusetts: Massachusetts Institute of Technology, July 1974.

Simpson, Robert W. *Scheduling and Routing Models for Airline Systems.* FTL Report R68-3. Cambridge, Massachusetts: Massachusetts Institute of Technology, December 1969.

Simpson, Robert W. *Summary and Recommendations NASA/MIT Workshop on Short-Haul Air Transportation.* FTL Report R71-4. Cambridge, Massachusetts: Massachusetts Institute of Technology, October 1971.

Smith, Cynthia L., and Williams, Louis J. *An Economic Study of an Advanced Technology Supersonic Cruise Vehicle.* NASA TMX-62,499. Moffett Field, California: Ames Research Center, October 1975.

Taneja, Nawal K., and Kneafsey, James T. *The State-of-the-Art in Air Transportation Demand and Systems Analysis.* FTL Report R75-7. Cambridge, Massachusetts: Massachusetts Institute of Technology, August 1975.

Taneja, Nawal K., and Simpson, Robert W. *A Multi-Regression Analysis of Airline Indirect Operating Costs.* FTL Report R67-2. Cambridge, Massachusetts: Massachusetts Institute of Technology, June 1968.

The Port Authority of New York and New Jersey. *Transatlantic Air Travel "Fifteen Years in Review," 1956-1971.* New York, June 1975.

Ultrasystems, Inc. *Examination of the Costs, Benefits and Energy Conservation Aspects of the NASA Aircraft Fuel Conservation Technology Program.* Report prepared for NASA (Contract No. NASW-2859). Irvine, California, November 15, 1975.

Vitek, Richard L., and Taneja, Nawal K. *The Impact of High Inflation Rates on the Demand for Air Transportation.* FTL Report R75-6. Cambridge, Massachusetts: Massachusetts Institute of Technology, May 1975.

Vittek, Joseph F. *Air Service to Small Communities: Directions for the Future.* FTL Report R73-5. Cambridge, Massachusetts: Massachusetts Institute of Technology, February 1974.

Journal Articles

Annable, James E., Jr. "The ICC, the IBT, and the Cartelization of the American Trucking Industry." *The Quarterly Review of Economics and Business,* Summer 1973, 13:33-47.

Bain, Joseph S. "Output Quotas in Imperfect Cartels." *Quarterly Journal of Economics,* 1948, 62:617-622.

Beechy, Thomas H. "Quasi-Debt Analysis of Financial Leases." *Accounting Review,* April 1969, 44:375-381.

Bierman, Harold, Jr. "Analysis of the Lease-or-Buy Decision: Comment." *Journal of Finance,* 1973, 28:1019-1021.

Blanchet, Robert. "Fuel Consumption and Environmental Needs: New Key Factors in New Airliner Design." *IACO Bulletin,* June 1975, pp. 18-20.

Bower, Richard S.; Herringer, Frank C.; and Williamson, Peter J. "Lease Evaluation." *Accounting Review,* April 1966, 41:257-265.

Crooker, John H., Jr. "Airline Mergers in the 1970s." *Journal of Air Law and Commerce,* 1973, 39:143-166.

Davidson, Vic. "Canadian STOL-Commuter Service Demonstrates Early Success." *IACO Bulletin,* December 1974, pp. 14-15.

Eads, G.; Nerlove, M.; and Raduchel, W. "A Long Run Cost Function for the

Local Service Airline Industry: An Experiment in Non-Linear Estimation." *Review of Economics and Statistics*, August 1969, 51:258-270.

Glenn, C.H. "Factors to be Considered in Airline Scheduling." *Canadian Aeronautics and Space Journal*, June 1972, pp. 149-156.

Hyman, Warren, and Gordon, Larry. "Commercial Airline Scheduling Technique." *International Journal of Transportation Research*, 1966, 2:23-29.

Johnson, Robert W., and Lewellen, Wilbur G. "Analysis of Lease-or-Buy Decision." *Journal of Finance*, September 1972, 27:815-823.

Johnson, Robert W., and Lewellen, Wilbur G. "Reply." *Journal of Finance*, 1973, 28:1024-1028.

Keyes, Lucile S. "Notes on the History of Federal Regulation of Airline Mergers." *Journal of Air Law and Commerce*, 1971, 37:357-387.

Koontz, Harold D. "Domestic Airline Self-Sufficiency: A Problem of Route Structure." *American Economic Review*, 1952, 42:103-125.

Mansfield, E. "Size of Firm, Market Structure, and Innovation." *Journal of Political Economy*, No. 6, December 1963, 71:556-576.

Narodick, Kit G. "What Motivates the Consumer's Choice of an Airline." *Journal of Retailing*, Spring 1972, 48:30-38 and 96.

Nerlove, Marc. "Distributed Lags and Estimation of Long-Run Supply and Demand Elasticities: Theoretical Considerations." *Journal of Farm Economics*, May 1958, 40:301-311.

Povinelli, Frederick P.; Klineberg, John M.; and Kramer, James J. "Improving Aircraft Energy Efficiency." *Astronautics and Aeronautics*. American Institute of Aeronautics and Astronautics, February 1976, pp. 19-31.

Reid, Samuel R., and Mohrfeld, James W. "Airline Size, Profitability, Mergers and Regulations." *Journal of Air Law and Commerce*, 1973, 39:167-178.

Schultz, Randall L. "Market Measurement and Planning with a Simultaneous-Equation Model." *Journal of Marketing Research*, May 1971, 8:153-164.

Simpson, Robert W. "Get Ready for the Great Debate on Transportation." *Astronautics and Aeronautics*. American Institute of Aeronautics and Astronautics, February 1976, pp. 38-45.

Wyman, Harold E. "Financial Lease Evaluation Under Conditions of Uncertainty." *Accounting Review*, July 1973, 48:489-493.

General References

Air Transport 1975. Air Transport Association of America. Washington, D.C.: August 1975.

Air Transport World. Stamford, Connecticut: Reinhold Publishing Co.

Aviation Daily. Washington, D.C.: Ziff-Davis Publishing Co.

Aviation Week and Space Technology. New York: McGraw Hill Book Company.

International Civil Aviation Organization Bulletin. International Civil Aviation Organization. Montreal, Canada.

Official Airline Guide. The Reuben H. Donnelley Corporation. Oak Brook, Illinois.

The State of the Air Transport Industry. International Air Transport Association. Geneva, Switzerland.

World Airline Record. Roadcap Associates. Chicago, Illinois.

World Air Transport Statistics. International Air Transport Association. Geneva, Switzerland.

Unpublished Material

Allen, William Bruce. "A Model of the Demand for Transportation: The Case of Air Freight." Northwestern University, Department of Economics, 1969.

Bartlett, Hale Carlyle. "The Demand for Passenger Air Transportation, 1947-1962." University of Michigan, Business Administration, 1965.

Blackburn, Anthony J. "A Nonlinear Model of Passenger Demand." Massachusetts Institute of Technology, Economics, 1966.

Blood, Dwight Melvin. "A Cross-section Analysis of the Domestic Intercity Travel Market." University of Michigan, Economics, 1963.

Chan, Y. "Route Network Improvement in Air Transportation Schedule Planning." Massachusetts Institute of Technology, Aeronautics, 1972.

Clerman, N.S. "An Airline Fleet Planning Model." Massachusetts Institute of Technology, Aeronautics, August 1969.

Cochran, Douglas Lessel. "An Evaluation of the Use of Gravitational Formulae for Estimating Potential Air Passenger Traffic Between City-Pairs." University of Oregon, Business Administration, 1970.

Cooke, Blaine. "International Aviation Policy: Heretics at Home, Orthodox Abroad." Remarks before the Travel Research Association, The Waldorf-Astoria, New York, April 16, 1974.

Costantino, James. "An Evaluation of the CAB's Regulatory Policy with Respect to the Promotional Fares of the Domestic Trunk Air Carriers." The American University, 1971.

Demakopoulos, Steve Andrew. "Methods and Efficacy of a Long-Range Industry Forecast: A Case Study of the Domestic Air Cargo Industry." New York University, Economics, 1970. Volumes I and II.

Ebbs, George H. "Sensitivity Analysis as a Tool for Affecting the Rational Evaluation of Corporate Decision Alternatives: A Study of Capital Equipment Planning Process in Two U.S. Airlines." Columbia University, 1969.

Faulkner, Henry. "An Airline Fleet Planning Model with Financial Constraints." Massachusetts Institute of Technology, Aeronautics, June 1970.

Fritzsche, David Jerome. "The Relevance of Consumer Response Data for Regulatory Decision-making: The Commuter Airlines: A Case Study." Indiana University, Business Administration, 1972.

Fruhan, William E. "The Fight for Competitive Advantage under Regulation." Harvard University, Business Administration, 1970.

Fuchs, G.A. "IATA and its Regulators." Massachusetts Institute of Technology, Aeronautics, 1971.

Gellman, Aaron Jacob. "The Effect of Regulation on Aircraft Choice." Massachusetts Institute of Technology, Economics, 1968.

Greenberg, Barnet Alvin. "An Analysis of Airline Market Share." University of Colorado, Business Administration, 1971.

Gritta, Richard David. "Profitability and Risk in the U.S. Domestic Trunk-line Industry: A Case Study of Eastern Airlines, 1959-1969." University of Maryland, Economics, 1972.

Hiat, D. "The Impact of Charter Services on Scheduled North Atlantic Air Travel." Massachusetts Institute of Technology, Sloan School, 1974.

Johnson, Timothy Edward. "Financing of the U.S. Domestic Trunk Airlines, 1960-1969." University of Illinois at Urbana-Champaign, 1971.

Johnston, Everett Edward. "Problems in the Evaluation of Travel Time." University of Oregon, Business Administration, 1971.

Jones, Thomas Owen. "An Analysis and Evaluation of Future Vertical Lift Aircraft in Scheduled Commercial Airline Operations, 1972-1977." George Washington University, Business Administration, 1972.

Joun, Yound Pyo. "The Demand for Air Travel." University of Washington, Economics, 1966.

Joy, Okie Maurice. "The Value of Limited Monthly Information in Forecasting Airline Price Relatives." University of North Carolina, Business Administration, 1969.

Keintz, Rita M. "The Demand for International Travel to and from the United States." Boston College, Economics, 1971.

Kingrey, J. "Lease versus Buy: An Application to Airline Equipment Acquisition." Massachusetts Institute of Technology, Sloan School, 1974.

Kleiger, Linda Jean. "Maximization of the Industry Profits: The Case of U.S. Air Transportation." UCLA, Economics, 1967.

Likens, James Dean. "The Welfare Costs of Non-Optional Airport Utilization: A Case Study of the Washington-Baltimore Airports." University of Minnesota, Economics, 1970.

Lu, Ming-Te. "A Computerized Airline Crew Scheduling System." University of Minnesota, Business Administration, 1971.

MacCallum, Robert A. "A Systematic Approach to International Civil Aviation Route Exchange." Massachusetts Institute of Technology, Political Science, June 1971.

Maxfield, Daniel Paul. "Federal Long-Range Planning for Commercial Air Transportation—An Appraisal and a Proposal." George Washington University, Business Administration, 1971.

McMahon, James Anthony. "Price Determination by a Cartel: A Study of IATA's Pricing of the Economy Class in the North Atlantic." Boston College, Economics, 1969.

McMillen, James E. "The Effect of Scale in the Airline Industry." Massachusetts Institute of Technology, Aeronautics, September 1971.

Mehring, J.B. "Toward Optimal Airline Fare/Schedule Combinations: Benefits and Costs of Alternatives in Three U.S. Transcontinental Markets." Massachusetts Institute of Technology, Civil Engineering, 1974.

Mertins, Herman. "Dimensions of National Transportation Policy Formation." Syracuse University, Political Science, 1970.

Miller, James C. "Scheduling and Airline Efficiency." University of Virginia, Economics, 1969.

Miller, John Andrew. "Air Diplomacy: The Chicago Civil Aviation Conference of 1944 in Anglo-American Wartime Regulations and Post-War Planning." Yale University, History, 1971.

Mize, Jan Lee. "An Econometric Analysis of the Demand for Airline Passenger Transportation—Domestic Routes." Georgia State College, Economics and Commerce Business, 1968.

Narodick, Kit Gordan. "Competition and Regulation in the Domestic Air Freight Industry." Columbia University, Economics, 1967.

O'Connor, William E. "International Cooperation vs. Nationalism in the Economic Regulation of the World's Airlines." The American University, Political Science, 1970.

Orior, Henry. "Domestic Air Cargo, 1945-1965: A Study of Competition in a Regulated Industry." Columbia University, Political Science, 1967.

Pierce, Burton Ross. "The Nature and Extent of Long Range Planning in the Transportation Regulatory Agencies." Stanford University, Business Administration, 1971.

Pomeroy, Leslie Klett. "An Evaluation in Terms of the Public Interest of the Civil Aeronautics Board's Route Strengthening Policy for Local Service Air Carriers." The American University, Economics, 1970.

Powers, Thomas Francis. "Toward a More Dynamic Travel Policy: A Critical Review of the U.S. Travel Service." Georgia State University, 1969.

Randall, Reed Heber. "Supplemental Airline Fleet Planning: A Mathematical Programming Approach." University of California, Business Administration, 1969.

Redenius, Charles Melvin. "The Railway Labor Act and the Airline Industry." University of Michigan, Political Science, 1968.

Renard, Gilles. "Competition in Air Transportation: An Econometric Approach." Massachusetts Institute of Technology, Aeronautics, 1970.

Rugg, Donald Dix. "The Demand for Foreign Travel." University of California, Economics, 1971.

Sackrey, Charles Melvin. "Overcapacity in the United States International Air Transport Industry." University of Texas, Economics, 1965.

Schad, Thomas Wayne. "An Econometric Study of the Demand for Air Freight in the Domestic United States." Wayne State University, Economics, 1970.

Schultz, Randall L. "The Development of a Marketing Planning Model through Simultaneous-Equation Multiple Regression Analysis: An Airline Study." Northwestern University, Business Administration, 1970.

Seddig, Robert George. "Regulatory Policy-making in the Civil Aeronautics Board." Princeton University, Political Science, 1971.

Sercer, R.W. "Airline Profitability: A Case Study." Massachusetts Institute of Technology, Aeronautics, 1975.

Simpson, Robert W. "An Analysis of Airline Costs." Lecture notes for M.I.T. Course 16.74—Air Transportation Economics. Massachusetts Institute of Technology, Cambridge, Massachusetts.

Simpson, Robert W. "Technology for Design of Transport Aircraft." Lecture notes, Massachusetts Institute of Technology, Cambridge, Massachusetts, July 1972.

Stanley, Marvin M. "Incrementalism for the Wide-Body Jets in the Domestic Air Cargo Market: Toward an Improved Profitability for the Domestic Trunk Airline Industry." The American University, Business Administration, 1972.

Strom, Harold Kjell. "The North Atlantic Air Transport Market: A Study of the American Competitive Position." University of California, Los Angeles, Economics, Commercial Business, 1964.

Stuart, Merrill Middleton. "The Use of a Gravity Model in Interpreting Air Passenger Traffic between Hawaii and the Conterminous States." Columbia University, Education, 1968.

Varga, G.J. "Financial Methods and Instruments in the Air Transportation Industry." Massachusetts Institute of Technology, Aeronautics, 1970.

Verleger, Philip K. "A Point-to-Point Model of the Demand for Air Transportation." Massachusetts Institute of Technology, Economics, 1971.

Wiley, John R. "Class Notes From Courses on Airport Planning." Flight Transportation Laboratory, Massachusetts Institute of Technology, 1972.

Index

Index

Advertising, 68-73; competitive, 69; institutional, 69
Air Commerce Act of 1926, 2
Aircraft selection criteria, 93-97
Air Freight Rate Investigation, 218-219
Airline labor legislation, 115-130
Air Mail Act of: 1925, 1, 3; 1934, 4
Airport and Airway Development and Revenue Act, 17
Airport and Airway Trust Fund, 17
Airports, 296, 303-304
Air taxi carriers, 10, 293
Alaskan air carriers, 24, 237
Allegheny-Mohawk merger, 244-245
American-Western merger proposal, 245-246
Antitrust, 255, 293
Aviation Act of 1975, 19. *See also* Deregulation debate

Balance of payments, 257, 283
Bermuda Agreement, 8, 259-261
Bilateral agreement, 2, 6, 258-262
Break-even analysis, 42, 54
Break-even load factor, 40

Capacity agreement, 17, 57-59
Capital requirements, 77-85
Cargo, 4, 13, 292-293, 304-305; carriers, 23; domestic rates, 216-223; international rates, 271-276
Chandler controversy, 266-268
Chicago Conference, 7, 8, 117, 258-259
Chosen instrument concept, 9, 184
Civil Aeronautics Act of 1938, 5
Civil Aeronautics Board: air carrier data, 145-150; Civil Aeronautics Act of 1938, 5; deregulation debate, 291-298; Domestic Passenger Fare Investigation, 197-216; Federal Aviation Act of 1958, 11-14; General

Passenger Fare Investigation, 192-195; mergers, 246-250; Mutual Aid Pact, 125-130; rate-making, 189-223; Route development, 153-186; subsidy, 225-239
Civil Aeronautics Board data bank, 145-150
Classification of carriers, 21-27
Class rate formulae, 233
Collective bargaining, 116-130
Commuter carriers, 10, 26, 235, 297
Competitive bidding system, 236
Costs, 31, 43-57, 95-96, 298-299
Cross-subsidization, 41-42, 213-216, 234

Data: industry, 27-29; sources, 144-152
Debt financing. *See* Capital requirements
Decision Number 83, 116
Demand, 71, 131-145
Demand scheduling, 111-112
Denver Service Case, 164-166
Department of Transportation, 16, 180-181, 250-254, 291
Depreciation, 198
Deregulation debate, 291-298. *See also* Aviation Act of 1975
Derived demand, 61
Detroit-California Case, 169
Differential fares, 42, 66, 202-205, 269
Direct operating costs. *See* Costs
Discount fares. *See* Differential fares
Discrimination, 13, 65, 67, 204-205
Distribution system, 73-75
Domestic Air Freight Rate Investigation, 220-223
Domestic Passenger Fare Investigation, 18, 197-216

Econometric method, 135-141

337

About the Author

Nawal K. Taneja is Assistant Professor at the Flight Transportation Laboratory of the Department of Aeronautics and Astronautics at the Massachusetts Institute of Technology. Prior to this he was a Senior Economic Analyst with Trans World Airlines in New York City. At M.I.T. he teaches graduate courses on airline management. On the research side, Dr. Taneja's interests center on the application of econometric methods for forecasting the demand for air transportation. He is the author or co-author of several articles in this area and has served as a consultant to major industrial and government organizations in the U.S. and abroad on subjects related to air transportation planning.